SEEKING FIRST THE KINGDOM

SEEKING FIRST THE KINGDOM

NORTHWEST NAZARENE UNIVERSITY

A CENTENNIAL HISTORY

by

Richard W. Etulain

Northwest Nazarene University
Nampa, Idaho

SEEKING FIRST THE KINGDOM:
Northwest Nazarene University,
A Centennial History

Published by:
Northwest Nazarene University
623 S. University Blvd.
Nampa, ID 83686

ISBN: 978-0-9857155-0-2
Printed in the United States of America.

Author: Richard W. Etulain
Designer: Paul Kinsman
Printed by: Caxton Printing, Caldwell, Idaho

For Nazarene founders and educators
who courageously embraced a
Christian liberal arts tradition

Contents

Foreword

RICHARD A. HAGOOD
President Emeritus

The founders of any noble enterprise most assuredly begin their quest with an idea in mind of what could happen if their dreams were to come true. If what they had hoped for somehow came to reality. Such is the case with the founders and early leaders of Northwest Nazarene University—this noble enterprise that is now at the doorstep of its centennial. Early in his brief tenure as the administrator of the fledgling school in Nampa, Idaho, C. H. French was asked by skeptics if there was a future here. His answer was both faith-filled and prophetic. He is quoted as saying: "Yes, in time God will build a great school in Nampa." His answer reflected the belief and commitment of a hardy band of pioneers who, in 1913, had faith that the vision God had given them would, in fact, be fulfilled. It was a faith as grand as any explorer of any territory.

The centennial year of this noble enterprise which today bears the name Northwest Nazarene University is an opportune time for celebration and reflection. Centennials, as a rule, are not easy to come by, either for individuals or institutions. So, it is right and customary to celebrate what is often a rare occasion—to give praise as a Christian university to God for His providence and to say thanks to those who lived out the mission and purpose of His calling. It is also a time for reflection—to think back constructively on how this divine-human partnership worked its way through the years. Reflection allows those of this current era, and those to come, to analyze what worked well or less well.

The centennial history that follows in this book is a significant tool in helping us realize many of the ways in which this university has been God-inspired and God-directed. We have all heard that often times it is only by looking to the past—often through the rearview mirror of life—that we most clearly see the hand of God at work. This history may also be a tool in analyzing what has allowed the institution to prosper in the midst of its changing environment or at some times to struggle for viability and sustainability.

Because our desire has been for a centennial history that can be instructive in reflection and analysis, as well as celebratory, it was appropriate that Dr. Richard Etulain, alumnus and renowned historian of the Western United States, be commissioned to write a history of Northwest Nazarene University. He was asked to write with an historian's methodology and objectivity—although that would be a challenging assignment for one whose loyalty and passion for his alma mater are so genuine and intense. This book is truly a labor of his love.

A centennial history could well have a third significant benefit to those entrusted with fulfilling the mission of our university into the years and decades ahead. More than celebration and reflection, a centennial history and the accompanying centennial events provide a golden moment to project aspirations for the institution's future. And, resolutely, to pray for a future that is as God-directed and God-inspired as those times past.

Recently, I came into possession of a family treasure—an old trunk that had been my mother's repository for a collection of photo albums, family genealogy, notes, diaries, letters, and so forth. As I have gone through the trunk's contents, stories that I had heard in my younger years took on an expanded meaning and things I had never heard nor seen enriched my view of my family. So, it is with a centennial history, I suggest. The archives of the university have provided the historian over 100,000 documents from which to craft this history. It serves as the university's treasure trunk. Those archives and Etulain's research at other locations and numerous interviews form the basis of this history of our noble enterprise.

However, like my family trunk neither the university archives nor the human and written resources beyond, contain the whole of our history. There are thousands upon thousands of stories—some written, most only oral tradition—which also are part of Northwest Nazarene University's history. I am pleased to know that there is a companion piece to the centennial history that captures many of those stories. But, even beyond these wonderful gifts of memory and information, there are more stories to be told. Behind every name on, or within, a building, garden, or field there is a book-length story to be told. Behind each of the more than four hundred endowed scholarships there is a story to be told. Behind each lifetime friendship formed at our university there is a story to be told. The centennial is the right time for alumni and friends of the university to tell their stories.

During the latter years of my tenure as president, and with the centennial looming, I wrote and spoke a good deal about fulfilling the promise of greatness that the early founders and leaders had envisioned for our university. Of course, it is unlikely that any of these pioneers could have imagined what Northwest Nazarene University has become in this modern era in terms of campus infrastructure, excellence in curricular and extracurricular programs, regional, national, and global recognition, and more—these examples of temporal greatness. I would like to think, however, that our pioneers would not be surprised today that our university has continued to fulfill the promise of eternal significance they so valued at the very beginning of Northwest Nazarene University.

It is appropriate that this centennial history bears the title *Seeking First the Kingdom: Northwest Nazarene University, A Centennial History* for in this phrase, excerpted from the school motto of more than eight decades, we see the integrating theme over the length of the institution's history. It is this commitment to seeking the will and ways of God and to bringing to bear on contemporary culture the Kingdom perspective found in the teachings of Jesus Christ that has motivated and driven generations of NNU folks. This is the noble enterprise, this seeking the Kingdom, as daring and daunting as any exploratory adventure, that has captivated the minds, hearts, and souls of all who have embraced the mission of Northwest Nazarene University for these one hundred years.

Preface

Pungent earthy smells cycled up from the Treasure Valley as we drove down out of the Blue Mountains of eastern Oregon, crossed the Snake River, and entered Idaho. It was the fall of 1955, and as a just-turned seventeen-year-old freshman I was on my way to Northwest Nazarene College in Nampa, Idaho. Innocence reigned. I knew the college would be like an extended Nazarene summer camp, which I had relished for nearly ten summers. I had loafed through high school, more interested in sports and girls than studies. A similar frolicsome college career with minimal attention to academics danced in my mind.

Northwest Nazarene College proved to be both what I expected and something much different. Sports—intramural and intercollegiate—were available. And the plethora of attractive young women, Nazarene coeds, made college all the more inviting.

But the classes were not what I thought. They opened in prayer and included frequent and explicit references to religious experiences. My courses were refreshing, encouraging, and stretching. Soon I was taken with the literature and history classes, beginning to think I had a brain worth cultivating.

Campus spiritual life combined the old and new. As a lifetime Nazarene I recognized much in the chapel and church services. Familiar hymns, testimonies, revivals, evangelistic preaching—they were all there. But Sunday services in cavernous College Church with a pealing organ filling the sanctuary and sometimes an auditorium crowded with 1,000 attendees were new to me. So was the full run of superb speakers; they had not come to my small Nazarene churches of less than fifty.

By the end of three semesters I had been won over to academic excellence. I was entranced with the combined spiritual, academic, and social atmosphere of the small campus in Nampa. That appreciation and attachment grew during the next three and a half years (it turned out I was on the five-year plan) as I made spiritual decisions, decided on an occupation, and won over a young woman who became my lifetime partner.

Not surprisingly, my experiences at Northwest Nazarene College (NNC) were similar to those of hundreds—even thousands—of other students who came to the Nampa campus. It was a journey into NNC country—physically and emotionally. It was also an experience that shaped a lifetime. For me, those early emotional bonds expanded when I returned to teach two years at NNC and later served three years on the Board of Trustees after it became Northwest Nazarene University (NNU). In between I went on to become a professional historian, teaching at Idaho State University and the University of New Mexico.

So as a Nazarene, a graduate of NNC, and an academic historian I was asked by President Richard Hagood to write a "scholarly history" of my alma mater. At first I hesitated because of other commitments, but once I agreed to do the history, I vowed to produce a centennial history as strong as I could make it.

As I have now moved ahead with the task of recording a scholarly history of NNU, unexpected tensions have emerged. My love for the institution pushed me toward an entirely positive, upbeat story of NNC/NNU. There was much in the archives, campus publications, and student and alumni memories on which to base a cheery narrative. But, simultaneously, the same sources also revealed periodic dilemmas, conflicts, and even a few failures—in administrative leadership, in student and faculty activities, and in the decisions and actions of others involved with the college. How was I to write a story only about happy sunbursts when disappointing shadows were also clearly a part of the college's history?

In the past, several college leaders and some of its chroniclers chose to overlook the less-positive aspects of NNC/NNU's history. In their presentation, letters, and histories they omitted the down sides of the past. As one of the important pioneering deans of the college, Albert Harper, wrote about early historical accounts of NNC, "we were better Christians than historians; we recorded the pleasant and positive, and forgot the tension and headaches."

Once I began to write I decided that I would produce a full, complex history of my alma mater. I would not tell an incomplete and slanted story, omitting less pleasant details. After spending more than a year researching the NNC/NNU archives, reading the campus publications, and talking to numerous persons about the university's past, I became more and more convinced that I must relate an inclusive story that included ups and downs, successes and failures, positives and negatives. As a professional historian of nearly fifty years I could do no less. Reluctantly, I also decided to publish the book without footnotes, but those who wish to follow the documentation for the NNC/NNU story will find fully noted copies of the manuscript in the NNU archives in Nampa and in the Nazarene archives in Lenexa/Kansas City.

In my commitment to balance my love for NNC/NNU with writing sound history, frequently heart and head have conflicted. In the end, my major goal became to provide a sympathetic account of a much-admired institution and its leaders, faculty, students, and alumni.

I am grateful to two NNU presidents—Richard Hagood and David Alexander—who have encouraged and supported this project. They have read this history thoroughly, in manuscript, and commented extensively on it in its preliminary forms. I have benefitted greatly from their reactions but have not always followed their suggestions. Because this is my history, my point of view on the NNC/NNU story, I hold responsibility for the content of this narrative and its conclusions.

Prologue

THE FARAWAY NEARBY: 1913-16

Sunday morning dawned clear and warm. It was July 4, 1915, in Nampa, Idaho, a small farm town in the Boise Valley, a few miles from the mighty Snake River. After church services and by early afternoon the heat had begun to mount. Nearly fifty men, women, and children clustered in an arid, sagebrush space on the southern and western edges of Nampa, adjacent to the Kurtz Park addition. It was an auspicious moment, the groundbreaking ceremony for the first buildings of what would become Northwest Nazarene College (NNC/NNU). The group had come to this isolated, remote corner of the Pacific Northwest (PNW) hoping to turn ground for a holiness school, as a part of the Church of the Nazarene, for their children and for the study of the Bible. If the school was in its beginning stages, its setting and its supporting denomination were also in their infancy. A sense of newness and promise shadowed and shone on the people gathered in Nampa on that Independence Day.

The groundbreaking ceremony simultaneously built on a brief, recent past and looked to a hoped-for future. Two short years earlier in 1913 a courageous and committed Nazarene layman, Eugene Emerson, had nearly single-handedly launched the Idaho Holiness School. But, surprisingly, so many students and their families came to the school that new buildings soon had to be erected. Several persons gathered that mid-summer were central to the founding of NNC. Members of the Emerson and Parsons families were there, as was Charles V. Marshall, a pioneering professor and principal. Sherman Ludlow, a member of the school's Board of Directors, was in attendance. And standing in the center of the group, shovels in hand, were two Quaker ministers: the Rev. Lewis I. Hadley and the Rev. Harry Hays, now aiding the Nazarenes. This hopeful group embodied the dreams and aspirations springing up among the early Nazarenes of Nampa.

The Nazarene denomination was but a few years older than Northwest Nazarene College. In 1895, Phineas F. Bresee, a former Methodist bishop, had organized a Church of the Nazarene in Los Angeles. Several pressures had pushed Bresee out of the Methodist Church. For several years he found it increasingly difficult to preach the doctrine of "Second Blessing" holiness, or Entire Sanctification. Bishops in California did not encourage—some actively opposed—that emphasis. Nor had he found support for his desire to focus primarily on the needy and poor. His

On July 4, 1915, a small group of enthusiastic Nazarenes met at the current location of NNC to break ground for new buildings. (Fig. 0.1)

Methodist denomination preferred to serve, by and large, upward mobile southern Californians, especially the solid middle-class Americans flooding into the region from the mid-1880s onward.

Finally, and probably most importantly and certainly most immediately, Bresee was without a church in the mid-1890s. His work with an independent but Methodist-supported institution, the Peniel Mission, ended abruptly when he was let go by the mission in the summer of 1895. So, at 57 years of age, Bresee "stepped out under the stars," on his own to found a new church, which he called the Church of the Nazarene. He had no other goals, explained one of his later chief lieutenants, than to "preach the gospel of full salvation to the poor in Los Angeles."

Understandably, Methodist leaders discouraged Bresee from leaving their denomination and founding a new one. But without a church or church position and increasingly frustrated with his status among the Methodists, Bresee was convinced he must do so. After establishing his first Nazarene church in Los Angeles in 1895 and others soon thereafter in southern California, Bresee branched out to organize still more Nazarene churches in the Pacific Northwest. These churches were planted in such cities as Spokane (1902), Boise (1903), Seattle (1905), Yakima (1905), and Portland (1906), with others organized in smaller towns like Garfield, Washington (1904), Ashland and Milton, Oregon (1905), and Monroe and Plainview, Washington (1906).

By 1915 about 50 Nazarene churches had been established in Idaho, Washington, and Oregon, with slightly less than 2,000 members listed on these church rolls. Meanwhile, uniting Nazarenes with other holiness groups across the United States, the church had become a national denomination, first in Chicago in its initial General Assembly in 1907 and even more so at Pilot Point, Texas, in 1908. Four years later, the expanding Northwest District was divided into the Northwest and Idaho-Oregon districts. The infancy of the national denomination, as well as the newness of its regional districts, added to the rapid change and organizational challenges but also the enthusiasm that marked Northwest Nazarene College in its first years.

Overnight transitions were also remolding NNC's physical surroundings in southwestern Idaho. At the turn of the twentieth century the state of Idaho was but a decade old, with legacies of pioneer mining and agricultural economies still in evidence. By 1900, however, railroads were replacing covered wagons, stagecoaches, and horse carriages as the new mode of transportation. Within the next two decades automobiles invaded Nampa, including a few owned by NNC leaders. First platted and settled in the 1880s, Nampa had evolved into an agricultural and transportation center a decade or so later. With 799 residents in 1900, the town expanded to 4,205 in 1910. Visitors and early residents described Nampa as a wide-open frontier town, with more saloons than churches and schools. Ringed by arid areas and huge stretches of sagebrush, the town was beginning to capitalize on the newly laid-out irrigation systems bringing water to nearby farming areas. The stuttering steps of the Idaho Holiness School to become Northwest Nazarene College took place in these shifting sociocultural and physical environments.

Layman Eugene Emerson played the leading role in the founding of Northwest Nazarene College. A remarkably diligent man of fortitude and courage, he was also a decisive and immensely generous person. Others shared in the college's brave beginnings, but Emerson, more than any other person, provided the needed focus and financial support for a new holiness school in Nampa, Idaho, and one linked to the Church of the Nazarene. In the tripartite division of founding and nurturing that St. Paul provides in the New Testament, Eugene Emerson was the seed planter, and later, others watered, cultivated, and harvested. Emerson's leading role was all the more notable considering his humble, rural background, and his modest public school education.

Eugene Emerson was born on June 22, 1866, in Spring Mountain, Ohio. He moved with his family to Kansas and from there to Idaho in 1882, where the Emersons settled in northern Idaho in American Ridge, Latah County. Emerson's father James, by his death in 1900, had amassed an estate of more than 1,000 acres of farmland. His mother, Martha Emerson, sold the farm and relocated to homestead in Marsing, Idaho. As an ambitious young man, Eugene had purchased livestock and grazing lands of his own. Returning to Kansas, he married Indiana Bogue, his childhood friend and sweetheart. After a bit of wandering, Eugene and Indiana settled in Nampa where sons Calvin (1902) and Earl (1907) were added to the family.

The Emersons were not a church-going family, although Indiana Emerson was of Quaker heritage and Eugene had some church background. That quickly changed when Martha Ulrich, who attended a holiness church, the Mennonite Brethren in Christ in Nampa, invited the Emerson boys to Sunday school. Attentive to his sons' interests, Eugene began attending the church and was soon converted. In the meantime his businesses were expanding, especially his lumber dealerships in Nampa and other nearby communities. Enjoying these financial successes, Eugene and his family began spending winter months in southern California, where they planned to build a home.

In Pasadena, Emerson made new acquaintances and decisions that redirected his life and soon led to the founding of NNC. Making contact with the Nazarene Church in that area—itself less than a generation old—and hearing the inspired preaching of Phineas F. Bresee and Seth Rees, Emerson became sanctified. That is, he experienced what Wesleyans and Nazarenes called "a second work of grace," in which one's heart is cleansed from sin and he or she is empowered, through the Holy Spirit's help, to live a holy life. As part of this new religious commitment, Emerson vowed to establish a holiness school in the Nampa area. He would replicate in Idaho what his new holiness friends were doing in Pasadena with the Nazarene University.

With Emerson at the controls, a new engine whirled into action. Indeed, the frenetic activities of the spring months of 1913—that stretched through the following summer and fall—were testament to Emerson's drive and diligence. Although a Nazarene church had opened in Boise as early as 1903, none existed in Nampa. Emerson single-handedly changed that. In spring 1913 he built, with his own funds, the Chapel located at 15th Ave. and 6th Street, near where the First Church of the Nazarene now stands. After the Rev. M. E. Ferdinand held a revival meeting at the Chapel, eleven members joined the first Nazarene Church in Nampa. A few weeks later, from June 25-29, the newly organized Idaho-Oregon District of the Pentecostal Church of the Nazarene met in Boise. The proceedings read: "Bro. Eugene Emerson...was then introduced to the Assembly as the man who built a Nazarene church at Nampa, and was unanimously extended the courtesies of the floor." Revealingly, although Emerson may have testified to his vision for a holiness school in Nampa, he was not added to the district's Education Committee.

In fact, the report of the Education Committee made no specific reference to the founding of a holiness school in the Pacific Northwest. It did echo, however, the sentiments of other Nazarene district reports: "We recommend," the report read, "that all who know the value of souls either educate their children at home by private instructors or as soon as practicable arrange for private schools." Holiness people should "secure Christian teachers," obtain "good books for our boys and girls to read" and "call attention to our accredited schools and universities...." But nothing appears in the minutes about an Idaho Holiness School, launched three months later.

The decision to open the school seems to have been largely in the active hands of Eugene Emerson, aided by a clutch of friends and supporters. Less than a decade later, Emerson recalled the decisive moment: "One day in July [1913] while sitting in the Ford the decision was finally made to start the Idaho-Oregon Holiness School." In the same month, Emerson, Rev. Ferdinand (then pastor of Nampa First Nazarene), and S. E. Parsons organized as a Board of Directors. Their actions quickly shifted into high gear.

More than any other person, Eugene Emerson deserves the title of "founder" of NNC. (Fig. 0.2)

The first move forward occurred on July 23, when Rev. Ferdinand wrote to Carlton H. French, a public school teacher in Troy, Idaho, inviting him to move to Nampa and head up the new school to be organized in September. A week later Ferdinand repeated the invitation, asking French to be the "whole cheese" of the new school. "We expect to open a Primary and Preparatory Holiness School," Ferdinand indicated and then added, "and lift it to a University as soon as God permits." Ferdinand reported that he was still in a revival in Nampa where "about sixty plowed thru to God. We also have a fine church of thirty-one members. So far we have about fifteen for the school."

Emma French (Smith), Carlton's wife who later remarried, many years afterwards recalled the difficult decisions their family faced in moving to Nampa in August 1913. They would have to leave family members in northern Idaho, and the future of the new school was, at best, shaky. The Frenchs were promised $100 per month, a furnished house, and groceries; but Carlton and Emma, as well as her sister Gladys Bellamy, were to be heavily involved in teaching. And the Frenchs were already the parents of four young girls. Emerson met the French family at the train depot. Carlton and Emma had vowed never to ride in a dangerous automobile, but when Eugene "put our luggage in his car, we looked at each other and crawled in. We felt strange, but it was only one of the things we did that we had never thought we could do." Disorganization and near chaos reigned that late summer and into early fall.

Area newspapers in August-September carried news of the opening of what became Northwest Nazarene College. "Nampa is to be the home of a new college founded by the Idaho district of the Nazarene church," reported the *Nampa Herald-Leader.* "The college, although under the direction of the Nazarene Church, will be open to all denominations. It will commence with teaching only practical academic courses as are taught in public schools, except that it will teach the Bible. Later," the story continued, "it will develop into college work with a view toward enlarging into a college of recognized standing." The following month, in a story datelined from Nampa, the Boise *Idaho Statesman* added that C. H. French had arrived in Nampa and that the college would soon open. It was "the first to be organized in the northwest by the Nazarene church, and it is due wholly to the efforts of Eugene Emerson of this city that the institution is to be located in Nampa."

A planned school building had not yet materialized, so the school opened in the recently closed Mennonite Brethren in Christ Church at 13th Ave. and 8th Street. On the warm day of September 13, 1913, thirteen students came for opening classes. The beginning was inauspicious. As one account insightfully concluded, "Those were pioneer days, days of beginning, days of small things, unimpressive and sometimes scorned by those later on the scene." Nearly a decade later, one of the first students recalled the church/school building as "gloomy, dusty and even musty." The windows were stained, "blurred by rain and dust." And the building's exterior, roasted by the bright sun and suffering from lack of upkeep, featured "blistered and curled" paint. The furnishings included only a few chairs, "seven homemade tables," and "a pulpit to be used as the principal's desk."

The first semester of the Idaho Holiness School betrayed its newness and instability. The facilities were inadequate, the curriculum disorganized, and the students very young ("only three...were considered old enough to sit on the front seat...and to support the preacher with many amens." The finances were even more unfixed. Indeed, as H. Orton Wiley, later the first NNC president, noted, other Nazarenes of the Pacific Northwest hesitated to support the Nampa school because they were convinced that if a denominational college were to be established it should be placed in "Portland, Walla Walla, Spokane or some other large city."

Before buildings were erected on the current NNC site, most classes met in the vacant Mennonite Brethren in Christ church building. (Fig. 0.3)

Still, the school opened, and Carlton French served as principal while his wife Emma and his sister-in-law Gladys Bellamy taught part time. Emma, only twenty-three with four young children, felt the stress of home and school pressures. As she remembered fifty years afterwards, "We worked very hard at the school, taught in the morning and made calls in the afternoon, and attended a mission at night which M. E. Ferdinand had charge of." Pastor Ferdinand was also in charge of raising money for the school, but "the finances did not come as planned." The French family failed to receive its promised monthly salary of $100, but with a furnished house and groceries provided, they were able to survive for a few months.

Toward the end of the first semester, Rev. Ferdinand asked the Frenchs if they would continue their work if the school were organized on a separate basis, independent from the Nampa Nazarenes. The pastor thought the separation would enhance his ability to raise school support. But Carlton and Emma, not wanting to accept the change, resigned. Emma French retained unpleasant memories of those events for many years. Eugene Emerson, she recalled, "was a loyal Nazarene and had no other intentions at any time," but Ferdinand "was a cunning man. Many did not detect his cunningness when first becoming acquainted with him. I was afraid to trust him from the first time I saw him, but Mr. Emerson did not mistrust him until he suddenly resigned the Nampa Church and moved away leaving him [Emerson] to take over." Others did not share Emma's distaste for Pastor Ferdinand, but all appreciated Eugene Emerson's steadfastness in keeping the school alive—and barely afloat.

Adding to the mounting insecurities were the financial hard times in Nampa in 1913. A terrible fire had ravaged the town in 1909, a recently completed sugar beet factory had closed, and controversies over prohibition had divided Nampa and undermined its fiscal stability. So severe was the financial depression that in September 1913, the very month the Idaho Holiness School had opened, Nampa's oldest financial institution, the Bank of Nampa, shut its doors. Clearly, without the hoped-for financial support from students and their families and from the Nampa community, additional pressures fell on the school's leaders, especially Eugene Emerson. As always, he was up to the tasks.

Emerson moved quickly to replace Carlton and Emma French when they expressed their unwillingness to continue as the school's principal and teachers. Driving to nearby Greenleaf, Emerson invited Lowell H. Coate, a Quaker and public school teacher, to be the new school principal. Coate agreed to serve, and on December 24, he and six other men had the school's articles of incorporation notarized in Nampa.

Two days later the Idaho secretary of state signed the document and affixed his official seal. The Idaho Holiness School of Nampa now stood as a legal institution; its official date of founding was listed as December 26, 1913. The central purpose of the school, the document stipulated, was to "provide courses of study preparatory for business and professional life, or for general culture, to establish classical, mathematical, scientific, technical, theological, agricultural, musical, oratory, physical culture, and general courses of study."

The articles of incorporation additionally noted that the school should sponsor lectures and conferences, and should secure and publish needed books. "In the theological department," the school must "conserve, maintain, advocate and promulgate the great New Testament Doctrine of Entire Sanctification or Christian Holiness." If the latter goal were attained, the school would be especially an "institution committed" to the holiness tradition, sometimes referred to in Nazarene teaching and preaching as "Perfect Love." This attempt to balance heart and mind, to become a school offering both religious instruction and strong academics, would be the central challenge for the college/university in the coming decades.

Curricular experiments and rapid change marked the school's organization during the second semester of 1913-14 and in the following school year, 1914-15. By the end of spring 1914, nearly 40 different persons had attended during the school's first year. That fall, counting duplications, about 30 students were enrolled in primary, grammar, Academy (high school) programs, with 15 more in theological courses and 24 in the music classes. Lowell Coate remained as principal, and Miss Estelle Curray joined energetic Grace McHose in music; Charles V. Marshall, with a master's degree, came to teach science; and the Rev. Earl Perry and the Rev. Harry Hays (the latter also of Quaker background, had become pastor of Nampa First Church) taught the theological courses. Hays, in addition, served as superintendent of the Idaho District of the Church of the Nazarene. All classes during the second year remained in the former Mennonite Church facility, save for the Bible classes meeting in Pastor Hays's home.

Shortly before the fall 1914 semester opened, the school published the first of many catalogues, *First Annual Catalogue of Idaho Holiness School 1914-1915.* This small pamphlet not only included the expected school calendar, but also lists of trustees and faculty members, costs for tuition and room and board, and a few photographs. It also provided a revealing description of the school's academic expectations, religious guidelines, and a list of the rules of social conduct. Together these latter descriptions reveal a new institution searching for its identity but simultaneously demanding in its sociocultural standards.

The catalogue descriptions also indicate the school's desire to marry high academic and religious standards. The Introduction informed prospective students that the leaders of the Idaho Holiness School were sparing "no pains to secure the most capable teachers in scholastic intelligence as well as spiritual preparation." But one of these goals must not crowd out the other: "God can have His way with man only when man's spiritual development is at least equal to his intellectual development." Obviously school officials reasoned that students should expect, and welcome, the school's endeavor to maintain this balance.

Lowell H. Coate was secured as principal in late 1913 and filled that position well for NNC. (Fig. 0.4)

If students were counted upon to be present in all their classes, they were also to attend Sunday services (morning and evening). Likewise compulsory were daily religious assemblies before classes began. In addition to these regulations, students were warned to obey all other rules: "Implicit obedience to every regulation will be required." "Positively forbidden" were "card-playing, the use of tobacco, profanity, obscene language, and the reading of trashy literature...."

Guidelines for other social behavior and recreational activities were equally demanding. Because a "healthful, refined and cheerful social life is an education in itself," the catalogue continued, the school would promote social gatherings for young adults. School leaders considered "the co-mingling of young men and women...as helpful to both," but those experiences and events would be structured "social privileges as might be enjoyed at home." Indeed, young men were enjoined "not to habitually accompany...[young ladies] to and from services, about the campus, or elsewhere." Of note, nothing was said about modest dress or the use of make-up for holiness young women, even though these would be dynamite issues to surface in years to come.

The expanding student body at Idaho Holiness School necessitated major changes. Land and buildings were needed to host and house the growing school. Soon, closer and more supportive connections with Nazarenes in Nampa and the larger Pacific Northwest had to be forged. As he so often did, Eugene Emerson personally took care of the immediate needs. He secured nearly ten acres of land, including blocks 75, 76, 93, and 94 in the Kurtz Addition section of Nampa, and offered them on May 14, 1915, to the school for $4,000 at eight percent interest. A few days later Emerson and other school trustees drove stakes in the newly acquired land, symbolizing it as claimed for the Lord's work. In October 1916, changing his mind, Emerson gave the land to the school and scribbled on the deed: "for the within a ... mtg [mortgage] was given but fully donated several months later and note destroyed."

Groundbreaking occurred on July 4, 1915, and the administration building and women's dormitory rose out of the Idaho sagebrush as rapidly as funds and labor allowed. The buildings for the school, now officially known as Idaho-Oregon Holiness School, were not completed by its fall opening. When the last nail had been driven, the campus community met November 24, 1915, to dedicate the administration building. "We were so delighted and satisfied," Olive Ingler recalled a few years later, "that we walked on air."

School officials also began to reach out beyond Nampa and link the new institution with Nazarenes of the Northwest. Changing its name to the Idaho-Oregon Holiness School in 1915, the board likewise contacted Nazarenes in Washington State to solicit their support for the Nampa school. In the spring of 1916 the name changed again—to Northwest Holiness School. The final name change in the early years—to Northwest Nazarene College—occurred in December 1916, at the suggestion of the new NNC president H. Orton Wiley. Eugene Emerson and other school leaders also encouraged Nazarene families to relocate to Nampa so they could enroll their children in the holiness school. Among those who moved to Nampa were members of the Parsons, Dooley, Harper, and Dean families. Even before the 1920s and out on its sagebrush fringes, Nampa was becoming a northwestern Nazarene enclave.

"The Shack" served as a primitive dormitory for men before Gideon Hall was erected. (Fig. 0.5)

1

Brave Beginnings

THE WILEY YEARS: 1916-27

The selection of H. Orton Wiley as NNC's first president in early 1916 turned out to be a wise decision from every perspective, then and later. Continuing growth had brought demanding but healthy changes. By the spring of 1916 enrollment had expanded to about 65 students. At that time, after laboring under a teaching and administrative overload, Professor Marshall is reported to have said, "What you need is a college president." Hearing that Wiley, the president of Nazarene University in Pasadena, had just resigned, Eugene Emerson, Lewis Hadley, and their colleagues invited him to assume the presidency of the Nampa school. After a few days of negotiation that gave Wiley an extended contract and something of a free rein in hiring faculty (the Pasadena school had refused to grant Wiley these two requests), he notified the board he would accept their offer. For nearly a decade he would provide the enthusiastic, genuine, and balanced leadership the nascent Nazarene institution needed, even amid challenging conflict.

Although Wiley would become arguably the leading theologian and intellectual of the Church of the Nazarene for two generations, he never seemed to abandon the modesty and approachableness of his midwestern and far-western farm and small-town backgrounds. Born in a sodhouse in Nebraska on November 15, 1877, he was reared in Nebraska, California, and southern Oregon. Finishing high school in Medford, Oregon, Wiley matriculated to Oregon State Normal School (now Southern Oregon University) and trained as a pharmacist. Later, after his conversion in 1894 and his sanctification following seven years of seeking the experience, Wiley pastored a few years as a United Brethren Church minister, moved to Berkeley, California, and completed a Bachelor of Arts degree at the University of the Pacific (then in San Jose), and also a bachelor of divinity degree at the Pacific School of Religion, in Berkeley. In the meantime he had joined the Nazarenes and held several pastorates. In 1910, he accepted the deanship at the Nazarene University in Pasadena and succeeded to its presidency in 1913. A man of both strong religious emotions and sound intellectual development, Wiley tried to balance these sometimes conflicting drives in his early college work.

In the years surrounding 1915, the Church of the Nazarene was itself going through an important transition. Phineas F. Breese, the church's founder and most important early leader, died in that year, and so did another newly elected general superintendent (GS), William C. Wilson. Soon, R. T. Williams and J. B. Chapman, young men without much leadership experience, were elected as new Nazarene general superintendents. At first they, and hold-over general superintendent, Hiram F. Reynolds, were much less open and pliable than Bresee in holding the church's reins and guiding it through coming controversies. Their inexperience would eventually lead to something of a leadership crisis from 1915 into the 1920s.

Another kind of shakiness that beset Wiley at Pasadena, during three presidential years there (1913-16), followed him into his presidency at NNC. As long as Nazarene Church founder Phineas Bresee stayed close to the college in southern California and provided sympathetic encouragement and direction, the diverse opinions dividing the university bubbled up but did not boil over. After Breese's death in 1915, the lid flew off the roiling caldron of discontent, and waves of controversy and conflict flooded over the Pasadena campus. Seth C. Rees, who joined the Nazarenes in 1911, and now served as pastor of the University (Nazarene) Church after a rocky career in other religious groups, won over Wiley through his fiery and assertive preaching. Rees, whose son Paul dubbed him a "warrior saint," was an emotional man who seemed to relish a good battle. But it was Rees's actions, more than his ideas, that were the primary source of controversy.

Rees was a militant, strong-willed, and individualistic leader. Throughout his career in several denominations he stirred up opposition primarily because of his dramatic and sometimes erratic behavior. His foes in 1915-17 were A. O. Hendricks, pastor for the Pasadena Nazarene Church and Professor A. J. Ramsay, a man of Baptist background teaching at the Nazarene University. In the early months of the controversy, Wiley was clearly on Rees's side. From early 1915 to the spring of 1916, the Nazarene unrest in southern California gained in intensity, eventually claiming several prominent victims.

General church and district authorities, concluding that Rees was fomenting rebellion and division, disbanded his University Church. As a result of this dramatic and probably unwise action, Rees left the Nazarenes to begin the Pilgrim Holiness denomination. In 1915-16 the Nazarene University teetered on an uncertain edge, fraught with division, indecision, and falling revenues. When the university refused to grant Wiley the afore-mentioned requests, he shook off the dust of southern California and went elsewhere. Before the invitation came from Nampa, Wiley turned down a tentative offer to become president of Olivet [Nazarene] University, resigned at Pasadena, took a pastorate in Berkeley, and announced his intention to work toward a master's degree in systematic theology at the Pacific School of Religion. After accepting the NNC presidency, Wiley was a college president in absentia during the 1916-17 year, pastoring the Berkeley church, completing his master's, and traveling to Nampa for consultation on two or three occasions.

H. Orton Wiley learned several lessons from the traumatic uprising in Pasadena in 1915-1916, and those lessons would serve him well in his decade with NNC. Once the University Church in Pasadena was disbanded in February 1917, some former members joined Rees's soon-established Pentecost-Pilgrim Church (later the Pilgrim Holiness Church) and supported his nascent Bible school launched nearby. Others from the disbanded church moved to Nazarene congregations, and still others searched for a new church home. Wiley was caught in the maelstrom of the varied discontents and controversies, and many years later would recall the dilemma he faced in the midst of the incident. "The Rees revivalistic approach," Wiley opined, "brought on a lot of opposition and the division between the Pilgrims and the Nazarenes. I said that the Nazarenes were to blame but I couldn't feel free to join the Pilgrims…."

Carefully balancing spiritual emphases and academic programs, Dr. H. Orton Wiley, here with his wife Alice, served as NNC's first president (1916-26). (Fig. 1.1)

Some congregation members and students from the Nazarene University followed Wiley to Berkeley, while others enrolled at NNC. During his year in Berkeley and while serving as president in absentia, Wiley received letters from Nazarenes in Nampa sympathetic to Rees, warning that if Nazarene authorities refused to "retract" their actions in southern California, the general church would "burst from end to end." Arnold Hodgin, Rees's brother-in-law then pastoring the Nampa Nazarene Church, had been a part of Rees's church in Pasadena. Later, Hodgin would be at the center of a large upheaval at NNC in January 1918. When Wiley moved to Nampa in late spring of 1917, disgruntled elements from the Rees imbroglio and others sympathetic to Rees were congregating in the Boise valley. Another explosion like that in Pasadena nearly broke out as the school year began in late September.

Wiley had neither fully backed the firebrand Rees nor disowned him in the southern California squabble. Convinced that General Superintendent E. F. Walker and District Superintendent (DS) Howard Eckel had acted injudiciously—if not illegally—in disbanding the University Church, Wiley urged the general church to rescind that action, even while greatly troubled with Rees's actions as pastor and as the founder of a new church group. Bent on finding a middle-of-the-road, more peaceful route, Wiley endorsed a previous Nampa invitation to Dr. Fred Matthews and Rees as speakers for the opening campmeeting. He also invited Hiram F. Reynolds, now the senior general superintendent of the Nazarenes and an opponent of Rees, to lead a missionary rally alongside the campmeeting. Wiley's attempts at peacemaking nearly exploded in his face.

As some participants got wind of who was coming to lead the campmeeting and missionary gatherings in Nampa, they reacted in heated dismay. When General Superintendent Reynolds heard that Matthews and Rees were to preach at the campmeeting, he fired off an emotional letter to Wiley. Addressing the president as "a Brother and Dear Friend...whom I love very dearly," Reynolds proceeded to upbraid Wiley for inviting these critics to be the campmeeting speakers, even questioning if Wiley intended to "REMAIN A TRUE PENTECOSTAL NAZARENE." (Reynolds was undoubtedly referring here to the original name of the church, the Pentecostal Church of the Nazarene.) He wondered if the unsettling preaching of Matthews and Rees would lead to a repetition "of the School and Church conditions, now pending in Pasadena?"

When Wiley explained his peacekeeping reasons for bringing the diverse—even warring—elements to Nampa, Reynolds came on to NNC, still doubtful of the chancy arrangement. Concurrently, Wiley let Rees and Matthews know that he and the Nampa college were Nazarenes and would remain so. Rees had promised beforehand "to forget the past, and ignore all that the Nazarenes have done against us....And go on [to] do Something for God and Souls." At the same time R. T. Williams, one of the general superintendents, although "deeply" upset about Nazarene information appearing in Rees's *Pilgrim* magazine before it was published in a Nazarene publication, nonetheless told Wiley, "One of the greatest joys that has come to my heart is the attitude you have and are taking." But a pastor of one of the largest Nazarene churches in the Pacific Northwest expressed his consternation to Wiley after hearing disconcerting information: "A rumor has reached me that Rees and Matthews are coming to Nampa to hold a meeting. I said to the party who told me this, 'I cannot believe it,' and I cannot until I hear from you that it is not so."

Despite the threat of discord, the campmeeting and missionary conventions were highly successful. Shortly after the meetings closed, the October issue of the new campus publication, the *Nazarene Messenger*, praised the large accomplishments of the gatherings. Matthews, Rees, and the Rev. Fred St. Clair preached to crowds of 1,000 to 1,500, and more than "500 seekers for salvation and sanctification" graced the meetings. At the missionary rally Reynolds preached a strong message, and an excess of $1,750 was quickly raised to provide financial and passage support for missionary candidate Myrtlebelle Walter, a student at NNC. In addition, an educational rally raised $2,000 for the college, and another Hallelujah March paid the needed support for District Superintendent N. B. Herrell. Privately, Wiley was more ambivalent, reacting both positively and less so. He emphasized the achievements of the meetings' outcomes in reassuring Reynolds, but he was more pessimistic in a letter to a Portland pastor, confessing that "no reconciliation will ever be possible" between the dissenting factions. To a rural pastor in Montana, Wiley would write that he was "convinced that the Pentecostal Church of the Nazarene cannot have the smile of God upon her and hold the respect of her people unless that action [in Pasadena] is repudiated."

In the coming weeks Wiley seemed to have a premonition that further difficulties were on the horizon. A pastor in Hutchinson, Kansas, wrote the president reporting that the Rees virus was infecting their region and asked Wiley's opinions on the controversies. Wiley testified to his loyalty to the Nazarenes and his "experience of entire sanctification," but he admitted his continuing discontent with the dissolution of Rees's church, without supporting Rees's establishing a new denomination based on "radical congregationalism." Wiley was convinced it wouldn't work. But the clearest inkling of Wiley's worry about the situation in Nampa came when the Hutchinson preacher asked him about the Nampa pastor, G. Arnold Hodgin: "How is Brother Hodgin on the matter?" Wiley's answer was vague and evasive. "In regard to Brother Hodgin," Wiley wrote, "I would rather make no statement in regard to him, thinking that he should state his own position. We hold Brother Hodgin in high esteem here, and he is doing a work that is owned of God." Then came the warning of oncoming problems: Hodgin "is very closely related to the affair in southern California [Rees] and his sympathies must of necessity be there."

The explosion came the next month. In late January Wiley told a California pastor that "Just now we are kept pretty busy taking care of some of the Pilgrims," but the watch care was not sufficient. Three days later student Ira Shanks recorded in his diary: Monday, January 28, 1918: "Back to Nampa this morning. Found things in a chaotic condition at the school. Brother Hodgin resigned yesterday...." Six faculty members, the matron of the girl's dormitory, the cook, and twenty to twenty-five students withdrew from NNC in the last days of January. They gave no reasons for their resignations and withdrawals, but Wiley provided what he thought to be the general and specific reasons for their decision to leave.

The Pilgrims, as Wiley referred to those leaving, were convinced that Nazarenes had "lost the fire" and were now with the "cooled off crowd" and that Wiley had "sat down on the fire" and was backslidden. "They expected me to swing this school and district for the Pilgrims and I gave them very plainly to understand that I wouldn't be a tool in anybody's hands....They then dropped me flat, and this seems to be the spirit of the thing,—do as I say or you are backslidden." But more specifically when "some of the Pilgrim students...got to smashing chairs, kicking plaster off the walls, and had a potato fight in the furnace [room],—all of this in the name of religion," Wiley told them he "would not stand for any such nonsense." Such admonitions, evidently, were enough to spark fire with those already discontent with the situation at NNC. In a few days, most headed south to Pasadena, to become involved in the new Pilgrim church and Bible school just beginning.

For weeks, Wiley was consumed with writing dozens of letters explaining what had happened. In these explanations he made clear that many of those who had resigned had come from the Rees fallout over the past year; they never seemed completely satisfied with what was occurring in Nampa. He was undoubtedly a bit overly optimistic in telling his sister Elsie that the Pilgrim exodus would "scarcely make a ripple in the college and in a few weeks we will be on a better foundation than ever." Indeed, Wiley had to scramble for faculty replacements, and there were scars of discontent at NNC and around the Nampa area for months to come.

But a few days after the dissenters left, an enthusiastic revival broke out, with several refreshing times of "singing, shouting and crying." A "VICTORY CAMPAIGN" to raise $10,000 for the college was underway, with good results already emerging, and a "beautiful spirit of harmony and confidence" had swept over the student body, which, to Wiley, was "the truly Christian spirit." Most important, as Wiley wrote to a Canadian couple, "We have learned the difference between the leadings of the Spirit and mere impression and can never take sides with anything, however good it may seem, which is in direct opposition to the Scriptures." He also recognized the irony of his position in the recent affray in writing to a minister in southern California: "I know that the dear people of So. Cal. had some very wrong conceptions about Bro. Rees dominating me," Wiley explained, "but I do not blame them. Now, the Pilgrims...are telling that I am but a tool for the Nazarene Church. Strange how things will change isn't it?" Wiley would face demanding challenges at NNC during the next eight years but none so traumatic as these two in 1917-18 that threatened to split the Nampa Nazarenes, if not the larger general church, into warring factions.

Other quandries Wiley faced were the kind administrators might relish: what should the president and college do with the swell of students who came to Nampa, filling classrooms, dormitories, and the dining hall to overflowing? The unexpected booming enrollment in the grammar school, Academy, and college sections of NNC forced President Wiley and the school's Board of Directors to make important decisions more quickly than planned. As dozens of new students came to Nampa, a fast-track, more-expansive building program was launched; more faculty hired; and expanded and idealistic plans for financial support put before the college and its surrounding districts. The most reliable of several notoriously inexact lists of enrollment figures in the first three years of its existence reveals that the Nampa school enrolled 13 students in the fall of 1913; 64 in 1914; and approximately 70 in fall 1915, including a few new college students. A year later 166 students attended NNC, with those numbers jumping to 232 in 1917, and to 342 by 1918. In September 1920, enrollments in the college, Academy, and grammar school reached their largest total in the first years of the school, 385 students.

In these booming years, several buildings went up as rapidly as shaky finances allowed. Trying to avoid going into debt, the college leaders were caught between needed classroom spaces and dormitory rooms and very limited financial support from a small constituency. The administration building and the first section of a women's dormitory (Hadley Hall) opened in fall 1915; in 1916, a men's dorm, Gideon Hall; the Club (dining hall) and a grade school building in 1917; and a heating plant in 1920. Wiley dreamed of an elegant, visually balanced, and appealing quad of Spanish-style buildings, on the pattern of Stanford University's architectural style; but limited monies forced the college to erect much more modest cement-and-wood frame structures. Nampa Nazarene layman W. D. Parsons, indefatigably and at much cost to his family, served as the chief construction engineer for most

The ramshackle Administration Building, later Emerson Hall, was the first building erected on campus in 1915. In the background is "The Club," renamed the Speech Hall, built a bit later. (Fig. 1.2)

of these hastily erected buildings. Gradually, trees, shrubs, and a few spaces of lawn pushed back the everywhere-present sagebrush surroundings. But depressed prices and spiraling costs for farmers in the West in the immediate post-WWI years made it difficult for agricultural Nazarenes to increase their giving to the college. As Wiley wrote the Rev. J. B. Chapman at the end of the school year of 1920-21, "Everything here in the west is in a very depressed condition financially," but he hoped, "if we have good crops here, or rather if the market is in any sort of condition," "it will be comparatively easy to raise...money at that time." But those good times did not come, and gathering additional monies seemed like grabbing straw in a stiff wind.

When Wiley had first accepted the NNC presidency in 1916, he promised to secure an academically strong and spiritually committed faculty. Retaining Charles V. Marshall (science and mathematics), Mary Forsythe (English), Grace B. McHose (music), and Lewis I. Hadley (theology) from the school's first professoriate, Wiley added in the first half of his decade-long presidency other such faculty as Wesley Swalm (history and education), Francis C. Sutherland (modern languages), Dr. Thomas E. Mangum (medical missions), and several other teachers for the grammar school and Academy.

Another faculty member Wiley hired was Bertha Dooley. Diminutive (well under five feet), but dynamic Dooley served as a dedicated teacher for thirty-five years at NNC. A magna cum laude graduate from Whitman College, Dooley earned a master's degree at the University of Washington and began teaching at NNC in 1917. A superlative instructor in English, Greek, and Latin courses, she inspired her students with her commitment to them and her attention to detail. Looking back on her long career in the classroom, Dooley optimistically told an interviewer "I am happy that I could engage in such a rewarding profession." In 1960, NNC dedicated a new women's dormitory in honor of Dooley.

None of Wiley's decisions on new faculty was of more consequence to NNC than his invitation to Olive M. Winchester to join the college faculty. Winchester came to NNC in the fall of 1917 and served as professor of Biblical literature and theology until her resignation in 1935 to become dean of the Division of Graduate Studies in Religion (1935-47) at Pasadena College. While at NNC she became dean and later vice president. A superb scholar, a dedicated churchwoman, and a joyful promoter of holiness and missionary work, Winchester added much to the academic and religious missions of NNC for nearly twenty years under the leadership of four presidents. Had attitudes toward women serving in top administrative positions been different in the Church of the Nazarene during her tenure, she may well have been president of one of the denomination's colleges.

Olive Mary Winchester was born on November 2, 1880, in Monson, Maine. After attending public schools in New England, she graduated in 1902 with honors from Radcliffe College, the women's division of Harvard. Ten years later

Dr. Olive Winchester, a loyal and strong Wesleyan theologian, was the first NNC professor with an earned doctorate. (Fig. 1.3)

Winchester received her Bachelor of Divinity degree from Glasgow (Scotland) University Divinity School as the first woman to gain that degree from Glasgow. After several years of teaching in Scotland and at Pentecostal Collegiate Institute of North Scituate (Rhode Island), a forerunner of Eastern Nazarene College, Winchester left New England to enroll in graduate school at Pacific School of Religion in Berkeley, California, where H. Orton Wiley was also a graduate student. Both received their Master of Sacred Theology degree in the spring of 1917, and both arrived that summer in Nampa to begin their full-time residence. Wiley and Winchester remained friends and mutual supporters in their years together at Nampa (1917-26) and at Pasadena College (1935-47). In 1925, Winchester took a leave of absence to gain her Th.D. at Drew Theological Seminary, a few years before Wiley was awarded an honorary doctorate at Pacific School of Religion. Winchester was the first NNC professor to hold an earned doctorate in a liberal arts field. (Mangum's degree was a doctorate of medicine.)

Winchester, like Wiley, taught courses in theology and Biblical studies, later adding courses in religious education and sociology. She demanded much of her students. In upper-division courses students were expected to research extensive lists of factual questions and to build a thorough card file of answers, prepare a 25-page research paper, and write three book reports on collateral reading. As her student Ross Price noted, "the student always felt he had earned whatever grade he made for the course." Winchester was convinced that this research would be of use for a lifetime, especially for ministers and other church workers.

An heiress to part of the large Winchester rifle estate, Dr. Winchester was financially secure, and able to live independent from the modest—even meager—salaries NNC could afford its faculty. With her funds she heavily supported mission, campus, and other general church projects. She also purchased a huge seven-seater car, which she cheerfully drove and loaned out to college and student bands involved in missionary and fund-raising projects throughout the Northwest. She even advanced the money for President Wiley to build his commodious house near campus (now the Alumni House), and when Wiley was unable to make his payments on the house (because NNC fell behind in paying his salary), he and Winchester gave the home to the college.

On a few occasions, however, Winchester and Wiley would fall into conflict. Winchester thought Wiley too idealistic, often promising achievements that neither he nor the college could deliver. She sometimes lost confidence in his statements because she saw too many failures. In addition, Winchester had loaned money to Wiley—as she did to Eugene Emerson, NNC, and the Nazarene Publishing House—and none of these loans were repaid on time; some not at all. In Wiley and Emerson's cases, Winchester's lawyer—and Winchester herself—had to apply pressure to get the Nazarene leaders to fulfill their financial promises. But Winchester also admitted that her own personality sometimes drove her into conflicts. As she told one general church leader, "I am a chronic scrapper....I think that I would be lost if I did not have something to scrap about. There is no telling what you will have to pull me out of the next time you come."

NNC colleagues provide intriguing personal glimpses of Winchester. They describe her as a confident woman, ambitious, and one who did not suffer easily those who sternly or off-handedly tried to bully her or other professors. That self-confidence would lead her occasionally into conflicts with equally self-assured male leaders such as Russell V. DeLong, the NNC president from 1928-32 and 1935-42. But with sweet-spirited men like Presidents Wiley and Reuben Gilmore (1932-35), who got along very well with faculty, students, and many supportive laypersons, she was a rock of stability and devotion.

Colleagues and students often chuckled at the New Englander Winchester's difficulty in pronouncing western placenames. Her strong accent made hash of Nampa ("Namper"), and Parma became "Palmer." Still others pointed to Winchester's willingness to laugh at herself. On one occasion she hurried into class to begin with a usual word of prayer, but forgetting where she was, uttered a quick, before-a-meal blessing. Along with the class, "she threw back her head and laughed uproariously."

Besides securing academically strong, religiously committed faculty like Olive Winchester, Wiley had to raise increasing amounts of funds for the burgeoning college. In the first two or three years of his administration he tried several methods to bring in needed monies. Indeed as the school rapidly transitioned from a small grade school into an institution of mushrooming grammar, Academy, and college departments, the college administrative leaders quickly broadened their fund-raising efforts. First, Wiley and others appealed for funds from individual churches, which numbered only six in the Idaho-Oregon District in 1913 and twenty-one by 1919. Meanwhile, the Nazarene General Board of Education, meeting in Portland, laid out a Northwest Educational Region (Zone) that in 1919 included Washington, Oregon, Idaho, Montana, the Dakotas, and parts of Wyoming and Colorado. Four years later Minnesota and the Canadian provinces of Alberta,

Saskatchewan, and Manitoba were added. To cover these expanding educational areas, Wiley, Winchester, other faculty members, missionary candidates, and student music groups, like a group of dedicated traveling salespeople, visited as many district assembles and churches as possible.

Special debt-reduction and campus-expansion programs were also launched. In 1919 a newly announced Victory Campaign for $100,000 spilled across the pages of the *Nazarene Messenger,* the college administration's voice, calling for the large amount to fund new dormitories, a gymnasium, a music conservatory, a missionary building, a heating plant, and expansion of the administration and Student Club buildings. The next issue of the *Messenger* revealed that a bit more than half ($52,000) of the funds had been raised, but "We want $48,000," the report enjoined. Not all the needed funds arrived.

The shortfalls in fund-raising were not because of lack of effort. Repeatedly Wiley and others encouraged district assemblies to increase their support of the college. For example in 1919, "To Shout Up the Walls" at NNC, college representatives at the Idaho-Oregon District Assembly meeting in Nampa took assembly delegates to each proposed site for new buildings on campus. Moving from one place to another, the attendees sang, prayed, and whirled their way across campus, hoping to increase giving to the college. At the evening service following the enthusiastic campus tour "a storm of...genuine old-fashioned shouting" broke out. One brother rose to promise funds for the grammar school, another to pay for expanding the chapel to seat 1,000 persons. "By this time," a reporter told his readers, "the audience was having 'spells'. They marched and shouted and sang" and then marched again around Eugene Emerson's nearby home and the Nampa church. It was an enthusiastic, even sacrificial time of giving "in true Nazarene style."

During Wiley's administration NNC rarely received the funds it needed. Building a campus overnight for an exploding student body seemed beyond the financial means of the small band of Nazarenes heroically supporting the school, especially agricultural laypersons particularly hard hit by the depressed economic times of the early 1920s. In the fall of 1922, Wiley had to send an alarming letter to a member of the college's Board of Directors: "We have to draw out all of our funds to apply on three [one] thousand dollar bank notes. This leaves us nothing for salaries or monthly bills. The case is desperate." Competition for these sorely needed dollars was also increasing. Until a general church system was organized to support missionary candidates, they too visited the same district assemblies and churches to fund their efforts in foreign fields. Before long, Dr. Mangum was also encouraging the same Nazarenes to support his new missionary and medical buildings and programs just emerging adjacent to the NNC campus. The wary wolf of insufficient funds for the operation and expansion of the NNC campus lurked at its door until at least WWII.

The financial challenges, however bleak, could not douse the flame of the spiritual development at NNC that shone as a bright and hopeful beacon. President Wiley, himself, on numerous occasions, was a much-needed source of light for the college's religious pilgrimage. Timothy L. Smith, historian of the Nazarenes, portrays Wiley as a "spiritual firebrand" who knew how to balance head and heart. True enough. The intellectual advancements Wiley encouraged among faculty and students equaled his clear spiritual leadership and mentorship during his decade at NNC. Like Nazarene founder Phineas F. Bresee, Wiley wanted to "keep the glory down," to maintain a red-hot gospel on campus. His students frequently recalled his wandering the platform in church services, half-praying and half-shouting when emotionally caught up in altar calls. There is good evidence, too, that around 1919, Wiley selected the NNC motto "Seek Ye First the Kingdom of God."

Wiley's experiences from the Rees incidents also taught him that undisciplined and overly wrought up emotions could lead to disastrous campus cataclysms. He wanted to avoid those by discouraging rowdiness such as the breaking and throwing of objects while "in the spirit," and he was on to students who wanted to pray throughout a class period, especially if they had come unprepared for an exam or oral presentation. Also, he did not agree with those who seemed, primarily, to look for evidences of the Holy Spirit in one's dress or appearance. Wiley's correspondence and published writings during his presidency rarely mentioned the length of women's sleeves or dresses, their hair styles, makeup, or jewelry. Those and other similar issues were much less important to him than to pastors and laypersons succumbing to a rigid, legalistic fundamentalism threatening Nazarenes in the early 1920s.

Channeling the religious emotions of students in the right direction, without dampening their spirit, remained a continuous challenge. One fall the spiritual barometer hit a new high point in what some called the "Students' Revival" because it included later Nazarene missionary luminaries such as Prescott Beals, Louise Robinson (Chapman), and Fairy Chism. Revival-like sessions broke out in classrooms, the dining hall, and the college chapel, with an unusually spontaneous overflow of spiritual enthusiasm during general church leader Dr. Goodwin's visit to campus.

Among that year's students was a perky young woman from Indiana known for her shouting. Standing beside her chapel seat or near the altar, she would call out: "Brother Wiley, I want to testify." Then would come increasing volatility of words and crescendo of voice, until rapid shouting broke out. With the shouting came footsteps and then running, more shouting and circling the chapel. It was a pattern, and her fellow students, recognizing her transparent honesty, were moved by her emotion.

On the first morning of Dr. Goodwin's chapel talks, he announced his text from Acts 2: "This is that...." Before he got any further the excited young woman from Indiana began shouting, and soon the long altar was filled. Hoping to allow Dr. Goodwin to be able to speak the next day, Wiley called for a "waterlogged song" and sedate praying to keep down the emotions. It was not to be. The song blew on the embers, and the prayer set things ablaze. Wiley told Goodwin the service was his, and the visitor began with the same text "This is that." The Indiana lass took off, shouting, the altar filled again. Goodwin, realizing what was happening, put down his Bible, saying, "Oh, well, what is the difference? This is that."

Such outbreaks, Wiley was convinced, were beneficial for the college and its constituency, as this one was. The revivalistic atmosphere spread throughout Nampa and into churches surrounding the town.

On the other hand Wiley tried to avoid encouraging or allowing emotional Nazarenes to carry their religious views to illogical ends. When a devout brother and sister wrote from Melba to deplore "Red Cross signs hanging in the windows of our brethren," thinking of them as evidences of "our leaders even shaking hands and compromising with the world," Wiley had a helpful answer for them. He first testified to the spiritual high tide at NNC, stating that, "The college was never in a better condition spiritually than at the present." He also urged the couple to rethink their attitudes about the Red Cross, for, said Wiley, "I could not be a Christian and refuse to help in this worthy cause." Referencing the Good Samaritan story, he wondered if the Red Cross help for the sick and wounded was not akin to what Christ said about the Samaritan. "Does not our Lord mean to teach us clearly that anything which does not take a deep interest in the welfare of our fellow man, whether temporal or spiritual, is of little account in His sight?"

Wiley sought the difficult middle road between the extremes of liberals and fundamentalists. A half-century later veteran missionary to India, Prescott Beals, one of Wiley's early admiring students, succinctly summed up Wiley's position: Wiley, Beals recalled, "somehow or other had the knack of holding things steady—staying away from fanaticism on the one hand and cold formality on the other.... He just held to the middle of the road."

Not all ingredients of NNC's early campus life came, like directives on high, from the president's or professors' offices, however. Some parts of the campus social mosaic gradually emerged from students' needs and aspirations. Others were clearly partnerships among administrators, faculty, and students. Still others had unclear origins. Whatever the source, several patterns of social life were coming into focus by the mid-1920s.

Religious, literary, and music groups were soon at the center of NNC's student life. Photographs appearing in the student-organized yearbook, the *Oasis*, from 1917 through 1926 illustrate the sustained interest in religious organizations. Articles in the *Nazarene Messenger*, the periodic newsletter sent out from NNC by the administration, and presidential letters substantiate this ongoing participation in religious groups. Preacher, missionary, and Home-Band groups both encouraged students to prepare for the future as well as to participate in at-hand opportunities for ministry. Over the years from these missionary groups came some of the heroes and heroines of Nazarene missions: for example, Prescott Beals (1919), Bessie Littlejohn Beals (1920), Louise Robinson (Chapman) (1920), Moses Hagopian (1921), Fairy Chism (1923), Andrew and Daisy Fritzlan (1924), Esther Carson (Winans) (faculty), F. C. (faculty) and Ann Sutherland.

In 1924, of the dozen students pictured as graduating seniors, ten were preparing for special work, six as pastors and evangelists, and four as missionaries. Two years later twelve again were listed as 1926 graduates, half preparing for the mission field, and two for the pastorate. At the end of 1926, NNC had graduated seventy-four young women and men; nine were serving as missionaries or called to the mission field, seventeen as pastors or evangelists, and twenty-four as teachers. Dr. Winchester often encouraged students to minister in the PNW, by filling her expansive Studebaker touring car with evangelistic teams. Dubbed "the flying squadron," the Northwest Band of Winchester evangelizers raised monies for new buildings, gathered food supplies for the Student Club, and gave young preachers an opportunity to ply their pulpiteering.

Students may have spent as much time in religious gatherings as in class. With daily chapels, church service times twice on Sunday and another on Wednesday night, and several revival weeks each year, NNCers were surrounded by a profoundly encompassing religious atmosphere. President Wiley gave an inkling of this ongoing spiritual fervor in a letter in 1920 to recent graduate Myrtlebelle Walter, who was then a missionary in India: "This last revival meeting has been great. It lasted seven weeks and looks as if it might break out again any time."

Early on, music organizations, immediately and continuously, also captured the attention of students at NNC. Building on the natural complementary bond in evangelical circles between evangelical preaching and stirring musical presentations, the college emphasized vocal, piano, and other instrumental lessons from the beginning. Grace McHose and A. M. Paylor were pioneering professors in musical instruction. Musical groups such as the Men's Glee Club, Women's Glee Club, orchestra, and instrumental ensembles soon appeared. All these groups, as well as smaller vocal teams, became often-invited representatives from the school in revival meetings, fund-raising events, and regular church services. Although President Wiley, Professor Winchester, and some of the college's representatives usually traveled with these groups, the most successful of the musical outreach ventures were the traveling quartets, which in 1923 began traversing the NNC

Singing groups, sometimes experiencing travel problems, were very popular out on the NNC educational zone. (Fig. 1.4)

educational zone to meet prospective students and to encourage constituents to expand their giving. So prized were the summer quartets or other traveling musical groups that they became the most requested representatives from the college—and their popularity continued well into the future.

A smaller number of students became intrigued with the campus literary organizations. English Professor Mary Forsythe, with a sound academic background, was instrumental in encouraging the literarily inclined to write creatively in her classes and for the *Oasis*, which began publication in 1917. A few student writers were published in the monthly *Nazarene Messenger,* which H. Orton Wiley also launched in 1917. When tight times silenced the *Oasis* in 1920 and 1921, NNC students utilized essays intended for that annual in issues of the *Messenger,* which included stories about graduating seniors and other student-centered articles. Not surprisingly, many of the student authors wrote about their spiritual journeys, but more than a few also dealt with environmental subjects, seeing God's work in nature or enjoying the beauty and wonder of Idaho landscapes.

Some of the best of this nature writing in the *Oasis* came from missionary candidates Louise Robinson and Fairy Chism. Robinson (Chapman) found beauty and insight in studying and admiring the ubiquitous hearty sagebrush that surrounded the NNC campus. She expressed joy in realizing that the God who could care for "the little sagebrush" could also look after her. Also seeing God in nature,

Chism was convinced that once a human "breaks through the wall [of understanding,] the finite gives place to the infinite....Then, when man is found, man is lost and God is found."

Patterns of social life at NNC also began to emerge during the Wiley years. Since a majority of the students lived on campus, as they have during the college's century-long existence, important segments of their nascent social life revolved around dormitory activities. Dorm life has always provided a place apart: a setting to form lifetime friendships, a refuge from class and campus pressures, a halfway house between families to eventual homes away from home, and a lively domicile where unplanned antics and memorable pranks were hatched. Information about dorm life, although scant, nonetheless testifies to its importance in the teens and twenties at NNC.

A few years elapsed before women and men's dormitories provided comfortable and adequately furnished accommodations. Hadley Hall (1915) sufficed for women, and Gideon Hall (1916) replaced the slapped-together "Shack" that, almost tent-like, housed men in the first years. Once heating problems were addressed, these two dormitories served reasonably well as the principal housing for on-campus students in the 1920s. They worked well, too, as agents of social organization. Friday night dormitory gatherings—exchanges in which women invited the men as guests and then the men reciprocated—were substitutes for dates, which were not then allowed at NNC.

Most social relationships between young women and men were clearly proscribed in the college's first years. Students took classes, went to chapel, met one another on campus, and ate together. They might even sit together in church services, but they were discouraged from meeting together on campus or walking together as a couple to church. One student, Charles Howard, remembered forty years afterwards that "some old folks both men and women...got it in their heads...to pray through on who should marry who[m]....They had nearly everyone of us lined up with someone, and said we would have to go through with it, as the Lord through them, had made the decision." But Charles did not follow this prescription: "I know I wiggled out of it, and married the girl of my choice," Marion Benton Howard. Revealingly, when Charles proposed to Marion he did it indirectly through President Wiley. Wiley helped out a bit reluctantly because Marion had a call to the mission field but aided them, nonetheless, in their stuttering steps to marriage.

Charles Howard also spoke of one way that young men and women gathered in unexpected ways in unexpected places. In the first years of NNC's existence there were no sidewalks stretching across the several blocks between the campus and the Nazarene Church. During winter months and rainy times, puddles and mini-lakes formed and had to be crossed in making the journey to church. "It was up to some of us boys and men," Charles recalled, "to carry the girls and young ladies over the small lakes and puddles....We rather enjoyed it as it was about the only time we got to hold the girls." Missionary Prescott Beals had similar memories of these incidents: "the mud puddles were quite broad and deep so that gave the boys an opportunity to form a kind of saddle with their hands and carry the girls across those mud puddles. Of course, the boys liked that, and I think the girls liked that too."

In the early 1920s, rules regulating campus social life were codified into a rather extensive list. Some of these rules had appeared in successive issues of the college catalogues and elsewhere, but now they seemed more extensive—and stringent. Dated June 1924, the three-page, single-spaced "Rules Governing the Social Life of Northwest Nazarene" dealt with college and Academy students, the social privileges of each, dormitory regulations, other "miscellaneous regulations," and the penalties assessed for rule-breakers. Although the code writers, said to be both the faculty and students, promised that, "In matters unspecified the widest latitude is given, always considering that the individual student is entitled to the utmost freedom of activity," freedoms were as tightly controlled as those for inductees at a boot camp.

No college young man could accompany a young woman anywhere without a female chaperon. Moreover, Academy males could not enjoy that limited privilege—that is "the public keeping of company by young men and women." Men and women were not to be seen together, "loitering with each other about the

These two coeds, on the "Big Road" (Holly), were traveling the challenging unpaved streets between campus and the Nampa Nazarene church. (Fig. 1.5)

halls, classroom or other public places." That would be "a breach of propriety." So watchful were college officials that they even blacked out the male figure in an *Oasis* photograph showing a young man and woman talking, standing next to one another. No college man could call on a coed in her dormitory without first securing a dean's permission to do so. And "the number and frequency of such calls should always be within the limits of propriety." Finally, undergraduate students must show respect for upper-division students and the faculty. In turn, upper-division students ought to consider their deportment as model behavior for younger students. If NNC men and women broke these rules, their social privileges would be revoked until the Social Committee of the Faculty restored those privileges.

Despite pressures to swing right and become more prescriptive and legalistic, NNC usually remained ensconced in the middle of the road in its attempts to become a Christian liberal arts college. In this challenge of balancing heart and head NNC was following a faith and learning tradition among the Nazarenes stretching back to its founding. Phineas Bresee, the church's principal early leader, supported liberal arts colleges while a Methodist in Iowa and southern California. When a group of holiness women laypersons in the Los Angeles area began efforts to organize a Bible college among the Nazarenes, Bresee "was slow to respond to their urgings." He had reservations about the narrow focus of a Bible college, preferring the wider, more challenging emphasis in liberal arts programs. But he was "slowly persuaded" and swung his support behind what became Nazarene University and later Pasadena/Point Loma Nazarene University. Before his death in 1915, Bresee committed H. Orton Wiley, a devoted Bresee disciple, to supporting Nazarene University, including its expanding Bible and liberal arts program. Indeed, Wiley founded the liberal arts program at the university while he served as its dean from 1910 to 1913. Wiley had brought this balance between Christian faith and liberal arts training when he came to NNC as its first president.

Undoubtedly Wiley's wise, warm, and supportive ways did much to relieve tensions in NNC's first brave beginnings. There were few major disagreements during his administration. In his ten-year presidency, not many issues after the Rees incidents of 1917 and 1918 threatened campus equanimity. No more than a handful or two of disgruntled parents and pastors wrote to the president to harp on religious, dress, or disciplinary issues. Wiley was the key to these peaceful times. He rarely spoke or wrote about exteriors: the dress, adornment, or the behavior of students. Campus residents, their parents, and their home churches—all seemed to trust Wiley and what he and the faculty were doing in Nampa. At any rate, without disagreements among the president and trustees, the administration and faculty, and the college and its supporters, the campus remained remarkably calm compared to the disruptions that exploded on the scene in the 1930s.

In 1921 President Wiley agreed to a second, five-year term, extending his presidency until 1926. But his duties and administration ran in different, more complex directions in that second term. Part of these new bearings resulted from changes occurring in Wiley's career. The general Nazarene Church, taking note of Wiley's training as an academic and of his spiritual maturity and balance, called on him with increasing frequency to participate in a variety of activities. He became a member of the Nazarene General Board of Education, where he spoke for, and helped lay out, the division of the Church of the Nazarene into educational zones linked to the several Nazarene colleges then in operation, as well as those founded later. Because of his presidential experience at two Nazarene institutions, Wiley was looked up to as one the church's veteran educators to be heeded in making educational decisions for the Nazarenes.

Wiley probably was as widely quoted on educational matters as any early Nazarene leader. Realizing that he already had served in Nazarene higher education for more than a decade, church leaders and its publications asked for his advice. Answering requests for his opinions, Wiley wrote often on the value of college training and what it should be in Nazarene institutions. First in the national Nazarene periodical, the *Herald of Holiness*, and later in NNC's *Nazarene Messenger* Wiley pointed out that "the college period is one of self-discovery" in which young persons learn about their intellectual worlds and about themselves. In addition, the Christian college provided "for symmetrical development of the whole person, spiritual, moral, mental and physical." Nor should anyone overlook how much a college education taught young people discipline, "an appreciation for hard work," and "a love for study and a taste for good books." Considering these and many other benefits of higher education, Wiley urged his Nazarene readers to provide much more financial support for the church's colleges.

Wiley also warned of dangers in Christian higher education, whose perils must be avoided. For example, "Christian Education means more than merely placing the Bible in the school and surrounding the students with a spiritual atmosphere," he told a Nazarene professor. On the other hand, too much of "a critical attitude toward the Bible" could "destroy the most holy environment." For Wiley, although Nazarene colleges had to follow government standards for degree programs, they also must be careful not to worship at the shrine of every form of accreditation. If Nazarene schools tried to be like state colleges, they would cease to "be Christian in the truest, deepest sense."

Mounting responsibilities eventually piled time-consuming duties on Wiley's already burdened shoulders. He wrote numerous essays for church periodicals,

The Nazarene Missionary Sanitarium and Institute, founded by Dr. Thomas Mangum, was central to the preparation of missionaries and nurses in the early years of NNC. (Fig. 1.6)

and in 1919 he accepted an invitation for the huge task of writing a survey of theology for Nazarene colleges, pastors and church leaders, and laypersons. (Because of a press of mounting duties and Wiley's own perfectionism, the three-volume study *Christian Theology* was a generation in the making and did not appear until 1940-43.) When the church also launched a book-publishing arm, they called on Wiley to serve as a manuscript reader. He warned them that "I am afraid I am rather a severe critic along some lines, but I am anxious that what goes out under our imprint [Beacon Hill Press] shall be worthy of a place in holiness literature." Apropos of that warning, he said of one manuscript: "Certain portions should be entirely re-written." And much more uncharacteristic of Wiley: "Ten years of study and practice would make an excellent writer of the author."

New duties and obligations for the hard-working president also surfaced on the NNC campus itself. One of these added much to Wiley's involvement in foreign missions. Even before coming to Nampa but especially after he arrived, Wiley was a cheerleader for missions. That enthusiasm spilled out in his teaching, his writings for church publications, and his college leadership. More directly—and personally—he found time to write dozens of letters each month to missionaries in several world areas. His newsy missives of encouragement went out to, among others, Louise Robinson in Africa, Prescott and Bessie Beals and Myrtlebelle Walter in India, Esther Carson Winans in Peru, and F. C. and Ann Sutherland in China. On some days, especially Sunday afternoons, he wrote nearly twenty pages of single-spaced supportive, and very welcome, letters to NNC missionaries scattered in these worldwide mission stations.

A new kind of missionary effort was also surfacing on campus and consuming more of Wiley's time and energy. In 1918, Dr. Thomas Mangum, a recent graduate of the University of Texas Medical School at Galveston, and his wife Emily came to Nampa to found what was eventually called the Nazarene Missionary Sanitarium and Institute. The Mangums felt called to provide medical training to help missionary candidates to prepare for their work in foreign fields. Wiley had invited them to move to Nampa to establish "an Infirmary and Missionary Training Institute." At first the goals of Dr. Mangum's work were modest, but interest in the sanitarium expanded, necessitating the broader emphases of training of nurses as well as of missionaries. Wiley encouraged these efforts, even as they competed with his college work and demanded his increasing involvements.

No less taxing even if more limited were Wiley's efforts to help Nazarenes in western Canada who desired post-high school training for ministers and other students. On a handful of occasions he and Professor Winchester traveled to Calgary and other locations to offer courses of several weeks in Bible and theology to aid Canadian Nazarenes. These energy-sapping duties added to his heavy administrative and fund-raising tasks, as well as his normal teaching load of four or five—sometimes more—courses each year on the Nampa campus. Those mounting duties and their demands were enough to make a stone groan with the effort.

Wiley's expanding obligations were not without their costs. Although committed to a strong academic curriculum, he was unable to maintain his desired high standards for his faculty in the last two years (1925-26) of his administration. In those years only he, Olive Winchester, and F. C. Sutherland had master's degrees. (Winchester gained her Doctor of Theology degree in 1925.) No new faculty members with advanced degrees replaced the loss of two faculty members with master's: Marshall in science and Forsythe in English.

The pressures on Wiley's family also increased. Beset by periodic health problems Wiley's wife Alice had difficulties parenting their four children with her husband and their father so often absent—including summers, holidays, even Christmases—and enmeshed in so many deadlines. Alice's warm but heart-rending letters reveal how burdened she was with family duties and in entertaining guests. On more than one occasion she asked that he hurry home as soon as possible.

Still, in all, and as late as 1923, Wiley was optimistic about his NNC presidency. Now in the eighth year of his administration, he told missionary Louise Robinson, "I suppose if it is agreeable to all that I will continue for another ten years." Wiley thought he would remain in Nampa because he did not like "moving around," undoubtedly recalling how often his own family had moved in his boyhood and young adult days, and he, his wife, and their children in their first years of marriage. Besides, in November 1923 the Wiley family had moved into their sturdy, handsome, new brick home on the edge of campus. Adding to Wiley's optimism was the additional administrative help the college had given him, freeing him to work on his delayed theological volume and to write for church periodicals.

But dilemmas continued to surface, and freed time shrank to a minimum. Family problems also reared up. Alice Wiley's ill health returned, the Wileys' older daughter Pearl also had health challenges and was encouraged to move to a drier climate, and Ruth their younger daughter was badly injured in an accident. To recoup their health, members of the Wiley family began spending several weeks at a time in southern California. Perhaps Wiley was also disappointed about the lack of financial support he and NNC received from the Nazarenes of the Northwest. In a revealing essay for the *Nazarene Messenger* Wiley raised a series of probing questions: why were Nazarenes of the region not supporting the college as they should, why were they sending their sons and daughters to state schools where evolution and other secular theories were taught with regularity, and why were Northwest Nazarenes seemingly unconcerned about placing their children in a Christ-centered atmosphere that would help them with their later lives? It was a hard-hitting essay, uncharacteristic of the mild-mannered Wiley.

In the midst of this period of great need for enlarged support in midsummer 1924, Wiley wrote another unusual missive—three-page and single-spaced—to the NNC Board of Directors. In the previous school year (1923-24) he had not been paid his full salary and had been forced to borrow money to pay family expenses and other costs incurred when traveling for the college. Yet over the years he had donated $1,500 of his meager salary to the college. Until recently he was paid less than the Nampa Nazarene pastor. He also pointed out that he could have supported his family better on a salary of $1,000 less than his NNC salary—if it had all been paid. He could not continue this way, for he would be unable to support his wife and four children.

So, what should the board do for him? Make certain he got his full salary—on time. Take care of his expenses when traveling for the college. Provide "a month's vacation on full salary each year" and allow him to preach and serve at "camps and conventions" during the summer and keep for himself the remuneration paid for this work. Wiley had not wanted to write this directly worded letter, he told the directors, but he was forced to. "I believe God wants me to have an adequate support for myself and family in harmony with the demands of the position with which you have honored me," he concluded, "and this not for personal benefit alone but that I may worthily represent you and the institution I so dearly love." The directors raised Wiley's salary, but the financial problems continued for the president and the college.

More than thirty years later, Wiley recalled the stresses of his NNC years. "I always remember our years in Nampa with a great deal of pleasure," he told long-time acquaintances in Nampa, but "they were hard years for the college and us. We seem[ed] to be always in the pioneer stage of things...." To another friend in Nampa, Wiley would write: "I remember the days at Nampa with a good deal of pleasure, although they were intensely hard and trying days. However, I had my family and enjoyed them very much." Wiley often sounded these ambivalent notes in speaking of his days as NNC president.

Quite possibly all these challenges, once joined, prepared Wiley to make a move. Another was becoming increasingly clear: finances. Even though Wiley gave a rosy report on the fiscal status of the college at the end of his presidency, there were rumors of mounting debts, which two years later had exploded to nearly $100,000.

Wiley was like an immigrant, both pushed and pulled. NNC's mounting debts, Wiley's dissatisfaction with the lack of support from Nazarenes of the Northwest, and the college's unanswered financial questions helped push him out of Nampa; and the warm and persisting invitations of his California friends to return to Pasadena beckoned him southward for what seemed a promising and less hectic future. But before Wiley decided to go, he made an unusual offer to Olive Winchester, even though she continued to advise him not to leave NNC. Winchester revealed that Wiley "had an idea that he would take" Pasadena, "build up a seminary et cetera, and I would take this school here [NNC]," she told R. T. Williams. "I said at once that I [Winchester] would not consider any such proposition," Winchester continued; "my position in school work was vice president, not president." Wiley was not through: "then he wanted to know if I would take the school as vice and carry it on, and I replied that that would entail all the responsibility without the full authority, and I would not consider." But Wiley seemed to have made up his own mind for the future. He resigned from NNC in the spring of 1926, and by that fall was back for his second stint as the chief administrator of Pasadena College.

H. Orton Wiley, surely one of the heroes of NNC and Nazarene history, epitomized the requisite qualities of a founding president of an evangelical college. A strongly committed churchman and enthusiastic spiritual pilgrim, he was an equally driven advocate of academic achievements, intellectually linked to the pursuit of liberal arts education. In his balance of spiritual and academic realms, Wiley set NNC on a course of symmetry, centered on its stated goal of becoming a Christian liberal arts college. Apt Wiley images proliferate: astute founder, man of balance, and person of uncompromising integrity. Others jostle for accreditation: warm supportive father and older brother figure, leader of increasingly mature wisdom, commitments, and dreams.

Joseph Grant (J.G.) Morrison came to Nampa as NNC's second president in the fall of 1926 under unusual circumstances. Without a completed college degree, just four years a Nazarene, and innocent of higher education administration, Morrison did not seem a logical candidate for a college presidency. (Graduating seniors had more college training than their president.) In other ways, his selection was not surprising. In January 1926, two months before Wiley resigned, Morrison held a revival in the Nampa Nazarene Church and at NNC. His powerful preaching had moved laypersons and students alike and endeared him to the college and local Nazarenes. He was also a member of the NNC's Board of Directors. When the presidency came open, college leaders, recalling Morrison's uplifting revival, asked him to assume the presidency. Understandably, Morrison had reservations about accepting the position. He was a preacher, evangelist, and district administrator, not an educational leader. Twice he refused the nomination. But when Morrison reportedly overheard Eugene Emerson's fervent prayer, "send us a man, Lord," that earnest petition melted away his hesitancy, and he became the college's new president.

J.G. Morrison came from sturdy Iowa and South Dakota heritage, similar to that of H. Orton Wiley's in Nebraska. Born on March 27, 1871, the last child of a family of ten, Morrison grew up in a sodhouse, near a small town, and with a Methodist Church background. After abbreviated college training and a stint as a journalist, Morrison began as a Methodist pastor. Following service in the Spanish American War, he returned to pastoring and became known for his stirring holiness preaching and writing in North Dakota and Minnesota. As the Methodists increasingly silenced or sidelined preaching on sanctification, Morrison became more involved with the Layman's Holiness Association (LHA) of the upper Great Plains. Over time he rose to the presidency of this organization, which noted historian Timothy Smith labeled a species of "Wesleyan Fundamentalism." Bit by bit Morrison gravitated toward the Nazarenes and joined that church in April 1922. He and others brought nearly all of the 1,000 members of the LHA into the Church of the Nazarene later in 1922, with Morrison named district superintendent of the Minnesota-Dakotas areas. Serving four years as the leader of what became the Minneapolis District, Morrison resigned that position in the spring of 1926 and came somewhat hesitantly as acting president of NNC. He was fifty-five years old.

Morrison spent less than a year as president before the general church called him to Kansas City as the Foreign Missions secretary. During Morrison's few months in Nampa he was out on the zone much of the time, introducing himself and raising funds in churches spread from Minnesota to Washington and Oregon. He had just begun putting his imprint on campus when he was gone.

Morrison was an ambitious man, often telling listeners "Where there's a will, there are twenty ways." Biographers often cite an anecdote to illustrate this facet of his personality. When the Morrison family first arrived at NNC, they thought of the college buildings as "rather ordinary old structures sadly in need of paint" and the campus as "quite unsightly covered with overgrown weeds and wild grass." Following a plan that the Alumni Association had formulated during the last months of Wiley's administration, Morrison encouraged the campus and its supporters to raise sufficient funds to give all those dull buildings a fresh coat of blindingly white paint. As the money came, students and other volunteers wielded dozens of paintbrushes to whiten up the campus. "Paint, white paint! More paint—everything is going white at old NNC," the *Messenger* told its readers. The enthusiastic workers sided and painted both dormitories and the Student Club building and were now waiting for more funds. The "money is all gone...But we Must, Must, Must ornament, decorate and rejuvenate the other two....Reader," the reporter pleaded, "send us a dollar with which to buy paint." The dollars came in and the painting was soon completed, to the evident satisfaction of the new president.

J. G. Morrison served briefly as NNC's second president (1926-27). Fig. 1.7

Morrison was also a person of military bearing and discipline. These characteristics surfaced in an enigmatic manner. When students arrived for classes in the fall of 1926, they discovered the initials SUS on sidewalks and near building entrances. What did these three letters stand for? Although speculations were rife, no one knew for certain. Later, it was revealed that the ramrod president wanted the student body and faculty to "Stand Up Straight." Diligent exercise was important to Morrison. A decade later he privately encouraged his successor, President R. V. DeLong, to make sure he did his "health exercises." "Games, walks, athletics, gymnastics...will not do, they are not regular enough. You must undertake something that will be as regular as the coming of the dawn. Be religious about it...Do them strenuously, and as near in the nude as you can."

Although Morrison whitened the campus and taught students to "stand up straight," he evidently did not devote much attention to two other crucial areas of administration. First, there is no evidence he spent much time revitalizing the faltering faculty or in securing new faculty members. Undoubtedly without much formal education himself, he had neither a grasp of faculty needs nor the necessary contacts to secure new professors. That void would remain.

Second, and of much more immediate importance, Morrison paid scant attention to finances, his own and perhaps those of the college. As his wife would reveal, he left money issues to her, and to God. "He never paid attention to finances except from necessity," Mrs. Morrison wrote later. Well and good for the Morrison family, but NNC was in debt, had not put in place a well-organized plan to address that debt, and seemed unable to think of its financial future when present financial needs were so demanding. Wiley had not been a strong and successful fund-raiser in his final years, and now Morrison compounded the problem, allowing the college to fall deeper in the red. It was the most crucial problem facing NNC, and the faulty financial oversight nearly led to disaster two years later.

Although Morrison remained at the NNC helm for less than a year, his colleagues, students, and college supporters remembered him fondly. His farewell send-off to Kansas City for his new position included genuine thanks for his standing in the gap and filling in the hedge of need. A bit more than a dozen years later, after Morrison had served as missions secretary and then general superintendent from 1936 until his death in 1939, NNC dedicated a new women's dormitory, Morrison Hall, in his honor. Perhaps his successor President R. V. DeLong, who confessed to Morrison that he had the "utmost confidence in you" and that "I would take your advice quicker than any other man in the Church," was instrumental in honoring Morrison in this manner. Interestingly, many years before a building was named for the first president, Wiley, one for Morrison had been erected. None was ever built to honor DeLong.

For the most part, NNC leaders and students were so overcome in launching a school in far-away Nampa, Idaho, keeping up with its sudden expansion, and keeping it afloat financially, that they showed little interest in the intellectual and cultural currents swirling about them. True, World War I and the flu epidemic in 1918 impacted the campus, but many students were not of age and thus did not serve in the war. Financial, staff, and spiritual needs—and sometimes controversies—devoured the time, energies, and monies of administrators, faculty, and students. They rarely mentioned larger regional, national, and even global tensions and conflicts. The bubble of provinciality, which many later students tried heroically to avoid, hermetically sealed off NNC from much of the outside world in the 1920s.

The decade of the twenties did impact NNC, however, but in rather unexpected ways. The years from 1920 to the Crash of 1929 were quite different from the rather glib, misleading description of them as "the roaring twenties." In fact, some of the downsides of the decade influenced Nazarenes of the Northwest: a harsh agricultural depression that blindsided farmers in the early 1920s, the huge and unsuccessful campaign to foist prohibition on the American public, the flawed leadership of Presidents Warren G. Harding and Calvin Coolidge, and the failures of Congress and states to address pressing economic needs bubbling to the surface as the decade wore on. Even the up sides of the decade disguised mounting dilemmas: isolationists like Idaho Senator William Borah helped swing the U. S. away from international commitments, leading to the unpreparedness in the face of evil expansionists like Adolph Hitler in the 1930s. Seemingly, superficially happy economic times also masked, below the surface, a widening chasm of wealth between the rich and the needy.

Other social and moral issues complicated the 1920s. Influenced by regional, ethnic, and religious prejudices widespread among Americans, Congress enacted immigration barriers for migrants from Asia and others whom Americans considered "lesser peoples." Animus toward Catholics and Jews—and sometimes African Americans—drove the Ku Klux Klan and similar hate organizations. Less harsh but nonetheless restrictive laws were enacted nationally and locally, as social conservatives attempted to shape a society and culture they thought hell-bent in its attitudes and actions. Some of these restrictions carried over into Nampa. When Eugene Emerson was elected and served as Nampa's mayor from 1923 to 1925, he supported several measures that undoubtedly would have pleased most Nazarenes but alienated others of opposite persuasions. As one disgruntled newcomer put it, "Nampa was controlled by Nazarenes...we had a Nazarene mayor, Eugene Emerson, and he closed up everything...They had the theaters shut down. They couldn't have motion pictures, and they couldn't have games in the clubs or pool halls. They made 'em quit playing cards, and the only thing that the men could do in those places was play dominoes...." The critic's sour conclusion: "There wasn't any social life to speak of."

Not surprisingly, these economic, social, and cultural transformations impacted NNC and its community of supporters. When President Wiley decided to keep tuition and room and board charges at lower than low rates in the late nineteen-teens, he made what seemed then wise and frugal decisions. A bit later, Wiley told students in 1923 that if they "could earn from $50.00 to $60.00 per month for the four months of the summer vacation," they could expect to study full time when they returned in the fall. That meant students could attend NNC for an eight-month academic year for about $200 to $250.

But what college leaders—and national political and economic advisors too—were not prescient enough to plan for was the disastrous downturn that bludgeoned American agriculturists following WWI. Farmers around the Pacific Northwest—as well as those in other U. S. regions—saw markets, deluged with postwar products, dramatically shrink nearly overnight. Because of the agricultural downturn, many—if not most—Nazarene students from agricultural and rural areas had fewer dollars for college. Dozens of parents and students wrote to President Wiley, asking if enrollees could not work off most of their college expenses. Committed to helping these students, the college found itself cash poor, unable to fully pay faculty salaries and other pressing accounts. Wiley understood the major source of the financial crunch at NNC. "Our books will show now quite a shrinkage in subscriptions due to the great financial stress we are in here in the West," he wrote to church leader J. B. Chapman; "I am told that it is much worse here than in the East on account of the high freight rate."

The dangerous Spanish influenza also invaded the NNC campus. It came in the fall of 1918, threatening the lives of students and leading to the quarantine of the campus. The flu epidemic eventually forced the closing of the college for several weeks and the resultant loss of needed revenue from tuition and room and board charges. The year 1918-19 closed deep in the red, sinking into the unwelcome quicksand of further debt. Rallying some in the midtwenties, NNC would plunge to new lower depths and would be nearly forced to close in 1927-28.

Meanwhile, by the mid-1920s the general Church of the Nazarene and Northwest Nazarenes had begun to establish discernable identities. The church had expanded steadily with numbers mushrooming especially in the upper Midwest, South, and Far West. Several Nazarene colleges and universities, most of them struggling financially, had been organized, and Kansas City, Missouri, had become the swelling Nazarene headquarters with administrative offices, a publishing house, and missionary headquarters. But Nazarenes had not yet established clear, strong stances on controversial subjects of the mid-1920s. On political issues, most Nazarenes were moderate to conservative Republicans, and would remain so in the coming decades. On

The male "dog pile" represents the informal, unstructured social life in the early years of NNC. (Fig. 1.8)

cultural and social issues Nazarenes generally steered a middle path, avoiding the Modernist or liberal stances on the left or rigid Fundamentalism on the right. Prohibitionists, denouncers of higher criticism, and critics of flappers they were. But on the issue of evolution, they were surprisingly moderate considering that church growth in the 1920s and 1930s came more in rural areas rather than from the urban places of many Nazarene founders.

General Superintendent J. B. Chapman clarified some of these positions in an essay he prepared for the *Herald of Holiness*. Were the Nazarenes Fundamentalists? Yes and no, Dr. Chapman answered. If "fundamentalism" (common noun) meant believing in the existence of God, the divinity and virgin birth of Christ, the inspiration of the Bible, the existence of the Holy Spirit, a born-again experience, and sanctification (the work of the Holy Spirit in a second work of grace), the Nazarenes were fundamentalists. But if the definition was Fundamentalism (proper noun), the Nazarenes were not Calvinists, did not believe in "once saved always saved," and varied from Fundamentalists in their interpretation of the Second Coming. Keeping these clarifications in mind, according to GS Chapman, Nazarenes were true fundamentalists.

By the end of Wiley's administration in 1926, it was clear that the college, like the Church of the Nazarene itself, was steering a course between the opposite polls of Modernism and Fundamentalism, though the latter still crouched at the edges to the right. On issues of higher criticism—that is, the rational, scientific study of the Bible as a literary document—Nazarenes throughout the general church and at NNC were clear: they believed the Bible to be the inspired Word of God and thus not to be considered on the lesser plane of a great work of literature. A few years later H. Orton Wiley would play a (if not *the*) central role in formulating the Nazarene *Manual* statement in 1928 on the Scriptures: "We believe in the plenary inspiration of the Holy Scriptures...given by divine inspiration, inerrantly revealing the will of God concerning us in all things necessary to our salvation." This statement, following a path between Higher Criticism on the left and the more conservative total inerrancy position on the right, remains the central, middle-of-the-road position of the present-day Nazarenes. Revealingly, this stance was hammered out in the 1920s, when many other evangelical groups and leaders were moving to the far right into Fundamentalist camps.

NNC sought both fellowship with, and separation from, non-Wesleyan Fundamentalists. Both groups spoke of the increasing secularism of public schools and universities, including their teaching of Darwin's theory of evolution. Perhaps the leavening effects of its Christian liberal arts colleges were already impacting Nazarenes, keeping them from embracing Darwinistic evolution on the one hand, but finding in theistic evolution a system of ideas consonant with the Biblical Genesis account on the other.

Nazarenes did find community, too, with Calvinistic Fundamentalists on rather pronounced anti-labor stances, in their separation from Pentecostal enthusiasts like Sister Aimee McPherson, and in castigation of Germans (the locus of much Higher Criticism) and Communists. If there was nary a "Modernist nor a Higher Critic" among the Nazarenes, there were increasing numbers who worried too much that emphasis on academics and social gospel work would detract from getting the real "glory down" of individual, red-hot salvation and sanctification. In the 1920s, one heard fewer references to founder Phineas F. Bresee's statement that the *raison d'être* of the Church of the Nazarene was to spread holiness among the poor. Preaching holiness, yes; but much less about serving the poor.

There would be other differences between the Nazarenes of NNC and leading Fundamentalists of the 1920s. Even though Nazarenes tended to turn inward upon themselves, they were rarely as bitterly hostile in their attacks on American society and culture, of other religious groups, or of those within their ranks holding differing viewpoints, for instance, on the doctrine of sanctification and Biblical inspiration.

As in so many other areas, H. Orton Wiley was a model of balance. He seemed in full accord with founder Bresee's declaration that Nazarenes must have unity in essentials and liberty in nonessentials. Although Wiley warned against the dangers of Higher Criticism, he said very little about evolution and tried to find a middle-of-the-road position on the controversial issue of Scriptural inspiration. Much less academic and more conservatively Nazarene than Wiley, J. G. Morrison preached practical sermons on "Achieving Faith," majoring on one's spiritual walk rather than on nonessentials. Perhaps NNC Business Manager J. C. Henson spoke best for college leaders of the 1920s—this beginning era—who tried to avoid on one side the shoals of liberalism and sharp rocks of excessive legalism on the other. He visited one church that wanted to define true holiness by one's dress or daily behavior, to launch darts at NNC for not doing more in these areas, and to avoid paying any support to the college unless it preached this restrictive credo. Returning home, Henson uttered in frustration: "Great God, rain brains on us."

And so the NNC journey would begin.

2

Pressing Forward

THE DELONG AND GILMORE YEARS: 1927-42

Russell V. DeLong, the third president of NNC, was a boy wonder. Born in Massachusetts in 1901, the son of a Nazarene minister, DeLong was on the fast track even as a college student. Early on he gained a reputation as a superb speaker, tireless traveler, and industrious promoter while still a collegian. In spring 1927, just three years beyond his bachelor's work, less than a year after completing graduate studies, and seven months among the professoriate, DeLong was still in his swaddling clothes as an academic. Only twenty-six years old when named president of NNC, DeLong learned how to administrate on the fly. But blessed with a brilliant mind, abundant energy, and spotless Nazarene credentials, DeLong perceived overnight how to hold, pull, and sometimes jerk the reins of a still-new and balky evangelical college in the Far West. He soon proved he was as ambitious for the college as for himself.

DeLong was named acting president of the college in March 1927. He was promoted to chief administrator, just a few days after J. G. Morrison left NNC to become executive field secretary and assistant foreign missions secretary for the Nazarene General Church in Kansas City. The next year DeLong became the full-blown president and served until 1932. The following year, 1933, he was president in absentia while he pursued doctoral work at Boston University and traveled widely as an evangelist and frequent guest speaker. After a hiatus of three years, DeLong returned to NNC for his second stint as president, 1935 to 1942. Later, keeping up his peripatetic life, he was a district superintendent in Indiana (1942-45), dean of Nazarene Theological Seminary (1945-52), and president of Pasadena College (1957-60). He also became the voice of the Nazarenes, the chief speaker for the Nazarene radio program "Showers of Blessing" while keeping up a near-frantic schedule as a revivalist, world traveler, and attendee of the Olympic games. The same could be said of DeLong as was expressed about one of his heroes, President Theodore Roosevelt: all accelerator and no brakes.

Unfortunately, in fact, there was a down side to DeLong that plagued his otherwise very successful career. He seemed to be too assertive for some, and no matter how hard he tried, that irritant remained—and was bothersome. DeLong had difficulty not alienating others in moments of tension, competition, and crisis. He turned sour and tendentious when students, colleagues, or church leaders questioned his assertions, motives, or conclusions. All three of his administrations at Nampa and Pasadena were marred with such conflicts, leading to calls for his lay-off or firing before resignations occurred. Alongside his clear talents and achievements, DeLong seemed insecure, often betraying feelings of inadequacies in his frequent bragging about his accomplishments. His critics, stressing his darker side, thought of him as arrogant, quarrelsome, and unable to admit to or learn from his mistakes. The two DeLongs—the man of success, the man of drawbacks—were like two horses harnessed together; when the less secure one slipped, he undercut the rapid gait of the more able partner.

But the energetic and forceful DeLong led NNC directly and successfully in the first years of his presidency, especially in 1927 and 1928. Although the youthful president faced a multitude of challenges, he first devoted his attentions to getting the college out of debt and pushing for accreditation, even as he tried to deal with other needs. DeLong's Out-of-Debt campaign is one of the heroic stories of NNC's history as it saved the college and won high regard for the new president.

Comparatively, H. Orton Wiley, although a superb spiritual and academic leader, was not as adept as DeLong at raising funds. And, J. G. Morrison had been too briefly in the president's office and too often on the road to pay much attention to the college's deteriorating financial situation. By the time DeLong took office NNC was nearly $100,000 in the red, unable to pay its debts, and was (in fact) in the hands of a receiver, Nampa Investment Corporation (largely operated by Eugene Emerson), and rapidly losing the confidence of its creditors.

Within days after taking over the college's administrative reins, DeLong had a dramatic plan for re-paying the entire debt. In mid-April, relying on the advice of General Superintendent R.T. Williams, a handful of district superintendents and pastors, and working in tandem with NNC Business Manager J. C. Henson, fund-raiser extraordinaire, DeLong announced his plan in an emotional Sunday night prayer meeting with about 150 persons in attendance. One account recalls the memorable gathering: "Sometime after midnight the group prayed through, and the presence and manifestation of the Holy Spirit was wonderfully sensed." The next morning in chapel DeLong presented the college's straitened circumstances, led in prayer, and called for contributions from the faculty and student body. In moments of "hilarious giving," faculty members (who had not received full pay in recent years) and students raised more than $13,000 to pay off the huge debt. The corner of faith had been turned; a tipping point seemed not too far in the future. The campus community was now convinced the needed funds could be raised and spread the story to the uttermost parts of the NNC zone.

Following the momentum, DeLong, Henson, and the Out-of-Debt committee launched an unusual campaign. All the debt must be raised—every dollar of the $93,000—or the funds would be returned to contributors and the college closed and sold. It was an on-the-edge-of-the-cliff strategy. To that precarious position the fund-raisers added an ultimatum: the entire amount must be raised by November 1, 1928—all of it—or the college would no longer exist. From April 1927 to the early fall of 1928, NNC leaders visited the churches of the college zone, spoke to individuals said to have funds available, and contacted businesses in the Boise Valley. By February 1928, only $15,000 more was needed, but that final amount seemed the hardest to raise, like getting the camel through an eye of a needle. The following September, once fall semester opened, DeLong led a prayer meeting each Friday night to address the debt. Beginning in October, telegrams, letters, and other notices went out across the districts. Special days of prayer were called for, and Dr. Williams implored Northwest Nazarenes to save their college. The night before the zero hour of November 1, a final $5,000 was still needed. Feeling the need to give more, hard-pressed faculty and students raised $1,000 in one more prayer meeting, followed by more zone telegrams and phone calls.

Dr. Russell V. DeLong, here with his wife Doris and their daughter, was the energetic, forceful third and fifth president of NNC (1927-32, 1935-42). (Fig. 2.1)

The next day, promises and funds flooded in. Nampa businessmen followed through on their promised contributions. Students emptied their pockets, pledged funds previously saved for the next semester's tuition, and promised even more. Together, they had gone over the top; the debt would be paid.

With a notable penchant for publicity, Russell V. DeLong captured such an auspicious moment by spreading the glad tidings far and wide. He and the finance committee telegrammed the dramatic news to the *Herald of Holiness*, and ran the same telegram in the November issue of the *Nazarene Messenger*. "VICTORY," read the oversized headline, "The job is done...the college is entirely free from debt." Expressions of gratitude were delivered to Dr. Williams, college officials, "and to all our people who so loyally supported the campaign, and above all to God for

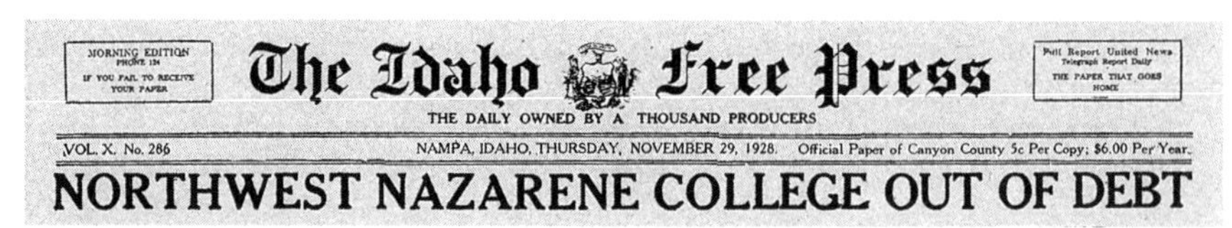

MORNING EDITION
PHONE 134
IF YOU FAIL TO RECEIVE YOUR PAPER

The Idaho Free Press

Full Report United News
Telegraph Report Daily
THE PAPER THAT GOES HOME

THE DAILY OWNED BY A THOUSAND PRODUCERS

VOL. X. No. 286 NAMPA, IDAHO, THURSDAY, NOVEMBER 29, 1928. Official Paper of Canyon County 5c Per Copy; $6.00 Per Year.

NORTHWEST NAZARENE COLLEGE OUT OF DEBT

President DeLong engineered a vigorous, successful campaign to raise nearly $100,000 in 1927-28 and saved NNC from closing. (Fig. 2.2)

victory." It was a mountaintop experience that DeLong remembered—and recalled to others—for the rest of his life.

Not surprisingly, the ebullient, indefatigable president was soon on another quest. Beginning in the late twenties, and for a full decade, DeLong pushed for informal, and then formal, recognition of the college's academic programs. NNC must become an accredited institution.

DeLong moved simultaneously in several directions to gain accreditation. First, he tried to hire a more academically prepared faculty. Next, he wrote to several state-sponsored institutions in NNC's zone: for example, University of North Dakota, University of Idaho, University of Washington, and University of Oregon, requesting acceptance of NNC's graduates in their graduate programs. He also made contact with Idaho's state educational organizations, trying to get recognition of NNC's undergraduate programs and its preparation of teachers. When DeLong saw inequities, opportunities, or advantages, he pursued them, sometimes like an offensive, persistent bulldog.

At the time DeLong became president in March 1927, only three faculty had completed a master's beyond the bachelor's degree. Olive Winchester had the only terminal degree, a doctorate in theology. Francis C. Sutherland (history, education, and languages) had a master's, and so did DeLong, in philosophy and theology. The other thirteen faculty members listed for college work did not have master's degrees. Knowing he needed a strong faculty to gain positive reactions from an accrediting commission, DeLong went on the hunt for other professors with at least an MA. By 1932 he had secured a new group of faculty members, all with master's degrees: May E. Bower (education and science), Albert F. Harper (debate and expression), C. V. Marshall (science), Bertha Dooley (English and classical languages), Kent Goodnow (modern languages), Ira N. Taylor (modern languages), as well as several others at work on advanced degrees. Several of these persons—especially Bower, Harper, Marshall, and Dooley, along with Sutherland and Winchester—were long-time and very valuable faculty members in the 1920s and 1930s, and some beyond.

As he worked at adding new faculty members and making the important contacts with other institutions of higher education, DeLong realized how much accreditation would mean to NNC graduates and to the reputation of the college. If NNC students, as undergraduates or as graduates, transferred to state colleges and universities and could not gain acceptance of their credits, they would soon realize that their years at Nampa would rank them behind their peers academically. They might also think their expenditures for an NNC education would have been in vain.

To press even more thoroughly toward accreditation, the president kept close tabs on students who graduated from NNC and went off to do graduate work at such institutions as the Pacific School of Religion in Berkeley, Boston University, universities in Idaho and Washington, and several other colleges and universities. When an NNC graduate did above average or superior work, DeLong made sure their achievements were part of his badgering of accrediting associations to pay more favorable attention to NNC and its academic programs.

Consider, for example, how much President DeLong courted Idaho educational administrators, officials at the University of Idaho, and Frederick Bolton at the University of Washington. He first contacted Idaho's commissioner of education and asked for accreditation for NNC's high school work; then he worked with several educators at the University of Idaho to secure their support. DeLong asked them what NNC needed to do to receive initial accreditation for standing as a junior or two-year college and, eventually, for its recognition as a four-year liberal arts college. Most important of all, DeLong pursued Professor Bolton, chairman of the Commission of Accreditation of the Northwest Association of Colleges. Inviting Bolton to campus, the president also made sure other important educational officials and businessmen from Nampa and Canyon County were in attendance. The banquet hosting Dr. Bolton was orchestrated with finesse. "It was the opinion of all who attended," the *Nazarene Messenger* reported—in an account perhaps written by DeLong himself—"that the banquet was one of the most inspiring and beneficial social events of the college this year." The visit and NNC's record of progress sufficiently impressed Bolton that two days later in Spokane he recommended that the first two years of college preparation at NNC be accredited.

The formal recognition came the next day, on April 10, 1930, with accreditation as a junior college. The Northwest Association would now put its stamp of approval on the first two years of NNC's academic offerings. That achievement, DeLong told a Portland Nazarene preacher, symbolized how much "God has helped us in the last few years," but the president added he now was looking toward four-year recognition: "we must make plans to go on and reach that goal." DeLong undoubtedly was pleased to hear from another minister on the district that the president deserved "hearty congratulations on your most excellent achievement in this direction."

Even though DeLong continued to press for other types of academic recognition for NNC, he was forced in new directions by unexpected circumstances. In fall 1929 the worst depression in the history of the United States fell like a suffocating wet blanket on the whole country. If that financial disaster had come a year or two earlier, it is doubtful that DeLong would have been as successful in his Out-of-Debt campaign. Now he had to face new, even more dramatic challenges in keeping the college financially afloat.

The two largest evidences of the negative impact of the Great Depression on NNC were its falling revenues from student payments and its inability to pay the full salaries of its faculty members. Other fiscal challenges were also soon evident. How were all these to be handled?

There was a further irony: students coming to NNC were arriving in greater numbers even though they had fewer dollars to fund their college education. The Out-of-Debt campaign had wiped out nearly all capital debts—buildings, grounds, loans, and interest on loans—but it did nothing for the annual budgets. Once the $93,000 shortfall had been wiped out, NNC had to live within its financial boundaries and not spend more than was coming in, largely from student payments and the budgets of NNC's educational districts. There was the rub. Since student enrollments were continually growing from 1928 to 1931, older buildings needed to be expanded and new ones erected.

DeLong, with the aid of the college's trustees, attempted a series of experiments to keep NNC afloat financially. But he was chary of making large structural changes in these years of financial pressure. Revealing his essential conservative outlook, DeLong told an Oregon pastor it was unwise "in an abnormal time to endeavor to completely revolutionize the policy of any business concern or institution that has been followed in more prosperous days." Instead he and the college would try less radical innovations.

Beginning in 1928, the college offered a reduced rate of $250 for a year's tuition and board if students would pay that amount upfront rather than the $310 charges over time. At first this offer helped bring in larger amounts of cash, but by 1930 and 1931, cash income had dropped off $4,000 and $2,000 respectively, and yet, as Vice President Olive Winchester noted, "at the same time we [have] had increased enrollment."

Faculty members took an increasingly large hit as the Depression pressed the college from every side. Although salaries—about $125-135 per month for 8 ½ months for a faculty member with a master's degree—remained much the same in the depression years, they often were not fully or promptly paid. Gradually a system of barter—known as "transfer"—was put into effect. A professor might sign a contract for $125 per month, but only 50 percent of that amount was guaranteed, with the remainder coming in "transfer" (the vegetables, fruit, and meat that students sometimes used to pay college charges) or tuition payments for faculty family members. As the depression deepened in the early to mid-1930s, more and more faculty members received only partial salaries and increasing percentages of transfer. On a few occasions, DeLong was forced to let faculty go because the college could not pay their salaries.

On occasion financial pressures out on the NNC districts flooded onto the Nampa campus. Many farm families had been experiencing bad times since world agricultural markets collapsed following World War I. Then inadequate rainfall and other climatic disasters blind-sided agriculturalists in the late twenties and early thirties. Those continuing dilemmas meant that many rural churches and districts with predominantly nonurban churches were unable to pay their budgets. In these dire circumstances some districts made decisions that hurt NNC financially. In North Dakota the district superintendent diverted educational funds meant for the college to other pressing needs. Hearing of that decision, DeLong wrote direct—even pointed—letters to the district treasurer and superintendent telling them that he was upset with what the district had done.

Sometimes DeLong merely put off creditors or pushed in other directions to raise funds. Two months after he assumed the presidency, a letter threatened suit against the college if it didn't pay a bill of $125. DeLong replied "at present time it is absolutely impossible to pay the bill which you have undertaken to collect." The president looked for other sources of much-needed funds. In DeLong's papers are lists of donors who might have abundant resources; "parties that promised to give liberally to the school." And on one occasion he wrote to a fund-raising agent for the college urging him to find out about a widower who was rumored to be well-to-do: "[Pastor Hugh C.] Benner and I will try and get in his will." When the president wrote to trustees or other boards helping administrate the college, he gave upbeat reports but also tried to relay the difficult financial circumstances the college faced.

Besides urging districts to pay their budgets, churches to take up special NNC offerings, and cutting faculty salaries and numbers, DeLong tried more unusual methods to save money or raise funds. He repeatedly pointed out that the chapel or dining hall could not accommodate all the students, and the library had inadequate space too. The president also noted that nearly 70 students, about half the student body, were taking his Introduction to Psychology class in a room meant for 40 students. The expansion of one building and the erection of a new building, DeLong contended, would take care of most of the problems. The administration building should be remodeled, including the construction of a chapel wing

The all-purpose College Chapel in the Administration Building hosted religious, dramatic, and other student activities. (Fig. 2.3)

and the remodeling of other parts of this central building. In addition, the college needed a gym. The president was convinced that NNC's accreditation as a four-year college would be held up if a gym were not constructed. But how were these projects to be undertaken when the college was already financially strapped?

DeLong had ideas for these projects, as he almost always did when pressed. He floated a dream that included the rental or purchase of brick-making and cement-mixing machines, a request to Nazarenes across the educational zone of each one purchasing a single brick for $1, and the hiring of several college boys to help construct the addition to the administration building. The idea caught hold and was immediately put to work. Not only was a chapel wing completed but also the remainder of the administrative building veneered from the bricks that the whirring machine, like a well-oiled automaton, turned out by the thousands. Once finished in 1931 the building was dedicated as the Emerson Administration Building.

For the gym there was another plan. The Idaho-Oregon district wanted a place for its annual camp meeting. What if the district and the college student body joined forces to fund this much-needed building? The idea seemed fortuitous since it would cost the college almost nothing. Students agreed to tax themselves

$1 each semester to help fund the physical education building, and the district would raise the other dollars. It would be a multi-use building even before the term was invented—a gym for college students during the school year and a large gathering place for the district for its annual camp meeting. Most amazing of all, the two projects were completed even in a time of near-zero funding. Unfortunately, however, the college had to take out a $30,000 loan to construct the rather extensive addition to the administration building, and most of that debt was still hanging over the college at the end of the decade.

In the middle of it all, DeLong never forgot the need for spiritual direction on campus. In this area he was outstanding. He was a clear, invigorating, and authoritative—if not authoritarian—leader in spiritual matters on the NNC campus. A strong pulpiteer and a committed revivalist, DeLong kept the spiritual temperature on the warm—if not fiery—side. He learned early on, too, that many NNC supporters cared much more about its religious than its academic emphases. Understanding this bias, DeLong made sure that news of revival outbreaks and emotional break-throughs in regular chapel services got out to these onlookers. His periodic reports to college administrators also accentuated spiritual matters. "Some of the most gracious scenes of spiritual power have been witnessed in the past four years," he noted in 1929. "Revivals have broken out each year and scores of young people have been saved and sanctified at the altars of the college chapel." As a result more than a few students felt special calls to the ministry and mission fields. "Northwest Nazarene College is serving the Church and endeavoring to keep her motto always to the front, 'Seek ye first the kingdom of God and His righteousness,'" one report concluded.

An insightful and discerning analyst of the NNC student body, DeLong also clarified to board members the differences between the first students enrolled in the college and those arriving in the second decade of its existence. In his presidential report to the college's Board of Directors in November 1929 he pointed out clearly the differences between the two groups and suggested this was a "matter which you have possibly not thought of before." Those who came first, he began, were "made up of an older group of students who were getting their education later in life and came with a definite goal and objectives." But the more recent students were younger, more diverse religiously, and coming from more varied "homes and communities. Many come without the ideal of such an institution as Northwest Nazarene College. It takes time and tact and much prayer to keep them here and keep them satisfied until they become imbibed with the spirit of the school." This was an important and revealing observation, and had DeLong been given several more decades of perspective, he would have seen that each generation of NNC/NNU leaders has faced this increasing diversity of student backgrounds and their lessened links to the Church of the Nazarene.

Undoubtedly, DeLong derived a good deal of satisfaction from the very positive responses to his preaching and spiritual leadership on campus and out on the Northwest zone. Repeatedly pastors and district superintendents called for his return to speak at churches, district assemblies, and other lay gatherings. And they asked him to bring along singers, quartets certainly, but also his wife Doris Gale DeLong, a talented musician and gifted soloist. DeLong often gave glowing testimonies of his work in letters to others, and there is every evidence he was a strong spiritual leader then and later.

In his connections with campus students and with parents and their children, DeLong faced stressful dilemmas. In these relationships he sometimes betrayed the personality flaws that undercut his otherwise skillful and energetic leadership. Still, being fair to the president, he was forced to deal with truckloads of small, vexing problems a modern president would have farmed out to his fellow administrators. DeLong had no such staff. Disgruntled parents, having been notified that their son or daughter had been disenrolled, often fired back defensive missives attacking the president or the college. Surely their offspring had not been guilty of misdeeds; there had been a misunderstanding, the college had been unfair or unyielding in the treatment of their son or daughter, or shouldn't a Christian college forgive and move on. DeLong frequently became a substitute or directive father trying to straighten out the erring young persons, hoping to redeem them for the college, their families, or themselves. As many of these attempts at redemption failed as succeeded.

The expectations of parents were amazing. Here was a president of a booming, church-related college, under pressures from bulging enrollments, tight budgets, and other extraordinary leadership demands expected to keep track of the daily life of nearly 400 high school and college students. Additional pressures from pastors, church officials, and friends added to the load. It was enough to make a cat bark. Consider one nervous mother in Portland. She had not heard from her son for three of four weeks—even though she had sent him letters, clothes, and a cake—so she wrote to Dean Albert Harper; having no answer from the dean, she fired off a letter to the president. Could he "personally investigate" and let her know about Bob? Probably a bit annoyed by the distraught mother's request, DeLong reported that Bob was all right and would soon write. He was only 14.

Another experience was the tip of the iceberg. A devoted mother had "prayed through" about her son Eugene coming to campus, but she lacked the needed funds to send him. So, DeLong suggested that Eugene not come. He wrote her straightforwardly: "I took it upon myself, at our expense, informing you that it was not my judgment that he should come...." Eugene came anyway, and financial, academic, and other problems, by the bundle, followed—and for several years.

And then a letter came from Canada. "I would just like to drop you a line to-day to tell you that there is [sic] a disappointed and brokenhearted father and mother up here in the north country." The man and his wife wanted "to find a friend that would cooperate with them in trying to locate their boy." John had come to NNC to register and then disappeared. The father had written before, and DeLong had answered, but still no John. Now the father wanted some action: when John "did not complete his registration I do not see why someone did not notify me of the conditions....Someone in authority could have seen that something was wrong and that the parents of a child should be notified." DeLong had written, had made contact; but he could not locate John; that was not enough for the worried father and mother.

Dress requirements were another problem banging at the president's door. These guidelines were shifting in DeLong's first years in office. The 1926-27 NNC catalogue stated the "Dress Regulations" in specific detail: no "thin dress materials" were acceptable unless "suitable under slips were worn"; "skirts must be of such length as not to expose the calf of the leg; sleeves must be not less than four inches below the elbow; dress necks are not to be low in front or back." Women's hose could not be "flesh-colored or extremely thin," and "jewelry for ornamentation [was] prohibited." One year later all the concrete details had been dropped and replaced with the statement: "Students will be expected to dress in conformity with the standards of the Church of the Nazarene." And in the next year's catalogue the statement on "Dress Regulations" read: "Students will be expected to dress in conformity with the standards prescribed by the Faculty Committee on Dress."

These continuing shifts in this minefield of controversy among evangelical and fundamentalist schools raised unanswered questions among students, families, and churches. And the queries came. One member of a prominent Nazarene family in the northern Rockies wrote to ask about the subject. DeLong told her "Dress requirements demand that sleeves should come at least to the elbow and that skirts should be six inches below the knee." But she could bring her portable phonograph as long as she did "not play it in study hours." Another young woman's question was the more remarkable. She had flunked French, and admitted that, but she really wanted to know about a possible dress code at NNC. "I heard a rumor that we were only supposed to wear blouses and skirts. Is that so?" In answering, Olive Winchester wrote more about making up the failed French course and then added, "Regarding wearing apparel the rules will be the same as they have been heretofore"—e.g. the guidelines in the 1926-27 catalogue.

Sometimes the questions or problems were even more complex. One young coed became infatuated with a young man from Canada, and when he was dismissed for smoking, she grew even more homesick and listless. But one Friday she made her way to the altar and "seemed to pray through in good style and professes a Christian experience now." DeLong had hopes for her future at NNC, but also told her father the college would "keep an eye on her associates and let you know from time to time how she is getting along." Another young woman refused to abide the college's dress code, traveled homeward with a young man without the permission of her parents and the college, and bruised NNC's expected standards while she lived off campus. The president apprised her mother of these happenings and pressured her daughter to leave her off-campus housing and come back into the dorm. When still another young woman seemed smitten with homesickness, fell "under conviction," and "bobbed [her] hair," DeLong telegraphed her relative advising her to encourage the young woman to "get down to work [and] observe [the] rules of school. She has fine talents." The young woman went home but soon seemed to find herself. She asked for the president's forgiveness because she had accused him of "trying to work Psychology on me and bribe me....I intend to go deeper into the things of God. I covet your prayers," she told DeLong.

All the more challenging were the problems with the offspring of pastors and even district superintendents. DeLong had to tell a Nazarene minister in Weiser, Idaho, that his son had broken several NNC rules and had taken a negative, defiant attitude toward the college. The discipline committee had been lenient, but after repeated offenses they were now recommending dismissal. The president was writing the pastor father that his son would be allowed to reapply at a later date but that the dismissal was probably good for the son; "he certainly needs something to awaken him," the president wrote. The father seemed to agree with the college's decision. Perhaps hearing that a DS's daughter had repeatedly and purposefully broken several code-of-conduct rules was even more disconcerting, especially when she did it because she "*thought* there was a tendency on your [Delong's] part to have favorites in school." But when she wrote to confess her misdeeds, asked his forgiveness, and spoke of being "reclaimed," she seemed to satisfy the president. There were a surprising number of ministerial sons and daughters who got into trouble, and an equally surprising number who went on to become ministers, missionaries, and other special workers.

Russell V. DeLong was a hands-on president, the kind later observers would call a micro-manager. His tendency to watch every campus activity carefully meant that many of the students' social activities were linked to presidential leadership. Close ties between the president's office and student activities were particularly evident in the Athletic-Literary societies and debate program that flourished in DeLong's administration and well afterwards.

The Athletic-Literary societies had begun in a rather desultory fashion in the Wiley administration and had continued during Morrison's presidency. But those men were like father figures compared to the youthful DeLong. Active, athletic, and committed to the arts, DeLong reorganized and revitalized the societies. They became the arena for social activities on an isolated and protected campus—and would remain so for several decades—at least into the 1960s.

DeLong entered the world with competitive genes. He enjoyed vigorous games of tennis and played in basketball games into his thirties. Contests of skill and academic achievement seemed part of his heritage. A lifetime sports fan, he later crisscrossed the globe attending Olympic Games on several continents. His post-NNC letters often overflowed with fulsome accounts of his travels, achievements, and successes. All the more reason to understand, then, his promotion of Literary-Athletic (later, Athletic-Literary) societies, a gym for competitions, and a first-rate debate program.

Sensing the need for additional social, cultural, and physical activities that would capture students' interests and keep them tied to campus life, DeLong reorganized the Literary-Athletic societies in the first semester of 1927-28. Terminating the groups begun during Wiley's administration—for the academy and the college—he arbitrarily divided all students into three new societies: the Olympians (later Oly's), Alpha Delta Phi (ADP's), and Sigma Lambda Alpha (SLA's). (The Lambda Sigma Pi, or LSP's, were added in 1938.) Intense competitions in athletic, literary, and musical activities were launched, and students became emotionally attached to their societies, working to win the coveted Faculty Loving Cup. At first the Oly's led the way, but soon the ADP's and SLA's also won the cup competitions. One observer, looking back more than thirty years, concluded that these new literary-athletic organizations "formed perhaps the most significant phase of the internal organization of the school." DeLong was certainly pleased. He referred to them as "splendid programs," generating "great interest." Until the first intercollegiate sports program (men's basketball) was launched in 1933-1934, these societies furnished the physical exercise and other competitions the students apparently wanted and needed. Although church-nurtured young people might have experienced musical competitions, the societies also fostered literary projects hitherto unknown among pre-college Nazarenes. The society activities undoubtedly played another signal and important role: they helped capture the time and energies of students who might otherwise have left campus to become involved in entertainments forbidden in the church and college. When the Athletic-Literary societies fell out of popularity later in the century, it was a clear sign that the NNC campus was beginning to look outside itself for additional social activities.

Debate activities, previously limited to campus competitions, quickly became more extensive and expansive under DeLong's encouragement. He hired professors whose specific assignments included work with NNC debaters and urged them to set up contests with debaters from other colleges. In spring 1931 the president rehearsed the expansion of forensics with the Board of Regents. Tryouts and intense preparation led to a very successful series of NNC debates on several Northwest campuses, including the University of Oregon, Oregon State College, and University of Washington. Another team went south to do battle with debaters from University of Utah, Stanford University, and the University of California. When students participated in these debates, DeLong was convinced, NNC "made quite a name for itself and these larger institutions are glad to welcome our boys, knowing that they will put up a good stiff argument which will be profitable for the debaters of these other institutions."

Building on these initial successes, the debate program expanded even further. Debates were initiated with Nazarene rival, Pasadena College. A women's team was also established and sent out to other campuses. But the victory of victories—and an event remembered long in NNC annals—was the debate on February 26, 1932, between the NNC men and visiting team from Stanford. More than 700 people, including Governor C. Ben Ross, jammed into the chapel to watch debaters Donald Harper and Theodore Martin and their opponents. Although the NNC debaters lost a close 2-1 decision to the seasoned Stanford duo, the event did much to put the Nampa school into the memory banks of attendees and readers of local and regional newspapers. A reporter for the *Nazarene Messenger* probably came close to the truth in calling the match "one of the truly epochal events in the history of Northwest Nazarene College...."

Understandably, DeLong put even more emphasis on spiritual matters than the erection of buildings and the Athletic-Literary and debate groups. He was a genuinely religious leader, but he also knew that he must report the campus' spiritual victories to keep the college supporters happy. His letters and reports overflow with accounts of revivals and other spiritual outbreaks. Some of the breakthroughs came in the two or three revivals scheduled for each school year, others in faculty-led chapels, and still others that spontaneously erupted in church gatherings, prayer meetings, or devotional times. In spring 1931 he wrote a college schoolmate in the East that "God has given us a very wonderful school year. We have had the greatest revival I have ever witnessed." The president was even more effusive in a brief piece in the school paper. The revival was unscheduled; "no special evangelist was called," he wrote. But chapel services exploded with fervor. As DeLong put it, "Tears flowed, shouts rolled, fervent exhortations were given until at times it seemed that heaven was very near." He thought two outcomes of the revival were particularly noteworthy: "First, it was a deep, far reaching time and, second, it was a time of unusual religious freedom." Refreshing times like these were like warm spring breezes blowing in after a cold, bleak winter, freshets that

Nazarenes in and around the Nampa campus hungered and thirsted for.

Despite the accomplishments of the DeLong administration, despite his personal achievements, and despite the good news going out from the campus, discontents were also bubbling beneath the surface at NNC. How those rumblings began and precisely why is not clear in the written records. The president obliquely mentioned dissenters and his desire to complete his doctoral work, but he was neither specific nor extensive in his descriptions of discontent. It is clear, however, that in the spring semester of 1932 petitions began to circulate calling for an investigation into DeLong's presidency. A change in organization also complicated matters. Previously a Board of Directors, all from Idaho, was the primary board of administrative control. But a change in Idaho law allowed the organizing of a new Board of Regents that included members, ministerial and lay, from all regions of the NNC educational zone. For several years after 1929 both of these groups functioned as boards of control but not always smoothly and consistently.

The cover of conflict and controversy pitched off in the late spring and early summer of 1932. The dramatic story emerges gradually, in bits and pieces, from minutes of regents and directors meetings. Much of the story remains mysterious. In spring 1931 the Board of Regents had thanked DeLong for his "splendid leadership and excellent report." The report was "received with a rising vote." Later in the meeting DeLong recommended that Dr. Winchester be continued in office as vice president and dean of the College of Liberal Arts. In a closing motion the regents moved and passed that DeLong be rehired as president for the next four years. So far everything seemed sweetness and light.

But in the next year division reared its ugly head. Although the regents voted to express "appreciation" for DeLong's "excellent and comprehensive report," they were evidently stunned with the "important communication" from Dr. Winchester, resigning as NNC's vice-president. They immediately named a committee of three to interview Winchester. That afternoon the report of the interviewers was received, with the regents asking Dr. Winchester "to meet with the Board for an interview concerning her work in the future." She appeared "and made statements concerning her work in the future." DeLong was evidently not at this meeting.

The next afternoon the drama took a more ominous turn. Although President DeLong recommended that Winchester be continued as vice-president, dean of the college, and head of the Department of Biblical Language and Literature, which the regents unanimously favored, she wrote the board "declining the office of executive vice president as offered by the Board." The regents passed a resolution of regret, expressing their "appreciation of her services these many years in this institution." Within minutes, DeLong (now in attendance) nominated Rev. Donnell J. Smith as vice president and Mallalieu Wilson as dean. Both nominations passed unanimously.

Four days later on March 14, the Board of Directors also met in Nampa. In the afternoon session, with President DeLong in attendance, the directors named a committee to meet with Dr. Winchester and talk to her about what DeLong had "said relative to her non cooperation and insubordination." The three-person committee quickly reported, "Dr. Winchester denied insubordination but acknowledged she had not cooperated with the forward program and gave as her reason that Dr. Williams was not in favor with the building program." Then, thinking over what the regents had done in electing Smith and Wilson, and with legal advice from a local lawyer, the directors reconsidered the regents' actions, deciding they were "illegal." That motion "carried...with opposition." Donnell Smith resigned as vice-president, with DeLong then nominating him as executive secretary. The directors accepted the nomination. The following day the directors wrote to Winchester to inform her of their decision, telling her "your name was again placed in nomination." They hoped "the work in the school ... [would] proceed harmoniously."

What happened in the next month is seen through a glass darkly. Clearly the critics of DeLong and the defenders of Winchester were now in the lead. On June 16 a report of a subcommittee of the regents, addressed to DeLong, directly and bluntly asked for a "clear understanding between you and the Board of Regents concerning your present attitude and your future policy." The report went on: some regents, faculty, alumni, and supporters of the college were convinced that he was "tyrannical and [had] not always given fair treatment and proper consideration." Further, it appeared he had "endeavored to make the institution a one man school and eliminate everything which did not and everyone who does not harmonize with your program." Directives followed these harsh words from the regents to the president: he must be more democratic in his actions, more humble, and cooperative, apologizing to those he had harmed. And in actions that clarified DeLong's relationships with Winchester, he was instructed to make sure she would reassume her "former position on the Faculty for a period co-terminus with your own." Finally, he and she were to issue a "joint statement" of their agreement to work together in a forthcoming issue of the *Nazarene Messenger*. This demanding, proscriptive report was delivered to the regents meeting in Wichita, Kansas, where Nazarenes were gathered for the General Assembly.

The damning report was put in DeLong's hands and his response requested. His reply to the subcommittee was presented on June 21 (no copy is extant), but the next day he also presented his drafted contract for 1932-33 to the regents. It stated specifically the amount of his salary and how it should be paid. Once a standing debt of $3,000 was paid off, payments due DeLong "shall have prior claim to any other obligation." Without yet voting on DeLong's contract, the regents listened to Dr.Winchester's written reply (copy lost) to their requested information. Next they asked for comments from two general superintendents. As those comments were being heard, three regents resigned, suggesting their discontent with the proceedings.

Confused, undecided about what to do, the regents made several motions without passing any, until General Superintendents Dr. R. T. Williams and Dr. J. W. Goodwin recommended that DeLong be given his requested year leave of absence and that "Dr. Winchester take her place, as vice pres. and go on." "She would cooperate in this plan." The contract terms of DeLong's proposal were accepted and passed. The regents then passed a resolution that "Brother DeLong" be given "a letter of recommendation both as to his ability and natural qualities," one that expressed their "confidence in them; and that [they] regret[ed] that it seemed advisable for him to resign." But they also decided that a committee of three should be named "to negotiate with someone as acting President of the College for the ensuing year, with power to act."

Although the regents had made difficult decisions, a modicum of peace seemed on the horizon. As Olive Winchester confessed, "we have been through some of the worst storms that I have ever experienced." Once the future seemed settled with DeLong seemingly out of the picture, Winchester tried to talk H. Orton Wiley, then editor of the *Herald of Holiness* periodical published in Kansas City, into returning as the NNC president and move the campus back to things of the spirit. But the unsolved difficulties would soon reappear. Indeed, even though DeLong would serve as president on leave during most of the 1932-33 school year, a new acting president was named, and Dr. Winchester returned to her previous roles as vice president and dean, those decisions were severely tested in the next three years and never completely solved. Within two months evidences of lingering discontents were re-surfacing.

The conflicts and disarray at NNC in 1932-33, although of a different kind, mirrored the dire situation and traumatic changes confronting the nation as well as the Church of the Nazarene in the early 1930s. During the winter of 1932-33 before Franklin D. Roosevelt's inauguration as president, the country plummeted to its nadir economically. In 1933 farmers were earning but half of their 1929 incomes, lumbermen selling for only one-third what they received in 1926, and fish canneries, wheat farmers, and livestock ranchers were in a bad fix. Many urban workers were laid off and unable to find new jobs. These depressed times meant that many Nazarenes had little or no cash to send their young people to college or to support those institutions. College officials would have to come up with new systems of financial support to survive during the depressing days of the early 1930s.

Transitions in the Church of the Nazarene added further stress to the status quo in Nampa. While the church kept at its forefront central Christian doctrines and specific emphasis on entire sanctification, it had more difficulty explaining how holiness should display itself in the actions, attitudes, and appearances of its members. When General Assemblies met in 1928 and 1932, they attempted to rewrite the church *Manual* to provide more specific lifestyle guidelines for Nazarenes. In the *Manual* of 1932, for example, those who wanted to join the Church of the Nazarene were "required" "to show evidence of salvation from their sins by a godly walk," including "avoiding evil of every kind." Some of those evils were profanity, reading Sunday papers, tobacco, "liquors as beverage," and "indulging of pride in dress or behavior." And Nazarenes must avoid "the theater, the ball room, the circus, and like places... [and] lotteries and games of chance." If those prohibitions were in the main sections of the *Manual*, the "Appendix" noted that the General Assembly was "on record as being unqualifiedly opposed to our people's patronizing promiscuous public bathing places."

These behavioral guidelines, now made explicit in the church *Manual*, were difficult to maintain on college campuses and among church young people. So it was, and so it has been. There may have been a unity of spirit among early Nazarenes, but simultaneously a competing diversity of opinion about such actions as reading Sunday newspapers, using a public swimming pool, or wearing stylish clothes. As the NNC records of the 1930s demonstrate clearly, it was a stressful task for college administrators to deal with these standards and encourage students' universal acceptance and adherence to them.

The months between DeLong's presidency and the beginning days for the new president were fraught with these and other difficulties. Even before someone could occupy the chief administrator's chair, money had to be found to pay the college's bills, enough cash even to pay for postage.

The huge challenges facing the new president, Reuben E. Gilmore, in summer 1932 are reflected in the brevity of his administration. Most of the NNC/NNU administrators have served for nearly a decade or more. Only three were much briefer. J. G. Morrison (1926-27), as noted, left Nampa in less than a year to take an important administrative position in the Nazarene General Headquarters in Kansas City. Later, the abbreviated presidency of Leon Doane (1992 -93) was cut short tragically by cancer. The administration of Reuben Gilmore also ended tragically but one of another kind. Accused of encouraging religious modernism and expressing uncertainty about explicit details of holiness doctrine, Gilmore resigned under immense pressure. The resignation need not to have happened.

Reuben Eugene Gilmore came from humble origins. Born on August 22,

Reuben E. Gilmore, a warm and devoted man, served as NNC's fourth president (1932-35). (Fig. 2.4)

1902, raised in rural Arkansas in less than modest circumstances, and from a very conservative religious home, Gilmore attended Arkansas Holiness Academy and Bethany-Peniel College in Oklahoma. He then transferred to Oklahoma City University to gain an accredited degree in 1924. The next year he finished a master's degree in psychology at the University of Oklahoma and then completed three years of doctoral work in philosophy and religion at the University of Chicago. Ordained while at Bethany, he dropped out of graduate school and began pastoral and evangelistic work. He also taught philosophy and religion at Olivet Nazarene and Bethany Nazarene. When President DeLong resigned, General Superintendent R. T. Williams recommended Gilmore for the Nampa presidency. Gilmore was named acting president on June 26, 1932. Even though Gilmore was an outstanding student and a gifted pulpiteer, he had limited classroom training and no administrative experience.

Financial and other dilemmas shadowed the three months between DeLong's leaving and Gilmore's arriving. Dr. Winchester, who ably and energetically carried out administrative duties in Nampa between the presidents, warned Gilmore that "financially there will be a fight on." (Winchester persisted in calling Wiley, DeLong, and Gilmore "Dr." well before they officially gained their honorary or earned doctoral degrees, which all eventually did.) The vice president also informed R. J. Plumb, chair of the Board of Regents, that the finances were "rather serious," "the building payments are delinquent a thousand dollars," and "money is not coming in." To a prospective faculty member she was even more pessimistic: "it would be doing a person an injustice to...bring them to a place where they might not get enough for the bare necessities of life before the year is over."

NNC was clearly on the edge of financial collapse. The new president had to act—and overnight. Enrollment had plummeted to 308, a 20 percent drop from fall 1931. Even worse, only $19,000 had come in by registration time, less than half that of the previous year. There was virtually no money for faculty salaries, and too little for debts and fuel and electricity bills.

The needs called for extraordinary measures. The variety of plans put forth to deal with the financial chaos seemed almost as spur-of-the moment as President Roosevelt's precipitous New Deal programs. The exception was that President Gilmore had little or no money, and he couldn't deficit spend because banks and lending institutions would not give the college any more money. The debts to these lending institutions were already too high, and they weren't being paid.

So attempts to save money and to get by without spending any cash were several and often entirely experimental. Probably the most widely employed was the previously mentioned transfer system. Since the college was unable to pay anything like full salaries, many faculty families moved into dormitories where board and room were available. President and Mrs. Gilmore and their young daughter Roselyn were among these dormitory newcomers. One student recalled an unusual example of transfer. "In early 1935," he remembered, "I had a used 1926 Essex and needed tuition for the second semester. One of the Associate Professors needed a car. So, a transfer was arranged....The faculty member got the Essex as part of his salary, I got credit for an amount of tuition and not a penny of cash (something neither the college, the faculty member nor I had seen recently) changed hands." For fuel, college boys, utilizing any vehicles at hand, gathered nearby sagebrush, which burned hot—and briefly—in wood-burning stoves, all the while giving off a strong, unfamiliar aroma. In spring 1933, the school was put on a six-day schedule, allowing for earlier dismissal in the spring and the possibility of a longer summer for more student work.

In the dining hall a democratic labor system was put to work. Daughters of Nazarene leaders and preachers, young women who later became a pastor's wife or a wife of a church leader, as well as daughters and sons of needy laypersons—all worked for 15 to 25 cents an hour. In that way they paid off room and board; no cash was exchanged at a dollar-depressed college. The gender division in the dining hall was unbalanced, with but two or three men among the dozens of cooks, servers, and food preparers. Work in the campus kitchen and dining hall provided hundreds of NNC students' jobs in the midst of a pressing depression.

But the food that was served caused problems. The menu was heavily weighted toward starches and other fatty foods. Bills with Nampa, Boise, and Salt Lake City suppliers ran toward potatoes, cheeses, and pasta dishes. Bread, crackers, soups, beans, canned peaches, canned vegetables, spinach, and beets were also among the food items most often listed. Fresh fruit and vegetables were a rarity since the college year ended in late May and began at the end of September. But more than a few students provided, in the form of transfer, fresh beef and pork to pay off their tuition charges. Truly, on occasion, the students were able to eat "high on the hog." The files of the kitchen and dining hall bills indicate that fruit, vegetables, and meats were often canned in summer or early fall months to provide student and faculty fare in winter and spring before new crops became available. In fall 1934 the campus was blessed with 3,100 quarts of canned food that a Mrs. Mulligan had prepared at the cost of 15 cents per quart.

Revealingly, almost no students complained about the food served at NNC. Perhaps they realized that what they ate at the Nampa campus did not differ that much from the hard-pressed and sometimes bleak dinner table fare they faced in their own homes. The family names of Nevin, Irwin, Wiley, Powell, Kincaid, and Dean, all families whose members would play notable roles at NNC and in the Nazarene church, appear on the dining hall work roster. So does that of L. Guy Nees, later president of another Nazarene college.

Gilmore also favored student-operated industries as a way to put collegians to work and gain income for the college. A fledgling laundry, wood shop, dairy, print shop, and pressing and cleaning business were part of these student industries. In beginning this plan Gilmore was following popular ideas sponsored by Roosevelt's New Deal and implemented at colleges across the country. None of the industries was very successful, and none lasted beyond Gilmore's administration. They were, however, another indication of how much the president was willing to experiment to provide jobs for students and to right the fiscal NNC ship. By the end of his presidency half of the on-campus students were working part-time at the college.

Gilmore went in other directions, off campus to raise needed funds. Launching a Life Saver Plan modeled after a giving strategy borrowed from Bethany-Peniel College, Gilmore traveled out on the zone, making a good impression, and dispelling some of the ill feelings that arose in the final months of DeLong's administration. As Vice President Winchester put it, Gilmore "has captivated the hearts of the people everywhere as he has here." Although Winchester had locked horns with DeLong, she found Gilmore a soft-spirited, approachable person very willing to let her help him with the school's administration. Gilmore and Winchester were a solid, complementary team during his three-year tenure at NNC.

Even though cash was as scarce as Democrats among the Nampa Nazarenes, the college located enough funds to keep the debate program alive and to launch another controversial form of competition. NNC was proud of their debaters because, like David of old, they could take on the Goliaths of West Coast academic institutions. In March 1934 the Nampa debaters defeated Stanford, winning for the affirmative on the debate question: "Resolved: That the powers of the President of the United States should be substantially increased as a settled policy." The local newspaper described the atmosphere of the contest: "The house was filled with an enthusiastic audience which represented the student body and citizenry of Nampa and neighboring cities and communities." Under the able leadership of Albert Harper, who was completing his doctorate in education at the University of

Although intercollegiate sports were controversial, the "preachers" basketball team helped to defuse some of the conflict. (Fig. 2.5)

Washington, the NNC debaters proved to be a strong forensic team up and down the Pacific Coast and in the northwestern states.

In another area the NNC campus moved to new, uncertain ground. Since its beginnings the school and then college had frowned on competitive athletics. Following in the footsteps of Nazarene founder Phineas Bresee, NNC leaders disapproved of football and other violent, competitive sports. The 1915-16 catalogue was explicit in this stance: "we do not tolerate Rugby foot-ball, nor any other brutal or demoralizing games, nor permit the students' minds to become detracted from their school work by indulging in numerous interscholastic meets…." But the intramural contests between the Athletic-Literary teams had encouraged a competitive spirit over the years; so had the successful forensic program. Why not competitions between an NNC basketball team and other nearby schools and other groups—in the form of exhibitions? In 1933-34, evidently with the encouragement of President Gilmore, the Board of Regents voted to allow such competitions. In January, in its own gym, the basketball team won the Intermountain Tournament by beating Gooding College and Boise Junior College and then Gooding a second time for the championship. "After due deliberation," Gilmore wrote to the board chair, "we decided to let our college team participate." Some thought the intercollegiate team was allowed since so many of the young men were preparing to become ministers—the "preachers" team, as it was known. Later in the spring baseball and track teams scheduled games and meets with teams outside Nampa. When an Oregon pastor expressed his disappointment with the athletics program, the president asked him to "withhold judgment" until the one-year experiment was tested. He was certain that the regents would "vote unanimously against continuing it" if there were negative reactions. Besides, Gilmore added, "Our whole situation here at Nampa is different from any place I have ever been," probably referring to the isolation of NNC and its distance from Nazarene populations, "and the program grew out of our many problems here in connection with the school." The "noble experiment," Gilmore told the president of Bethany-Peniel College, resulted from "the general sentiment of our constituency," which "is different from that to which we are accustomed." Whether intercollegiate sports should be allowed—since the general Nazarene Church continued to frown on such activities—remained a contentious subject well into the 1960s.

The tough financial times began to loosen up after Gilmore's first year as president. Nazarenes out on the educational zone were able to contribute more than in 1932-33, and the administration was able to land government funding through one of President Roosevelt's New Deal plans. Civil Works Administration funds became available in early 1934, putting twenty young men to work for five weeks. "This brought several hundred dollars into our treasury," Gilmore explained, allowing some faculty salaries to be paid at the fifty percent level. Although these government-sponsored programs provided much-needed funds, board members and pastors expressed reservations about becoming involved in the programs. They smacked of socialism, some complained.

The varied discontents voiced over the course of Gilmore's brief presidency coalesced in the spring of 1935. The president began to feel the mounting opposition. In early 1935 he wrote to the regents, saying that he, personally, had "prayed and worked, seemingly to little avail....It may be," he added, "that there is not sufficient confidence in my administration." If that was the case, he was willing to step aside. "I should like very much that the Regents feel perfectly free to plan a different administration if they so desire."

When a pastor from Washington wrote in with other reservations, the president noted, "Dame Rumor is not dead." He urged the pastor to speak to members of the Board of Regents to get his information first hand. When rumormongers spread the story that NNC "teachers...do not believe in Holiness," they should know that the music teacher has joined the Nazarene Church, he told the pastor, and he should be aware that the principal of the Academy would not be returning the next year. Just because the principal had supported a controversial political campaign in California that Upton Sinclair mounted did not mean that the principal was "a communist or Socialist." H. Orton Wiley, then president of Pasadena College, said Nazarenes in southern California were not holding it against the principal for supporting the Sinclair campaign. Wiley was surprised that NNC constituents might make it "impossible to ever use ... [the principal] again" because of his political stances.

Outspoken critics raised other issues. The participation in intercollegiate sports rankled some, although the regents did not overturn these activities. Still others thought the president was not preaching about and supporting holiness doctrine as explicitly and enthusiastically as he should. And they worried that he brought too many non-Nazarenes to campus to speak. In the spring of 1935 a pastor from the Methodist Church in Yakima, Washington, preached in chapel, and ten days later the pastor of the Nampa Methodists spoke. The next day a presenter advocating peace and asking the college students to become supporters of peace movements appeared on campus. Undoubtedly these presentations made some NNC supporters nervous.

When the Board of Regents met in March, Gilmore asked them to "thoroughly investigate the criticisms which were directed at the school with reference to its spirituality and that steps be taken to clear up the misunderstanding." In dealing with these issues, the regents moved that all teachers hired at NNC should be "required to sign a contract stating their belief with reference to some of the things for which our church stands." District superintendents on the board were asked to investigate the criticisms. Their report stated that not all of the cardinal Nazarene doctrines were being emphasized as they should and that chapel speakers were sometimes undercutting these doctrines. So they recommended that the president, vice-president, and faculty take "steps...at once to correct this." Gilmore moved the adoption of the report. Later in the meeting faculty members came before the board, and "statements were made which seemed to clear up some of the misunderstandings." One week later the president wrote to an Idaho pastor "everything came out fine in the Regents meeting. They seemed to be unanimous in their appreciation of all that I have tried to do."

Gilmore apparently misunderstood the continuing discontents. Critics seem to have congregated in the Nampa area. When the Idaho-Oregon District Assembly convened in early June, attacks on Gilmore's leadership heightened rather than diminished. Although the published report of the district assembly says little about the other criticisms, the education committee's report did point out that since increasing numbers of students were coming to NNC "with inadequate spiritual knowledge and with no specific Christian call," the faculty will have to "bear a larger share of the burden than previously because of the absence of the older Christian students." By implication, the administration would have to take on this burden too.

Still more was going on behind the scenes. Although no extant record exists, a rump group of the assembly—or perhaps members of the Board of Directors, since most of them lived in the Nampa area—met and proceeded to write up a report urging Gilmore to resign because they were convinced he had failed as a spiritual leader and was leading the college in wrong—even dangerous—directions. Critics of the president—but not his supporters—appeared before the group to make their complaints. After receiving the gist of the complainants, General Superintendent J. B. Chapman, presiding at the Idaho-Oregon assembly and long-time friend of the president, "burst" into Gilmore's office and bluntly told him, "Gilmore, I think you ought to resign." "That was just the little push I needed," Gilmore recalled forty years later. He wrote out his resignation and handed it to Rev. Guy A. McShane, the chairman of the Board of Directors. It read in part: "Believing it to be for the best interests of the Northwest Nazarene College, of myself and all others concerned, I am hereby tendering my resignation, as President of this institution." Almost as quickly Dr. Chapman, after talking to others besides the critics, returned and hurriedly told the president "Gilmore, you should not have resigned, for these people like you." But it was done; the burden had been lifted.

As for criticisms of Gilmore, no one was harsher than former president J. G. Morrison. He and Gilmore evidently quarreled when Morrison traveled to Nampa and conversed with the president. "Doctor Gilmore stated to me," Morrison reportedly told DeLong, that "if you old men force me out, I will take two-thirds of the student body with me, for they are loyal to me, and will not stay under another leader." Morrison knew and had experienced "the rape of Methodism," he asserted, and he "smelled that same stench at Nampa, Idaho, when I interviewed your recent predecessor," he told R. V. DeLong. Instead NNC ought to "have keen, up-to-date culture and scholastic training, and yet possess the hottest of hot orthodox spiritual power, truth, doctrine and blessing." Morrison then followed with a statement that revealed his own bias: "This is what our youth need in these hectic communistic, atheistic days."

Soon after his resignation, Gilmore retreated to New England to take a pastorate and to enter a doctoral program at Boston University. When rumor arose indicating he was leaving the Nazarenes, his supporters wrote to question his decision. He was not immediately withdrawing from the church, he told General Superintendent R. T. Williams, but he had "given [his] word to join the Methodist Episcopal Church." He thought he "should leave the Church of the Nazarene... because of [his] liberal views." In the end, he could not "feel badly toward the brethren in the northwest, for from their point of view I am guilty. From my point of view, which I think is a higher point of view, I am not guilty."

Four decades later, reconsidering the unfortunate events that took place in the spring and early summer of 1935, Gilmore provided further information from his perspective. Unfortunately the records of the critics and of the Board of Directors remain unavailable. Gilmore did not contest the charges or the recommendation that he resign because, though upholding the spirit of the Nazarene doctrine of sanctification, he had trouble with "the letter" of sanctification. "Even when doubts were growing in my own consciousness" about Nazarene doctrines, he told former NNC dean Albert Harper, he "consciously continued to preach Church doctrines." To do otherwise he would have "felt [himself] a double hypocrite to teach or preach other doctrines as long as I was a member of the Church of the Nazarene. My battle was with my own conscience."

While admitting his own uneasiness about doctrine and his continued role as president, Gilmore disagreed with another perspective about his resignation. Veteran missionary and NNC professor F. C. Sutherland suggested that political and economic positions were behind the resignation. Sutherland wrote in his unpublished fifty-year history of NNC that the Roosevelt "program captivated a large majority of Americans, and, behind the college walls, the political philosophy set forth by the more ardent New Dealers, began to captivate some of the students and several of the faculty....This was a passing phase, but at the time it had attraction. This philosophy declared that the profit system was immoral and called for a highly socialistic type of government.... Unfortunately, criticisms aroused by the conflicting political theories and by charges that the specific doctrines of our church were not being defended led to Dr. Gilmore's resignation in the spring of 1935." Gilmore begged to differ. These statements, he countered, "stand undocumented. And so far as my knowledge extends is [sic] not wholly true."

Usually, President Gilmore shied away from being explicit about his views in 1935—and much later—but sometimes he offered a few hints. "The record that indicates that I was less than a fully orthodox Nazarene," he admitted later to Dean Emeritus Thelma Culver, "is not wholly false." He added: "The letter of the doctrine of holiness, entire sanctification, gave me problems and still does. Because I felt deficient in the letter of the doctrine I leaned way over to emphasize the spirit of love and service implied in the doctrine." Or, as he told NNC President John Riley in the early 1960s, "my roots go deep into the holiness movement and those roots are still live ones. While I may not be orthodox in doctrine, I shall prize the spirit of 'perfect love.'" Ironically, in his stress on holiness less as an instantaneous work of grace and more as a gradual, long-range growing into "perfect love," Gilmore was ahead of his time, foreshadowing some of the shifts in Nazarene theological emphases in the post-1960s era. But those emphases in the mid-1930s did not fly, especially with conservative Nazarenes in the Nampa area. They wanted him out of the president's office.

Whatever the charges and whether they were right or unfounded, the deed was done. NNC was again without a president. In troubled times college officials must find a new president—and do it quickly. They did.

The minutes of the Board of Regents convening in July 1935 reveal their uncertainty about the future. Fifteen of the regents were listed as present, but when Gilmore's letter of resignation was passed on from the Board of Directors, only six voted on the motion to accept the resignation—two for acceptance, three against acceptance, and one blank. Nine of the regents had not voted on this important decision. Quickly, motions were made to take care of pressing financial needs and to grant Dr. Winchester a year's leave of absence. Then one regent moved that they wire Dr. T. W. Willingham (president of Olivet Nazarene) and Dr. A. K. Bracken (president of Bethany-Peniel) to see if either would be interested in the NNC presidency. The next day Dr. Orval J. Nease (recently president of Pasadena College) was also suggested. Before any of these contacts were decided on, the same nervously active regent moved that R. V. DeLong be contacted to see if he would return to NNC. Another regent moved that the board at once vote on giving DeLong a re-call to the presidency. The vote was 12 "yes" and 0 "no" of the 15-person board. If DeLong accepted the position, his salary was to be $225 per month on a 12-month basis. He would be returning for his second try at the presidency and the fifth president of NNC.

Speculations about this unusual turn of events are certainly normal. How did DeLong feel about getting the telephone call and then telegram from Spokane offering him the presidency—after the board had essentially driven him out of town three years previously? In early summer of 1932, DeLong told J. G. Morrison later, he went "through some very dark moments....It looked as though our air-castles and life were completely annihilated. I was tempted of the Devil to do everything." In 1935 DeLong's first reactions were to reject the offer, but after "more pressure was brought to bear to assist me, and after much prayer, [I] had the clear conscience that it was God's will I come to Nampa."

What about the board? They had essentially cashiered DeLong and now were calling him back. The minutes of the board meetings are silent on their motivations. Perhaps they concluded that having the assertive, brash, and blunt DeLong was better than Gilmore, whom they reputedly considered too liberal in politics and too modernist in religion. Whatever the board's motivations, the DeLong who returned was still the controversial mix of strong, bold leadership combined with the impatient, shoot-from-the-hip administrator they had known. Thankfully, the strengths reappeared before the limitations, although those surfaced before too long.

DeLong was surprised at the positive consensus of support he received when he returned to campus in early fall 1935. "You will be glad to know that I have received a very cordial and warm welcome locally," he told General Superintendent

R. T. Williams. "There does not seem to be much opposition. Both the Board of Directors and Regents are unanimous. I am greatly encouraged about the situation." And the regent who had nominated him in July and was DeLong's strong supporter informed the new president, facetiously, "If you find any persistent foes there, just gouge out their eyes and spit in the hole, or cut their hearts out and then bawl them out for bleeding."

Red ink—multiple columns of it—stared NNC and its leaders straight in the eye. DeLong went after the problem as directly and energetically—and successfully—as he had eight years earlier in the Out-of-Debt Campaign. The combined enrollments at the college, Academy, and grammar school were up. The president was pleased with "the finest personnel we have ever had at N.N.C," he reported to a GS, but he had to admit that "financially the out-look is not so bright." A loan company was demanding $5,000 on the building debt, principal and interest. Plus, mounting debts necessitated taking an additional $7,000 from the current income to pay last year's debts, a dangerous precedent that could only worsen unless the financial picture was redrawn.

DeLong set about to do just that. With only a matter of days to raise the needed $5,000 he and the DSs of the zone divided up the debt among the districts and churches—and went after them. No systematic way of raising funds for annual NNC budgets yet existed—that was to come—so this crisis method was launched. It worked. On November 7, DeLong and Campaign Manager Earl C. Pounds wrote to zone pastors that 185 churches had responded, and offerings totaled $5,513. DeLong was encouraged with the giving; some of the "quotas were hilariously met." What he didn't mention was the large capital debt still hanging over the college and its inability to pay faculty their full salary. Still, DeLong had achieved again what he had done so well in the past: engineered a fund-raising campaign that garnered much-needed funds and united Northwest Nazarenes behind NNC.

The glow of the financial success had barely dimmed before DeLong set out on his next foray: to achieve full accreditation for NNC as a four-year institution of higher education. It was important to address some of the fiscal instability of the college before approaching the accrediting commission because they would want to know about NNC's finances as part of their accrediting procedure. In a December 1935 faculty meeting DeLong listed necessary changes to achieve full accreditation: a better library and science facilities, eight college departments headed up by persons holding at least a master's degree, a separation of the college and the academy, and improved classrooms. He also outlined how a better financial support system for the college could be put into operation.

DeLong also reached out to important officials. Making contact again with Dr. Frederick E. Bolton, the chairman of the cumbersomely titled Commission of

Accrediting of the Northwest Association of Secondary Schools and Institutions of Higher Learning, DeLong asked for an interview to bring Dr. Bolton up-to-date on NNC's advancements. It also helped that Albert Harper, a recent doctoral graduate from Bolton's department at the University of Washington and now dean at NNC, was described as "a brilliant student" whom the education department considered "one of their most promising graduates" in his work at Seattle. In the coming months DeLong kept Bolton apprised of what the college was doing to improve its faculty, facilities, and funding.

Nazarene Messenger

Northwest Nazarene College Monthly

Volume XX April, 1937 Number IV

Educational Sunday April 25, 1937

ACCREDITATION AND THE EDUCATIONAL BUDGET

Victory

Northwest Nazarene College Accredited

On Wednesday April 7, 1937, by unanimous vote of the Northwest Association of Colleges accorded Northwest Nazarene College, full, unconditional and permanent accreditation as a four year senior college.

May issue of Messenger will carry full details.

MY FIRST IMPRESSION OF N. N. C.

Under the strong leadership of President DeLong, NNC became the first fully accredited Nazarene four-year college in 1937. (Fig. 2.6)

DeLong marshaled the charge toward accreditation like a skilled field general. He took no chances of failure, looking closely after every detail. He invited Bolton to NNC, brought other dignitaries to campus, and, perhaps most importantly, shanghaied nearly 150 NNC graduates who were teaching in the greater Nampa-Boise area—all for a finely turned dinner to highlight the achievements of NNC as an academic institution producing first-rate teachers. Perhaps the grand display worked. At least Bolton was impressed. He told the president: "I wish you to know how much I appreciated the many courtesies extended to me on my trip to Nampa," and then went on to say more than he probably should have: "I am hoping that the Commission will see fit to extend full four-year accreditation to the college. I feel sure that it is worthy of such accreditation."

That wonderful news came on April 7, 1937, less than a month after DeLong's carefully orchestrated hosting of Bolton on the NNC campus. Declaring April 25, 1937 "Educational Day…and Victory Offering," DeLong sent news of the achievement to the uttermost parts of the Nazarene world. Noting that the commission had voted unanimously for NNC's accreditation, DeLong called it "a tremendous and colossal achievement." And not missing a beat of his tub-thumping, he added: "Northwest Nazarene College is the first Nazarene institution to gain such recognition."

The president also set out to revive the college spiritually. No one in the past had accused DeLong of being too liberal or modernistic, and those criticisms would not surface in the next few years. He was a skilled, direct, and enthusiastic preacher. Turn him loose in the pulpit and usually audiences were moved with thought and emotion. (Indeed, these clear homiletical and vocal strengths were a major reason that later DeLong became the chief speaker on the Nazarene international radio program "Showers of Blessing.") At NNC, revival fires had burned in the past, were banked, and now they would soon reignite.

In fact, DeLong was heeding the strong suggestions of church and regional leaders in firing up the NNC spiritual engine. His first predecessor, J. G. Morrison, wrote from Kansas City to say, "I know that things out there are in a mess…save it again financially, and save it spiritually; the latter is where it has been the most nearly ruined." Invoking familiar words of the previous decade, Morrison knew that God "will help you save the school and make a great, red hot, glorious, Holy Ghost filled institution of it."

At the first faculty meeting in September returning president DeLong stressed "professional adequacy," "social responsibility," and "spiritual emphasis." He placed particular stress on the third item. "The president plead [sic] for a vital and dynamic religious program during the school year." The next day a series of recommendations—"Rules for N.N.C," formulated by the Board of Regents—were read and adopted by the faculty. The regents desired, they said, "to maintain a school of the highest scholastic standing possible... [and] to keep the school fundamentally spiritual and evangelistic at all times." These stipulations asked that one chapel each week be evangelistic, that no speaker be invited to speak on campus who would "speak at variance with Nazarene Doctrines," and that the "chief aim in maintaining the school is to perfect the salvation of our young people, to train them scholastically and develop Christian character, as well as also train religious workers." Clearly this list aimed at correcting the spiritual failures that critics pointed to in the Gilmore administration.

And revival came that fall. In November, Rev. Dorothy Bridgewater and her song evangelist husband R. E. Bridgewater led a revival series that the *Nazarene Messenger* called the "Greatest Spiritual Tide Witnessed in Years." The Rev. Bridgewater, "preaching the old Gospel without compromising in the least," delivered sermons that were "clear-cut…and understandable." Seekers flocked to altar services lasting four or five hours. The closing Sunday of the special services, according to one eyewitness, was "one of the greatest days we have ever seen." Reports of the revival spread out through the district, prompting a pastor in Yakima to write to DeLong that the outbreak was a "seal [of God] upon his return." "First was the great financial response of the people. Second is the great Revival given by God.... It makes us out in the districts feel JUST as good."

Unfortunately, in early January 1936 a major shock swept across campus, Nampa, and the NNC zone. In January the NNC community was stunned by a headlined story about the college founder in the Nampa newspaper that read "Eugene Emerson of Nampa Takes Own Life Today." Depressed, unable to keep up with his financial obligations, and breaking under the load of his extraordinary leadership responsibilities, Emerson, at age 70, had taken his own life. There were a few earlier telltale signs that Emerson sometimes stumbled under his numerous large assignments. When college officials called for audits of the NNC giving and expenditures records, Emerson was greatly bothered by that decision because he had taken care of such duties—through his own businesses, and sometimes from his own pockets. On another occasion, under the pressures of decisions and duties, he nearly went off track, Dr. Winchester told a leading Northwest layman.

Nearly 1,000 friends and acquaintances crowded into Nampa First Nazarene to remember and memorialize Eugene Emerson. Undoubtedly many gathering for his service already realized how important he had been to the history of the college since 1913: without Emerson, NNC might not have existed and certainly not in Nampa. His heroic and personal commitments gave birth to and sustained the institution. His name on the central administration building still testifies to his enduring central importance to NNC/NNU.

Despite this major disappointment and other challenges, growing enrollments led to the expansion of the faculty and the erection of new buildings. In 1935-36, 165 students were attending NNC; by 1937-38, 219; in 1938-39, 309; and in 1940-41, 361, the highest until 1946-47. When DeLong reassumed the NNC presidency in 1935, Albert F. Harper and James R. Garner were the only professors with earned doctorates (Olive Winchester chose to leave NNC for Pasadena in 1935, probably because she couldn't abide DeLong's style of leadership). Soon embroiled in controversy, Garner left, but Harper continued for several more years.

Dr. Albert F. Harper, professor of education and psychology and debate coach, later served ably as college dean. (Fig. 2.7)

In these years of transition and controversy, including three presidential changes, Albert Harper was a bulwark of steady,

Bertha M. Dooley, strong scholar and gifted instructor, taught English and Greek for many years. (Fig. 2.8)

dependable leadership. A graduate of NNC and perhaps its first graduate to gain a PhD, Harper began teaching at the academy; later he was an instructor at the college in the fields of philosophy and education and a very successful debate coach. Through the first DeLong administration, the three up-and-down years of Gilmore's presidency, and the equally challenging second DeLong administration, Harper got along with clashing campus groups. In 1935 he became dean of the college and was a central figure in helping NNC gain accreditation. During the summers when DeLong was often absent on speaking engagements, Harper was virtually acting president of the college. In 1943 Harper left NNC to take a position in the Nazarene headquarters in Kansas City.

In 1935, seven faculty members had master's degrees, with May Bower, F. C. Sutherland, Bertha Dooley, and C. V. Marshall among the long-time faculty members. Seven years later there were still only two PhD's on the faculty (Harper and Maude Rice), but DeLong had nearly doubled the number (thirteen) of faculty holding a master's degree. Among the newcomers were several who stayed for many years: Mallalieu Wilson, Joseph Janosky , Guy Sharp, and Marian Washburn. Adding these new faculty members was an important step toward achieving accreditation as well as offering a more varied and broad-based curriculum.

In a brave attempt to bridge the gap between tuition dollars and church contributions and mounting costs for salaries and other campus expenses, DeLong followed in Gilmore's footsteps in securing government funding. Like his predecessor, DeLong tapped the New Deal Works Progress Administration and National Youth Administration for work-study grants for NNC students, supplying some years well more than $4,000 for working students. He also wrote to Idaho's Senator James P. Pope hoping to secure funding from the Reconstruction Finance Corporation to refinance "the capital obligations of Northwest Nazarene College." He was unable to secure these monies for capital debts.

Soon after the Out-of-Debt Campaign, DeLong turned to other financial needs. Early in 1936 he launched The Faculty Emergency Offering to pay off faculty salaries much in arrears. But it didn't go well. Writing the chairman of the Board of Trustees, DeLong told him that the campaign was "rather discouraging." He was not sure what would happen "unless we get a greater response." Then the chief administrator, as he did all too frequently, turned his presidential guns on the chairman, "I really feel that you should assume some responsibility for the payments of the faculty salaries and see that your own church [Spokane First Church] and district does it's [sic] part." He also reminded the chairman that the "present situation is due in great measure to recent difficulties for which I am not responsible." DeLong added he was afraid of losing his faculty; one had already resigned, saying, "he could not live on the salary we pay."

After this disappointing program came to very little, DeLong and the regents tried to take advantage of a special occasion to wipe out NNC's existing debts. In celebration of its twenty-fifth anniversary the college launched a Silver Jubilee Campaign, with the motto "To owe no one and no one owe us by December 31, 1938." The program aimed at addressing all the major debts facing the college: $23,000 for a first mortgage, primarily on buildings; $2,000 for a furniture fund; and $9,000 of unpaid faculty salaries, for a total of $35,000. Were DeLong and the regents thinking of their huge success a decade earlier in raising $93,000 to save the institution? The extant records reveal no such thoughts, and the Silver Jubilee program enjoyed no similar success. Not only did the fund-raising fall short of the goal, the chain of reminder letters to those owing debts to the college, mainly former students, stirred up surprisingly hostile reactions. When the debtors failed to respond or pay what they owed after three letters, their bills were turned over to bill collectors. A number of ministers pled home mission salaries, even though the college badly needed their dollars.

Nonchurch funds were available for constructing new buildings, although they were not easily secured because of the college's lack of an endowment and its shaky financial history. But something had to be done; more than 200 coeds were attending NNC, and the sole women's dormitory, Hadley Hall, housed only 70 women. The rest were staying in off-campus homes, a touchy situation for parents and college administrators unable to control the rhythms of their daily lives. NNC must have a new women's dormitory, but government funds were not available for the project, churches were already stretched to their maximums, and the college's current debts loomed as another barrier to loan-makers. Carefully courting a St. Louis real estate mortgage loan company, raising guaranteed backup notes at local banks, and acceding to the company's demand for a professional architect and bonded builder, the college secured a much-needed construction loan in spring 1940. Construction proceeded in high gear, and just before fall classes in 1940, Morrison Hall (named after NNC's second president) opened its doors to a new generation of NNC women.

A financial drive for another building was begun almost immediately. A new

The R. T. Williams Library (1942) was NNC's first library building; it later became home to its Division of Philosophy and Religion. (Fig. 2.9)

library was obviously needed, so in concert President DeLong and the regents, in the spring after opening Morrison Hall, launched plans for a new library. They decided to mount a pay-as-you-go funding program, building only as gift dollars arrived. Although the system did not work out, the careful and less costly construction work of W. D. Parsons, helpful financial contributions from many Nazarene laypersons, and the student-work-for-tuition program allowed construction to move along, despite some delays. In fall 1942, the R. T. Williams Library opened to greatly pleased faculty, students, and college supporters.

Not surprisingly it was in the organizational and social life components of the NNC campus that most of the controversy arose during the second DeLong administration. For example, in bragging about NNC's new accreditation, the president alienated other Nazarene administrators and not a few laypersons. Or, consider another conflict. When DeLong wrote to the representative of a company doing business with NNC that he "resent[ed]" and felt "so disgusted" about the company's policies, but still felt "most cordial" toward them with no "bad spirit," they might have wondered which DeLong was speaking, and when. And one letter to the father of a son recently dismissed from NNC illustrates many such letters going out from the president's office. "I am rather amazed at your attitude," DeLong told the father; "I will not be held responsible for the wrongdoing of your boy and then blamed for it." One student who attended NNC in the late 1930s remembered that DeLong too often stood before the student body in chapel to berate them for their recent actions. That student, who became a Nazarene pastor, recalled those negative sermons sixty years later. Still another student and later a NNC professor remembered a chapel service in which the president called out a student's name, asked him to stand, and told him to leave the service and college as punishment for his recent infractions. The professor wondered, much later, if DeLong could have ever after spoken to that embarrassed student concerning spiritual matters.

DeLong also wrote a fiery letter to H. Orton Wiley, then president of Pasadena (Nazarene) College, accusing him of poaching on Nazarene students in the Northwest for Pasadena. After Wiley calmly and rather fully answered the complaints, DeLong replied with vigor and hot dissent, ending his letter "I challenge you to produce any evidence of my transgressing on your Zone in the same manner you have transgressed on ours." One cannot imagine any other early NNC president replying in such words.

In another all-too-typical conflict, a father wrote the president about his daughter's unpaid bill. He was upset that she could not obtain a copy of her records so as to gain a teaching position and pay off her $92 bill. That was a NNC policy, but in replying to the distraught father DeLong told the North Dakota farmer that he, the college president, was in "no sense responsible for the present condition." In fact he was trying to save the Nampa school, "making a fight, getting less than half my salary and only about one-third of what I would receive in other lines of work." He disliked the father's attitude and did not "feel very much encouraged that you do not appreciate" NNC's help and were accusing the college of "unjustly holding credits." To be fair to DeLong, he was in ticklish situations here and in other dilemmas, but too often he alienated persons like this father with his abrupt, opinionated, and self-defensive reactions. Eventually in 1942, those negative treatments of students, faculty, and constituents would sink DeLong, ending his second presidential term.

NNC continued to evolve as other social transformations were at work on campus. More and more non-Nazarene students, others less committed to Nazarene behavior standards, and returning veterans in the early-to-mid 1940s—all these newcomers made it a larger challenge to keep to the disciplinary rules that NNC had maintained since its inception. Those standards were strict. In 1936-37 couples could see one another for two hours on Sunday afternoon—as long as those meetings had been prearranged with a dean. In addition, couples could be together in an automobile only with a faculty member or dean as a chaperone. And if a couple wished to marry during the school year, they had to secure permission well ahead of the ceremony. Regrettably, not all couples that married followed this rule and thus were dismissed from school. The minutes of the Faculty Committee on Discipline reveal that the most-often broken or bruised guidelines were those disallowing NNC girls to ride in automobiles with non-NNC young men and staying out after curfew. The faculty, sensing another mounting problem, also "voted that no mixed groups be allowed to go to the Nat [swimming natatorium] together." Young men and women were also expected to sit separately in the library, with one section of the library set aside for men and another for women.

Dress standards were equally demanding—and sometimes controversial—as they frequently were in the early history of NNC. In 1942 the faculty "Ideals and Standards" committee, in conjunction with the administration, listed their "Dress Regulations": "lipstick, colored fingernail polish, and rouge are forbidden," the rules read, "and the deans are to eliminate them": skirts must be long enough to "cover the knees at all times": women or girls were not to wear slacks, "riding breeches," or overalls; nor should they wear "ankle socks" on campus or in the dining hall; instead, they must don "full length hose," except in "gym, tennis, and outside athletic activities"; and "the wearing of jewelry for adornment is not allowed." Interestingly, the archival records indicate these demanding dress requirements seemed not to have troubled students as much as dorm hours, limited social times, and specific requirements on the uses of automobiles.

Conservative Nazarenes on the NNC zone and in the Nazarene headquarters also worried about the college's intercollegiate athletic program. The general church on more than one occasion expressed its negative opinions about intercollegiate sports. Phineas Bresee, from the very beginning, urged Nazarenes to stay out of the violent and cutthroat competitions he thought ruled athletics. For the next generation and more Nazarenes followed his advice. In the 1930s NNC was the only Nazarene college to sponsor intercollegiate sports, and that action upset conservatives on the NNC zone and in Kansas City.

But like Gilmore before him, DeLong thought an athletic program benefitted NNC. In 1938 DeLong wrote a long, strongly worded letter to the General Board of Superintendents supporting athletics. He had polled the faculty, and they had voted 22 to 0 for the program, and when he took the issue before the Board of Regents, they voted unanimously—16 to 0—for sports. So, DeLong told the GSs that DSs, pastors, college administrators, faculty, and students were overwhelmingly for intercollegiate sports at NNC. The athletic program had "not been a detrimental influence but rather... [had] been a contributing factor in the salvation of several young men....Some of these have been gloriously saved and sanctified and called to the work of the Lord." He was not writing to the generals to ask their approval, for what they had at NNC was "purely temporary, probationary and experimental." Was DeLong whistling through the breeze? The "temporary" athletic program had already been in place for five years, and it would be "probationary and experimental" for years to come.

At the very end of DeLong's second administration, the campus newspaper *The Crusader* appeared for the first time. Launched in February 1942 as a campus newspaper to appear every other week, *The Crusader*, carrying the NNC motto "Seek Ye First the Kingdom," was, in its first issues, primarily a paper devoted to campus religious, academic, social, and athletic news. The founding editor, Victor Bundy, in his leadoff editorial stated the paper's major purposes: "build student morale," "promote proper conduct, high scholarship, sportsmanship, spirituality, and a well-rounded program of campus life." The early issues stuck closely to these traditional goals, offered little social or cultural criticism, and thus pleased the administration and NNC supporters with its noncontroversial coverage. Later, from the 1960s onward the campus newspaper would often be at the vortex of controversies, exhibiting its desire for a clear freedom of the press on campus and also often speaking for activist students. Simultaneously, outspoken articles in the paper frequently upset administrators as well as laypersons out on the educational zone.

Periodically, criticisms surfaced of DeLong's sometimes-abrasive leadership style and his tendency to be brash with dissenters and especially with students. But his abundant talents as an administrator, his clear energies as a forceful president, and his especially transparent successes as a strong academic and spiritual leader often kept criticisms at bay. That all changed in early 1942.

When the Board of Regents met for its semiannual meeting in March 1942, they were faced with troublesome reports. The regents' minutes read that early in their spring meeting "the president...gave a survey of some serious matters in the school...during the past months and explain[ed] a number of accusations which have been brought against him and which have led up to the present situation in the school." A student-generated questionnaire and an anonymous letter, given to the regents, were explicit testimonies of mounting student and also faculty discontent with DeLong's leadership and his controversial methods of handling those discontents. Three members of the faculty, so DeLong thought, "got together and agreed to start an agitation among the students and faculty against" him. These criticisms and others, "led on and encouraged by the wife of the Chairman of the Board of Regents [,] produced a situation...which made it difficult." It was an especially "ticklish situation" because DeLong was close friends with the board chairman and did not want to embarrass "one of my best friends." Disagreeing with the findings of the questionnaire and the letter, the board called in faculty and staff members and students said to have been associated with, if not authors of, the criticism. Nearly all recanted or apologized for their attitudes and actions.

But the wrangling and criticism were too much for DeLong. On March 12 at the regents' meeting the secretary of the board read the president's letter of resignation. After a back-and-forth discussion, a tabled motion, and a time of prayer, the board voted. From the 17 ballots cast, twelve voted to accept DeLong's resignation, with 5 against. Later that evening, after consultations between the president and the board, the regents authorized the business manager to pay DeLong $3,000 the next day, March 13, 1942, "in exchange for Dr. DeLong's five year contract." The next day his resignation was announced in chapel, and on March 18 the same notice appeared in the campus newspaper. "The strain and responsibility of ... [the NNC presidency] under the present national crisis" and the need to protect his wife's health, DeLong told the *Crusader*, were the reasons for his resignation. The Board of Regents immediately began the search for a new president, and two months later the *Crusader* front-page headline read "Dr. Corlett Accepts Presidency."

Several signs reveal the major changes invading NNC in the twenty years from roughly World War I to World War II, from the early years of H. Orton Wiley's presidency to the closing years of Russell V. DeLong's second administration. For one, the tone of the college changed in this full generation. Like a man with many irons in the fire, Wiley was a multi-tasking leader, but his missions seemed tied most of all to the habits of the heart, to religious/spiritual goals. He was clearly an exception in the unusual combination of revivalist and intellectual, even though his desire to keep NNC "red hot" with an intense gospel trumped academic emphases during his presidency.

Consider his participation in church efforts. Wiley often preached in Nampa, in churches of the Pacific Northwest sending their students and dollars to NNC, and in revivals and summer camp meetings. He enjoyed preaching, and urged churches to have him fill their pulpits as he traveled throughout the Northwest educational zone with college quartets. He presided over a nascent college that he personally infused with a revivalistic aura. Wiley spoke often of chapel times that broke from schedules to erupt into emotional altar calls, testimony times, and hours-long meetings. He seemed to joy in these unscheduled emotional breakthroughs, seeing them as signs of "keeping the glory down."

Even more noteworthy was Wiley's stress on missions. In no period of the college's history was more emphasis placed on missions and missionaries than during Wiley's ten years at NNC's helm. Year after year he spoke of and led the college's extraordinary devotion to missions. Wiley brought missionaries to campus, he personally helped young missionary candidates raise their support (before the general church had a program to do this), and attempted to keep missionary stories and called-out ones before the college faculty and student body. Most impressive of all, week after week he wrote two and three page letters to missionaries—especially those early in their careers in foreign fields—encouraging them, raising financial support, and particularly bringing them up to date on NNC campus and district news. Although never a missionary himself, H. Orton Wiley was and remained an enthusiastic cheerleader for missions while at NNC.

A decade later much had changed. After Morrison's less than a year as NNC leader, Russell V. DeLong and Reuben E. Gilmore led NNC from 1927 to 1935, after which DeLong returned to lead the college a second time from 1935 to 1942. The transition in emphasis under these two scholarly leaders is clear in their personal correspondence, in their leadership emphases, and in their attention given to shifting policies.

DeLong and Gilmore were more interested in emphasizing the preparation of ministers and teachers than in enthusiastically pushing missions. It would be a mistake to say they were uninterested in missionaries; it would be equally mistaken to state that they fully shared Wiley's extraordinary stress on missions.

Like Wiley, DeLong and Gilmore were scholars. But the emphases of the two later leaders were more philosophical and psychological than the theological direction of Wiley's intellectual journey. True, all three men embarked on graduate programs while leading NNC, but Wiley, as true for most of his career, stuck closer to theological topics than his two successors. Eventually DeLong would spend a large part of his career as a preacher, Wiley—and Gilmore—as scholarly theologians.

The three leaders also differed in their academic leadership. Wiley was often forced to hire faculty members who were available Nazarenes, even if they frequently lacked the academic preparation needed for a school hoping to launch, sustain, and improve its liberal arts emphases. Wiley was committed to making NNC a liberal arts college rather than a Bible school, but DeLong, and to a lesser extent Gilmore, was even more motivated to push the Nampa college toward accreditation. DeLong did so by hiring better-prepared faculty, trying to put the college on a more solid financial foundation, and leading by example. Without a doubt, DeLong's ongoing graduate education at Boston University with some of the country's leading scholars in the Personalist philosophy—just before he became president and between his two stints as the NNC leader—encouraged the increasing academic tone that he brought to NNC.

DeLong, particularly, wanted NNC to gain accreditation, to become something well beyond a Bible college. In the goals he laid out for the college, in the better-educated faculty he secured, in the contacts he made among the colleges and universities of the northern West, and especially in his courting of administrators and accrediting agencies, DeLong led the college down the clear path of a heightened emphasis on academics.

The content and tone of DeLong's and Gilmore's correspondence from the late 1920s to the early 1940s demonstrates that the college was moving in directions different from the policies of Wiley in the late teens and early twenties. In his desires to strengthen NNC, DeLong faced ongoing, unrelenting financial pressures. Wiley spoke infrequently about these pressures; perhaps he should have done more to raise funds, but he seemed reluctant to push his own needs or the finances of the college. His successors, while almost always saluting Wiley's pioneering and encouraging leadership, also hinted that he did not leave the institution in strong financial standing when he resigned in 1926. J. G. Morrison's very brief presidency added to these financial woes. As we have seen, DeLong took on that huge financial load while a young man in his mid-to-late twenties and, with the sustained and emotionally charged aid of students, faculty, and laypersons—and the much-needed support of Nampa businessmen—captained the miracle giving program of 1928, raising nearly $100,000 to get NNC out of debt. Those monetary challenges continued to lurk at NNC's door during the DeLong and Gilmore years, as the nation and Nazarenes faced the deepest depression the U. S. had experienced. Wiley had faced tough financial times, too, but quite different ones from those during the Great Depression of the 1930s.

DeLong and Gilmore also emphasized the spiritual matters at the college. Both spoke and wrote about the revivals that invaded the campus, broke up classes and dormitory gatherings, and flooded out to nearby Nazarene churches. They too invited the best special meeting speakers at their command to provide encouraging and life-changing campus revivals. No one from outside or inside the campus could say—and didn't—that these two presidents were not gifted speakers and revivalists themselves, even though some thought Gilmore light in his emphases on Nazarene doctrine. The two later presidents seemed, too, to joy in preaching and in conducting special services where special outbreaks of emotion and grace crowned those services.

The changed tone between the early 1920s and late 1930s became clearer to observers by the end of the Depression decade. Conservative board members, pastors, a few faculty, and particularly upset laypersons were convinced that vestiges of modernism and liberalism had sneaked onto campus and were dangerously replacing the earlier revivalistic and traditional emphases of denominational founding fathers like Bresee and Wiley. Their discontents and criticisms were undoubtedly major reasons Gilmore resigned in the early summer of 1935, and their negative reactions continued to flummox DeLong during his dozen years as NNC president.

Were changes in words and terms yet another symbol of a transitional wind blowing across the NNC campus and its constituency? During the first dozen years of NNC's existence, and particularly under Wiley's direction, college administrators, faculty, and students, as well as pastors on the college zone, spoke of keeping a "red hot" spiritual fire burning on campus. In the supposed equilibrium at a "holiness school"—Jerusalem (spiritual fervor) and Athens (academic excellence)—the balance favored a strong, emotional religious experience. The campus and district vocabulary so illustrated.

But a decade or so later—by the end of the 1930s—the widely used words had changed. Now, instead of celebrating NNC as "a holiness college" of emotional spirituality, the presidents and college leaders spoke of the institution as a Christian liberal arts college. Revivals, yes, but also new emphases on accreditation, better-educated faculty, intercollegiate sports, and much-needed funding from the federal government. Wiley's huge emphases on missions, calling NNC a "missionary school," were much more muted, with more stress on ministerial and teacher preparation.

This revealing tension between the intense spirituality of the founding years of NNC and during the decade-long leadership of H. Orton Wiley and the later, developing quest for a strong Christian liberal arts college of solid academic standing was much in evidence by the end of the 1930s. The increased emphases on accreditation and teacher preparation and the appearance of intercollegiate sports were but symbols of this notable transition. These changes and the tensions arising from them continued both to sustain and vex the college in the coming years.

3
WWII and Its Aftermath
THE CORLETT YEARS: 1942-52

Lewis T. Corlett, the sixth president of NNC, came to a college in turmoil in the summer of 1942. Besides the upset at the end of DeLong's second administration, other upheavals derived from changes in the nation and in the Church of the Nazarene. Fortunately, Corlett was a warm-spirited, emotionally balanced, and strongly committed person religiously. All those positive character traits were immensely challenged as the new president attempted to steer the NNC ship through some of its most stormy years of change. He proved to be a valuable man to have at the helm for the next ten years.

As we have seen, Dr. DeLong, as talented and energetic as he was, had difficulty in his interpersonal connections with students, faculty, and constituents. As the chairman of the NNC Board of Regents bluntly put it, "Dr. DeLong's one weakness is his lack of ability to get along with folks." DeLong "has done a great work here," he added, but "he has remained long enough." The chairman was sure that if Corlett became the new president he would "be able to iron out the few difficulties by the help of the Lord." Corlett did just that, quieting most of the discontents and calmly calling for loyalty and commitment to the college. Under Corlett's leadership, there were to be no rumors of or any actual palace revolts that often threatened and sometimes plagued the two DeLong administrations.

Very soon it became clear that the largest challenges from change were coming from outside the NNC campus. The United States, especially the American West, was being transformed under the onslaught of World War II, globally and nationally. These changes dramatically altered the American West, especially in California, but also in the Pacific Northwest, the heart of NNC's educational zone. The transformations resulted primarily from a giant infusion of federal funds to start and keep humming the war machines of national defense. Millions—even billions—of dollars poured into the PNW to build or expand shipyards, airplane factories, and military bases. Army bases (e.g. Fort Lewis), naval bases (Bremerton and Camp Farragut), and air bases (Mountain Home) mushroomed as thousands of new servicemen were stationed at these military installations. Huge amounts of funds also poured into nuclear production sites in Hanford, Washington, and near Arco, Idaho.

Much of this influx of funding went to private builders working on government contracts. Boeing Company in Renton, Washington, and Henry J. Kaiser's three shipbuilding companies in the Portland-Vancouver area were major recipients of this new funding. As one historian of the Pacific Northwest has pointed out, "Seattle alone secured war contracts totaling $5.6 billion, making it among the nation's top three cities in per capita war orders." At the same time more than 100,000 workers flooded into Kaiser's shipbuilding firms. These gigantic new sources of funding and the resultant floods of workers inundated PNW cities. Seattle, Portland, Tacoma, and Bremerton boomed. The state of Washington gained 500,000 in population between 1940 and 1945, Oregon nearly 200,000. Overnight 35,000 workers and their families crowded into Vanport, the jerrybuilt town thrown up near Portland, making it Oregon's second largest city. As one of the gateways to the Pacific and the major war theatre there, the PNW was rapidly becoming a central part of Uncle Sam's West.

These rapid and moving changes had notable economic, social, and cultural consequences for the PNW, and by extension NNC. WWII "created unprecedented prosperity," allowing parents and students alike to pay for college educations nearly impossible to fund during the preceding Depression Decade. But throughout the war years—1941 to 1945—many men (and some women) were in the service, unable to attend college. As a result most college enrollments, as at NNC, were heavily weighted toward coeds. True, some colleges such as NNC initiated new majors or curricular emphases to draw new students; these included a Civil Aeronautics Program, pre-induction training, shop training, and even release time to work in nearby fields. But these innovations were insignificant compared to the traumatic changes wrought by the returning veterans at the war's end.

Dr. Lewis T. Corlett, here with his wife Elba, was a balanced, pastoral administrator as NNC's sixth president. (Fig. 3.1)

At the same time, less momentous transitions at work in the general Church of the Nazarene also influenced the NNC campus. Because strong general superintendents from the earliest years had played a signal role in activities of the college, changes in those positions impacted the Nampa campus. Hiram F. Reynolds died on July 13, 1938, after serving thirty-one years as general superintendent and emeritus superintendent, especially as a cheerleader for missions throughout the teens, twenties, and into the thirties. The next year, J. G. Morrison, former NNC president, died on November 23, 1939—the first sitting superintendent to die in more than twenty years. He too had encouraged mission programs on the NNC campus and much influenced President DeLong in several of his decisions. The two new general superintendents included Howard V. Miller, former dean of religion at NNC, and Orval J. Nease, a student of Dr. Wiley and a close contact with other NNC presidents. In the same years, the quadrennium between 1936 and 1940, half of the denomination's district superintendents changed, including the incoming Glenn Griffith (Idaho-Oregon-Utah) and D. I. Vanderpool (Northwest) on the NNC educational zone.

Still other changes in the church were more closely linked to the war itself. The general church, and President Corlett as well, tried to reach out to servicemen, through letters, servicemen organizations, and the preparation of a new corps of Nazarene chaplains. Although the war had a direct, negative impact on Nazarene missions in China, Japan, and the Philippines, it helped to establish a mission program in Alaska, which eventually became part of NNC's educational zone. The largest impact of the war was in draining off so many male—and many fewer female—students early in the worldwide imbroglio and the return of thousands to college campuses at the end of the war under GI bill auspices.

Even though the war reduced material and human resources, it also primed the economic pump throughout the country. As one authority has noted, "Constantly improving economic conditions enabled all the [Nazarene] colleges to pay off their accumulated indebtedness." This mounting financial base allowed NNC, for example, to build new buildings and to pay full salaries, the latter of which it had not been able to do for several years.

Surprisingly, another change during World War II had minimal impact on the NNC campus. One scholar calls the religious reforms sweeping through conservative Protestants during the war years "the reawakening of American Fundamentalism." This upsurge in fundamentalism and evangelicalism manifested itself in such happenings as the national popularity of radio evangelist Charles E. Fuller and his program "The Old Fashioned Revival Hour," the rise of Billy Graham and Youth for Christ, and the organization of the National Association of Evangelicals. All these movements and several other similar organizations swept across the U. S. in World War II. But they made little impression on NNC. The Nazarene bubble kept Nampa isolated from these new reforming upsurges in American conservative Protestantism.

Lewis T. Corlett was both a surprising and not-so-surprising choice for the next NNC president. Born in Pennsylvania in 1896, he was taken into the Church of the Nazarene with his parents in 1909. After falling away from faith, he was reclaimed, sanctified, and called to preach in 1915. After one year at Penn State and two others at Arkansas Holiness College, he completed his undergraduate degree at Peniel College in Texas in 1918. He taught a few months, was ordained, and then continued teaching. At age 23 he was even named president of Arkansas Holiness College for a few months. Then followed fourteen years of teaching and pastoring. In 1934, Corlett was named dean of theology at Bethany-Peniel College, where he served until called to Nampa as president in late spring 1942. This meant that save for J. G. Morrison, who had no college degree, Corlett was the least formally educated of the first six NNC presidents. After his bachelor's degree, he took about a year of seminary training in 1931-32 in Dallas, but did not complete a graduate degree. In 1938, Bethany-Peniel College awarded Corlett an honorary Doctor of Divinity degree.

Despite his limited formal education, Corlett had a good deal of administrative experience and was a seasoned pastor and classroom teacher. In addition, he fit the mold of many early Nazarene teachers of theology. Unlike Olive Winchester and a handful of others, most professors of religion and philosophy in Nazarene colleges were more likely veteran preachers called to teach than scholars with advanced degrees. Moreover, Corlett had just held a revival at NNC, and the very positive reactions to his preaching and personality made him a winsome candidate, especially after the fractious recent DeLong years. Perhaps even more important for the early 1940s, he had the strong recommendations of Nazarene general superintendents, an endorsement that carried much more weight then than later in selecting a college president among the Nazarenes.

Corlett did not arrive with any well-organized plan of administration or mission for NNC. Devoted pastor and teacher of theology that he was, Corlett was primarily interested in practics, preparing Christian workers and finding ways to teach the doctrines of salvation and sanctification in a practical, understandable way. In addition, other than his most recent years at Bethany-Peniel, he seems not to have had wide-reaching communication with other Nazarene academics, although he was well connected with general and district superintendents and pastors across the country. These rather limited academic horizons meant that Corlett was stretched early on—and for most of his years at NNC—in securing the needed new faculty. He had to rely heavily on the advice of others—church leaders, other Nazarene presidents, and NNC administrators—to reach out to new faculty. He especially drew on his acquaintances and connections at Bethany-Peniel College for NNC faculty and administrators. On the other hand, during his ten years at Nampa he hired more than a few professors who stayed for most of their careers at the college and made outstanding contributions to the institution.

What Corlett lacked as a strong academician proved less a drawback than some might have thought. Corlett was a warm-hearted man, able to communicate with students, faculty, and regional Nazarenes. In a short period of time he won over the college and its supporters to his leadership. He began by building bridges with his ebullient predecessor, now residing in the East. "I wanted to write and express to you our appreciation for the wonderful loyalty to the College that we are finding everywhere we go," Corlett told DeLong. "You have certainly done a marvelous work in binding the members of the constituency to the College and its interests." A few weeks later he added to the fulsome compliments to DeLong: "I want you to know that your good work is showing up more and more as I get into the work of the college. You certainly did a wonderful job in bringing the institution up to its present position."

The next spring when General Superintendent R. T. Williams was unable to attend the dedication of the new library named for him, Corlett asked DeLong to give the Dedicatory Address. The invitation, DeLong told Corlett, meant "more than words can tell." But in other actions, early on, Corlett revealed how much he differed from Dr. DeLong. When Corlett discovered the unreturned diploma of one of those students whose graduation was held up as a disciplinary measure in DeLong's administration, he made sure that graduate, now a pastor in Canada, received his diploma. He had thought it had been mailed four years ago and now apologized: "I regret this [the oversight] very much as I wanted to clear up everything I could regarding the past."

In the usual frictions that shake all college presidents Corlett was extraordinarily calm and non-vindictive. Such was his kindness that former NNC Vice President and Dean Olive Winchester could write Corlett that she and others who were long-time faculty at NNC "felt very happy" about his presidency and rejoiced with him "in the advance of the work." When a former student asked about his "sweet and calm" actions, the president replied that it was "a miracle of God's grace." He was convinced that his experience of sanctification "took out the nature that was upsetting me and took away the carnality and the hot-headed temper I had.... I believe loving God supremely and people sincerely has developed more patience within me than any other one thing."

That charitable disposition surfaced in dozens of letters to and from the president. When an elderly churchgoer in Walla Walla indicted Nazarenes for not attacking beauty parlors—"that is one of our outstanding sins"—makeup, and other "worldly attire," Corlett replied in a soothing, sunny manner, thanking the man for writing. "Your good letter came yesterday," the president wrote; "I appreciate very much your suggestions and your interest.... We are anxious to do everything just the best way we possibly can." And on another occasion when a misunderstanding seemed in the making, Corlett quickly wrote to a pastor apologizing "for my seeming act of rudeness." The president "felt badly that the way I expressed myself seemed to be in opposition to you. I had no idea of that in mind but I know my positive way of speaking sometimes leave[s] a wrong opinion."

Rather than mounting a stiff and sometimes alienating self-defense under criticism, as DeLong so often did, Corlett tried to explain to critics why differences of opinion might exist. In reply to a veteran pastor who attacked basketball players in shorts for "their nudeness," their "undress," Corlett pointed out that he and the writer had divergent backgrounds. The pastor had joined the church in 1914 and thought "this condition would have caused a church split," but Corlett, who became a Nazarene in 1909, had "never heard anything about boys not playing in shorts until I went south in 1915." "There are different viewpoints," Corlett continued, "but we admire you all for your convictions regarding [these] matters." Another elderly Nazarene woman wrote to criticize a photograph in the *Nazarene Messenger*, which displayed "costly, low necked, sleeveless dresses…that are a temptation to the boys." Was "worldliness…sweeping the Nazarene church like a flood," she asked? "In the face of another world catastrophe…in the face of starving millions,—in the face of the soon and eminent coming [sic] of our Lord, can we afford to ignore vital issues… and play with fire?" Two days later Corlett answered and explained that he had been out of town and that the staff member in charge of pre-viewing the issue of the *Messenger* had "failed to check this picture as carefully as he should have." The president confessed he was "embarrassed" about the picture (several others had written in about it), but he also told the letter-writer that he appreciated "so much your sincere letter and agree with you in your ideas and standards." (Revealingly, although this controversial photograph, which Corlett wished had not been published, appeared in the November issue of the *Nazarene Messenger*, it was reprinted several months later in that year's *Oasis*. Had the censors again failed in their work?)

Corlett's self-control and his willingness to deal with such comments and criticisms presumably arose from both personal experiences and his growing interest in applying holiness teachings to lives buffeted with physical and mental health challenges. For example when another devout Nazarene woman in Oregon wrote in about the afore-mentioned photo, she also asked President Corlett whether this controversial photo was not substantiation of the "trend to worldliness at N. N. C." that she had heard in several stories about the college. In fact, what was "worldliness," she asked? If such immodest dress was a sin when she was a student at Nampa in earlier years, wasn't it still a sign of sin? "The problem you raise regarding worldliness is one of the most difficult ones to define or draw a line on," the president told her in his long, sympathetic answer. Since "customs change and styles vary from year to year," he pointed out, "it always will be a point of discussion as to how much a Christian can conform to the changes that come without compromising." For him, "worldliness [was] something of the spirit and comes from the inner nature." He admitted that he could not tell her "how much we should conform to changing customs; [but] I try to keep the students from going to extremes on them." In the end, he was attempting to move students away from the dress and behavioral standards they followed in public high schools toward the higher, more demanding guidelines at NNC. He would appreciate it if she prayed for them in this difficult area of decision-making.

As pastor, professor of theology, and president, Corlett was forced to think about and comment on more pressing and controversial issues than students' dress. On several occasions early in life he had to deal with his own nearly overwhelming physical and psychological dilemmas. As he confessed in one of his books, *Holiness: The Harmonizing Experience* (1951), he had suffered several such bouts of nervousness. In these experiences, he, like others similarly afflicted, was "so tense that often what is said and done does not register in the memory and consequently cannot be recalled." He too had "experienced this personally in times of nervous prostration." As a result of these personal and professional experiences, Corlett had been laboring several years on publications dealing with the impact of the holiness experience on every-day human attitudes and actions.

Corlett's most extensive discussion of the healing power of holiness teachings on human behavior appears in the afore-mentioned *Holiness: The Harmonizing Experience.* His thematic emphases are not startling—in fact quite traditional: believers must not try to re-adapt their beliefs to shifting liberal worldviews that change over time; they can find harmony only by attuning themselves to God's eternal plans of perfection. "Holiness," Corlett was convinced, "is adaptable to the problems of every age and will meet the needs of this present one." Larding his text with numerous scriptures and long quotes from a handful of books sympathetic to his viewpoints, Corlett concluded "God's standard is Christian perfection for everybody.... God has a majestic harmony

Dr. Corlett authored several books on daily holiness living, including Holiness in Practical Living (1948) *and* Holiness: The Harmonizing Experience (1951). *(Fig. 3.2)*

in all of this, and it is all performed in accord with His ideal of perfection."

The president was particularly pleased with chapter four in his book, "Harmony amid Human Frailties." He noted that this section had been widely commented on in the Nazarene Church, and when one piece of his writing was to be included in his autobiography, he asked that it be this chapter. The content and viewpoints of this writing tell us much about Corlett as a thinker and administrator.

The origins of the ideas Corlett worked into his often-cited chapter are of significance. Asked to be a revival speaker for another person who withdrew a few days before the services, Corlett pondered his emphases. Deciding that one sermon should address "Holiness and the Physical," he was inspired by "the Spirit" and wrote for one hour and ten minutes. A few days later he spoke on the topic for one hour and ten minutes. His audience stayed with him—and listened. "As far as I know," Corlett wrote much later, "this was the first message in our denomination given on the relation of nerves and nervous problems to Christian experience."

"Harmony amid Human Frailties," like the book of which it is a part, is a very traditional treatment of a very untypical subject for the time. "This is a nervous generation," Corlett told his readers. And the answer to nervousness was not in following the new pied pipers of psychology and other behaviorists. Rather, those hoping to find help for their nervousness needed to rediscover that God is "a tender Heavenly Father who cares for those who try to please him." Understanding the goodness of God, developing empathetic encouragement for sick people, disciplining one's passions, advancing a positive attitude toward life and others, and following the guidance of the Holy Spirit—these were the keys in dealing with nervous conditions and finding harmony in one's spiritual life. Corlett was certain that "An experience of Christian perfection can operate successfully in relation to all frailties and limitations of humanity. A person can be perfect in heart while biased in mind, warped in judgment, harassed by nerves, and handicapped by physical suffering." It was an optimistic, caring, and convincing message for many Nazarenes.

But for believers of a more analytic, interpretive cast of mind, large questions might have surfaced—then and now. Scholars in psychology and cultural anthropology might have blanched at some of Corlett's expansive, unscholarly assertions. They surely would have wondered about the implications of the writer's essentialist conclusions that "different races have different traits," that "those living in warmer climates naturally move and act more slowly than those in cooler atmosphere," and that those "who have been reared in industrial areas are usually more systematic and punctual than those who have lived in rural areas...." Others would have difficulty accepting the large contention that "All sickness is the result of the effect of sin on the race...."

But one must keep in mind Corlett's intended audience. He was writing for general Nazarene and evangelical readers, not primarily for scholars. His message was uplifting and beneficial for chronic worriers and for others beset with a variety of psychosomatic maladies. Plus, his book encouraged fellow journeyers to be sensitive to those beset with nervousness and depression. Listening to the guidance of the Holy Spirit, disciplining themselves, and following the promises of a loving, empathetic Heavenly Father, he thought, could help all.

Corlett in this volume, in an earlier book *Holiness in Practical Living* (1948), and in his last book, his autobiographical *Thank God and Take Courage: How the Holy Spirit Worked in My Life* (1992), provides valuable glimpses into his philosophy of Christian education and how he would administer a Christian liberal arts college. His primary emphasis was on developing the Christian character of students, but he was also much taken with training young men for the ministry. From his own personal and professional experience he was naturally much more drawn to the Jerusalem, or the spiritual, side of a Nazarene college than to the Athens, or academic side. Not surprisingly, then, Corlett did much to advance the religious side of NNC but was daily challenged to keep up with the academic side.

Corlett's presidential correspondence overflows with letters to other Nazarene leaders and pastors but especially to his beloved "preacher boys." As he told one young minister who attended his classes at Bethany-Peniel, "I am anxious more and more to provide those things which will prepare our young men for active work in service to the church." Another young preacher who studied with Corlett at NNC warmly and fulsomely thanked his mentor: "When the going has gotten rough, I've unconsciously gone back in my mind to homiletics class and listened again to your lectures and stories of your pastoral experience." Even more memorable were the times for personal counseling: "You have been more than a college president, you have been a counselor, a friend, a classic example of a God-made Christian. I'll never forget the times when you took time in the midst of a multitude of business to talk with me about my spiritual problems...." Letters such as this and dozens more warmed the president's heart and affirmed his call. As he wrote to still another pastor who thanked him for his tutelage, "One of the great pleasures of my life now is found in the successes of those who have been in school under me. It was with difficulty that I left the pastorate and returned to the school work and the only reason I did was that God assured me that I would be able to do a larger work in [the] training of young men to go out into the ministry." After nearly twenty years as a teacher and administrator, he was "beginning to receive the rewards of this promise."

Corlett proved, in his religious leadership of NNC, to be the balanced person he exhibited in his own life. From the beginning the new president had to re-establish warm connections with some of the Nampa Nazarenes who had become alienated from NNC during the last months of DeLong's second presidency. As the chair of the Board of Regents warned when offering Corlett the presidency, "there are many adversaries and problems of course." For the most part Corlett was able to overcome and move beyond those bad feelings. He brought sound and well-known Nazarene revivalists to campus and made sure that district superintendents from the NNC zone were invited to speak frequently in chapel and occasionally to hold revivals. Those invitations were important to bring about stronger and more enthusiastic bonds between Nazarenes of the Northwest zone and their college. Unlike DeLong, at no time during his presidency did Corlett face serious dissention from his constituency, let alone an open revolt.

The president, faculty, and student body also experienced seasons of refreshing spiritual renewal. During the fall and spring revivals the spiritual temperature on campus often reached new highs. Even the chapel services experienced breakthroughs. In late fall 1943 he wrote a serviceman "We had a wonderful chapel service last Tuesday with around forty people at the altar." That tide of fervor remained high, with the president reporting in 1948 that of all the students enrolled at NNC nearly 10 percent had "calls to mission fields."

A new spirit of unity and cooperation emerged on campus after John E. Riley arrived as pastor of the College Church of the Nazarene, which met on campus in the NNC chapel for its worship services. When College Church began under the forceful encouragement of President DeLong in 1937 and was authorized by the Board of Regents, bad feelings between the college and Nampa First Church surfaced. But the new College Church gradually grew under the able leadership of its first two pastors George Franklin (1937-42) and U. E. Harding (1942-44). When Harding resigned in 1944 to return to evangelistic work, College Church, in conjunction with President Corlett and acting under advice from the Board of General Superintendents, called Riley to be their pastor. A New Englander by heritage and pastoral experience, Riley quickly fit into his new western setting and immediately established a strong rapport with faculty, students, and townspeople. From the very beginning Corlett liked Riley and enjoyed his preaching. As he told members of the Idaho-Oregon District Assembly, "It has been a privilege to work with Brother Riley, our good pastor, who has helped to relieve me of my burdens as well as fed my own soul when I was in the service[s] of the College Church." In college chapel services Corlett and Riley sat together on the platform, and the same was true for church services on Sunday, in the chapel and then in the huge new church opened in 1949 across the street, at the corner of Dewey and Juniper. The two men were symbols of integrity and solid leadership: Corlett in things spiritual and administrative; Riley, in matters religious and intellectual.

Periodically, however, a few religious tempests, disrupting Corlett's presidency, also revealed much about his spiritual outlook. Throughout the history of NNC discontent and criticism have come primarily from outspoken conservatives, from Nazarenes unhappy with professors and their teachings, discontented about such activities as athletics and dramatic productions, or upset with dress standards on campus. In late 1949 a series of events involving two women students and a first-year professor represented one kind of disruption Corlett had to face. The two coeds, whom the president considered "emotionally unstable," accused the new professor of teaching heresy. In fact, his perspective—that the Bible contained the Word of God but also "the words of the devil and the words of man," which God had allowed in the Scriptures "for our warning and admonition"—was hardly revolutionary. As Corlett told a pastor in Washington inquiring about the controversy, the young professor's point of view was "not far off from what all of us believe." The young professor may have "unwisely made that statement to the class," but he clearly "believed in our theory of inspiration." When Corlett tried to explain to the young women what the professor meant—and the president had conversed with the young teacher on several occasions—and had encouraged them "to attend the fine arts recitals and develop a cultural aspect of life," they "seemed as if they were determined not to be considerate." One of the undergraduates was "so set in her ways of extreme fundamentalism" that she "walked out of chapel" when he tried to explain such matters to the student body.

Two other events placed similar pressures on the president. When a Canadian district superintendent inquired about a possible ministerial student recently graduated from NNC, Corlett gave the young theologue a good recommendation. But then the president added that while the aspiring minister was waiting for a job, he and his wife had begun attending North Nampa Church of the Nazarene. The president was not quite sure if the ministerial student had imbibed that church's "ultra-radical stands." He thought a strong district superintendent, providing good beginning advice, could lead the young man "away from any extreme attitudes he might have acquired." Six months later a layman wrote from the Emmett Church to complain that his pastor was headed off into a controversial theological byway and was refusing to allow NNC publicity or presentations into their church. What could he do about this pastoral misdirection? Corlett asked the layman not to cast the problem into an NNC-Emmett Church controversy; that would be detrimental for the college and the local church. True, the pastor was putting the Emmett Church and its people in an "embarrassing position" through his arbitrary actions, but the president counseled patience. "God, in time, can bring about things which look impossible, so I believe if we only hold steady God has a way out." Actually, Corlett was sensing a radical turn to the right invading several churches in the Nampa area. The movement continued to gather steam and followers and finally burst out into a new church movement in the mid-1950s, the Bible Missionary Union (later the Bible Missionary Church).

On some other issues Corlett could be surprisingly conservative himself. Like nearly all Nazarenes of his time he could not abide "the tongues people." When a student, pastor, or layperson asked him about Pentecostals who spoke in other tongues, he was decidedly negative. For Corlett, the tongues advocates were disrupters. They like nothing better than for you to deal with that issue, he wrote, because they "like to feel that you are scrapping with them." Moreover, Corlett added, "they thrive on that so I would not directly face them." Besides, "God is on your side and he will aid you as you preach with the grace and blessing of God upon you."

The president also strongly urged students, faculty, and pastors not to be doubters. As he told one pastor of another church, "you will find a problem... in the question of supporting your denominational institutions when you have doubts unto their loyalty to fundamental faith." Doubting was a problem because "it produced neither loyalty in the mind of the minister nor the people with whom he is working. In fact, some ministers I have known became so antagonistic that they lost the sweetness that perfect love should manifest." Clearly Corlett did not think question asking, especially in matters of faith and church support, was an advisable route to follow.

In the faith and learning ingredients involved in the balance of a Christian liberal arts college Corlett tended to veer toward the spiritual side. As his good friend and successor John E. Riley pointed out, Corlett loved to prepare ministers and was a superb teacher of homiletics and practics but did not lead by example in the intellectual side of campus life at NNC. Indeed Corlett sometimes seemed reluctant to put needed emphasis on the strong academic preparation of his faculty. He worried that graduate school pushed young professors too far into analytical pursuits, undermining their faith. When asked about the origins and founding purposes of NNC, Corlett replied that the school was founded on a two-fold purpose: "First, a desire to train workers to carry forth the doctrine of Holiness as a second definite work of grace. Second, a desire to establish an institution where the children of the parents believing such a doctrine could have a spiritual school to attend." For Corlett, emphases on the schooling, academic, and intellectual side of a college education always took a back seat to spiritual training.

Corlett's hesitancy about academic matters continued to display itself when the Nazarene seminary began and organized its curriculum in the late 1940s (and where Corlett would be president from 1952 to 1966). Corlett expressed his opinion about the new seminary's lack of emphasis on theology and practics in a worrying letter to Eastern Nazarene President Samuel Young: "Personally, I think the Seminary is getting too many Philosophy majors in it, but since they didn't ask my advice I didn't give it to them." But he did tell them explicitly less than a week later. To Hugh C. Benner, the seminary president, Corlett wrote: "I think you are getting too many fellows with Philosophy backgrounds on your staff."

More revealing and of much larger consequence was the Report of the

Commission on Education 1948-52, a Nazarene commission that Corlett chaired. He also seems to have been the lead author of the commission's report to the General Assembly of 1952. Although the commission included such staunch advocates of the liberal arts as Dean Bertha Munro of Eastern Nazarene College and former NNC President Russell V. DeLong, the report dealt almost entirely with the shaping forces of religion that needed to be at work on Nazarene college campuses. The nine pages of text list and discuss the theological underpinnings of Nazarene higher education and the necessary strong links between Nazarene churches and their colleges, but these pages contain almost nothing about the academic content of Christian liberal arts colleges. It was a revealing document about the church, about its philosophy of Christian education, and about the commission's chairman.

Given L. T. Corlett's lack of academic leadership at NNC, it is all the more remarkable that he hired several superb faculty members who served the college very well and stayed for many years. Corlett was also responsible for selecting and hiring Thelma B. Culver, perhaps the strongest academic dean ever to serve at NNC. Probably these successes in hiring strong faculty members and a superb dean came more from the president's wonderful ability to get along with people than from his image or strengths as an academic leader.

Several of the key faculty Corlett hired stayed with the college for more than ten years, some as many as forty years. Among these notable professors were Donald B. Tillotson (mathematics), Alline Swann (music), Helen G. Wilson (speech and journalism), Juanita Demmer (languages), Geneva Mumau Bittleston (library), Ruth Long (art), Dorothy Long (art), Gilbert Ford (physics and chemistry), Double E Hill (music), James Feltar (education), A. Elwood Sanner (religion), and Ruby Sanner (music). Thelma Culver had joined the faculty earlier but became the academic dean in 1946. It was a remarkable lineup of long-time, highly committed faculty members.

Obtaining strong faculty was an arduous, time-consuming task for Corlett. He tried a variety of avenues to find new professors because during his presidency enrollments spiraled upward. He drew especially on his previous contacts at Bethany Nazarene College, he wrote to other Nazarene college presidents, and he worked through district superintendents and other church leaders. Nothing came easy. In 1947 Corlett wrote to another Nazarene college president to confess, "It certainly is getting to be a difficult matter to find the proper personnel for our faculties." He was convinced that Nazarene colleges and the church in general "ought to find some way to encourage [our] young people to take graduate work." But another barrier had arisen, as he told a general superintendent: "We are losing too many of our graduate students and I firmly believe that a little personal interest from some of us as leaders will help to settle them in the battles that they are fighting."

Truth to tell, Corlett had never experienced firsthand the pressures students faced in major graduate schools; all of his post-graduate work was at a conservative

Protestant Dallas seminary while he was preaching. Besides, he was a bit afraid of what graduate schools and strongly analytical seminaries were doing to Nazarene and other evangelical students. When a religion professor came under criticism from outspoken conservative students, Corlett said of the professor: "since he has had so much seminary work, he has brought various aspects of the critical study of the Bible into his teaching and taking the seminary approach left it to the students to make their own decisions, rather than declaring himself too well on what our stand is." "Trying to be intellectually honest on a research method," the president added about the professor, "he unwisely" made statements in class that were too open-ended. Unfortunately, these statements suggested that Corlett had a truncated vision of Christian liberal arts education, implying its major purpose was to indoctrinate rather than to educate. The most far-reaching academic decision Corlett made was naming Thelma B. Culver academic dean of NNC in 1946. Except for the presidents of the institution, probably no one had more shaping influence on the academic mission of the college than Dr. Culver. For nearly twenty-five years, while serving as dean, she was a strong advocate of NNC's major goal of providing a Christian liberal arts education.

Thelma Blanche Culver was a woman of the West. She grew up in a South Dakota family in which education was valued. Her father was an influential newspaperman in her hometown of Corsica, but after he was converted, he felt a call to preach and eventually moved farther west to pastor. In South Dakota, Thelma completed high school and two years of college and then finished her undergraduate work at NNC in 1932. Next, she took a master's in education at the University of Washington and became the first woman to complete her doctorate in education at the University of Colorado in 1946. Culver began her public school teaching career in South Dakota and then taught in Idaho, including at NNC's College High School. In 1942 she joined the NNC college faculty, having taught at College High since 1935.

Dr. Thelma B. Culver, with a doctorate in education, became a strong academic leader and a superb NNC dean (1946-70). (Fig. 3.3)

When negotiating her new role as a dean with President Corlett, Thelma Culver asked to be

Dr. Gilbert Ford, a Harvard-trained scientist, was a first-rate teacher and scholar and later served as academic vice president. (Fig. 3.4)

freed from disciplinary duties so that she could focus on curricular matters. For the most part that division of duties followed. Dean Culver's influence on faculty and NNC's curriculum soon became evident when she returned to campus as the new dean in fall 1946. In faculty meetings she urged professors to prepare position papers on their fields, in that way encouraging continuing education among her colleagues. She also made her opinions known about possible faculty members being hired. Stepping into the gap of Corlett's limited academic preparation, Culver added notable strengths to the liberal arts atmosphere on the NNC campus. It was a position she continued to hold well into the succeeding Riley administration.

On occasion, serendipity raised its helpful head to aid NNC's academic mission. In spring 1947 a young graduate student in physics at Harvard wrote to query President Corlett about a faculty position at NNC. Gilbert Ford was asking about a possible teaching slot for two years hence. "I have felt for several years that I would like to spend my life teaching in one of our church schools," Ford wrote, "and I believe I am in God's will in planning for such a career. I am particularly interested in Northwest Nazarene College." The president, replying rather noncommittally, seems not to have understood how much this letter to him promised. Nonetheless the necessary details were worked out, and Dr. Ford came to NNC in 1950. No other professor did as much as Ford to heighten the academic reputation of NNC in the next twenty to thirty years in his first-rate work in physics and the general sciences. He became a symbol of academic excellence linked to a gentle, devoted soul.

Academic challenges were not the most taxing problems Corlett faced, however. The most troubling dilemmas arose from economic matters. Surprisingly, too, these questions were rarely ones dealing with debts but more often those associated with more incoming students than facilities, faculty, and classrooms could accommodate. The war years and the immediate postwar era led to a student body expanding at a rapid rate and then shrinking. And the wartimes also led to a different kind of student body from what NNC had known previously.

When Corlett arrived in Nampa in time for the fall 1942 opening, the shaping impact of the war was already being felt. By early October more than 400 college students were at NNC, accounting for the institution's largest enrollment in history. All the dormitories were full, necessitating that older students find rooms in the community. Twenty more women than men students were at the college. Classes in the sciences and mathematics were overflowing, especially with the added programs enrolling young men in special naval and army programs. With nearly 140 other students in the Academy (high school) and Grammar School programs, the campus buildings were packed. These numbers, with some wavering, continued to expand in the war years, and by 1946 enrollments in the college had jumped to 450, with the K-12 programs claiming nearly 180 students. Now, about 630 students jammed the campus. President Corlett tried to deal with the expanding student body, but the new buildings were slow in coming. Alternatives had to be put in place.

Had Corlett been a DeLong he might have launched an immediate campaign to erect new dormitories for young women and men. But Corlett was more cautious, hoping to adopt a pay-as-you-go plan. Besides, the Board of General Superintendents, with increasing tuition revenues becoming available, were urging all Nazarene colleges to pay off existing debts before they launched new programs. Inclined to follow such advice from the church hierarchy, Corlett silenced the big guns of expansion to prime a program for paying off debts. Early in 1943, with regent support, Corlett launched a program to wipe away all the red ink. It was an "opportune time to take advantage of the financial conditions of the country," the board told the campus community, "and improve the financial position of the college." The debt-reduction campaign would endeavor to pay off about $25,000 of its total indebtedness of $66,000, resulting from earlier debts and the construction costs of Morrison Hall. After a few months of successful fund-raising, the regents voted to continue the campaign until the entire debt had been erased.

Decisions at the spring 1943 semi-annual meeting of the board illustrated the much-improved financial outlook at the college. Not only did the regents raise faculty salaries five percent, in addition to the ten percent raise awarded professors the previous fall, they authorized another ten percent salary jump in the coming year. Moreover, they voted to clear up all old salary debts carried over from the Depression and to raise the percentage of guaranteed annual salary to the faculty. That meant that the college now owed no back salaries. In addition, the regents authorized the programs and buildings needed to staff and house the War Service Programs expanding on campus.

Financial support from the Northwest educational zone and other funding from the federal government continued to mount up in the coming months and years. These additional dollars allowed the college to offer new programs and courses. One of these programs was the Civilian Pilot Training (CPT) course, which gave students two months of training in reserve programs for the army, navy, and air force. In late 1942 about thirty young men were enrolled, but in the spring semester of 1943 nearly twice that number were taking the CPT course. Working with the federal government's National Youth Administration, NNC also offered shop training for students interested in mechanical, drawing and blueprint, and other shop work. The college, in addition, inaugurated an accelerated educational program that allowed high school juniors who had already completed three years of high school, were in the top half of their class academically, and who had letters of support from a principal to enroll as college freshmen. At the end of a successful freshman year, these students would receive a high school diploma as well as credit for their first year of college. This fast-track program prepared young men and young women more expeditiously for war work and allowed academically talented students to move more quickly into their educational training. The college also made sure that young women, making up well more than half of the NNC student body, were apprised of all the new occupational openings for coeds who wished to take their place in the job market.

The burgeoning enrollments forced the Board of Regents and president to think about more dormitories and additional classroom space. In its fall 1944 meeting the board adopted the president's recommendation of an expansion program. The regents, realizing "that the enrollment this year of 572 is the largest enrollment the school has ever had for the first semester," approved Corlett's general plans for new dormitories and classrooms and called for architectural plans for buildings that would "maintain the harmony and the beauty of the campus."

But there was a conflict: both the regents and the president wanted to pay off the existing debt before launching an expensive new program of expansion. The conflict was resolved with escalating enrollments, increased giving, and a generally expanding U. S. economy. In the January 1945 issue of the *Nazarene Messenger* the front page headline read "Complete Victory Near at Hand for N. N. C.: Debt Entirely Paid on February 1, 1945." About two months later the regents announced a new building program of $700,000 that would include new dormitories for both men and women, an educational and a fine arts building, a science hall, a gymnasium, and a new heating plant. Other remodeling projects were also included. It was a bold and expansive program planned for a campus enrollment of 1,000. Perhaps too bold. In the next fourteen years (1945-59), only the men's dormitory, Chapman Hall, was completed, although a science hall (the incomplete hospital wing) and a woman's dormitory (Mangum Hall) were purchased.

Meanwhile more pressing and resource-grabbing issues captured the attention of President Corlett and the regents. In the years from the end of the war in 1945 until 1949, GI's, often with their families, came flooding onto the NNC campus. Where would they live, how would they be housed, and how would the additional needed classes be organized? These were the questions that NNC's leaders were forced to face—head-on and immediately.

The plan for development was two-pronged. Rev. L. Wesley Johnson, an experienced and newly hired field man, would travel throughout the Northwest educational zone speaking at churches and securing pledges for the Expansion Plan. At the same time, the campus would provide the necessary housing, even if very temporary, for the incoming veterans and their families. Since the G. I. Bill made new funding available to veterans—and through them to the college—NNC could afford a modicum of expansion on its own. The G. I. Bill provided up to $500 each year for tuition, board and room, and other expenses and additional support for a married man. Veterans were to begin their college work within two years of an honorable discharge from the army, navy, air force, marines, or coast guard. Returning servicemen under the age of twenty-five were allowed one year of school, plus additional months or year's equivalent to their period in the service. These funds did much to satisfy cash-hungry sections of the campus.

On the other hand, despite enthusiastic presidential and regental support for the expansion program, funds for new brick buildings came in slowly—too slowly in fact—in an uncertain postwar economy. Stopgap measures had to be quickly put in place. They came from an unexpected source. L. Wesley Johnson, working his previous connections with governmental agencies, and encouraging President Corlett to do the same, contacted Idaho Senator Charles C. Gossett, a resident of Nampa, for his help. Locating twenty-five housing units, comprising three buildings that were no longer needed in Mountain Home, Idaho, after the war, Gossett and the Federal Housing Administration worked out their transfer to the NNC campus. Later in the summer three other units came from Vancouver, Washington. Some were ready for occupancy; others needed considerable remodeling. The housing units, dubbed "Vetville," although at first government property, would be of critical use to house veterans and their families. When all the housing units were not completely ready by fall 1946, the college secured nearly forty trailers ("Trailer City") for the flood of incoming veterans. These too came on loan from the federal government. Finally, in late spring 1946 ground was broken for a new men's dormitory, Chapman Hall, but completion was delayed until well into 1947 because of unavailability of building materials. When ready for occupancy in fall 1947, Chapman accommodated nearly 160 men, the first brick-constructed men's dormitory on campus.

Other vexing challenges pushed at the college administration. Some extended from wartime into postwar economies. Rationing restricted gas, tires, coffee, film, and many other items during the war, and specific building materials, unavailable during the global conflict, were still in minimum supply after 1945. Supplying a

During WWII and afterwards, "Vetville" provided housing for returning servicemen and their families. (Fig. 3.5)

balanced diet in the dining hall also challenged NNC leaders both during the war and afterwards. Can you serve "more vegetables fruits, canned & dried apples both raw [sic], baked in sauce rather than so much starch," one Walla Walla mother asked? Later, a father in Oregon requested that his son be allowed "to come home to finish school because of the undesirability of the meals provided in the dining hall." He had examined the food complaints and found the "grub situation" terrible; "the dining hall provender has always been a reprehensible factor at NNC." Meanwhile, discontented students labled a curiously congealed main dish of meat and potatoes "elephant's hind leg" and described the apple crisp as "ground up shotput." In replying to these complaints from parents and students, Corlett admitted the problem, which was "entirely one of labor," he said. He had been unable to hire a "dietician who could fit into our program here and plan so the meals will be what they ought to be. I will not give up until I secure one," Corlett promised.

But the complaints continued. During the pre-holidays at the end of 1946 and in the early weeks of 1947, the negative comments about dining hall food reached a new intensity. Besides the chorus of criticisms coming from disgruntled parents, undoubtedly through their sons and daughters at NNC, a member of the Board of Regents, representing "several mothers of the local church" in Walla Walla, wrote to Corlett saying that one female student was urging "students [not] to enter N.N.C. next year because of the food situation." The regent was convinced that these "mothers are fine Christian mothers and I do not believe they would in any sense exaggerate the picture." Again, Corlett admitted the problem. The cook in the dining hall seemed "to go in spurts in her planning." In fact, "the kitchen is our big problem," he confessed. "If we can accomplish this [eliminate the kitchen problems] we will make a great step forward in N.N.C."

Still another concern that weighed heavily on Corlett and the college administration was the Samaritan Hospital complex. Since its humble beginnings in 1920, Samaritan Hospital, under the diligent leadership of Dr.Thomas Mangum and his family, had provided invaluable service to young women and men preparing for the mission field, medical service for the Nampa community, and other services for the general Church of the Nazarene. But the hospital had struggled financially because it had never been a recipient of general church funds and thus had to maintain and attempt to expand on a very narrow giving base. Often NNC and Samaritan Hospital were appealing to the same persons for support, mainly Nazarenes in Nampa and the broader Northwest educational zone. By mid-1946 it was clear that something had to be done. Two general superintendents urged that NNC take over the Nurses' Training program and make it part of the college's academic mission. Corlett was inclined to do that, but admitted that financial and housing dilemmas needed more study. If the nursing program became part of the college, the hospital itself would have to find a way to enlarge, and establish and keep an accredited program. The major difficulties were three: lack of necessary funding, dwindling numbers of nurses enrolled in the program, and an inadequate number of beds and patients for the hospital to receive accreditation.

The fiscal problems would not go away, and solutions did not arise. Four years later Northwest District Superintendent E. E. Zachary termed the persisting hospital problem "an 'A No. 1' mess." "I do not think it is hopeless," he added, "but my honest opinion is that the whole arrangement is going to have to be placed on a new situation." The downward financial spiral continued when the hospital was unable to complete a large concrete shell of a building intended as an expansion. Eventually, the hospital, without necessary funding and unable to garner sufficient church or community support, sold its dormitory for nurses, Mangum Hall, to the college for a women's dormitory, and later sold the unfinished concrete shell that, with considerable additional construction, became the college's new science building. When the hospital closed in 1967, the college purchased its buildings and, after renovation, they became the Fine Arts complex.

If expanding and then plummeting enrollments were Corlett's major economic challenge, he faced many fewer dilemmas in campus social life than his predecessor. Corlett succeeded in getting along with students as he did with opinionated pastors and disgruntled church persons, especially in the Nampa area. In addition to his winsome personality, Corlett also had on his side, for the most part, a more mature student body. When the college enrollments boomed from 1942 to 1948, many of the new students were returning veterans and their families, older students and less likely to cause headaches for the college disciplinary staff. Plus, Corlett increasingly passed on disciplinary matters to strong administrators as he did academic decisions to Thelma Culver. At first the head residents of dormitories served as dean of men and dean of women; then, adding numbers and experience, the college formed an informal personnel committee, which included persons whose major assignment was serving as dean of students. In addition to the head residents in the men and women's dormitories, A. Leslie Parrott and C. Edward Taylor were named, successively, deans of students in the late 1940s and early 1950s in Corlett's administration. In early 1948 Helen Grace Wilson was announced as dean of women. For most of the next generation she was in and out of positions dealing with disciplinary and campus social life matters. In the early years of her work she relied on a judicial board of dormitory and advanced students to help make decisions. Closely allied to and also serving important roles in advising and counseling students were Dean Culver, for upper division students, and Donald B. Tillotson, in charge of lower division students and student testing. For a time LaMont Lee also served in the important position of director of athletics and intramurals.

Athletics were a very important part of NNC campus life during the Corlett period, and the president was a sports fan. Often he wrote in his letters of how the basketball team was doing and what was happening in the intense competition among the Athletic-Literary societies. In his correspondence with one NNC athlete preparing to teach, he expressed his wish to carry on the sports program at NNC because it helped "to keep the morale of the school at the highest." During the war and postwar years, men's basketball was the central focus of the sports program. Ralph Allison, Oscar Reed, and LaMont Lee were the coaches of basketball teams playing competitors in Idaho, Oregon, and Washington. The teams rarely were top-notch, but they had an outstanding player in Morris Chalfant; if wins were secured against traditional foes like the College of Idaho or Boise Junior College, coaches and players seemed satisfied. By the late 1940s men were also much involved in intercollegiate competition in baseball and track. In 1950 the *Oasis* declared the baseball team the best in the Boise Valley and the track men among the top in the state of Idaho.

Before intercollegiate sports programs for women were launched, NNC hosted many women's intramural competitions. (Fig. 3.6)

Women's sports were limited to intramural competitions. In the early 1940s women played such team sports as softball, volleyball, and basketball—in dresses or sweaters and skirts. By the end of the decade they were competing in pedal pusher outfits. In 1949, the NNC Administrative Council was asked to consider the possibility of a "women's basketball team in intercollegiate competition." In response, the committee passed a motion that stated "it be our policy not to allow any expansion of our intercollegiate competition for women in athletics at this time." But if a young woman broke an existing NNC athletic record, she was offered a scholarship for the next semester. Individual sports for women and men also included ping-pong, archery, and golf.

Helen Grace Wilson, an enthusiastic speech teacher, later became Dean of Women and sat on the Personnel Committee. (Fig. 3.7)

Along with athletic expansions, the social transformations throbbing through American society in the 1940s, not surprisingly, impacted the NNC campus. Both the wartime and postwar transitions in American social life drove some of these social changes. They invaded Nazarene colleges. One reason for the changes, of course, was the veterans on campus who had global and nonevangelical experiences much at odds with what was expected of NNC students. But the records of disciplinary cases on campus rarely focused on veterans. They dealt primarily with college students in the normal age group. When such students were guilty of—or thought guilty of—campus code infractions, they were brought in front of the dean of students, dean of women, or dean of men, along with administrators. They were given a list of possible "sins" and were asked to respond if they had broken these rules and if so how many times during the school year. Some activities on the long list dealt with forbidden entertainments: movies, bowling (at bowling alleys), skating (roller skating rinks), dancing, or playing pool. Other listed misbehaviors included smoking, drinking, stealing, using profanity, leaving a dorm without permission, and the one that seemed most often bruised or broken, riding around in a car with undesirable citizens (e.g. soldier boys, townsmen, and other non-NNC companions).

Corlett largely remained distant from these disciplinary cases, but one such occurrence tried his legendary patience; perhaps nearly caused it to unravel. Shortly before Christmas 1944, a young woman enrolled at the NNC Academy, already under discipline for breaking campus and dormitory rules, left Hadley Hall with a friend

A traditional Tug of War often pitted classes or other groups against one another. (Fig. 3.8)

and skylarked to Denver. Her mother, coming to NNC to investigate and to secure the return of her daughter, fell ill in Nampa and was hospitalized for three or four weeks. She wrote to President Corlett demanding that NNC pay part of the costs for her hospitalization and the transportation charges for her daughter; if he did not, the mother warned, she would contact the college's Board of Regents and the parents of all other girls living in Hadley. When Corlett refused, calling her tactics blackmail, she followed up on her threat; the letters went out. Girls were unsafe in Hadley Hall, the woman from Corvallis wrote; first floor windows were unscreened, the dean of women "hardly treated the girls like human beings"; it was "a deplorable situation...to be regretted especially in a Christian school." Then Corlett was forced to write to all concerned trying to explain what had happened and why the mother was undermining the purposes of the college. "She is a Christian," Corlett wrote, "but is a neurotic, which affects her viewpoints and judgments." Two months later the mother was sure that what she had done was right since "God has blessed me with some peace and comfort." In fact, she wondered if "in some respect God may use even this seemingly unfortunate incident to bring blessing and help to your school." Corlett did not answer her last letter.

The persisting tensions among Nazarenes concerning social activities, entertainments, and dress standards continued under Corlett's leadership but at a less stressful level. When he became president, the NNC catalog stated: "The use of tobacco or alcoholic beverages, card playing, dancing, and theater going are strictly forbidden." All students not living with their families in the Nampa area were to reside in dormitories; off-campus living arrangements were possible only after special permission from an appropriate dean. While dress requirements were much less specific than a decade earlier, students were nonetheless enjoined to aim for "unobtrusiveness," "the first essential element of refined and beautiful dress...." One specific was mentioned: "Young women should use particular discretion in selecting party and banquet dresses that they conform" to NNC "standards and ideals." Ten years later at the end of Corlett's presidency, the stipulations on entertainments remained virtually unchanged, with the added statement "Those who do not cheerfully agree to these standards may be asked to withdraw from the college."

But the statements on dress had been dropped in the catalog, even though general guidelines on appropriate dress were stipulated once students were on campus.

One aftermath of the war furnished NNC students with a new outlet for their social needs. In the late 1940s one of the government surplus buildings that Business Manager L. Wesley Johnson secured was placed next to the Morrison Hall dining area to become a coffee shop. Later dubbed "The Bean," this small, intimate space provided a meeting place dear to NNC students. For more than a generation it was the watering hole for after-study-hours gatherings, as well as snatched breakfasts on the way to classes and coke and burger breaks during the day. It was the closest thing to a campus "hang out" that often sprouts up close to college and university campuses.

For the most part NNC was a campus-centered culture, but war and postwar experiences forced students to look outward a bit more often. So many young men and women were in the service—the 1945 *Oasis* listed more than 250 in the armed forces and five who had lost their lives—that campus residents were pummeled with war and service-related stories. Returning veterans added to these war front accounts. And other connections resulted, none more intriguing than when Japanese students came to the NNC campus in the late 1940s. There were complications in these new connections. One student from Japan, who later went into the ministry, confessed that "when I arrived at N. N. C., I had a fear in my heart, because I wondered if they were against the Japanese." But his fears were unfounded; he came to "feel everyone who belongs to N.N.C. has known each other for a hundred years."

Not all Japanese were so welcomed. When a young Japanese woman from Bethany Nazarene wished to enter the nursing program at Samaritan Hospital, she was rejected as "unacceptable because of her nationality." The president of Bethany thought this "a very unfortunate reaction." How was the girl to feel "when she realizes that her own church discriminates against her." Corlett thought differently. The hospital had hired Japanese women to serve as maids, "but the reaction of the patients made it absolutely necessary that they be asked to leave." He added that if the Japanese nursing

"The Bean," a remodeled government building, became a much-loved student hangout. (Fig. 3.9)

student came to Samaritan, "it would not be of any value to put a girl in nursing whom the people would react against." The Japanese young woman would be embarrassed and "would bring the institution to the place where it would be liable to lose a great amount of income from patients who would go elsewhere." Many associated with the hospital as patients and staff, unfortunately, seemed to agree with the president.

During his ten years at the NNC helm, Corlett won increasing praise and admiration from general church leaders, NNC regents, and students. They trusted him and found him fair-minded, full of encouragement, and always a ready listener. Even if he had not been a dynamic academic leader and a dreamer of expansion, he had kept things on an even keel, balancing the varied and sometimes competing agendas that supporters of the college had in mind. After the tumultuous years of DeLong's controversial leadership, Corlett was a peacemaker and counselor.

Then came a surprise announcement in June 1952. Corlett was resigning his NNC office to accept the presidency of Nazarene Theological Seminary (NTS) in Kansas City. While attending the General Assembly in June he had been offered the NTS reins and after a late night of prayer, decided he ought to move to the new post. In some ways the decision was not surprising: Corlett had always listed among his chief goals the preparation of "preacher boys." Now he would have the opportunity to focus his energies on that much-desired purpose. The NNC regents accepted Corlett's resignation "with regrets" and turned to electing a new president.

Nominating and electing NNC's seventh president was much more complicated and arduous than anyone expected. Indeed, two separate meetings of the regents, several sessions, elections but non-acceptances, and numerous ballots transpired before a candidate accepted the board's election. In the first meeting on July 15, after two ballots, the board elected Dr. Paul Updike as president. When he turned down the nomination, they elected one of their own, Northwest District Superintendent E. E. Zachary. When he expressed uncertainty, the board returned to voting, and after twenty-two ballots elected Zachary again and gave him all the time he needed to make a decision. Three weeks later the board reconvened in Nampa on August 5. Zachary, still uncertain about what to do, withdrew from election. The board had to make a decision with the fall opening only a month or so away. After a marathon process of twenty-nine ballots, Dr. John E. Riley, pastor of Nampa's College Church and good friend of Dr. Corlett, was elected. The next morning at 9:00 a.m. the board met with Dr. Riley, and he accepted the presidency. Had the long, complicated, vote-filled process led the board to God's man for the NNC presidency at that time? Many college supporters came to believe that in Dr. Riley's able leadership during the next two decades.

4

Redefining a College

THE RILEY YEARS: 1952-73

Dr. John Eckel Riley looked like a college president—and many thought he spoke and acted like one. Tall, handsome, tanned, masculine, a voracious reader, articulate; he was these and more. Equally important John Riley was a devoted spiritual leader, first as pastor of a series of Nazarene churches in New England and Canada, then at Nampa's College Church, a professor of theology and philosophy, and as president of NNC. Whether as a minister preaching Sunday sermons, a speaker in weekly chapel times, in his memorable public prayers, or as an administrator writing encouraging but direct letters, Dr. Riley made unforgettable impressions. As NNC's seventh president, he led the college for twenty-one years, nearly twice as long as most other NNC presidents, and longer than any other leader in the university's history.

John Riley arose from backgrounds quite different from those he seemed to display during his NNC presidency. Those acquainted with the sophisticated, erudite John Riley, the impressive president of NNC, might have assumed that he came from elite, intellectual New England origins. Not so. Instead, his Canadian-born parents arose from working-class backgrounds; his father ("Pa"), the most important man of his life, was a worker with his hands before accepting a call to preach as an adult. His mother ("Ma") was, most of all, a devoted wife and mother of six children. Neither parent was bookish. So when Riley enrolled at Eastern Nazarene College and majored in English literature, and later philosophy and theology, he moved in directions quite different from those of his parents. Probably the inspired tutelage of Dean Bertha Munro at ENC was the shaping influence in Riley's journey in the life of the mind. Dean Munro, Riley wrote more than a half century later, "raised my interest [in literature and language] to a new and higher level....I still feel the inspiration of those classes when 'the best ever written' was analyzed and found to have beauty and power in both thought and expression." He added about his early years, "If I was not a scholar, I was always a downright serious student."

Riley's boyhood and youthful years also display the first notable vestiges of what became his profound and lifelong delight in the outdoors. On occasion Nampa residents and NNC students thought Riley in western clothes flipping and serving pancakes at the college's annual Buckaroo Breakfast seemed an image out of focus. That was not the case. During his Nampa years Riley joyed in his hunting trips with men from College Church and NNC. These connections with nature and the relished hunting and fishing were already apparent in Riley's Huck Finn boyhood in Massachusetts and Maine. They would continue in his summer stays at Red Fish Lake, his Idaho Eden of relaxation and reflection.

Riley's presidential administration divides roughly into three sections. In the first years of his leadership, until roughly the end of the 1950s, he forged good connections with regents, fellow administrators, particularly his dean Thelma Culver, new faculty, and pastors out on the NNC educational zone. He learned to be a college president. Then gradually in the early 1960s, he began to dream of a much stronger and well-constructed campus, culminating in his ambitious plans for what he called Campus Plateau 1970. Third, in the late 1960s his largely peaceful previous years were disrupted by campus discontents, from both national cultural shifts sweeping across the country but also from transitions beginning to take place within the Church of the Nazarene. Although campus upsets settled down by 1971 and helped Riley regain a less stressful presidency, the difficult and yeasty late 1960s left their scars. In 1973 Riley was happy to retire early and take up new assignments, especially those that sent him and his enormously supportive wife Dorcas to several worldwide and stimulating but also demanding assignments.

What was it about John E. Riley that helped him transition from what seemed to be a serious, staid, and formal New Englander into a superb leader of a Nazarene institution and people in a faraway rural and very nonurban West? First of all, some misread his eastern backgrounds and overlooked his outdoor addictions and his nonelite origins. But most of all, Dr. Riley was, and increasingly became, a man of balance. Blessed with a first-rate intelligence, warmly committed to evangelical traditions, and driven to recognize and address the needs of faculty, students, and outlying districts, Riley, quite simply, developed into a leader of balance, or, as he would say, a man occupying the middle of the road. In this regard he followed in the mediating position of founding president H. Orton Wiley.

Riley's inaugural address "The Person and the Issues," delivered on November 5, 1952, briefly presented four major points of his views on a Christian liberal arts education. Firstly, reflecting his own commitment to a Personalist philosophy, the person-centered viewpoint that informed the outlook of all his NNC presidential predecessors save J. G. Morrison, Riley told his listeners that *"all education must be person-centered."* Secondly, "liberal [arts] education," he added, *"must also minister to the whole person."* Thirdly, this desired form of education must continue to display its *"rare and significant relationship between the teacher and the student."* To buttress this point, Riley noted that "it has been observed that a college president earns his salary if he finds one good teacher a year; if he finds two or three great teachers he has done a life's work." Fourthly, the new president asserted that *"liberal [arts] education* is *fundamentally religious."* Because education, like religion, was the search for truth, they were united in an organic whole. Riley's opening address was an invitation to Northwest Nazarenes to see anew the balance of heart, mind, and soul that had been NNC's major goal since its beginnings. The speech also caught the attention of a wider group and was reprinted in the well-known journal *Vital Speeches,* a signal salute of Riley's gift for words and ideas.

Dr. John E. Riley, here with his wife Dorcas, provided superlative spiritual and academic leadership as NNC's seventh president (1952-73). (Fig. 4.1)

In the first years of his presidency John Riley demonstrated that he was to be a different kind of leader from his predecessor. Dr. Corlett, though himself a professor of theology for several years at Bethany-Peniel Nazarene, thought more like a pastor and sometimes expressed his wish to return to the pastorate. He was moved to prepare young men for the ministry, whether at Bethany or as president at NNC or the Nazarene seminary. Dr. Riley shared Corlett's pastoral heart and later nostalgically recalled "the loss of a pulpit with a congregation, close-knit and challenging." But ideas, books, raw intelligence drove Riley more than Corlett. That meant that Riley had a clearer, more direct, and mutual link with NNC faculty and other Nazarene academics, which Corlett did not experience. Riley's intellectual and administrative bent showed up in his work in securing faculty with doctoral degrees. When Corlett became president in 1942, two professors with earned doctorates (Albert F. Harper and Maude R. Rice) were on the faculty; when Corlett left the presidency in 1952, five professors had earned doctorates (Alvin Aller, Thelma Culver, Gilbert Ford, Carl Hanson, Maude Rice). But Riley, pushed the number of doctorates during his presidency from five to twenty eight, with a half dozen others nearing completion of their doctorates. Riley's pursuit of these doctorates began slowly and then took off dramatically after a dozen years of his leadership in 1964. In the next nine years NNC professors with doctorates jumped from seven to twenty eight.

Before Riley could turn major attention to strengthening NNC's faculty and its academic mission, other pressing needs had to be addressed. Two weeks after accepting the NNC presidency, Riley wrote to Dr. Ed Mann, president of Eastern Nazarene College and life-time friend, that he knew the "first months and years... are going to be tough—but I believe I am in the will of the Lord, and so it will be all right." Still, he told Mann, a "$50,000 mortgage reduction campaign, a sick hospital, and a green president are quite a combination." On the same day, more than a week before he officially took up his duties, Riley revealed to the NNC regents that "the major item on my heart today is the $50,000 mortgage reduction campaign...." But he was also much concerned with the dilemmas surrounding Samaritan Hospital, and he needed to deal with a few other faculty, family, and campus details before College High and the college opened in a few days. There, in abbreviated form, were the most important challenges facing the new president: debt reduction, the Samaritan Hospital, College High (increasingly), and the faculty needs of the college. These issues were at the front and center of Riley's attention for the next half-dozen years.

The mortgage program went well. First aimed at reducing the total mortgage of $100,000 by half, the campaign soon turned a corner, and by the next year $70,000 of the debt had been eliminated. Riley and Business Manager L. Wesley Johnson visited districts and large churches in the NNC zone, urging them to give more than generously to get their college out of debt. Riley and Johnson, who forged a close-knit team over the years, were following well-worn paths of raising funds: announce a goal, first present the needs to the campus community and the Nampa-area churches, and then building on those encouraging reports, take the campaign to the outer rims of the NNC educational zone. In the late 1950s the design worked well, as it had so many times in the past.

The rising questions surrounding Samaritan Hospital and College High were more difficult to solve. In fact, they were unsolvable. Increasingly in the next half dozen years Riley and the regents wrestled with the hospital and College High problems, but eventually mounting debts and funding problems would do in both institutions.

Riley sympathized with the hospital, valued its important role among Nazarenes and in the Nampa community, and was close friends with Dr. Thomas Mangum, the founder of the Samaritan Hospital and Riley's personal physician. But that was not enough; other pressures were undermining the hospital. The lacks were the same as those during Corlett's presidency: insufficient numbers; not enough patients were utilizing the Samaritan Hospital to allow it to keep a full-fledged clinical program for nurses in operation, and not enough nurses were enrolling at Samaritan to keep it an accredited program. In addition, insufficient funds were available to support all the needed programs at the hospital. These problems increased in intensity during the 1940s and landed in Riley's lap when he assumed the presidency. Two years after taking the NNC reins Riley wrote to Mangum making clear his support for Samaritan and what the general superintendents had said about the issue. It boiled down to the two points of insufficient numbers of patients and nurses, as Riley tried to make clear. If those two numbers problems could be solved, Riley added, he wanted to express to Dr. Mangum "my strong interest in the reactivation of the Samaritan School of Nursing at such time as it can be accredited as a department or school within Northwest Nazarene College....I am vitally interested in the nurses' training if these [enrollment and financial] problems can be solved."

Unfortunately for the supporters of the Samaritan Hospital, the problems mounted rather than diminished. The financial woes continued and reached new peaks of distress. The general Church of the Nazarene could never see fit to adopt the hospital into its yearly budget, though it expressed a desire that Nazarene nurses be trained in Idaho. In a parallel way, Nazarenes of the Northwest zone tended to think of Samaritan as a Nampa hospital.

Seeing these problems and recognizing the precariousness of his and the hospital's position, Dr. Mangum had hoped, for nearly a decade, to reorganize the Nazarene Missionary Sanitarium and Institute into two separate divisions and gain support from the general Church of the Nazarene. He asked that one division be the Samaritan Hospital and the other division a school of Nursing Institution. The first would be primarily a hospital focused on local needs and concerns, and the latter "to serve the Church at large" and emphasize missions preparation. Most of all, Mangum wanted the Church of the Nazarene to support his plans financially. He regretted "that a definite financial program for expansion had not been approved and agreed upon." Unfortunately, Dr. Mangum's dream did not come to fruition.

Even though fund-raisers canvassed churches on the NNC zone and approached other churches and laypersons across the Nazarene movement, gifts were insufficient to meet the mounting needs of the hospital. As we have seen, the campaign to build a needed wing to the hospital fell far short, and only a concrete shell was completed. So a move began toward closing the hospital or putting it in other hands. Although accreditation was extended through 1954 to cover all the nurses then enrolled in the course of studies, by the end of the decade the buildings of the Samaritan Hospital and School of Nursing had become NNC property and were being rented out to a local Nampa board hoping to keep the facility functioning. That dream proved illusory, with the hospital closing all operations in 1967 and eventually becoming an NNC building.

Riley's early headaches also included mounting difficulties surrounding College High. Although enrollments at the Academy (College High) and the Grammar

First as the Academy and later as College High, this school provided precollege training until its closure in 1959. (Fig. 4.2)

School were 150 percent of the college numbers as late as 1930, by 1952 when Riley became NNC president the Grammar School had been discontinued, and the combined enrollments for grades 7 through 12 were 118 students while the college had a bit over 400 students. Even though College High expanded in the first years of Riley's presidency, the school was losing money, he had trouble attracting teachers for the minimal salaries paid, and the school was draining off the time and energies of the president. When James Feltar, the sturdy, veteran high school principal resigned to take a position with the college, and Virgil Vail did the same in 1957, Riley was convinced "it would be impossible and impractical for [him] to try to build a high school faculty for the next year."

In an attempt to reach a conclusion on the College High matter, Riley met with everyone involved: parents, students, administrators, PTA, and others. These meetings, Riley wrote, were "most interesting sessions," and he had come through them "bloody but unbowed!" The pastors of Nampa First Nazarene and North Nampa Nazarene were particularly driven to keep College High (and later Nampa Christian High) open, probably because several key College High and Christian High families attended their churches, and the superintendent of the Idaho-Oregon district seemed reluctant to call for the school's closing. In referring to this impending controversial decision, Riley admitted to an Oregon district superintendent that he did not "mind getting [his] shins kicked, but ...would hate to upset local morale so much that the thing would blow up in our faces."

Six weeks later Riley informed a general superintendent that he thought the college, Nampa community, and regents had reached what he considered "the soundest possible solution." Local supporters of College High were being given three years to take over control of the school, and he was trying to hire Elmore Vail ("he taught for a number of years and loved the high school and is loved by all of the local people") as the new principal. Vail was hired as the new principal, things quieted down, and in 1959 the school was closed, with the building, equipment, and other supplies given to Nampa Christian High, which began in a new location and continues to this day.

Even while he dealt with these two institutional dilemmas during his first years as president, Riley had to learn how to be a college administrator. He had to exchange his well-worn and familiar pastoral hat for a new, somewhat ill-fitting academic one. He had to learn how to deal with district superintendents and pastors on his board of regents, and perhaps, most important for the former pastor, he had to learn how to work with faculty who saw NNC from perspectives different from that of the president's office. In short, in the 1950s and early 1960s John Riley had to learn how to be a college president.

Riley's first huge academic hurdle in 1957 showed how much he had learned in five years. The Northwest Association of Secondary and Higher Schools came to campus to evaluate NNC's accreditation. Surprisingly, no re-accreditation visit from the Northwest Association had occurred since the initial accreditation under President DeLong in 1937. The usual practice was for a team from the Northwest Association to visit every ten years, if not more frequently. Why NNC received no visit in the twenty-year period from 1937 to 1957 is unclear. Whatever the reasons, the campus community spent much of 1956 and early 1957 gathering information, producing a 350-page self-study (for the committee to read before it came to campus), and preparing for the accreditation committee.

The report of the evaluators, issued in October 1957, contained few surprises. The president said the report "confirmed" what he already sensed. Most of the visitors' observations and recommendations had appeared in the NNC self-study; college administrators, faculty, and regents were well acquainted with the college's strengths, equally aware of its shortcomings, and knowledgeable of what needed to be done. After praising faculty for their support of NNC and their high morale, despite very low salaries and backbreaking teaching loads, the team pointed to several inadequacies at the college, some of them sufficiently glaring that they needed to be addressed as soon as possible. NNC administrators and regents must do something about several buildings on campus. The facilities for teaching the physical and biological sciences were woefully inadequate and a bit dangerous to the students. The Fine Arts and physical education buildings, as well as Hadley

Hall, were not satisfactory either. College High should be closed, a new classroom building erected, and something done about science teaching equipment and audio-visual materials.

Observations about and recommendations for the faculty were equally explicit. President Riley and the regents ought to think seriously about raising each professor's salary by at least $1,000 and reducing their horrendous teaching loads. "Faculty salaries are generally too low to attract and hold topflight staff members," the evaluators reported. There were far too few professors trying to do too much, spreading themselves too thin with numerous preparations and large enrollments. The college also must reduce the number of its majors, many of which could not be staffed adequately, add new faculty in the social and physical sciences, and buttress their mushrooming program in education.

Other shortcomings caught the eye of the evaluators. The library, while adequate in its textbook and general survey books, needed to acquire hundreds—even thousands—of volumes to support the college's liberal arts programs. The mushrooming teacher education program must be strengthened with additional faculty to allow the teaching of more subject-matter teaching methods courses. One-person departments, such as those in sociology, philosophy, chemistry, must be avoided; new faculty members must be added in several of the sciences, in economics and political science, and in some areas of religion. And these new hires should be PhD's, or persons in doctoral programs.

Dr. Riley, although confronted with these several suggestions for change and improvement, must have been pleased with the positive statements about his leadership sprinkled throughout the accreditation report. A key statement at the center of the report encapsulated the committee's very positive reactions to Riley: "Recent improvements in administrative policies have resulted in establishing very good relations between the Board of Regents and the President, and between the President and the faculty members and students." In fact, so impressed were committee members that they had no suggestions for improvement in the administrative structure of the college or of any of Riley's activities in heading up NNC. The strong endorsement throughout the report of Riley's leadership most certainly buoyed his confidence as a relatively new president.

The evaluation team recommended accreditation for NNC for the next five years but also requested arrangements for another visit to the campus "before 1962." It also requested that "a satisfactory progress report involving significant recommendations made" in the 1957 report be submitted to the Northwest Association's meeting in 1960. Riley filed that Progress Report in November 1960 and then updated it with further notes in October 1961. The operating budget almost doubled from $440,000 in 1957 to nearly $800,000 four years later. Faculty salaries had risen almost 50 percent in the same period. Much-needed buildings had been erected or were in the planning stage: Dooley Hall housed up to 120 women; the first floor of the old hospital wing had been remodeled and was in use for science classes and the rest was being worked on; and government funding for a new student center was in the planning stage. Fewer majors were being offered, College High had been closed, and stronger faculty had been secured. Improvement in library holdings, a new vice president for campus life, and stronger instructional programs were also now in place. Overall, Riley was able to point to marked improvement in the NNC program, noting how many of the accreditation committee's recommendations in 1957 had been addressed, or were receiving greater focus.

The accreditation report and the NNC reactions to it provide illuminating glimpses of the college as it pushed toward its golden anniversary. Some of the major problems remained, however: inadequate finances; understaffed, underpaid, and under-prepared faculty; inadequate space and equipment for some departments; insufficient library holdings; and outmoded buildings. But the accreditors, overall, were impressed with the results at NNC: although apparent needs remained, "maximum results [occurred] despite insufficient means." Faculty morale was "exceptionally high," and the same spirit infected students who "feel he or she belongs" at this college. Undoubtedly regents and faculty, as well as administrators, were pleased and gratified with the evaluators' explicit comments about the optimistic, can-do, and morally illuminating atmosphere on the NNC campus. Although the visitors would not have used similar words, Nazarenes might have seen this as evidence of the high spiritual tone on campus. All in all, the accreditation report of 1957 and NNC reactions to it indicated that things were going quite well. Yes, more money and new buildings were needed, and so were more and better-trained faculty. But those were coming. NNC seemed on the right track, as this important review from outsiders clearly indicated.

If the re-accreditation report revealed that Riley was progressing well in his academic leadership at NNC, parallel events provided windows into other facets of his generalship. Besides establishing good relations with the faculty, Riley had to forge workable connections with other administrators, regents, and pastors of the zone. He had a head start since he had served on the NNC faculty and had become acquainted with NNC leaders and many pastors from the Northwest, but as president he was wearing new clothes, having to come to the new links from other directions. Those fresh connections reveal a good deal about Riley as leader and person.

Early on, Riley fashioned smooth working relationships with Dr. Culver, dean of the college, and L. Wesley Johnson, business manager. When interviewed decades later, Riley opined that he and Dr. Culver worked well as a team. They shared duties, with Riley making most of the decisions concerning general programs and securing faculty, Culver dealing with curricular matters and often suggesting to the president what tinkering ought to be carried out in course offerings. She urged

President Riley, Dean Culver, and Business Manager L. Wesley Johnson worked well together at the helm of NNC. (Fig. 4.3)

him to formulate an academic structure for the college that he liked, and his staff and faculty would adhere to it. Riley and Johnson also agreed on a smoothly functioning division of responsibilities. The president depended on the business manager to find sufficient funds to keep the college out of debt and raise enough new dollars to support the faculty to be hired and the buildings to be erected. Johnson made clear in an upbeat and fulsome report to the Board of Regents how strong his new boss was. "Dr. Riley promptly demonstrated his ability as an able administrator upon assuming the presidency of the college," he told the regents. "He is one of the hardest workers I have ever seen, putting in long hours and accomplishing the extraordinary. I don't know what time he arrives at the office each morning, for when I arrive (which is always after 6 o'clock), he is on the job." Riley had many strengths, Johnson continued: "he has excellent business judgment, understands academic problems, is a natural leader, and, best of all, has a warmth of spirit and Christian zeal that permeates the entire constituency of the college." Those words were as honeyed toast to the regents; they had found a multitalented administrator to lead NNC for the foreseeable future.

Riley also made warm, encouraging contacts with the regents. He admitted that in going into his new job he thought of Daniel headed into the lion's den, but now, about two weeks later, he "felt like Daniel must have felt afterward." In connecting with the regents, he was "a man with twenty-eight new brothers." Moreover, he added, "I appreciate more than I can tell this new heart-warming relationship in a difficult task." Like his predecessor Dr. Corlett, Riley was able to win regents over to his vision of NNC. But their presidential visions differed, with Riley emphasizing more the new buildings, additional faculty, and stronger academic programs than Corlett.

Not all these connections with regents and pastors were sweetness and light, however. Dr. B. V. Seals, chairman of the Board of Regents and a man of wit, humor, and grassroots wisdom, was also a prize-winning curmudgeon who carried grave doubts about many academics. He seemed fearful that the bookish trends at NNC were outrunning the needed spiritual emphases. He was equally hesitant about intercollegiate sports and not shy about expressing those reservations. "I do not seem to find any way in my own thinking to justify what we are doing" in regard to intercollegiate sports, Seals told Riley. He was "really puzzled at how we can go ahead and ignore [the General Assembly] in the matter of athletics." Riley replied "that the statement [about sports] in the back of the [church] *Manual* should be changed." We ought to agree with the General Assembly and the *Manual*, conceded Riley, but he didn't think that, after more than twenty years of intercollegiate sports, NNC "ought to back up now." He hoped that the controversy could be soon resolved. Looking back on his years of working with Seals, Riley concluded that they were indeed friends but quite different men. Seals was a pastor, preacher, district superintendent but not an intellectual; academics did not interest him much, and he wondered sometimes what NNC was up to in its campus activities. As Riley put it, Seals would probably tell everyone "Watch John Riley," be sure he does what he ought to.

Not infrequently pastors wrote to Riley to express their opinions in hopes of changing polices that upset them. Others made Riley's administration more difficult by their attitudes or actions. One pastor of a large church bluntly told Riley "Say, doc...I'm wondering if you realize how much antagonism you build up when you come into town with 7 Nazarene Churches, and schedule your choir's program for just one of them? We feel, and I share the feeling, that the harm you do is far greater than the good you do...." In his two-and-a-half-page, skillfully worded response, Riley laid out the reasons why the choir had not been in the pastor's church (the previous year because of a cantata at the pastor's church and this year because of geographical demands) and asked the pastor to work with the college in securing a choir presentation for the next year that would please the grumbling pastor and others in the Spokane area said to be upset with NNC. Riley's answer was a tour de force in diplomacy and tact. It augured well for his dealings with pastors on the NNC zone.

In the first years of his presidency Riley was gradually displaying his personality, points of view, and administrative acumen with campus residents, the Nampa community, and the NNC educational zone. Following the urging of the accreditation committee in 1957, and also the feelings of faculty, Riley helped raise faculty salaries and pushed for a more specific and well-organized salary scale for NNC faculty and staff. By the early 1960s, when Riley had been president for a decade, there had been a clear, steady climb in faculty salaries. The president also tried to deal clearly with discontents from the past. When the son of a former faculty member accused the college of writing "a very nasty [letter] which stated that I owed a large sum of money and that I never intended to pay it," Riley sent a copy of the letter, which was neither nasty nor negative about the former student. He thanked the letter writer for paying his bill and wished the student's family "every success and happiness." When a troubled student wrote to Riley to express his disappointment in not finding a special avenue of service for God, being limited to a dead-end job, and thinking his college training all wasted, Riley took the time to write a helpful, encouraging letter to a student he barely knew. He urged the student to think of volunteer work outside what he considered his meaningless position, to put emphasis on the widened horizons his schooling brought him, and to realize that his education could "release his mind and his spirit into the great world beyond the ditch where he" or anyone else might be working. Even "though you are tied to a rather insignificant job," Riley added, "your mind is still not bound." These letters illustrated the time a busy president took to build good feelings with students and faculty, past and present.

Riley's strong connections with the Nampa community were revealed in his relationships with businessmen and his warm feelings about his new home. Riley's links with the Nampa community were already apparent before he became president. During the summer of 1952 as the NNC regents wrestled with the selection of a new president following Corlett's resignation, several Nampa businessmen, persons Riley had met and befriended as pastor of College Church, wrote a strong letter to the regents endorsing Riley as the needed new NNC president. Those previously established links to businessmen and with the local newspaper editor continued in the first years of his presidency. Meanwhile Riley was becoming more and more at home in the Far West. The born and bred New Englander was feeling increasingly comfortable in his rural western surroundings.

That expanding feeling of comfort suffused Riley's guest editorial "My Town" appearing in Nampa's newspaper, *The Idaho Free Press*. He told readers he enjoyed Nampa because it was small enough for him to know the mayor, city council, and other community leaders. "My town is a nice size," Riley wrote, "not so small as to be too provincial, not so big as to be impersonal." Besides its neighborliness, Nampa was "a wholesome place in which to bring up one's family." He liked that it was "a city of churches, where ministers and congregations of all faiths are on good terms and regularly in cooperative efforts with each other." Nampa had decent schools, "attractive parks," and "a superior program of recreation." Generally, the town exhibited a "good moral, social and cultural climate" that appealed to him. True, there were "areas which [needed] improvement." He wished the roads and streets were in better condition, that we could "eliminate substandard construction," and "raise the level of ethical and social behavior in certain segments of our society...." He admitted that "My town has faults...but this is my town," he closed, "and I am happy to live here." Riley's portrait of his hometown was a warm, clear-eyed salute of Nampa that would have appealed to campus as well as community citizens. Remarkably, that at-home feeling continued to grow with Riley, with Nampa remaining his home for the rest of his long life.

Sometimes newcomers thought Riley too formal in his demeanor and actions. He realized this possibility and strove to be more open and accessible in spite of his natural reserve. Perhaps one long-time faculty member put it most succinctly: "Dr. Riley is the best administrator I ever worked for, but I never called him John." Even more remarkable, Dr. Gilbert Ford, who replaced Dr. Culver as dean in 1970 never used Dr. Riley's first name, although they were elbow to elbow, increasingly, on academic matters. As Dr. Ford put it, Dr. Riley was a "presence," and it was difficult to push through that ethos to become a close friend of the president's.

In the 1950s, a few major outlines of Riley's academic plans and religious emphases for NNC were beginning to emerge, but his major planning and implementation of those programs occurred largely after 1960. In the first years of his presidency Riley spoke warmly of several faculty, especially women, who had stood by the college for many years in its formative years. He was convinced, however, that he had to hire more family men with PhDs if the school was to move ahead academically and present a more balanced social image. Riley's actions in this area gradually gathered force in the 1950s and dramatically expanded in the 1960s. His reputation as an academic leader was certain and widespread after he had served a decade as the NNC president.

In Riley's attempts at academic planning, innovations were linked to enrollments, as they have nearly always been at NNC. When he assumed the presidency enrollments wavered between 400 and 450 after reaching 500 or more from 1947 to 1951. After dropping to a low of nearly 350 in 1953-54, enrollment gradually crept up to a bit more than 550 in 1960-61. Then student numbers skyrocketed to 1,200 in the next seven years. That meant in the first eight years of his administration Riley was not only pressed with paying the bills and balancing the yearly budgets, but also with adding faculty, raising their salaries, and expanding course offerings. He tried to address all these challenges, with the report of the accrediting committee in 1957 encouraging him to move in all these directions.

Riley was much more energetic than his predecessor in strengthening NNC's academic mission. If Corlett wanted the preparation of preacher boys to be his major goal as a college president, Riley thought in larger terms. As he told the director of a Bible college in South Africa, "There is no greater work in the world than the work of Christian education, for evangelism, along with everything else, depends on Christian education." For Riley the central purpose of Christian education was not simply the preparation of ministers, although that too, but the training of the minds and hearts of all students at NNC to be educated Christians at work in their worlds. And central to his goal of the Christian education of students was obtaining first-rate faculty members with a strong commitment to evangelical higher education.

Riley's correspondence, his writings for church and college periodicals, and his public presentations reveal how strongly and directly he aimed at bringing a new crop of faculty to Nampa. Usually Riley counted on his colleagues—administrators and faculty at NNC, pastors and district superintendents, or other Nazarene presidents—to call his attention to a promising faculty member. Then he would make contact. Nearly every year, he made appointments to talk to graduate students or professors who had been mentioned. Repeatedly in his letters to regents and in his columns in the *Messenger* he harped on securing stronger faculty members for the college.

Those encouragements and pursuits definitely influenced the enhanced faculty that Riley gathered in the first years of his presidency. Among those who joined the NNC professoriate by 1960 and stayed at least a decade were a number of influential and well-known faculty members. Virgil and Elmore Vail, after teaching at College High, joined the NNC faculty in physics and physical education. Orrin Hills also became part of the physical education (PE) staff and served as the basketball and track coach. Several came to the music department, including Warnie Tippitt, Marvin Bloomquist, and Deloris Bloomquist Waller. Wanda Rhodes came in home economics (and shifted to PE), and Eula Tombaugh also arrived in home economics.

The core liberal arts departments and the library staff also expanded. Lillian Lewis joined the English department, and Arthur Seamans also arrived in English. Percival Wesche came in history, and Robert C. Woodward became his colleague in that department soon thereafter. Meanwhile Darrell Marks began his long career in physics, and Juanita Demmer returned to teach foreign languages. Also coming early in the Riley administration were Thomas Leupp and Edythe Leupp, in the fields of psychology and education. Later, Tom Leupp served as Nampa's mayor and then as president of Cascade College in Portland. During the same years Edith Lancaster and Helen Rambo came as new staff members to join Geneva Bittleston in the library.

Since the religion and philosophy and education departments continued to expand in the early Riley years, new faculty members were added in those areas. Joseph H. Mayfield came as vice president for campus life, but he also taught courses in religion, philosophy, and Greek. Eric Jorden offered biblical and theology courses. Marian Marsh joined the department of education as an elementary and reading specialist, and Fred Knight in general education.

Several faculty members, holdovers from Corlett's presidency, proved invaluable academic leaders during Riley's administration. Gilbert Ford, Alvin Aller, and Double E Hill were stellar scholars and organizers of important programs in physics, biology, and music. They also carried their learning lightly, endearing themselves through their modesty displayed before colleagues and students alike. Marian Washburn was also a notably important faculty member from the 1940s into the 1980s. Accepting huge teaching and administrative loads, she was a mainstay in the college's humanities programs. More an appreciator than analyzer of literature, she quietly and competently introduced thousands of students to the classics of world, English, and American literature.

Dr. Darrell Marks devoted long years to teaching, administering, and volunteering for NNC/NNU. (Fig. 4.4)

Morris Weigelt (religion) and Arthur Seamans (English) were also memorable contributors to NNC's academic mission during their decade-long stays. Like H. Orton Wiley, Weigelt rose from Midwestern farm origins to become a brilliant Biblical scholar. Students were fascinated—and stimulated—with his knowledge of the New Testament. He was also an enthusiastic teacher, always ready to engage students in conversation about the Scriptures and theology. Seamans was a New Yorker and New Englander who, according to one of his colleagues, may have been the most important professor on NNC's faculty during the 1960s. A skilled prep school instructor of writing with a doctorate in literature, Seamans revolutionized the teaching of English Composition at NNC, making it one of the most stimulating courses on campus. He also drew hundreds of students into his English literature offerings, which included lively outings into nature to gain new understandings of the Romantic poets. Robert Woodward also stood tall among the scholarly professors at NNC. His wide-ranging lecture topics in numerous courses, his sharp analytical mind, and his devotion to his history majors were legendary on campus for more than three decades.

As NNC added these new faculty during times of shrinking or modestly expanded enrollments, Riley was gradually formulating more professional attitudes toward NNC's professors. He was beginning to lay plans for sabbatical leaves, fringe benefits, a form of tenure; he also spent a great deal of time trying to raise faculty salaries and to establish a formalized, concrete salary scale. In writing to the president of another church-related college in the Pacific Northwest, Riley pointed out that NNC had raised salaries "in a limited way each of the last two years," but he also had to admit NNC professors were being paid less than those at Pacific Lutheran College; "our faculty salaries are still considerably below yours."

Marian Washburn spent many years as a professor teaching multitudes of students in her writing and literature courses. (Fig. 4.5)

Riley found himself on the horns of an unresolvable dilemma: on the one hand he wanted "to help worthy students secure a Christian college education," but he also wished "to be fair to the dedicated, well-trained men and women who teach on our faculty." Riley also got an inside view of higher education in the Pacific Northwest by serving on the commission that evaluated higher education programs in the region. "As we go over institutions rather thoroughly," he told former NNC president Russell V. DeLong, "I get cold chills when I realize how weak we are in some areas as compared with some of these great institutions that seem to have plenty of money and high enough salaries to pull teachers from everywhere." The clash of desires in keeping costs low for students and providing decent salaries for faculty continued unabated into the future, for Dr. Riley and subsequent NNC presidents.

The financial pinch grew tighter at the end of the 1950s. Wanting to strengthen NNC's academic programs, Riley tried to squeeze out as many new faculty positions as possible. The money watchers thought he might have gone too far. After a meeting with a faculty subcommittee in November 1959, Business Manager L. Wesley Johnson wrote a direct, hard-hitting, and he thought realistic letter to President Riley about NNC's financial situation. "We have...difficulty balancing the budget," Johnson told the president, because we have "too large a faculty for student enrollment." Johnson reminded Riley he had sung this tune before—to Corlett and Riley. "I felt my statements were conservative when I suggested the possibility of a reduction of seven or eight instructors with an annual saving of at least $20,000 as has been presented in recent years." Riley tried to hold in abeyance such belt-tightening suggestions, but he did encourage professors to go on leave for doctoral programs. Even worse, as we shall see, he was forced to cut a few faculty members in such departments as music and others.

On several occasions Riley stated that the "twin principles" at work at NNC were "competence and conscience." As he tried to strengthen and diversify the college's faculty and academic programs, he wanted to stay true to the campus motto: "Seek ye first the Kingdom of God." "God and spiritual values still loom large on this campus," Riley told college supporters. "NNC seeks the prayerful support of her alumni everywhere as she endeavors to keep in touch with God and in touch with our day at the same time." But gusty winds of transformation were blowing over the country and campus. Would NNC and her president be able to keep the balance between competence and conscience?

Several notable changes swept through American conservative Protestantism in the years of Corlett's and Riley's presidencies. Beginning in the 1930s but especially in the 1940s a "new evangelicalism" gradually replaced "the original fundamentalist condition of the 1920s," one specialist in American religious history has noted. Nazarenes could find fellowship with most of the "essentials of evangelicalism," which another scholar defined as "that the sole authority in religion is the Bible and sole means of salvation is a life-transforming experience wrought by the Holy Spirit through Faith in Jesus Christ." But for the most part in the generation beginning during WWII and stretching into the 1960s, Nazarenes were more denominational than ecumenical in their evangelical allegiances. They might join, eventually, the National Association of Evangelicals (founded in 1942), take minor roles in such groups as Young Life, Youth for Christ, and Campus Crusade for Christ, but those organizations were never front and center for Nazarene participants.

At the same time, the "warfare mentality" and antimodernism of more militant fundamentalists did not infiltrate the leadership of the Church of the Nazarene. Still, a strain of fundamentalism among the Nazarenes, which became apparent in the 1920s, remained at the lay level and even influenced a few districts and their superintendents. In addition, because of its amillennial stance—joining neither the pre- nor postmillennial camps—the Church of the Nazarene did not participate in the dispensationalist wars that frequently erupted among fundamentalists and later evangelicals.

The resurgence of conservative Protestantism in the U. S. after WWII in the form of a "new evangelicalism" also had little traceable impact on Nazarenes. True, some Nazarenes subscribed to *Christianity Today*, participated in Youth for Christ gatherings, and even attended Campus Crusade presentations; but most of all they read their own denomination's *Herald of Holiness*, took part in their own Nazarene Young People's Society's programs, and were encouraged to attend their own Nazarene colleges. Were Nazarenes isolationists? Perhaps. Indeed, had they not always been and would remain so? One of the isolating factors was the difference in theological perspectives. As

Dr. Arthur Seamans stimulated hundreds of young men and women with his inspired teaching of composition and literature classes. (Fig. 4.6)

Arminian-Wesleyans, Nazarenes felt uncomfortable in a Reformed or Calvinist atmosphere, as well as with the Pentecostal movement, that permeated many of the neo-evangelical groups that sprang up in the years following World War II.

Another circumstance kept Nazarenes tied to their own traditions and distant from fellowship with other evangelicals and fundamentalists. Always pressed for money to pay faculty salaries and to build necessary but modest buildings, Nazarenes had quickly realized that their financial salvation lay with the churches in their educational zone. To keep these churches, pastors, and district superintendents happy with the educational efforts of NNC and other denominational colleges became the major goal of most Nazarenes. Sending quartets and other college groups to the churches and districts during the summer and sometimes during the school year was always necessary. The college presidents, NNC's included, also attended as many district assembles and district retreats and camps as possible. College presidents were indefatigable travelers, frequently flyers, around their districts. The financial support of churches on each educational zone was so important that NNC and other Nazarene colleges focused their energies and programs to keep avenues of contact and constituents' billfolds and purses open. That meant not much time or inclination remained for the college and individual churches to take part in evangelical programs beyond the denomination and its colleges.

Timothy L. Smith, the leading scholar of the Church of the Nazarene, described evangelicalism in the postwar years as a kaleidoscope. It remained a group of shifting elements, often newly jumbled from the impact of change. Holiness groups, Mennonite churches, Pentecostals, Black churches, Reformed groups, conservative Episcopalians, and Southern Baptists—all were a part of the continually shifting group known as evangelicals. Perhaps the only viewpoints that united these disparate groups were their beliefs in a born-again experience, the Bible as God's Word, and the guidance of the Holy Spirit. "Other than that, they represented largely independent, even if related, traditions," Smith pointed out.

Just as Nazarenes had not joined ranks, generally, with the militant, rather negative and separatist fundamentalists in the 1920s and 1930s, so they were slow to find common and central ground with the emerging neo-evangelicals of the postwar 1940s and 1950s. Even from a distance, however, Nazarenes did agree with the militant fundamentalists that the chief reason for their spiritual existence was to help save souls. And when former fundamentalists such as Charles E. Fuller in his widely heard radio program "Old-Fashioned Revival Hour" turned from separation and controversy to more positive emphases on working for conversions, Nazarenes felt one with Fuller, even if not centrally involved in his support.

But, as one historian of the Nazarenes has pointed out, his denomination "tended to hold aloof from councils and associations of churches." A decade and half after the founding of the National Association of the Evangelicals (1942) and despite the strong support of Billy Graham for the organization, Nazarenes thought it "inadvisable" to join the NAE and continued their "traditional policy of cooperation without affiliation" with the National Holiness Association. Two generations after finding common ground among several groups to found a new denomination in 1908, Nazarenes were reluctant to join nondenominational evangelical and holiness groups that shared many common goals and emphases with Nazarenes.

As they had earlier, Nazarenes continued to struggle with the conflicting impulses of anti-intellectualism and the mission of liberal arts colleges in the decade or two after World War II. More conservative members of the denomination were convinced that holiness people should, above all else, emphasize the Bible and the guidance of the Holy Spirit as *the* sign posts for journeying toward the holy life. On the other hand, advocates among the Nazarenes of the centrality of a Christian liberal arts training, without disagreeing with the important emphases on the Bible and the Holy Spirit, were convinced that God wanted to train young minds so as to improve the outreach of the gospel in pulpits, mission fields, churches, and communities around the globe. Conservatives, worried that assigning "ungodly books" in classes would lead students toward liberalism and modernism, urged Nazarene educators to use only books that explicitly agreed with holiness tenets. Some moved even further away from the liberal arts tradition, hoping to keep colleges primarily Bible schools. They anguished over what they viewed as moves toward secularism, as their letters to NNC presidents in the first half-century of the college's history clearly indicated.

In the mid-1950s conservative elements in the Nazarene Church broke out in revolt. One part of the revolt sprang up in the Nampa area, challenging Nazarenes in that region. At first the movement seemed on the verge of tearing apart the entire denomination. Increasingly in the late 1940s and early 1950s conservative elements in the denomination, often through influential district superintendents or outspoken pastors, pushed for more restrictive statements in the church *Manual* or college catalogues on dress, entertainments, and recreation. One such ultra conservative preacher announced "his theme" as "bobbed hair, short dresses and painted faces." Another's three-part sermon inveighed against crew cuts, twin pipes, and open-toed shoes. When the Nazarene General Assembly in 1952 took a middle-of-the-road position on television, neither praising nor forbidding it, criticism of that mediating stance quickly heated up to a boiling point.

In autumn 1955, Glenn Griffith, a former long-time Nazarene pastor and district superintendent of the Idaho-Oregon and Colorado districts, conducted a five-week tent revival in the Nampa area. He had turned in his credentials as a

Nazarene pastor and was now undertaking a separate ministry. In November he announced the establishment of the Bible Missionary Union (shortly afterwards renamed Bible Missionary Church [BMC]) with 126 new members. Most of these charter members came from Nampa-area Nazarene churches. The next year another very conservative district superintendent in Louisiana, Elbert Dodd, brought several pastors and more than a few members from his district into the BMC. Other come-outers from several other districts joined the new church. Although the BMC church has experienced several secessions itself over similar dress, entertainment, and recreational issues, it remains in existence, the largest breakaway movement from the Church of the Nazarene.

At first NNC leaders and supporters worried that the BMC revolt might have a major impact on the college. It did not, to the relief of campus administrators. When Dr. Riley was asked about the new BMC, he wrote former President Russell V. DeLong that Glenn Griffith wasn't "making much of a dent out here [Nampa] or in Colorado....The fact is there is relatively little stir about it around here."

In the same month the Reverend Griffith published an essay entitled "Nineteen Reasons Why I Am Leaving the Church of the Nazarene." Griffith pointedly reminded Nazarenes that in allowing rings in their wedding ceremonies they were breaking with their founders, and he castigated their watching television programs, failing to support conservative preaching, and their building ostentatious parsonages and churches. Nazarenes should be ashamed too because in many of their churches "worldlings that are painted, bejeweled, show-going, shorts-wearers are acknowledged as Christians, and...given an official place in the churches." And modern Nazarenes, Griffith added, were giving preference to liberals and college-educated pastors more than to those "baptized with Holy Ghost fire" and self-educated. Most of all, Nazarenes were urging their pastors not to preach on negatives, to accentuate the positive. That, Griffith argued, was wrong: "the (law) or [the] negative must come first, then the positive (Calvary), or there will be no conviction of sin." Because Nazarenes had moved in so many wrong directions, Griffith, after nearly thirty years among them, was moving in another direction. The Nazarene Church he had joined was "virile, impassioned and prayerful"; "now it seems cold, anemic and formal in its worship...."

Fortunately, the BMC proved not to be a major problem for Riley, but other large challenges lay before him. Riley realized, as presidents before and after him did, the importance of forging and maintaining strong religious links between the college and superintendents and pastors on the NNC educational zone. Counting the fall and spring revivals, named presentations like the Staley and Miller Lectures, and other religious emphasis weeks and days, Riley had up to a half-dozen opportunities each year to invite influential church leaders to speak on campus. Usually one of the annual revival speakers was a general superintendent; district superintendents, evangelists, and noted pastors were nearly always also among the yearly speakers. In addition, since daily chapels were in effect, many other pastors and church speakers came to speak in chapel. There were, of course, pragmatic and idealistic goals in mind in these connections. By inviting church leaders to campus, Riley kept them aware of college needs and undoubtedly made them feel they were helping to keep high the spiritual tide at NNC. Pastors were also often key recruiters for prospective students and important cheerleaders for raising church and district budgets so central to the college's financial stability. Dr. Riley worked hard at keeping these vital connections alive and supportive.

From his first days in the presidential chair, Riley made clear his desire to maintain the spiritual balance that had characterized NNC in the first forty years of its existence. He believed in the "solid and progressive" heritage of the college; he wanted to build on that. But, Riley warned, even with a "string of Ph.D.'s on the faculty and a reputation for graduating brilliant students, with every bill paid and endowments piled high, [NNC] could lose her soul. She must ever keep intellectually alive, spiritually adventurous, and morally courageous enough to challenge each generation to dare to follow Jesus." It was a message the college supporters wanted and needed to hear. With that promise, Riley was off to a good start with those who feared that NNC was losing its soul to the academics and liberals.

Riley also followed, for the most part, what his predecessors had done in curricular affairs, chapel presentations, and revivals. All students were expected to take four semesters of lower division religion/theology courses: one course each on the Old Testament and New Testament, and two semesters of Biblical Theology, with a strong emphasis on Nazarene beliefs. The president usually preached each Friday, and at least two of the other daily chapel services were religious. Speakers for those chapels were usually local pastors, other ministers and district superintendents from the NNC zone, or visiting revival speakers at NNC or in the Nampa area. Chapel attendance was required, and students were expected to attend two Sunday services, and often midweek Prayer Meeting, at College Church, unless given permission to attend another local church. When church attendance seemed to dwindle, Riley formed a committee of Nampa Nazarene pastors whose assignment was to consider petitions to attend services other than those in College Church and, generally, "to work with the administration in maintaining regular habits of church attendance on the part of our students." "This is a great contribution which, together," he told them, "we have to make in the lives of these students."

The NNC community was blessed to have A. Elwood Sanner as chair of the department of religion during much of Riley's presidency. A devout man with an intellectual bent, Sanner was a superb teacher, good preacher, a scholar, and, perhaps most important of all, a balanced person. In the midst of controversy, Sanner could protect his faculty and speak for the religious and academic missions of

Dr. A. E. Sanner provided many years of balanced, provocative teaching in the Division of Philosophy and Religion. (Fig. 4.7)

the college without alienating those whose agendas were different from those on the Nampa campus. Other members of the NNC religion faculty during the 1950s—Dr. Carl Hanson, Francis Reeves, and D. Shelby Corlett—sometimes through their analytical approaches to philosophy and religion, sometimes through their sharp-edged comments, stirred up controversies among students and constituents. On one occasion, for example, the equally outspoken chairman of the Board of Trustees became so upset with the combative Corlett that he told Riley he ought to get rid of Corlett; keeping Corlett "is unwise for us to carry," the board chairman asserted, for it is "very hazardous to continue the man in the capacity he has there."

Yet in the midst of sometimes stressful, full days of a college year, the renewing presence of God rained on the campus. In spring 1955, a quickened sense of God's presence came in Dr. Hugh C. Benner's sermons during the spring revival. College High seniors and then all of College High felt the Holy Spirit invading their campus; "more than a hundred [students] fasted and prayed each noon hour." News of the renewal spread across the college campus and into the Nampa area. Even before the sermon began on Friday's chapel, the altar was lined with seekers. Spiritual renewal warmed the hearts of hundreds of students and townspeople. Days later, one writer reported, "the sense of great quiet power still lingers."

For many NNC students in the 1950s the campus overflowed with acceptable social activities. Most Nazarene young men and women came from small churches—of 75 members or less—where teen groups were miniscule and social gatherings and recreation largely limited to church activities since they were forbidden to attend movies or to participate in school dances. That meant dates for Nazarene teens were confined primarily to activities at local churches, district gatherings, or summer church camps. Some of these venues offered limited opportunities for dating.

That all changed on the NNC campus. Almost too many activities were available to everyone. There were Sunday morning and evening and midweek church services, sports contests, especially basketball games in the winter, Athletic-Literary competitions such as plays and Closed Night, and other campus presentations. Activities such as Homecoming, Sweetheart Banquet, and the Circle K Banquet provided still other venues for daters. In fact, some students and their faculty sponsors complained of being "clubbed to death." Freshmen men and women soon realized they had come into another world, with so many social activities and dating opportunities on their plates.

Formal and informal guidelines provided some structure to these activities. Although most students obeyed the stated rules, outright rebels and innovative young people frequently found ways around the stated limitations and established informal ones of their own. For example, few NNC students brazenly broke or abused the regulations disallowing movie attendance or dances (for which they could be disciplined, maybe expelled). For the most part they followed the established dorm hours for young women, and sometimes for young men. But on dress and makeup standards, on activities involving the opposite sex, and in other areas, NNC students often established their own traditions.

One especially important unwritten set of traditional standards seemed to "rule" dating activities—what one could do from the first through several dates. These were not guidelines handed down from college leaders but ones students inherited from upper-class men and women—and maybe from students of previous years. An informal guideline obtained: on the first date couples might hold hands, on the second, a young man might put his arm around the chair seat behind his date or, dangerously, around her shoulders, and on the third date, if everything seemed auspicious, a guy might peck his date goodnight. Veering decidedly away from these unwritten rules might label one notoriously or even disastrously "forward": if a young man tried to get in a kiss at the end of the first date, he might be labeled as "too fast" or even "hot to trot" among the coeds in their after-date gab sessions in women's dormitories. Or if a young woman made clear there was to be no kissing on the third date—and maybe for some time afterwards—she was labeled "really cold" or sometimes "not worth it" among the guys' bull sessions in men's dormitories. It became very clear very quickly to NNC young men and women that they did not want to gain reputations as being "too fast" or "cold" as dates soon after they arrived on campus.

Toward the end of a date and before looming dorm hours, NNC young people often sought out places of "special fellowship." If time allowed and the conditions seemed right, a young man might take his date to Lake Lowell to participate in the infamous "submarine races." If the clock provided some time, couples might check out "parking places" at the gravel pit, the cemetery, or the nearby campmeeting grounds. And if minutes were preciously few, there were always the alleys beside and streets in front of the women's dorms. In good weather and bad, Kurtz Park worked for other young couples, especially those without cars. These times of "special fellowship" were often conversation pieces for campus chatter; they were also important if stuttering steps toward friendship, romance, engagement, and marriage.

Some NNC observers worried about these dating times at the college. One pastor complained that a group of students from NNC came to work in Butte for the summer and seemed to be "training" the church's girls in "mugnastics." One of the Nazarene students revealed, in the pastor's words, that he saw nothing "wrong with girls and boys promiscuously [sic] tying themselves in little knots in the corner of a car seat for hours at night either alone or in the company of other young people." The minister added that he had just received a letter from a Butte girl at NNC who confessed "it's hard to know what's right and wrong regarding date conduct down here....You go with some guy who you think is a sincere Christian and a respectful guy and then he may expect more than you think he should so you don't know what to think." The pastor was anxious about such "loose conduct." Did NNC students "receive any teaching" about petting? He worried that lack of sufficient training and warning on these matters might lead to the "sadly soiled lives" of some of the young people he had tried to help.

Dr. Riley admitted that the "petting problem" the Butte pastor raised was a challenge on the NNC campus. But he asked the minister to see the subject in perspective: "It is not something new...; rather, it is as old as humanity," Riley cautioned. He also allowed that "among youngsters who profess to be Christians there has been quite a lot done in regard to this." NNC leaders, the president especially, had tried "to deal with [this dilemma] constantly on the campus in order to give young people a sensible, wholesome approach to the whole matter of relationships between sexes." The only thing for the college administrators and faculty to do was to keep working on the problem and that way save many students "from heartache and prepare them for full and happy lives later on." Even if students did not take heed—and that was true of too many, Dr. Riley thought—they "will nevertheless have heard me say something to try to warn them."

Extraordinarily campus-centered, NNC overflowed with social activities for its students. None gained more attention and participation than the Athletic-Literary and intramural programs. As the student body expanded, new societies were organized. In the fall of 1956, two new societies, the Athenians and Spartans, were added to the earlier ADP's, SLA's, Oly's, and LSP's. These six organizations included all students enrolled at NNC and offered sports, literary, dramatic, and other activities on a monthly and sometimes weekly basis. On some occasions, more than 70 percent of the college student body participated in these society-sponsored events. These activities rivaled church and chapel services as the most participation-intensive events at NNC. They also tended to keep students tied to campus and discouraged young men and women from venturing outside NNC and Nampa for their social activities.

Women's athletic contests, especially among the Athletic-Literary societies, became more numerous in the 1950s and 1960s. (Fig. 4.8)

Organized intercollegiate sports, although involving many fewer students, were nonetheless exceptionally important facets of NNC social life. Men could participate in basketball, baseball, track, and cross-country programs, and men and women could take part in tennis, the only coeducational athletic competition available to NNC students. (Women's intercollegiate activity was not yet in place.) Moreover, student attendance at sports events, particularly men's basketball games, was remarkable. The dorms emptied on Friday and Saturday nights when virtually the entire student body traipsed down to Central Auditorium, where most NNC home games took place, to cheer the Crusaders and harass visiting teams, especially those from long-time rivals College of Idaho and Boise Junior College.

The basketball team reached a notable high point in the 1956-57 season. For the first time a NNC team won its district playoff and gained an invitation to the national NAIA tournament in Kansas City. Although the Crusaders were thoroughly thumped by one of the high-ranked teams in the first round, the team and its numerous enthusiastic supporters never forgot that year's achievements. Led by standout players Dave Gardner, Tom Tracy, and the Peppley brothers Duane and Bob, the team powered to its best winning season thus far, with a 25 and 9 record. Even the staid and scholarly president Dr. Riley, less an ardent sports fan than his predecessor and successor, saluted the "wonderful impression for N.N.C." the team made, especially in the Kansas City area.

Other church leaders were less impressed with the intercollegiate sports program at NNC and wanted to end it—soon. Board of Regents Chairman B. V. Seals was among the more persistent critics of organized sports. His point, that the general church did not favor intercollegiate competition, was well taken; the 1956 church *Manual* stated in its Appendix: "We recommend that it be definitely provided that schools and colleges of the Church of the Nazarene engage only in intramural athletics." Seals could also remember an unfortunate incident of four

The men's basketball team of 1956-57 was the first NNC team to reach a national finals. (Fig. 4.9)

years earlier when nine of the thirteen members of the 1953 team got "mixed up in some little difficulties [gambling]"; they were quickly disciplined, disallowed from playing any further games after January. "It has been a rather severe jolt to the team and...to everybody involved," but Riley added, "We think it may be the finest thing that has happened to us in a long time if we can recover from the 'major surgery.'"

Despite these problems, other controversies, and continuing harsh criticism, the basketball and other sports programs remained. Riley realized the importance of these activities to an isolated, campus-oriented college and pointed out that significance to several correspondents. When General Superintendent D. I. Vanderpool, a former member of the NNC Board of Regents, wrote to express his opinion that there was "an overemphasis on athletics" on Nazarene college campuses, Riley had a tempered and revealing answer for the Nazarene leader. He didn't want "an overemphasis on [athletics]," Riley told Vanderpool, but he also thought that "it would be seriously hurtful for us to try do away with all athletics."

Besides the Athletic-Literary, intramural, and sports programs, several other venues were open to NNC's energetic and committed students. In addition to the numerous church services that occurred each week, more than a few students took part in the Christian Workers Band (CWB). The band sponsored Sunday afternoon visitations to Nampa nursing homes, hospitals, and the county jail. Each group of ten to fifteen students provided something of a church service wherever they went, including singing, testimonies, and a brief devotional. The presentations not only furnished residents with a time of religious celebration; they also gave students an opportunity to hone their own skills in singing and public speaking. Other CWB groups traveled to regions of the NNC educational zone to provide church services, young peoples' rallies, or musical presentations. In the 1956-57 year it was estimated that 200 students, about 40 percent of the student body, participated regularly in CWB activities. In that year alone "over 65 services were held...utilizing 330 students." CWB groups traveled nearly 12,000 miles to present these services.

"The Bean" remained the most popular hangout on campus in these pre-Student Center days. It was the primary evening gathering place for students after study hours—or in place of study hours for less diligent scholars. In the 1950s one could order a Coke for a quarter and a hamburger for 50 cents—indeed, eat any meals, including a tip, for $1-2. Although it was rarely allowed, a few students tried to avoid paying for board, attempting to live more cheaply with skimpy meals at the Bean. Other students, sleeping in and missing breakfast, wandered in at mid-morning between classes for a sweet roll and coffee, or even an early Coke. For nearly fifteen years, before the new Student Center in 1961, the Bean remained *the* gathering place for a socially hungry student body.

Two years before the Student Center opened another notable change took place in the dining hall. Previously, meals were prepared and served by women and men hired by the college for those duties, with students often employed to act as servers for the family-style meals in the dining hall attached to Morrison Hall. Then in February 1959 it was announced that Saga Food Service, a relatively new company "managing college food services" would take over the college's dining hall and coffee shop. Although students would pay $10 more per semester for their board (only about 10 cents more per day), student wages would be raised, and perhaps most interesting of all, charcoal-broiled steaks would be served each Saturday night. The president was convinced that "much improved campus morale" would result from Saga's appearance on campus. About the first Saturday night steak fest, he told the chair of the Board of Regents: "You may be sure I'll be over there in line as guest since they have invited me to come free for the first time." Once the switch to the professional food services occurred in 1959, those companies remained in charge of the dining hall for the remainder of its pre-centennial years. In fall 2009, the fiftieth anniversary of the food services was celebrated with root beer floats and mugs for all who came.

Traveling groups such as the King's Heralds provided important outreach and ministry for summer and CWB programs. (Fig. 4.10)

All the while, students continued their pranks. In the Bean, students might salt one another's Coke or slip a surprise into a friend's main meal. Other kinds of tricks entertained the campus. Nearly every year silverware disappeared from the dining hall, squirt guns and squashy fruit assaulted couples too involved

Dr. Joseph Mayfield, as vice-president for campus life, furnished structure for challenging decisions concerning students' social life. (Fig. 4.11)

in their socializing to be aware of the coming dangers, and dorm rooms were "stacked" or otherwise put in disarray. Sometimes the pranks got out of hand, causing danger or even injury to students or campus buildings. The campus needed persons or a disciplinary system to deal with these matters. In most previous years a former pastor was invited to help with campus discipline or to serve as head resident in a boy's dormitory and perhaps a minister's wife or other women in girls' dormitories. Another format called for a faculty member or two to deal with discipline in addition to his or her teaching load. This informal format did not work very well. Something more systematic had to be organized.

Riley put in place a more formal, orderly system for dealing with discipline in the late 1950s. Named to the new Personnel Committee in 1958 were Dean of Men Warnie Tippitt, Dean of Women Helen Wilson, and Director of Intramurals Elmore Vail. In their weekly meetings the "PC" (as students dubbed the committee) considered student relations on campus, chapel attendance, dormitory activities, and all student disciplinary actions. Previously the Administrative Council had handled the latter headaches; now the Personnel Committee would be able to spend more time with campus discipline and to investigate more thoroughly these time-consuming decisions. Two years later in another action indicating the larger emphasis being placed on campus life, Dr. Joseph Mayfield of Pasadena College was named vice president of campus life. Having served as dean of students at Pasadena since 1951, Mayfield was an experienced administrator in the area of student campus life.

Riley realized that he could not hold tightly the reins of all campus activities and understood that student social life particularly needed more attention. Although students of the 1950s seemed quiet if not quiescent compared to activist students of the late 1960s and beyond, a few hints surfaced that the NNC student body was beginning to become more thoughtful—and outspoken—in their activities. That growing awareness was evident in the student newspaper, *The Crusader*. Since its beginning in February 1942, the newspaper had evolved into a helpful source of information about campus activities in the 1940s and 1950s. While providing updates on religious, academic, and social happenings, it had not become the voice of the NNC students. It rarely published anything that would have raised eyebrows or stirred up NNC-watchers out on the zone.

But a few changes occurred in the mid-to-late 1950s suggesting the *Crusader* could become a different kind of student organ. In 1954, in an editorial entitled "Your Liberty, Use It" the newspaper's editors urged students to express their opinions in "letters to the editor." This was "one of the most advantageous aspects of a college newspaper," the editors wrote, and they asked students to "submit their views and opinions in a progressive and positive manner." If letter-writers wished, they could remain anonymous and count on the editorial staff to protect their identity.

Over the next few months more evidences of student opinion appeared in the *Crusader*. The editors weighed in on whether NNC should join a basketball conference. Noting that the Board of Regents were coming to town, the staff decided they should express "our position editorially on this vital issue." "The *Crusader* believes," the editorial stated, "that membership in a conference would be a wise move and that NNC would benefit greatly from such a step." In the *Crusader* the next fall, Marvin Brunson and Joy Tink, two well-known students, asserted that NNC was balancing Christ and Culture, faith and learning. "Man is at his best when he is an educated Christian," Brunson wrote. Presidents, regents, and faculty had stated their opinions on this needed balance since the beginnings of NNC; now students were beginning to make their voices heard.

Some of the letters to the editor were less muted, more outspoken. One writer argued that NNC was too close-minded, that students were not allowed to criticize less-than-best facets of campus life or to express their religious doubts without being branded "trouble makers." But, the writer continued, such historic figures as Jesus, Martin Luther, and the Founding Fathers were critics of the status quo and called for change. Why not allow such commentaries at NNC? The letter writer claimed that a student who had criticized the dining hall and pointed a finger at non-Christian behavior in Chapman Hall had been asked to leave, and when another student expressed his reservations about some aspects of campus life to important visitors, he "was practically tarred and feathered....Student leaders especially were struck aghast and horrified that someone thought beloved NNC wasn't perfect to the nth degree." NNC needed to be more open to such criticisms, the writer continued; no "human organization" or "man-created idea" was "without spot or blemish." Not surprisingly, the column ended "Name on file."

The *Crusader* was primarily a NNC campus newspaper although a few news stories from off campus appeared in its pages. None was more revealing than the headlines of the October 17, 1957, issue: "Russians Launch Satellite into Outer Space." That story, following on the heels of the dramatic announcement in morning chapel a few days earlier of the Sputnik's launching, set the campus abuzz. Another *Crusader* story about these outer space happenings revealed how little NNC was open to world happenings and how much the campus worried about the Russians and the threat of Communism. In the midst of the rumblings and frowns over Sputnik, Dr. Fred Schwarz, noted Australian anti-Communist speaker, appeared in chapel, stirring up faculty and protected students to the dangers of worldwide Communism.

Sputnik, the threat of Communism, and the shaking of American confidence leading to the Cold War invaded the NNC campus in the late 1950s. No one was, of course, leading the campus in fretful hand wringing over these incidents and trends, but the drama of these events forced the NNC community to think more about world events and global happenings. The protected womb of the Eisenhower years was beginning to open up to the stirring occurrences that made the 1960s such a watershed in American history and culture. NNC would share in some of the ramifications of this momentous transition.

In the first years of his administration during the 1950s, then, the Rev. Riley became a college president. On those important lessons he built a much stronger and expanded college in the next dozen or so years of his administration. With enrollments growing dramatically—NNC numbers doubled in six years—Riley was able to greatly improve the faculty, expand program offerings, and particularly erect new buildings. From 1960 to about 1968, NNC went through one of its most important developmental and expansion programs. Those Riley years, along with H. Orton Wiley's founding years, the financial and accreditation push under DeLong, and the later professionalization and coming university status under the able leadership of Richard Hagood were the most important forward moves of the college. Just as Riley was achieving so much in the forward push on the Nampa campus, whirlwinds of discontent began to blow forcefully across campus, disrupting the college, unsettling regents and other supporters, and adding huge new loads of stress on administration and faculty. In the late 1960s NNC was caught in the crosscurrents of student activism and discontent that swept across the country and invaded even an isolated campus in Nampa, Idaho. For a short but traumatic time from 1968 to 1970 NNC had its foundations shaken. Then quickly, even as the whole country seemed to settle down, the college also began to experience a less frenetic time. For John Riley these disruptive times were the challenge of his administrative career, but he rode them out and learned from the experiences.

Change rode on the backs of exploding student enrollments in the eight years from 1960 to 1968. In 1960, 566 students came to the NNC campus; in

1968 that number had more than doubled to 1,203, the largest college enrollment until 1977-78. In the previous five years, 1955-60, enrollments had grown only from 456 to 566. During the 1950s Riley had spoken frequently of needed expansion, but financial pressures reined in his desires to replace aging buildings, build new ones, and hire stronger faculty. The bursting enrollments in the early 1960s, however, both encouraged and forced the president and regents to expand the campus. These needs were more than enough to encourage an ambitious president already bent on strengthening NNC. In addition, he was able to win over doubtful supporters to the idea that capitalizing on available government funding for constructing new and necessary buildings was exactly the needed partnership to keep up with the students flooding onto the Nampa campus.

Dr. Riley launched and led the Campus Plateau 1970 expansion of the campus. (Fig. 4.12)

The engine that outlined and propelled the expansion program was "Campus Plateau 1970." Riley had spoken earlier of other needed enlargement schemes, but "Plateau 1970" was the full embodiment of what he dreamed for NNC. Once "Plateau 1970" began in fall 1964, the segments of that plan gradually glided into place, and by the early 1970s all the major buildings planned for the program were completed. Before "Plateau 1970" could be begun, however, Riley had to take care of other matters in the early 1960s.

Indeed, the president and the college student body were beginning to experience sea changes of feeling and mood sweeping over the country early in the new decade. So noticeable were the breaks between the Eisenhower 1950s and the so-called "60s" that historians have depicted a watershed separating two very different eras, one pointing back to more placid years, one jetting forward to more yeasty, path-breaking times. Not surprisingly, signs and symbols of this transition came earlier and more clearly to the country as a whole than to a Nazarene campus in faraway Idaho. Nationally, the election of the youthful John F. Kennedy, with his buoyancy, idealism, and Camelot aura, foreshadowed changes on the horizon. Many college-age Americans identified with Kennedy and his vivacious wife Jackie as their older brother and/or sister. The new U. S. president particularly appealed to collegians when he told Americans "Ask not what your country can do for you; ask what you can do for your country" and launched the Peace Corps.

The Kennedy mystique was slower in infiltrating the NNC campus. Perhaps this was primarily because most Nazarenes were Republicans, had been and would so remain. When a straw ballot was taken in 1952, for example, 430 of 490 students and faculty voted for the Republican Eisenhower rather than for Democrat Adlai Stevenson. Indeed, every one of the 37 faculty members taking part in the poll voted for Eisenhower, not one for the Democratic candidate. In the election of 1960, many Nazarenes were even more reluctant to vote for Kennedy, the Catholic candidate for the Democrats. The dissonance between NNC campus opinion and that of the country was made explicit three years later in the days after Kennedy's assassination. In the first issue of the *Crusader* published following the tragedy, the front page headline and two full pages dealt with the annual Homecoming court and activities; one page was devoted to sports; and most of the rest of the issue treated visiting speakers, the Northwesterners singing group, and faculty activities. Only Gaymon Bennett, the newspaper's editor and later a long-time NNC faculty member, dealt with the Kennedy assassination in a brief editorial. He wrote that "The Lord gave America a president who gave his nation a new youth, a new vigor, a new decisive leadership, continued peace, and much more than we can or ever will realize." True enough, but other NNCers were slow to come to these realizations.

For that matter, the growing discontent that washed over Americans following the death of Kennedy, the difficulties surrounding the Vietnam War, the assassinations of Robert Kennedy and Martin Luther King, and campus turmoil, inundated other areas of the country more quickly and dramatically than in Nampa. But it did come. The enthusiastic spirit of the early 1960s, under the onslaught of the tragedies and untoward events of the mid-1960s, turned sour, negative, and increasingly dark. Within a half-dozen years after Kennedy's death the United States had become another country. Some of that disillusionment hovered over and then descended on the Nampa campus.

But Riley and the regents had been hard at work in their forward push before most of the discontents invaded NNC. Nearly every year in the 1960s a new building was erected or a major renovation or addition completed. A majority of the dollars came from low-interest federal loans, but Nazarenes across the educational zone also upped their giving, providing the necessary funds for the campus expansion. In 1960 Dooley Hall, a women's dormitory honoring a longtime NNC faculty member, opened. In the same year two of the less satisfactory frame buildings were razed, the Speech Hall (the old Commons) and Gideon Hall, a men's dormitory. The next year an impressive Student Center was dedicated, providing a social meeting place for students and a new dining area. In NNC's Golden Anniversary Year—1962-63—an addition to Morrison Hall was completed, and the following year a men's honor dormitory, Oxford Hall (now Sutherland), opened. Expansion hit a new high point in 1965-66 with the completion of Culver Hall, a women's dormitory, the Science Lecture Hall, the John E. Riley Library, and the remodeling of the old R. T. Williams Library into a home for the Division of Philosophy and Religion.

The expansion continued the next two years. The old Samaritan Hospital was transformed into a Fine Arts building, the impressive Wiley Learning Center opened, and a new wing of the Fine Arts building for choirs and bands constructed. The razing of venerable but substandard Hadley Hall, by turns a women's dormitory and Fine Arts building, signaled the end of old buildings as new surrounding ones sprang up. Finally, in 1971, after several delays because of lack of federal funding, the Montgomery Physical Education building was completed, including a sparklingly new gym, an indoor swimming pool, and other areas for numerous activities. Two years later the old gymnasium was demolished.

In all, twelve new buildings or major renovations or additions were completed in the years from 1960 to 1973. At the same time, most of the second- and third-class campus buildings were razed, some of them thrown together more than fifty years earlier. Nothing better illustrated the college's dramatic move forward in these watershed years than the erection of so many key, well-constructed buildings.

Abandoning its earlier hesitancy to seek and utilize government funding, the college community took advantage of post-Sputnik federal monies to expand its campus infrastructure. In 1957 only $433 in federal funds came to the NNC campus; in 1960-61, with government loans for Dooley Hall and the Student Center, the total for those two years climbed to more than $800,000. When "Plateau 1970" was announced in 1964, it included plans for six new buildings, totaling more than $2.5 million dollars. Approximately two-thirds of the funding would come from low-cost loans from the government or other lending institutions, one third from other grants and gifts. Gradually during these years and into the early 1970s Nazarene districts in the Northwest raised the percentage of their total giving for education from below 4 percent to as high as 7 percent in some larger, more well-to-do churches. This added funding from the districts was invaluable as a bargaining point when the college president and regents approached the government and banks for grants and loans. Some funders viewed the expanded annual contributions from the zone's districts as equivalent to a dependable endowment, which NNC did not have.

The Riley Library (1966) provided an attractive, modern library facility for the NNC campus. (Fig. 4.13)

Keeping pace with the physical expansion were strengthened faculty and academic programs as well as several new experiments in the college curriculum. Riley was tenacious in his pursuit of better-prepared professors, especially those with completed doctorates or those willing to enter doctoral programs with the college's financial support. Several that Riley secured in the 1960s remained on the faculty for nearly twenty years and were instrumental in its growing academic strength. Art Imel (chemistry) and Joe Tracy (chemistry) added to the hard sciences faculty as did C. Dene Simpson and Bernard Seaman (psychology) and Harrold Curl (sociology) in the social sciences. Reginald Hill proved to be a stable and diligent addition in English, as did Earl Owens in speech. The education faculty, already strong under the leadership of Thelma Culver, expanded its offerings with the addition of Lilburn Wesche. Physical education benefitted much from the long-standing work of Martha Hopkins, Paul Taylor, Art and Jean Horwood. And music would be stronger with the durable teaching and directing of Marvin Stallcop and Jim Willis. Irving Laird (religious education) and Howard Miller (business) ably served as classroom instructors and as administrators. Wanda McMichael and Geneva Bittleson continued their superb work as registrar and head librarian.

One new faculty member, Janine Lytle, and her long stay at NNC provide an illuminating, heart-warming story. A French war bride and a devout Roman Catholic who came to NNC as a student and then joined the faculty in languages, Madame Lytle—as her student addressed her—proved that persons outside Nazarene traditions could be wonderfully supportive of NNC's mission. In hiring Lytle in 1968, Dr. Riley told her directly "I understand you are a Catholic and that it would be impossible for me to recommend you for a permanent appointment to the faculty," but he quickly added, "we know each other so well and respect each other's faith," so the temporary appointment "will be worked out agreeably."

So well, indeed, that the "temporary appointment" lasted twenty-five years. Lytle's department chair praised her and her husband, active members at St. Paul's Catholic Church, as "the most 'Nazarene' Catholics one could ever meet," and the divisional chairman put it in terse nutshells: "Faithful to NNC. One of the college's most outstanding champions....One of the finest people ever and one of the best teachers at NNC." At Lytle's retirement the acting dean summarized the praises coming her direction: "I want to thank you for the quiet, diligent, and faithful way you have discharged your responsibilities, for your support of NNC, for your caring relationship with your students, and the manner in which you model for our Christian faith." It was an inspiring, uplifting story of acceptance, commitment, and understanding between an evangelical college and a devout fellow Christian.

The two school years of 1962-63 and 1963-64 were *anni mirabiles* for NNC. From fall 1962 to late spring 1963 the NNC campus was awash in a Golden Anniversary celebration. The next year not only did President Riley release proposals for the "Plateau 1970," with all of its ambitious building plans; he also unveiled a new three-term, semester credit restructuring of the academic year. As student enrollments spiraled upward, the campus was alive with activity and a positive outlook.

In the nine months stretching from September 1962 to May 1963 celebrations and visiting speakers dotted the calendar and graced the NNC campus. Wisely, Riley kicked-off the Golden Anniversary jubilee with an extraordinary convocation, a Northwest Conference on Evangelism. This huge gathering of several hundred persons, Riley asserted, "was truly the greatest campus convocation in NNC's history...." The preaching, presentations, music, and altar services provided "a fresh sense of the presence of the Lord with new vision of the future." At the end of the convocation, the president concluded "The Northwest Educational Zone was never more united or full of faith for the future."

Opening the fall session, a host of varied speakers provided religious and academic fare of the highest order. The Reverend T. E. Martin, an NNC grad, delivered the annual Miller Lectures, and Samuel Young and Norman Oke, well-known Nazarenes, led evangelistic services. But Leonard Spangenberg, Orville Walters, Timothy L. Smith, and George Reed also made presentations in the business, psychology, history, and sociology fields. And two lectures by noted Yale church historian Kenneth S. Latourette illustrated NNC's desire to bring first-rank scholars to lecture as part of the year of celebration. Not to overlook important connections in their immediate area, NNC also invited Robert Smilie, governor of Idaho and a friend of the college, to speak in chapel. He was a popular figure among the Nazarenes—and Republicans—of Idaho.

Homecoming, always an important and joyous in-gathering for NNC, was an extravaganza of memorable proportions at Thanksgiving time of 1962. In addition to the traditional class visits, chapels, and basketball games, a many-splendored historical musical pageant drew thousands of guests. Organized and directed by a multi-talented senior, Mel Schroeder, "Our Heritage" featured a cast of two hundred in magnificent scenes depicting national and regional themes. The finale celebrated a "Wheel of Progress," NNC's demonstrable moves forward in fifty years.

A salute to NNC leadership closed out the Golden Anniversary commemoration. All the living former presidents—DeLong, Gilmore, and Corlett (Wiley and Morrison were deceased)—came to campus to speak of their roles at NNC.

Together for the first time at the NNC campus, they provided revealing testaments of the steady progress the Nampa campus had made in its fifty-year history.

The next fall, after nearly two years of study, the NNC administrators and faculty inaugurated a new academic calendar for the campus. Dr. Riley had read the Ruml report urging small liberal arts colleges to adopt a student-faculty ratio of 20-to-1, which would allow these institutions to raise salaries substantially. Meanwhile, Dr. Culver had been reading research in the educational field calling for a new kind of annual academic schedule. The two administrators pushed for a change. Deciding not to adopt a traditional three-term schedule, the academic leaders embraced a hybrid system instead: three ten-week terms with the equivalent of thirty semester credits total being earned in the three terms. As President Riley told the academic vice-president at the University of Idaho, the "basic philosophy" of the innovative program would bring about a high student-faculty ratio and allow faculty and students to concentrate "more heavily on few courses in heavier concentration for a shorter period of time."

Generally, faculty would teach each term a nine-semester-hour load (faculty at state universities usually taught 18 hours per year rather than the extraordinarily heavy NNC load of 27). Students would enroll for the equivalent of 10 semester hours. An intense first week of registration and planning in the fall would develop a "unitariness" of program in which students registered for their full year of courses and arranged at one time for the payment of their entire year's charges. After these months of planning, Riley and the faculty seemed convinced that a new academic year of three terms with semester credit would bring about, for faculty and students, more concentration on fewer subjects and thus a better learning atmosphere.

Toward the end of the first semester of the new program, Dean Thelma Culver was certain that "students and faculty like[d] the plan, that better class work [was] being carried on and that the experiment should prove to be a success." Even the local newspaper took note of the three term-semester credit program, noting that several other colleges, including Dartmouth, Coe, Earlham, Goucher, and Carleton, had adopted the plan. Probably Dean Culver was the driving force behind the change; she had been one of the major advocates of this innovative program for some time.

Another indication of the academic innovation crossing into the NNC campus was the launching of The Institute of Asian Studies. The beginnings of the institute may have been rooted in serendipity. In spring 1963 the Madrigal singers (later the Northwesterners), NNC's superb singing group directed by Double E Hill, had been selected for a USO tour of the Pacific from April through June of 1964. During summer of 1963 Dean Culver and her ever-ebullient housemate, Helen Wilson, took courses while vacationing in Hawaii. In fall 1963 Business

Manager L. Wesley Johnson and his wife spent two months in Hawaii and the Orient. These experiences, especially the need to provide courses and credits for the traveling musicians, led to The Institute of Asian Studies in spring 1964. The institute would include course offerings in the Japanese language, in Asian culture, and in literature in translation. The new program was an unusual step for a small, provincial college like NNC. But reactions were so positive, the enthusiasm so manifest that for ten years the institute brought first-rate visiting speakers to campus, authorities on Asian history and culture. For a time Bart McKay, veteran missionary, was on campus to teach Japanese. On a few occasions, when a visiting speaker bruised the conservative religious and cultural outlooks of Nazarenes, controversy reared its head. But for the most part the institute was a sparkling example of the forward and outward perspectives that graced the Riley years of the early and mid-1960s.

Riley's nourishings of the NNC academic program demonstrated themselves in other areas as well. One of the most pleasing of these to faculty members was the commencement of a formal sabbatical program. In the fall of 1964 the Board of Regents adopted general policies about sabbaticals, and Riley moved quickly to implement those plans. Writing to the faculty and other administrators two months after the regents' decision, Riley asked faculty members to provide him with information about their length of service to the institution. He informed them that they must keep in mind the guidelines the regents adopted: leave time of one term and summer at regular pay, plus an additional allowance for each year of employment; additional funding for foreign travel and dependents; only four sabbaticals available in any twelve-month period; and, most important of all, the purpose of a sabbatical was "to render the recipient more useful to the college as a teacher, a researcher or as an administrator." Indeed, such leaves must not be rendered "solely on the grounds of length of service," but should be considered as "the investment of college funds designated to increase the efficiency of the faculty of the institution." Administrators and staff members would also be eligible for similar leaves, although with different time periods and financial support. This move did much to boost faculty admiration for Riley as their college administrator.

The faculty support for Riley clearly heightened too when he defended them against attacks, unwarranted or otherwise. Although these harsh criticisms did not occur often, they could be near vindictive in their ferocity. For example, in November 1964 a Washington farmer wrote to the president accusing Professor Robert Woodward, "who teaches Western Civilization," of being "somewhat short of a real Christian." The critic's agenda became clear: the professor had used

Dr. Robert Woodward stretched the minds and hearts of hundreds of students in his challenging history courses. (Fig. 4.14)

terms "that were invented, bought and employed by the Communists with reference to such patriotic programs and pastors and persons as Dr. Carl McIntire, Billie James Hargis, Dan Smoot, [Dean] Manion." The historian referred to these persons as "Radical" and "Ultra-Right"; since he used such terms "invented by the Communists don't you think he is guilty of breaking the eighth commandment? Unless he is one of them, of course." The letter writer also accused Woodward of attacking the Republicans, of seeking "to destroy their [students'] freedom to worship God." Professor Woodward and others like him should find positions "in an Atheistic institution where [their] efforts will be appreciated." In his reply to these harsh charges, Professor Woodward told President Riley "he did not attack the Republicans." In fact his own views were close to Republican leaders such as Nelson Rockefeller, George Romney, and Mark Hatfield and nearly the same on "extremism and Christian ethics" as those Editor W. T. Purkiser expressed in the *Herald of Holiness*.

The next day Riley answered the farmer from Washington. He thought the Othello man had categorized Woodward "pretty severely." The president asked why the layman, "on the basis of hearsay alone," could "write such a completely unjustified letter and cast innuendoes concerning Communism, atheism, [and] breaking the Ten Commandments." "Dr. Woodward is a fine Christian gentleman," Riley added, and "has been a Nazarene for many years, and is a loyal American." Even though Riley might not "see eye to eye on every political detail" with Woodward, he was sure that "we agree in the great basic principles....I believe in Dr. Woodward's fundamental soundness, and I am ready to stand back of him."

The critic from Othello was not to be denied. Seven months later he wrote another letter, to Vice-president Joseph Mayfield attacking professors for teaching evolution and denying the Bible as God's inspired Word. The district superintendent of the Northwest District, hearing of these difficulties, looked into the issues. After talking to the critic's pastor, he concluded the Othello man was "a bit eccentric" with his "own brand of legalism." The son of the critic, who had been asked not to return to NNC the next year for breaking the college's lifestyle guidelines, was now a Deist, his father lamented, "which, of course isn't Christian at all."

Mayfield's response was even more direct and explicit than Riley's earlier letter. "Your letter does reflect either a misunderstanding of or mistaken information about the position of NNC in the several items which you mentioned." First of all, Nazarenes did "not now believe or teach that the Bible is *verbally* inspired"; rather, they believed in the "plenary inspiration" of the Bible. That meant, as the church *Manual* pointed out, "the Bible is God's inspired Word, 'inerrantly revealing the will of God concerning us in all things necessary to our salvation.'" Plus, the critic's reactions to the possible teaching of evolution in an NNC classroom needed to be seen in context and not based, either, on hearsay. Mayfield added that even though the writer's son was alienated from his course in science, "other students sat in the same classes under the same professor with the same books to read, who have concluded the year with testimony of strengthened faith, greater commitment, deeper love for God, and appreciation for the ideals of the Church of the Nazarene." Then, the vice-president hit closer to home: "it could well be that ... [your son's] problem is not nearly so much his classes, professors, or an introduction to a new translation of the Bible, as it is his own attitudes and responses, which seem to be generally negative. He has consistently shown displeasure with his professor in history, science, Bible and literature, the Business Office and the Personnel Committee." Riley's and Mayfield's ringing defenses of NNC faculty in this and similar situations were a boon to professors' confidence in their administrative leaders. There were other ingredients of the tangled tale: the Othello man's daughter-in-law continued to write additional letters attacking NNC, and left a large, unpaid college bill.

Riley's academic agenda continued to move forward. The launching of the Topic of the Month program, book-of-the-year emphases, and the invitation of noted speakers to campus were also part of this agenda. He used the monthly thematic programs to spotlight college departments and professors and to invite challenging speakers to campus. Annually, he also announced a theme for the year, selected a hymn to emphasize, and chose books in common for faculty and students to read. For instance the "Suggested Book List for 1962-63" included the Book of Acts, the denominational history by Timothy L. Smith *Called Unto Holiness* (Smith was to be a campus speaker for the Golden Anniversary), John Bunyan's *Pilgrim's Progress,* Plato's *Republic,* Alfred North Whitehead's *Adventures of Ideas,* and Herman Melville's classic novel *Moby Dick.* A lifetime inveterate reader, Riley led by example and hoped faculty, staff, and students would join him in these annual

John Luik was the first NNC and Nazarene student named a prestigious Rhodes Scholar. (Fig. 4.15)

safaris through notable books. They often did.

By the mid-to-late 1960s, three departments had emerged as the college's strongest academic units. The Division of Philosophy and Religion maintained its eminence as a first-rank teaching department. Led in these years by A. E. Sanner and including Joseph Mayfield, J. William Jones, Chester Galloway, Irving Laird, Morris Weigelt, Alan Rodda, and President Riley himself, the department trained dozens of ministerial students and provided the introductory and advanced courses in which nearly all students enrolled. The education field, building on the strong foundations that Thelma Culver had established in previous years, maintained and even expanded during the 1960s. Lilburn Wesche provided leadership as chair of the Division of Education and Psychology, Culver remained as chair of the Department of Education, and Marian Marsh and Fred Knight, also with doctorates, provided strength in elementary and secondary education. James Feltar and Bernard Seaman were important administrators in teacher placement and educational psychology. Meanwhile the sciences had steadily improved since Dr. Gilbert Ford had joined the NNC faculty in 1950. A graduate of Harvard and a grace-inspired and committed teacher, perhaps the strongest academic in the college's history, Ford had helped draw several impressive scholar-teachers to the sciences. Joseph Tracy and Arthur Imel were the chemists, Darrell Marks and Ford in physics, and Milton Dean and Howard Morse in biology. Virgil Vail, a whiz in electronics and technology, provided much-needed wizardry in supporting laboratory and mechanical work.

Individual students were also garnering outstanding honors. In 1964, Stan Crow became the first Nazarene college graduate to gain entrance to Harvard Law School. At NNC he had served as editor of the *Crusader*, was active in debate, and served as president of the Young Republicans. Looking back over his four years in Nampa, Crow told a reporter "N.N.C. did all right, in my view." At Harvard he won honors for his work. Upon graduation he returned to Boise and became a well-known lawyer. In 1971, John Luik, a senior from California, was named the first Rhodes Scholar from NNC and from the Church of the Nazarene. A history and philosophy major, Luik was also involved in debate and managing editor of the *Crusader*. He went on to gain his doctorate from Oxford and begin a long career as a college teacher, an author, and a consultant on ethics issues.

An untoward threat to NNC's future occurred during the Nazarene General Assembly meeting in Portland in the summer of 1964. Not only did the assembly vote to organize a Nazarene Bible College, which eventually opened in Colorado Springs, on the NNC educational zone; the assembly also voted to begin two junior colleges in Kansas and Ohio that would disrupt the educational zones then in place. President Riley favored neither of these decisions because they added burdens to his job, reassigned the Dakota and Minnesota districts to other Nazarene colleges, and added the Colorado District, which did not want, at first, to become part of the NNC zone. But within the year Riley was writing to a variety of church and district leaders, laying out what these changes meant to the college's future, encouraging them to cooperate "in making the transitions involved in the beginning" of the colleges and the establishing of new educational zones.

The social life of the campus seemed to match the vivacity of the flourishing building and academic programs. Intramural activity, an active dating and matchmaking process, and campus clubs continued apace. And students persisted in

The Northwesterners, under the superb direction of Double E Hill, became NNC's premier musical group. (Fig. 4. 16)

pushing for later dorm hours and more student rights, including students on faculty and administrative committees. They also exhibited an independence of action that sometimes upset administrators and alumni, who called for clamping down on student activities. On a very few occasions, President Riley expressed his strong opinions about student actions. In early 1961, for example, he wrote a memo to student life advisors, telling them "unless I can have some assurance that there will be adequate supervision of women cheer leaders next year so that we will not have semi-dance steps and skirt swirling, to which I and a number of others have objected, there will be no women cheer leaders next year."

As before, music and athletic activities were at the center of campus life—and spread out to the education zone and beyond. To the Crusader Choir, traveling quartets, and other musical groups was added the Madrigals, later known as the Northwesterners. Ably organized and superbly directed by Double E Hill, chairman of the Music Department, this compact singing group became the college's premier musical ensemble. They traveled across the NNC educational zone for special meetings, sang at important and large venues in the Boise Valley, and in the 1960s were invited by the United Services Organization (USO) to tour the Orient and Europe singing at historic churches, public buildings, and before other prestigious gatherings. No musical group before or since has so resoundingly represented the college in so many important and attention-gathering events. In his able direction and promotion of the Northwesterners, Dr. Hill not only illustrated his front-rank talents, he also proved to residents of the Boise Valley that NNC had a first-class musical ensemble ranking with—or even surpassing—the best Idaho had to offer.

Gary Locke, a notable athlete, remains NNC/NNU's highest, all-time scorer in basketball. (Fig. 4. 17)

NNC athletic teams likewise expanded during the 1960s, keeping sports at the center of campus life. On most occasions the tensions over intercollegiate athletics seemed to diminish, only in isolated moments exploding into controversy. More exciting were the achievements of individual athletes, none more intriguing, in retrospect, than the career of basketball star Gary Locke. Coming to NNC in the fall of 1960 rather unknown and unheralded, Locke became a starter as a freshman. At 6′ 2″ he often played under the basket and impressed opponents and reporters alike with his agile footwork, superb shooting, and first-rate rebounding. As a sophomore he led the team with nearly 22 points a game and raised that average to 26 in his third year. His senior year he led the team in scoring for the third time and finished with a four-year total of 2,251 points, still the highest career total in NNC's history. And for two years he gained Little All-American honors. One of Locke's contemporaries on the basketball team, often feeding him for jump shots and easy lay ins, was Richard ("Goose") Hagood, himself a superb athlete and later NNC's eleventh president.

Other kinds of social life, of an informal and sporadic order, sometimes spiced campus life. Among them were the pranks. The usual dorm tricks,the dining hall antics, the misplaced automobiles on campus, and the chuckles in chapel kept administrators on their toes. On occasion a really innovative prank memorialized itself. Among these was one in early 1968.

Three ingenious male students began with diligent research. How long would it take an ice cube to melt? If attached to a poster, would the melting ice cube allow the poster to fall, to cascade down at just the right moment? After a few trial runs, the prankish experiment was ready. As burly Dean Wilder was intoning the joys of classical music—especially opera—in one of the Topic of the Month chapels, the poster with the ears and bow tie insignia of the Playboy Bunny dropped down from the chapel curtains, plopping in giant display alongside Professor Wilder. Gulping, gasping out "look a bunny," then chuckling, the nonplused presenter went on, accompanied by unrestrained howls from the students. NNC's network of prank detectives quickly spread out to apprehend the culprits. None were to be found; they had been seated in the audience to participate in the fun. No one "outed" the rascals, although they confessed to the deed many years later. Such talents promised clear future achievement: one merry prankster became the owner of an engineering firm, another a business leader, and the other a high up official in an educational think-tank. More especially, two became NNU trustees, one a top NNU administrator.

Such frolicsome times seemed increasingly to disappear, however, toward the end of the 1960s. The country—and the campus—was in no mood for more fun; serious problems had to be addressed, and the students increasingly wanted to be part of facing up to those problems and perhaps locating solutions.

The discontent among Americans bubbled up increasingly in the mid-to-late 1960s. Negative feelings toward the Vietnam War, heightened sensitivity concerning women's and minority rights, such organizations as the Black Panthers and the Red Power movement, and the enigmatic persons known as Hippies signaled the growing discontent in the United States. Alongside were the eruptions of student activism that characterized many college campuses. None was more widely noted than student actions at the University of California, Berkeley. When the activist student leader Mario Savio harangued a group gathered in front of the university's administration building, he told them: "There is a time when the operation of the machine becomes so odious...you've got to put your bodies upon the gears and upon the wheels, upon the levers, upon all the apparatus, and you've got to make it stop." No Mario Savio entered the NNC campus, but student discontent did arrive, and it was troubling for the administration, faculty, other students, and the broader constituency.

The student discontent came more slowly and much less vociferously to the Nampa campus than it did to Berkeley and other major state and private institutions scattered across the country. More pointed student questions and opinions first began to be aired in the mid-1960s. By 1967 they were appearing more frequently in the *Crusader*, now an outspoken student newspaper. When the newspaper doubled in size to eight pages, much more space was available for columns of opinion, editorials, letters to the editor, and news stories reprinted from other campus newspapers.

The lid flew off in the 1968-69 year—and beyond. Strong evidences of dissatisfaction and rising controversy appeared in fall 1968 issues of the *Crusader*. The October 18 copy of the newspaper, for example, included several stories on political contests since the controversial election of 1968 was near at hand, following on the heels of the violence and disturbances at the Democratic Convention the previous summer in Chicago. Students were airing their points of view, and so many Democrats and "liberals" were expressing their opinions in the campus newspaper that others thought the campus was veering dangerously to the left. One letter-writer, in fact, attacked the newspaper for including stories about folk-singer Pete Seeger, who had held a recent concert in Boise. In his letter, titled "*Crusader* Abets Communism," the writer told readers: "The ASB, through *The Crusader*, should not aid and abet the communist cause [which he thought it had done in printing a story on Seeger]. This unfortunately is what we accomplished." Another student worried that too many NNCers were blindly following new leftists when they should stick more to Nazarene traditions. More pointedly, a reprinted letter from the Eastern Nazarene College newspaper, titled "Pressure and Hypocrisy," attacked an ENC editor for being "very unfair to the student who protests against some administrative policies." The writer added, "The protesting students are spewing the administration out of their mouths because it is neither hot nor cold." Administrators, the writer suggested, were not living up to the ideals of balancing academics and spiritual life, on which ENC and other Nazarene colleges were founded.

Revealingly, this *Crusader* issue also contained an interview with the Rev. Gordon Wetmore, pastor of the Wollaston Church of the Nazarene on the Eastern Nazarene College campus and then holding a revival at NNC. In 1983 he became president of NNC. The interviewer very pointedly asked Wetmore that since he said the church "extends an invitation to those who dissent or strive for innovation or change," why were "the youth either ignored or rejected in their differing views and actions?" Wetmore thought "we're talking about two ends of a continuum here," and he was convinced the general church would "accept more and more the innovative force of the emergent." The next question was even more on edge: "Why does the Church of the Nazarene refuse or neglect to become involved in many social and political questions of our day...?" Again, Wetmore kept his cool and replied that evangelicals had traditionally relied on the impact of individuals and their concerned and upright lives to help to deal with societal problems and perhaps bring relief and remedy. He was convinced, too, that the other force of Protestantism was to commit itself to reforming social ills, and that he saw some inklings of that surfacing in the church.

Signs of discontent and controversy abruptly surged to a higher level. When conservative Republican George Hansen, then running against incumbent Democrat Frank Church for the U. S. Senate, appeared on campus to represent his positions and attack Church's actions, several students stood in the audience holding up black articles in silent protest to Hansen. The combative Hansen fired back, bluntly telling the protesters "You're doing a good job of being Americans." When a majority of the audience loudly applauded Hansen, he told the protesters "this proves that your type of thinking is on the way out." At the end of his speech, most of his listeners gave Hansen a standing ovation, but several refused to stand. In the question and answer session following the speech, the tables seemed to turn with students closely questioning Hansen, particularly his stances on the Vietnam War and on the draft. Why should eighteen-year-olds be expected to put their lives on the line, one student asked, when they couldn't vote to make decisions on war and peace?

Fiery reactions to the protest ripped across campus like a newly ignited firestorm, engulfing students and faculty. Then it spread to the Nampa area and out on the zone. Letters to the *Crusader*, local newspapers, and the president's office came in rapid order. One student told the protesters if they wanted to object to NNC happenings they ought to "go to a different school" and "don't ruin [NNC] for those who want something more to life than a black flag or protest signs." The secretary of the college alumni society took a similar tack. He found the "grade-school antics of a few dissidents" an example of discourtesy, unbecoming of a Christian college. In the same issue of the campus newspaper two students rejected these views. Dissent was a part of American traditions, one asserted. NNCers exhibited "an almost paranoiac fear of dissent"; instead they ought to recall their own country's history and see how dissent and protest had helped bring about the freedoms they enjoyed. One of the protesters, son of a NNC faculty member and later a president of a Nazarene college, provided a pointed defense of *why* he participated in the actions against Hansen. He stood in protest, the writer asserted, because he and others "believe so strongly that men like Hansen would hurt our country"—in fact, that the views of Hansen, et al., are "very dangerous to the survival of the human race."

As one can easily surmise, criticism from off-campus NNC supporters of the protesters was immediate and strong. A pastor of a large church in Washington, and a frequent letter-writer about the things he saw wrong at NNC, apologized for one of his church young people being involved in the protest against Hansen. He urged "that proper disciplinary action should be taken by the administration toward all of the students who participated in this demonstration….[He and his church board] give you full support in the enforcement of the rules, policies, principles, and traditions of our school and our church." One concerned Nazarene man and wife, with children at the college, pointed to scruffy beards, long hair, unruly music, SDS-like actions, and evidences of "Flower Children" actions as all of a piece. NNC was in danger of "allowing our children to drift into the line of thinking that is so prevalent on campuses of Universities and Colleges across the nation." "N.N.C. has stood as a fortress and pillar in our church"; but they were afraid those foundations were crumbling, so they wrote to the president with their very real concerns. Even veteran missionary and NNC booster Prescott Beals wrote a four-page, single-spaced letter to the *Crusader* editor, Dick Alban, registering his strong dissent from the kinds of essays, letters, and published articles being reprinted in the college newspaper. So upset was the much-esteemed missionary that he departed from his enthusiastic, upbeat support of NNC to elaborate on his misgiving about so much that was appearing in the *Crusader*.

Then, as the campus discontent continued to roil upward, an event occurred that, to some observers, illustrated the disconnects at NNC and other similar evangelical colleges. A brief news note appeared in the well-known periodical, *The National Observer*, entitled "Nampa, Idaho: Dancing's Out." Six students had been suspended, the story indicated, "not for taking part in campus riots, sit-ins, or peace demonstrations, but for dancing during an after-basketball game party at the student center." President Riley and a group of administrators and students had taken this disciplinary measure, the story continued, because the dismissed students had "violated the published NNC campus code of conduct." "Both the school and its sponsor, the Church of the Nazarene, forbid dancing."

When the Board of Directors (the executive committee of the Board of Regents) met in a special meeting in January in Portland, they focused much of their discussion on recent issues of the *Crusader*. The board seemed convinced it was best to allow the president to handle this problem, but then a letter from the Walla Walla Church Board was introduced, the same church whose pastor had just written Riley a grumbling letter and from which veteran missionary Prescott Beals would soon write. Now the secretary's notes indicated a "deep concern" over the newspaper and that "some definite actions should be taken to improve the content and tone of the *Crusader*." Plus, the directors would tell "all concerned that we are encouraging the administration to take such steps as are practical in this direction as soon as possible." And there was something of a warning shot across the campus bow when "it was suggested that faculty members could be contributing toward student protest and criticism by their own critical comments on the church."

When the full Board of Regents convened for its regular meeting in mid-March, the *Crusader* and general "Campus Climate" were much-discussed topics. About twenty of the regents asked the president, Dean Culver, and other administrators about the *Crusader*, campus discipline, and student outlooks. Riley assured them the college was "not going to give up the fundamental values, principles, and the faith of the church and of the college. Neither will we," he continued, "overreact and become solely a defensive, authoritarian institution." We need to hold steady and realize "that a significant segment of the student body is rallying to the cause of positive commitment to Christ and Holiness and are making the same known." Dean Culver said much the same: "it is not time to panic, but to hold steady." Besides, regents should realize that "our specific problems were not caused alone by a few students or a few faculty members, but basically the problem was caused by 'a rapidly changing society as reflected in moral standards, and social change. This changing society [is] having its influence also upon churches of our zone, as revealed in the conduct of many of the students now coming to NNC. For example—where did the students learn to dance?'"

As would become clear in the coming months, unexpected consequences resulted from Riley's push for well-trained, highly educated new faculty and added a new ingredient to the disruptive mix roiling on the NNC campus. Several of these new hires were young, activist professors who connected especially well with students. Among these was Dan Kirby.

Kirby came from strong Nazarene backgrounds and was a superb teacher who drew students to his classes, activities, and to his home. The son of a Nazarene minister and an NNC graduate, Kirby had public school teaching experience and had gained a master's degree. One of his school principals spoke of Kirby as "an exceptional teacher" with an "outstanding ability to build rapport, develop empathy, and identify with young people." Another administrator noted that Dan "has a keen understanding of young people, and he is able to easily gain their confidence and cooperation." With these strong recommendations and the encouragement of one of Kirby's mentors, NNC professor Art Seamans, Kirby was hired in fall 1967 to teach English composition and to direct some of the college's drama productions. At first things went very well.

But rumblings began in spring 1968. Kirby wrote a letter to the *Crusader* urging students to rethink their attitudes toward minority groups. "Racial prejudice

Dan Kirby, a stimulating teacher, became embroiled in a free speech controversy. (Fig. 4.18)

and the spirit of Christ are total strangers," he told readers. Then the letter veered into controversial territory. "I might say here," Kirby added, "that it has been difficult for me to understand why the [Nazarene] church has not been more forceful and courageous in proclaiming this....I likewise challenge the students of the campus to force the church to act courageously." (Earlier Kirby had challenged "radical conservatives" to rethink their attitudes about Vietnam and American diplomacy in an article he wrote for the student newspaper.) When a *Crusader* reporter asked Kirby about these letters and his other opinions, he told her that he stood by those comments and urged students to be a reforming force in their local churches "in tearing down the barriers of prejudice that exists within the walls of the church." Those were not comments that conservative church members liked to hear.

Then the crescendo of discontent rose sharply in fall 1968. Some thought Kirby had organized and led the protest against politician George Hansen in October. Others were upset with the play Kirby directed in the fall, *An Enemy of the People.*

The crunch time came the next spring. In April, under the general title of "Broken Stairways," Kirby directed three one-act plays: *The Hole, The Acting Lesson,* and *The Terrible Meek.* The purposes of the three plays, Kirby told a reporter, was to say: "OK, this is the way you are Materialistic. Full of clichés without meaning. And the answer is Christ." He knew there might be some fallout, so he tried to explain in the program the intentions of the plays.

The negative reactions came quickly: some faculty members left early on, not staying for the full evening. Others took swipes at the dress and the hair length of the male leads. The discontent came directly to President Riley's office. He reportedly told Kirby he had produced "controversial plays in a controversial year." Reviewing Kirby's much-discussed roles on campus, Riley told him he was "too threatening to college constituents." Rather than fire Kirby, who was in the first of a three-year contract, the college worked out an agreement whereby Kirby, rather than perhaps sue, would accept his full salary for the next year to attend graduate school.

When news of Kirby's "firing" hit campus, his supporters took to the streets. One student, writing in the *Crusader,* decried Kirby's being forced to leave as evidence of "Gestapo tactics" still going on at NNC. For that writer, Kirby had "brought a spirit of academic freedom in the classroom, a spirit which was previously unknown." And he heard that several other NNC professors had "already commented that they are hesitant and anxious about what they now discuss in the classroom because of Professor Kirby's fate." Elsewhere in this issue of the newspaper was the coup de grâce of discontent. Without permission from the newspaper's faculty advisor, the paper devoted an entire page with a picture of the Kirbys and nearly 200 names signed beneath the photograph. The head note read "We, the undersigned, feel that you add[ed] an irreplaceable [sic] element to academic freedom on our campus. Students will miss your leadership and honesty. We are sorry that you have to leave." It may have been this page, more than anything else, that led Riley to suspend the campus newspaper the following summer.

Why the Kirby incident? What happened? Did he have a "death wish," as one of his colleagues suggested? Was he merely a sign and symbol of the troubled times sweeping across the country and blasting through most campuses? Or were there other reasons? Revealingly, once Kirby left NNC, he completed his doctorate and became a distinguished scholar and consultant in the field of English education. And disruptions similar to these were in evidence at many other colleges including Nazarene campuses. Professor Seamans provided another insight into these events when he suggested that when Dan Kirby's father was asked to leave his pulpit in a Nazarene church, that action jarred the entire close-knit Kirby family. Kirby's actions and attitudes, Seamans posited, were tied as much to the resignation of the Rev. Kirby as to events at NNC. Besides, Seamans opined, a "repressive atmosphere" at NNC was all too ready to move Kirby off campus. Professor Marian Washburn also thought Kirby had not done anything that should have led to his being fired. Both Seamans and Washburn, Kirby's English colleagues at NNC, maintained that college officials should have been more understanding of his situation and more willing to work with him.

The controversies continued to boil over in the coming months. Wisely—and pragmatically—Riley waited to suspend publication of the *Crusader* until school was out in June 1969. That month's issue of the *NNC Messenger* announced the suspension "because of violation of policy and unacceptable tone and content on the part of the staff and paper...." The paper was to be suspended during the fall term 1969 while "policies and procedures" were ironed out for its resumption. Two months later in a memorandum released from his office, Riley explained that the suspension came to "call a halt to what I consider to be a very negative trend...." He was recommending the establishing of a Publications Board that would include a membership half faculty and half student. The president promised he would lift the suspension as soon as he was "satisfied that structure, procedures and policies have been established."

The committee worked diligently to get guidelines in place, and publication resumed in early 1970. Not everyone was satisfied with the compromises that led to renewed publication. Although students were given more responsibility in deciding what was in the newspaper, they were also asked to think through the implications of each story and column they published. Student editor Linda Nichols said her decisions would be guided by what had been the previous editorial policy: "We're trying to make people think and become aware not only of this campus, but of the world around them and of what they can and should be involved in." Two decades later recalling the tumultuous times of the Kirby incident and the turmoil over the campus newspaper, Riley wrote: "Suffice it to say...everybody learned something through those years, not the least of them the college administrators. One thing that was basic in my philosophy before and during those years was that while those in authority must be ready to make and stand by firm decisions, they must be wise enough to provide adequate time and adequate counsel before making them. Snap solo decisions are rarely advisable." Plus, he added, "The ultimate standard of behavior is Christ and the Bible interpreted by the best of human wisdom."

In early 1970 the Board of Regents realized that their strong president was bending—perhaps nearly breaking—under the mighty loads of pressures he was carrying. They urged Riley to take an administrative leave and embark on a world tour as a much-deserved respite from his college duties. (The regents also provided Mrs. Riley an additional $1,000, a "love offering" for her work in beautifying the campus and supporting her husband.) Just after graduation (June 12) the Rileys boarded a plane for Hawaii and the Far East. Before they returned on September 9, the president and his wife had visited missionaries, NNC grads, and other Nazarenes in India, the Middle East, Greece, Africa, and Europe. In all they had covered nearly 30,000 miles by air. Dr. Riley was particularly impressed with the missionaries: "The optimism, the absence of complaint, the bright happy service of missionaries, both NNC alumni and others, were a tonic whose exhilaration will linger long with us." The president, always an ardent traveler, arrived back in Nampa refreshed, jubilant, and recharged for his work.

He needed the renewed energies; more challenges lay ahead. Although the new publications board was in place to oversee the *Crusader*, problems lurked within the newspaper. In fact, the following spring, in the final issue of 1971, both the NNC faculty and Publications Board of the newspaper condemned its reporting and handling of controversial events and ideas. As the secretary of the board wrote, "It is the consensus of this Board that the *Crusader* has in certain issues, and more specifically in the last, violated the publications policy in respect to fair play, good taste, and courtesy."

Five months earlier student body president Duane Dale clarified student expectations. Apropos of his theme, "Bridging the Gap," Dale thought the NNC student body, like "students all over the country, [were] seeking ways to express and to put into effect their ideas and opinions." The key to achieving success in these ventures, the ASB president thought, was better communication—especially with the administration and with the regents. Riley agreed and moved to make sure new avenues of conversation were opened. Dale also wrote to the Rev. Raymond Kratzer, chair of the regents, requesting "some channel through which ... [student] ideas can be presented directly to the Board. This could be accomplished by allowing the A.S.B. President to be an ex-officio member of the Board of Regents." Kratzer's response both avoided and answered Dale's requests. He made no mention of the ASB president's becoming a member of the board, but he did encourage NNC students to channel their ideas through the Campus and Campus Life Committee of the board, which included one-third of all its members. Kratzer was sure, he told Dale, this approach was the best way to open the communication the students desired. He also urged the student president to be in touch with President Riley and the President's Cabinet, two other ways to improve communication between NNC and its student body.

Even though disruptive times continued to course through the U. S. well into the 1970s, campus life at NNC in those years moved in less frenetic channels, even some peaceful ones. In fact, Riley sensed "a radiant spirit [that seemed] to dominate." "'Fantastic' is a word heard frequently among the students. Active, positive service for Christ is in the air," he reported. Riley's joyous attitude probably derived in part from his rewarding world tour, but the spirit on campus and out on the zone was also more buoyant and positive. That spirit was reflected in the new directions on campus. Even before the "Plateau 1970" phases were finished, Riley and his advisors were planning "Mission 80."

In spring 1971, the official groundbreaking for the Physical Education Building, the final segment of "Plateau 1970," took place. Gathering government monies, a low-interest loan from an Idaho bank, and fees of $25 each term from all students, the NNC administration was able to fund this large and important project that had been long delayed for a lack of funding. At the same time the regents approved the largest budget on record, financing costs of the PE building, more sabbatical leaves for faculty, and other future programs. To fund these expansions and encourage support of "Mission 80," the regents asked districts to boost their educational giving from 5 to 6 percent of their yearly budgets. A year later some of the larger districts agreed to allocate 7 percent to education. This willingness to provide even more funding for NNC was further evidence that Nazarenes out in the NNC zone thought the crisis times of 1968-70 had passed and that Riley was leading the college in the right direction.

Riley saw "Mission 80" as a "qualitative" endeavor following "Plateau 1970," a "quantitative" program. He described the difference between the two concisely: "we are making the transition from a period of constructing buildings to a time of creative programming." In the next few months the president described "Mission 80" as it related to campus activities as well as NNC's outreach missions.

The pressures to expand between 1961 and 1967, when student enrollments doubled, greatly lessened in the next few years and impacted the type of programs needed on campus. From an apex of 1,203 students in 1967-68, enrollments leveled off and began to dip. By 1972-73 they had fallen to 1,007. In small colleges like Northwest Nazarene, with little endowment funding, programs were inextricably linked to enrollments. When fewer students came, innovative—and costly—programmatic efforts had to be curtailed. That was the case in the final years of Riley's presidency. Despite falling student enrollments, the energetic administrator found ways to keep morale high and a forward look before the campus.

Students began to work more closely with rather than at cross purposes with the administration. Problems concerning the *Crusader* diminished, a "Statement on Student Rights and Responsibilities" was adopted in April 1972, and student body officers seemed more inclined to embrace less troubling measures. For instance in 1971-72 the new student body president Steve Smith and his fellow officers attended the traditional faculty-only retreat and participated in discussions about planning campus activities for the next year. Smith told others that he saw "more uniting the NNC community than there is dividing it." That was undoubtedly soothing music to the troubled souls of administrators and regents.

Other programs solidified NNC's academic strengths. New faculty who would serve several years at the college were hired, including Ray Cooke (history), Mary Shaffer (art), Gaymon Bennett (English); others returned with newly completed doctorates: Martha Hopkins (PE) and Paul Taylor (PE). The Asian Studies program also continued apace, bringing distinguished speakers to campus. And important accreditations, in 1967 and 1972-73, provided significant salutes for the general college program as well as for its very strong work in teacher education and certification.

A major transition in NNC's academic history occurred when Thelma Culver retired from the deanship in 1970, after twenty-four years as the college's chief academic officer. She had been instrumental in leading NNC's general education programs, its curriculum, and work in teacher preparation. When she stepped down, Gilbert Ford was asked to be her successor, and he, reluctantly, took on those new responsibilities, a position he would hold for fifteen years. Culver enjoyed planning curriculum, but she wished to avoid the complexities of faculty hiring and determining salaries. When Ford became the new dean, Riley strode into his office with faculty folders and told him these were among his new responsibilities.

Ford's assumption of the deanship symbolized another qualitative change going on in NNC leadership. During the early years of his presidency, Riley seemed to take charge of most campus activities save for those Culver assumed. But over time and especially under the increasing pressures of "Plateau 1970" and campus unrest

Mel Schroeder directed the 60th Anniversary pageant "Teach the World to Sing," to universal acclaim in 1972. (Fig. 4.19)

during the late 1960s, Riley began to depend on other leaders and put together an expanding presidential cabinet. Besides Riley and Ford, serving on the cabinet were Howard Miller and Gerald Fosbenner in business matters and Joseph Mayfield and Irving Laird in campus and social life. Increasingly Riley consulted these advisors, without giving up the reins of general direction for the college.

The president also realized the importance of milestone celebrations as a unifying force for NNC. That being the case, he called upon NNC's tall and talented wizard of pageantry, Mel Schroeder, the director of NNU's Media Center, to plan and put together a 60th Anniversary shindig for 1972-73. As he had for the 50th Anniversary festival while still an undergraduate, Schroeder fashioned a huge gala event for the Homecoming gathering of 1972. More than 5,000 persons came to the seven performances of "Teach the World to Sing," involving hundreds of actors and stagehands. The pageant was presented in and became an auspicious beginning for the new Montgomery Physical Education Building. After attending a performance of the extravaganza, one viewer spoke of Schroeder "as Treasure Valley's own Walt Disney."

Early in 1973 a thunderbolt struck campus: Dr. Riley to retire. In some ways not unexpected and yet unknown to the campus, faculty, and most constituents, the announcement of his intended retirement on July 1, 1973, still took many by surprise. Riley, sensing the need for change on campus and in his own career, in February called the presiding general superintendent George Coulter and regent chairman Raymond Kratzer to inform them of his intentions. One month later, he gave his official resignation to the Board of Regents in its semiannual meeting in Nampa and urged them to move ahead quickly to select his replacement.

Riley had led NNC for more than twenty years with a firm hand through some of its most tumultuous times. It was only natural that many observers wanted to sum up his twenty-one years at the helm of the college. Regents and faculty pointed to burgeoning enrollments, an expanded campus, and stronger academic programs during his presidency. Others noted his balanced leadership among faculty, students, and alumni. In the February 1973 issue of the *Crusader* an article reiterated several of these achievements but also listed "Plateau 1970" and "Mission 80" and the implementation of new undergraduate and graduate programs as notable achievements.

Other accomplishments need to be mentioned. Riley was a strong religious leader, as pastor and president. As a chapel speaker, as a man of public prayers (gathered up by later General Superintendent Jerald Johnson into a booklet entitled *President Riley at Prayer*), or as college administrator, Riley moved his listeners and colleagues. He led NNC longer than anyone else in the president's office. An administrator who united vital piety and the life of the mind—what he called a balance of conscience and competence—Riley was an indefatigable cheerleader for the college and Nazarene higher education.

But what did he see as major achievements? For what actions and qualities would he like to be remembered? In his 75th Anniversary history of NNC, *From Sagebrush to Ivy*, Riley listed his major accomplishments under one major heading: it was, he said, "the development of the infrastructure that makes a college a college": these included "a strong Board of laymen and clergymen; an efficient administration; a competent and committed faculty...; a sound and balanced curriculum, supported by labs, library, and other educational media; a climate of Christian liberal arts learning; a 15- or 20-to-one student faculty ratio; and a growing body of loyal alumni and other constituencies." Although not the total of what others might say about Riley's achievements because he did not credit himself for all of what he had done, these comments were characteristic nonetheless of the quality of the man.

The Rileys stayed in Nampa and traveled the world after his retirement. In the next two decades teaching and speaking assignments took them to all corners of the globe. Riley also turned his fluid mind and fluent pen to writing the abovementioned *From Sagebrush to Ivy* and a 300-page unpublished memoir "R and R: Recollections and Reflections" (1992) for his family. He and his wife Dorcas also continued their summer sojourns to Red Fish Lake, his Idaho retreat, where his three daughters and their families could also enjoy a Riley get-together. And there were the mornings and sunsets to be relished from his home side patio. One person put it concisely: "John Eckel Riley was not only a great leader, he was a good man. He stretched our minds as he warmed our hearts."

5

The Transitional Presidents

THE PEARSALL AND WETMORE YEARS: 1973-93

The phone call came late at night—across the continent from the Pacific Northwest to the East Coast. Raymond Kratzer, chairman of the NNC Board of Regents, was calling Kenneth Pearsall, superintendent of the New England District of the Church of the Nazarene. Kratzer asked two pointed questions: Would Pearsall take the NNC presidency, and would he give his decision by the next morning? Surprised by the unexpected request and bothered by the need for a quick decision, Pearsall, after a night of prayer and uncertainty, rejected the offer the next morning. He did not feel free to accept it.

Why the offer of the presidency to Dr. Pearsall? Who was he, and how would he fit into the NNC leadership harness? He was a New Yorker by background, a graduate of Eastern Nazarene College, and a long-time pastor and then district superintendent, but had no graduate degree and was not a faculty member. He had served on the regents for both NNC and ENC, however, and was currently chair of the ENC board. During a pastorate in Yakima, Washington, and while serving on the NNC board, he had become acquainted with the Nampa leaders; they knew, liked, and trusted him.

The offer to Rev. Pearsall reflected the perspectives of most Nazarene church and college leaders in the early 1970s. Although President Riley had encouraged the regents to solicit names from and involve members of the student body, faculty, and alumni, the regents kept the nominating and election of the new president largely among themselves. These regent actions in 1973 were not unusual. No layperson had been seriously considered for the presidency heretofore, and none would be until the early 1990s. The ideal leader for a Christian liberal arts college, from the then-dominant point of view in the Nazarene church, was a pastor or a district superintendent. Laymen A. B. Mackey, president of Trevecca Nazarene College (1936-63) and Edward Mann (1948-70) of ENC, were distinct exceptions to this long-held "rule." Pearsall, as a seasoned pastor and an experienced district superintendent, clearly represented what the NNC regents considered an ideal leader for the college. Like his predecessor John Riley, Pearsall was the recipient of an honorary doctorate from his alma mater. This rather modest academic preparation for a college president seemed not to bother the regents, perhaps because only DeLong of the NNC presidents had had an earned doctorate. The regents could argue that

Dr. Pearsall, here with his wife Ruby, was a warm-hearted and positive man and served as NNC's eighth president. (Fig. 5.1)

the roles Pearsall had filled thus far in the church were not greatly dissimilar from those of his two predecessors, Drs. Corlett and Riley. Even a decade later, after announcing his resignation, Pearsall himself feared the future when a layman rather than church elder was selected as chair of the NNC Board of Regents.

Following Pearsall's rejection of the NNC presidency, the regents moved quickly to another candidate—another district superintendent. Ernest Martin, from Michigan, accepted the presidency, but after a hurried, eye-opening visit to campus revealing the multiple tasks of his new position, he resigned. The regents then returned to Pearsall and again offered him the presidency. This time, without much hesitation, he agreed to come as the eighth NNC president.

One month after Pearsall arrived on the Nampa campus, a group of students and faculty cornered him for an interview. Did the new president have plans for the future, the interrogators wanted to know. Pearsall wisely told them that, first of all, he intended to listen to students and to establish good connections with NNC supporters out on the educational zone. When the questioners pushed Pearsall for more about his plans, he admitted he had been most recently a district superintendent, and then he quickly added: "this is a new ball game and I'm going to need some time" to formulate plans for administering the college. In fact, he needed at least a year to acquaint himself with the campus and its constituents. Quite possibly increasing the college's enrollment and working "to secure funds" "would be at the top of the list of priorities." After one school year, he thought, the future might come into clearer focus.

This interview in the opening weeks of Pearsall's administration dramatized the manifold challenges he faced. He brought the good and extensive experiences of a pastor and church leader, of a kind and generous father of four children; and through his work as an ENC representative he had proven his ability to get along with young people. A skilled and impressive speaker, Pearsall also knew how to communicate with church members and pastors. One student writing in the *Crusader* summed up these strengths: "what this college needs most from a president is strong Christian leadership, goodwill, and a working intelligence. These are the qualities which we get from Dr. Pearsall." The "Prexy [was] qualified" for the job.

But in another area—academic leadership—Pearsall was an innocent abroad. A religion major with a bachelor's degree, he had not undertaken graduate work and had never been a faculty member. True, his work as a college representative and his service on two boards of regents acquainted him with the general operation of Nazarene colleges. But he was not, first of all, a scholar or a man of intellectual temperament. In that respect, he differed markedly from his predecessor.

In the first weeks of his presidency Pearsall repeatedly impressed laypersons and students as an approachable, warm, and encouraging leader. As new NNC presidents were prone to do, Pearsall went out on the Northwest zone to introduce himself and promote the college. Those initial meetings went well, with positive reports of the helpful gatherings and Pearsall's presentations trickling in to the campus. The honeymoon for the new president was in effect. It did not last long, however.

Within the year, snakes of controversy wriggled onto the Nampa campus. For one, new government regulations mandated equal treatment of men and women. These federal guidelines sparked fiery controversies that soon embroiled administrators, regents, students, faculty, and alumni—the whole matrix of the NNC community. But this imbroglio was much more than a verbal upheaval on campus and within the community; it was part and parcel of the sociocultural legacies of the United States in the 1960s and new issues that emerged during the next decade.

The rapid change and increasing diversity that characterized the Far Northwest in the 1960s continued to impact NNC and Nazarenes at large in the 1970s. New and returning students came to Nampa more aware of the social shifts in the U. S. that called for equal treatment of women and better conditions for minority groups. Nazarene young people proved to be out in front of their parents and church leaders in calling for institutional and educational innovations that would address the needs for these changes. Even though the lamentations of conservative laypersons that hippies and radicals had invaded the church campuses proved largely untrue, Nazarene students in the late 1960s and 1970s were more vocal and activist than they had been since World War II. Alongside these mounting social interests were other political, economic, and environmental concerns; the country saw the impeachment of a president, experienced the end of a military debacle in Vietnam, shared in mounting inflation at the end of the decade, and increasingly participated in moves to protect the environment. All these contested issues traveled to and spread out on the NNC campus. These pressures, and expanding student interest and participation in them, made Pearsall's administration far from placid in its early years.

New government regulations calling for equal opportunities for women engendered campus controversies over women's dorm hours. (Fig. 5.2)

Beginning in the fall of 1973, scarcely two months after Pearsall launched his presidency, a series of events stirred an extended controversy even while they illuminated interlocking federal, regional, and local influences on the NNC campus. In 1972 the U. S. Congress passed Title IX legislation, which stated bluntly: "No person in the U. S. shall, on the basis of sex, be excluded from participation in, or denied the benefits of, or be subjected to discrimination under any educational program or activity receiving federal aid." This landmark legislative expansion of civil rights codes in the country illustrated expanding federal guidelines for schools and colleges, especially those receiving federal aid for their students. Title IX would have a huge impact on educational policies and on athletics, illustrating advancements toward more equal treatment of the sexes, as well as racial and ethnic groups, and in other measures of the late 1960s and thereafter. These new federal guidelines worried some Nazarenes in the Pacific Northwest, as well as nationally; they often saw these changes as another dangerous government encroachment on personal and religious rights and standards.

Title IX, eventually, greatly impacted intercollegiate athletics on the NNC campus as well, encouraging a more full-fledged sports program for women. But in 1973 the new stipulations outlawing sexual discrimination first engendered dorm hour controversies at NNC. These conflicts erupted initially on campus and then exploded out on the college's educational zone. So contentious were the sometimes-angry reactions that President Pearsall might have wondered if his positive beginnings had not been transformed to a bed of hot coals through which he was being forced to stumble.

Kenneth Pearsall was an exceptionally positive man. He loved everybody and everything—his denomination and its leaders, pastoring and church administration, and serving his church. How shocking to him, then, when beginning in fall 1973 and increasing during the next two years the turmoil over dorm hours disrupted campus life, threw his relationships with NNC students into disarray, and stirred up discontent among the Board of Regents and NNC alumni. The explosive issue first appeared in the *Crusader*, as did much of the strongest campus criticism in the 1960s and 1970s.

Within a month after saluting Pearsall as an ideal NNC administrator, the *Crusader* carried stories flinging open the doors of controversy. Rather than stand by its promise to uphold the recently adopted "Bill of Rights and Responsibilities," one student wrote, the administration was curtailing rather than respecting women's rights in their dorms. Were administrators listening to the "female sector" of the campus, or was the "clamoring [sic]" of the "constituency" "so loud in your ears that it obscures our voice?" One month later another NNC coed, in a letter to the editor, complained of NNC's "adherence to a double standard." Treating women as a separate and inferior class and a compounding "overwhelming parentalism" at the college, she asserted, "can hardly be expected to facilitate Christian maturity in any student."

The dorm hours controversy heated up in the months stretching from spring of 1974 into fall of 1975. Students seemed convinced that NNC administrators were not listening to them, not heeding their urgent calls for changes in dorm hours, and not giving undergraduates more freedoms. One student wrote personally to the president, accusing him of muffling the controversy, of asking the Student Senate "not to talk to any member of the Board of Regents about the dorm hour's situation." When the regents met in fall 1974 they voted to retain the same dorm hours. As the campus debate on the issue continued red hot, Pearsall decided to back the regents' decision. Although the president said little about the issue, he was expressing himself to others in private. He told President Edward Mann of Eastern Nazarene that problems "had become too emotional" and would upset the college's recruitment plans, so he had sent an ultimatum to the director of student life at NNC, Irving Laird, "telling him that dormitory hours would remain the same."

The campus turmoil did not go away in the next year, but Pearsall took a different tack in handling the debate. Rather than speak out on dorm hours and federal influences on the contentious issue, the president backed away from speaking publicly in the college's publications. The *NNC Messenger* and the *Crusader* were largely devoid of Pearsall commentary on dorm hours. Behind the scenes, however, he agreed to meet more often with students, to listen to their desires and complaints. But in his personal correspondence he expressed himself even more forthrightly. On one occasion he complimented a college staff member on her observation about outspoken, activist students, especially as they expressed themselves in the student newspaper. "The last sentence of your memo was very well done," he told her. "Along with you, 'I am getting tired of these dumb "intelligent" kids and their rabble rousing.'" He admitted, too, to his predecessor that though the issue might have quieted down, it was still a "problem." "If we do not cooperate with the federal law [Title IX], we shall lose government assistance for our students."

True enough, the dorm hour dispute seemed to quiet down—only to be transformed into other campus contentions. These contested events from 1973 to 1975 reveal much about President Pearsall and the issues pressing in on him. An optimist, the president began to realize that "loving" his church, the campus, and his work was insufficient to solve these problems. He had to find other solutions. Although the general superintendents and most alumni respected and supported his steadfast stance on the unchanged dorm hours, he had not won over many students. Their reservations about his leadership soon surfaced in other traumatic issues, so much so that a handful of students questioned whether he should be the college president. Caught in the beleaguered center between church leaders and NNC alumni on one side and discontented students on the other, Pearsall made an important adjustment in his leadership style. He would continue to encourage students to find their complicated ways in their spiritual journeys, and he would urge them to remain devoted to God, but he would avoid taking public, up-front positions on controversial issues. He might explicitly express his opinions in private on these knotty issues but not in public. He would captain the NNC ship in a new, less confrontational manner in the next years.

Although the dorm hour quarrel sapped much of the president's time and energy, he kept the focus of the college on its motto "Seek Ye First the Kingdom of God." Through his own polished preaching on campus and out in districts and their churches, Pearsall was at his best. Even his critics usually admitted that Pearsall was a superb pulpiteer, while often disagreeing with the methods and content of his sermonizing. Pearsall was also convinced that chapel and special service speakers were vital in increasing the spiritual temperature on campus, so he was careful about which preachers, evangelists, and faculty he invited to speak on campus.

President Pearsall had learned much about preaching from G. B. Williamson and his wife Audrey Williamson. President of Eastern Nazarene College and later general superintendent of the Nazarene church, Williamson urged Pearsall to preach without notes. The president followed that method of delivery when speaking at NNC. Pearsall also credited Audrey Williamson, a college speech teacher, with showing him how to overcome his reluctance to speak before audiences. Even while yet an undergraduate at ENC, he took a church in New York City and traveled by train each weekend to preach his Sunday sermons. After nearly twenty years in the pastorate and several others as a district superintendent, Pearsall was a polished and persuasive preacher. Those strengths stood him in good stead as he represented NNC out across its sprawling educational zone.

Pearsall's sermons and his frequent writings in the *Messenger* reveal a good deal about his mind and religious commitments. In his conversations with denominational leaders and traditionalists among the NNC regents, Pearsall was encouraged to make NNC "more a Nazarene school." These advisors thought Riley, in his drive toward academic excellence and strength of faculty, might have allowed the college to veer away from its religious heritage. They wanted Pearsall to bring it back on course. A loyal and devoted Nazarene to the core, Pearsall set out to do just that. His commitment to what he believed the spiritual center of the college endeared him to many pastors, churches, and district superintendents; but faculty and students, especially, worried that he was trying to turn NNC into a church rather than a college.

Pearsall set the religious tone of his administration in his investiture sermon in early 1974. NNC needed another reminder of its origins and purpose. "We openly and without apology declare that we are a Christian college," he told his listeners. As a Christian college, NNC was committed to the marriage of mind and heart, to the union of "education and religion." He mentioned that American author Ralph Waldo Emerson had told his New England friend Henry David Thoreau that Harvard, begun as a Christian college, "taught all of the branches of learning." But, Thoreau replied, "Yes, all the branches but none of the roots." Pearsall strongly and persistently concluded "We must not forsake the 'roots.'" As the NNC community sought excellence, it must remember that "The Christian scholar is likely to be a better scholar because of his motivation. A good investigator wants to learn truth, if he can; but the committed Christian has an added motive in that his intellectual task is a sacred trust because it is God's truth that he is trying to learn." Quoting several Christian leaders and writers about the necessity and purposes of Christian education, Pearsall ended his investiture presentation with a celebration of NNC's motto. By seeking first the kingdom of God, NNC would become a "Kingdom College." That would be the goal of his presidency, and he diligently pursued that end throughout his administration.

The president's columns in the *Messenger* sent out from NNC to its alumni sounded similar strong notes. From the very beginning Pearsall told readers he was impressed with NNC and particularly rejoiced in hearing the students sing the college anthem, "Hallelujah, Amen," and their turning out in such numbers for the fall revival. He urged alumni to become devoted and enthusiastic recruiters for NNC. They should sell the college as a place "in which to prepare for life in its entirety." Their reward for this work: seeing students "high with a sense of HIS presence." At the end of his first presidential year, Pearsall quoted his life-shaping verse from Joshua 1: "As I was with Moses, so I will be with thee." Just as this scripture had been a lifetime sustaining promise for the president, so it could be for students and alumni.

No references to the early campus upsets made their way into the pages of the *Messenger*. Instead Pearsall chose to present the positive, urging professors, students, and alumni to do the same. The opening convention of 1974, for example, with evangelist Paul Martin was characterized as days of "love and unity," in which "many victories were won at the place of prayer." In those same days students were roundly criticizing the administration—and president—for what students considered their heads-in-the-sand reactions to dorm hours inequities and other student-generated suggestions for change.

In the early years of his presidency Pearsall continued his uplift pattern in plumping for the spiritual integrity at NNC. At the end of the 1976 school year he summarized his dreams for the college in the *Messenger*. Among these visions were his hopes that NNC would be a "catalyst to communicate Christ and holiness," keep "her [Christian] objectives clearly in view," remain "uniquely Nazarene," and that the "sun [would] never set" on the college. Moreover, as he told NNC supporters, there was "a danger that we shall develop the mind first and then the heart"; that tendency must be avoided. And, finally, the college must be "accountable for her stewardship." The president did not talk about what his critics pointed to as his shortsightedness: too much emphasis on religious matters, too little on academics, too much stress on balanced budgets, too little on expansion, including new programs and added faculty. Conversely, Pearsall's backers highly regarded this presentation, urging its publication.

In the second half of his presidency Pearsall wrote fewer articles for the *Messenger* and turned to subjects other than religious topics. In spring of 1980 he presented a report to the regents about the state of the college. Academics, finances, communications and development, and the physical plant—these topics and the mention of faith in relation to learning were his emphases. But not much on spiritual challenges on campus. Had the president concluded that explicit calls for adherence to Nazarene standards and lifestyle guidelines raised more student hackles than he wanted to arouse? Not by nature a confrontational leader or spokesman, Pearsall evidently preferred to avoid controversies in his writings and sermons.

NNC students were not chary, however, about expressing their distaste for or attraction to speakers who came on campus. If these often sharp comments appearing in the *Crusader* reflected widespread campus opinion, the views of NNC students were similar to the opinions of increasing numbers of Nazarene students across the movement. The newspaper scribes savaged several well-known Nazarene speakers. One of these was W. Donald Wellman, pastor of Denver First Church, among the largest churches in the entire denomination. In his opening convention chapel talk in spring 1975 Wellman pointedly criticized movies and "demanded" that students "return to church standards." According to the student report, Wellman "lambasted"

theater going as the "major moral problem in the Church of the Nazarene." "Mark it down," Wellman asserted, if Nazarenes did not restate and follow their anti-movie stance, "we won't have a stand to take in five years time."

Wellman's pugnacious approach did not play well on the NNC campus. Two of the *Crusader* editors took on the Colorado pastor. His chapel talk, they wrote, was "a rather pathetic and sorry display of Nazarene egotism." Wellman's "harangue...lacked credibility," particularly when he championed the Nazarenes (but not other evangelical churches) as "*the* Wesleyan church which will win the world." Moreover, they continued, his questionable use of statistics and other evidence "concerning the evils of attending the theater" made a "major issue out of something with little significance." Wellman and like-minded preachers and other leaders, the journalists concluded, allowed "no room for the individual within the Church of the Nazarene." Nazarenes must realize that their *Manual* was a series of guidelines for holy living and not irrefutable law; such realization, not narrow-minded legalism, would ensure "the future of the Nazarene Church."

If pastors became targets for harpooning, so did those in Nazarene leadership. When District Superintendent Hoyle Thomas appeared in chapel he delivered, according to one outspoken *Crusader* reporter, a "speech...full of historical inaccuracies, and...totally out of place." Dr. Thomas did not know his American history, the student wrote; he mislabeled some Founding Fathers as Christians who were Deists instead, and he misunderstood that Abraham Lincoln was more doubter than believer. The district superintendent also overlooked mentioning that Christians were guilty participants in the reprehensible dislocation of Indians in the move westward. Thomas seemed to believe, like the Rev. Jerry Fallwell, that the U. S. was the "greatest nation on earth, a special Christian nation, chosen by God." That was a dangerous notion that often led to intolerance, witch-hunts, and, perhaps, "a new McCarthyism, and imperialism," so the reporter thought. He was convinced, too, that "the last thing we need are nationalistic speeches filled with jingoism during a time that is set aside for learning about truth and love for one another—whoever he is...wherever he lives...."

The journalistic outbursts must have discomfited Pearsall. These sharp attacks were but three of the many that appeared in the student newspaper. And the criticisms targeted colleagues of Pearsall—a leading Nazarene pastor and a district superintendent, two positions Pearsall had held on his way to the NNC presidency. Whatever Pearsall thought about these examples of brash student journalism he kept to himself. Perhaps he was comforted by the positive reactions of students to other campus speakers on religious topics. There were plenty of these too.

The chapel speakers the students appreciated most were of four kinds: the intellectual preachers (e.g., Timothy Smith and Morris Weigelt), the personal "sharers" (Bob Benson), the talented and "open" pulpiteers (H. B. London and Kent

Dr. Timothy L. Smith, a noted Nazarene scholar and devoted preacher, encouraged and challenged the NNC student body. (Fig. 5.3)

Anderson), and those who pointed out how the gospel should include social dimensions (Tom Nees). During the 1960s and 1970s no major Nazarene speaker visited the NNC campus more often than Timothy L. Smith. Son of Nazarene pastors, ordained, a doctoral graduate of Harvard, he was a professor of history and education at the Johns Hopkins University. He had also authored a path breaking study of the shaping influences of evangelicals on social reform, *Revivalism and Social Reform in Mid-Nineteenth-Century America* (1957) and a superb history of the early Church of the Nazarene, *Called Unto Holiness* (1962). Smith embodied for many Nazarenes the balance of head and heart. He was an intellectual with a warm heart, devoted to the church, and open to all kinds of student questions. They took to him, the kind of person they wished to chat with, to discuss the big questions of their spiritual and academic lives without his shaking legalistic mandates or church rulebooks at them. As one student leader put it after Smith's spring 1979 presentations, "There have been few, if any, students who were not affected in some way....Our campus needed a tone of healing and love and he [Smith] provided an excellent platform to work from." The feeling was mutual, with Smith later praising NNC as "among the best... liberal arts colleges...in the United States." These remarks, first delivered at an international meeting of Christians and repeated at the Billy Graham Center at Wheaton College, gladdened the hearts of NNC administrators and other cheerleaders.

Morris Weigelt garnered similar positive reactions as a campus speaker. A graduate of NNC with his doctorate from Princeton, Weigelt taught at NNC for ten years before taking a position in 1975 with Nazarene Theological Seminary in Kansas City. When he returned to deliver the Staley Lectures, the popular professor, known for his "warmth, wit and wisdom," received an encouraging welcome. Weigelt "appreciated the spiritual openness of the campus" and sensed in his absence that NNC students were placing a greater reliance on faith based on reason rather than emotion." A *Crusader* columnist also praised Weigelt's "great sense of humor" and his "infectious enthusiasm for the scripture." In Morris Weigelt, NNC students found another model of the balance of mind and heart that so attracted them.

Other speakers such as Bob Benson came as "sharers," a warm, confessional approach to preaching that Reuben Welch, chaplain and professor at Pasadena College/Point Loma Nazarene College, made so popular among the Nazarenes from the 1960s onward. Students much appreciated speakers like Benson and Welch who seemed to "walk with them" rather than "preach at them." Benson, offspring of the well-known Benson Publishing Company family of Nashville, Tennessee, reminded listeners of Welch in his sharing, confessional approach. His low-key, informal presentations captivated and encouraged his audiences. The Fall Revival in 1978 with Benson was a "Quiet fall renewal," read a *Crusader* headline. NNC liked Benson, the reporter said, because he "created an attitude of mutual respect and caring" and his "chapel presentations seemed to reach the student body as a whole."

Two pastors from large Nazarene churches, H. B. London of Salem First and Kent Anderson from Eugene First, also drew raves from NNC reporters. In a memorable Friday chapel London gave students a paper "God Bag" and urged them to give their "impossible" problems to God. That encouragement, as well as London's "scholarly and professional manner," resonated with his listeners. "If we are fortunate," one journalist wrote, "other speakers of Rev. London's caliber will again grace our platform, adding to the spiritual dimension of our campus in a realistic and honest fashion." Equally impressive was the youthful, vibrant Kent Anderson in the Fall Revival of 1979. His sermons drew on his "personal testimony, marked by a sharing of the gospel and an invitation to all students to present themselves to God." In an enthusiastic editorial the *Crusader* editor stated that Anderson's "messages, his viewpoint, and his unique preaching style have made going to chapel five days in a row worth every minute spent." The sermons were so "uplifting and beneficial" that the editor wondered why many other chapel services and convocations were so disappointing. That question surfaced nearly every year of Pearsall's presidency.

Another speaker who impressed the NNC student body in 1975 was Tom Nees. A graduate of the college and a preacher, Nees had just resigned as pastor of Washington, D.C., First Church of the Nazarene to take leadership of a new urban ministry in the nation's capital, which became known as the Community of Hope. Nees's sermon hit home, telling Nampa students what they were hearing increasingly from evangelicals about addressing the social needs of the country. In adopting what was labeled a generation later as a "compassionate ministry" and a "missional" approach, Nees had examined his Wesleyan heritage and found that it provided the encouraging impetus to focus his attention and energies on the low income, homeless, illiterate, and medically needy in a downtrodden section of Washington, D.C. Nees's illuminating and supportive presentation was consonant with the social outreach desires of Nazarene students across the movement and

Dr. Morris Weigelt, NNC and Nazarene Theological Seminary professor, attracted students with his enthusiastic, warm-hearted preaching. (Fig. 5.4)

particularly apparent on the NNC campus during the 1970s.

The ambivalent reactions to still another speaker, Ann Kiemel, illustrated conflicting attitudes among NNC students vis-à-vis religious presentations. A pastor's daughter, an NNC alumna, a former youth worker, and now dean of women at Eastern Nazarene College, Ann had become a nationally known speaker. During Kiemel's talk in chapel, she received, according to one report, "the well deserved undivided attention of her audience and a standing ovation, supposedly for the significance of her message." The *Crusader* devoted an unprecedented four to five full pages to a positive interview with and photos of Kiemel. Most of the student body embraced Kiemel enthusiastically and gave her the attention of an evangelical star. But there were questions too: one writer wondered if the primary response to her talk wasn't "one of emotionalism" and questioned the depth of that response. Another doubting letter-writer thought, and claimed "several on campus" felt the same way, that Ann and other ministers "played on emotions to lead souls to the Lord, in my opinion a bit too much." Undoubtedly the question-askers were too critical of Kiemel, but they illustrated the increasing dissatisfaction of college students, including students at NNC, with answers from speakers and college leaders that, to them, seemed too pat—and perhaps a bit dated.

The varied and sometimes conflicting reactions to these religious presentations on the NNC campus vivified the complex, shifting attitudes of many Nazarenes in the 1970s. For most students, the intellectual speakers with warm hearts utilizing a confessional mode of presentation went over best. The more assertive, authoritative preachers often alienated students, and they seemed unsure about speakers who invoked emotions and, they thought, seemed light on content.

Revealingly, the theological upsets that later convulsed campus and district Nazarenes from the 1990s onward were almost nonexistent during Pearsall's presidency. Perhaps for three reasons. President Pearsall, unlike Wiley and DeLong among his predecessors, remained isolated from such discussions. Like a loyal pastor and district superintendent he followed the suggestions of general superintendents and boosted general Nazarene policies. Nor did the religion faculty raise the hackles of constituents. Although good scholars, Elwood Sanner, Morris Weigelt, Dan Berg, and Ralph Neil, for example, did not participate much in the theological frays of the time. In addition, most of the campus visitors giving religious presentations were not outspoken revisionists. Although Mildred Bangs Wynkoop's *A Theology of Love* (1972) would become a widely discussed new look at holiness thinking, it did not engender, at first, extensive discussion on the NNC campus. No one was saying much, either, about the creationist and scriptural interpretation differences that would in the next generation catch fire across the NNC zone and burn through the college campus. Students saved most of their criticism for campus guidelines, associating them with what they thought to be an out-of-date church in these areas. Ironically, two or three of the most gifted student thinkers of the 1970s would be embroiled in theological contentions from 1990 onward.

In another area, the raising of funds and balancing budgets, President Pearsall experienced great success. In the opening months of his administration and throughout his decade in office, Pearsall embraced one of the two approaches Nazarenes often employed in fund-raising. Tensions between the two methods had vexed the church for several decades. Ever the cautious conservative in financial matters, Pearsall believed that budgets should not be based on dreams of the future but tied to here-and-now, solid, present-day giving. The previous president epitomized the other method: plan for the future, dream of budget-stretching plateaus and missions, and then encourage NNC supporters to dig deeper and pay for these expenses over and above normal educational budgets. Whereas Pearsall hesitated to launch new calls for capital funds to erect new buildings and programs, John Riley sponsored them. Pearsall joyed in keeping each year in the black, but Riley had willingly faced red ink to fund needed expansion. In a few subtle but direct words Riley expressed his differences with his successor's fund-raising policies: "After the years of capital funds appeals for construction during the sixties, some church leaders developed something of a reaction. However, this meant that when the two housing units were built [the Olsen and Corlett apartments], it became necessary to borrow all the money for construction and at very high current interest rates. In the eighties the impact of high cost borrowing eventually awakened the Board to the need for capital appeals programs."

The center pivots of Pearsall's economic planning and strategy were to encourage churches on the educational zone to pay their educational budgets in full and to recruit larger numbers of students for the college. He believed that if he forged warm connections with pastors, churches, and their districts, they would support NNC financially and send their daughters and sons to Nampa. For the most part he achieved both of these goals. Those were the more demanding parts of his economic design. Other goals demanded less of the president: keeping a ceiling on campus expenses, not hiring additional faculty, not greatly expanding a needy library, and not launching new programs. These he managed expeditiously. Two very dependable and fiscally conservative business administrators, Howard Miller and Galen Olsen, were also exceptionally helpful in keeping NNC in the black.

The architecture of the president's economic plan was clarified in letters he wrote in early fall 1974. He urged his fellow administrators, who were soon to visit district pastors' and lay retreats, to stress "that we are very positive and optimistic about the future of NNC. At this time we do not share negative and pessimistic feelings about the work of our college [e.g. controversies over dorm hours and the upsetting content of the *Crusader*]." Play up the fall revival with evangelist Paul Martin and the Heritage Day presentation by leading layman Gordon Olsen, he told them. They ought also to mention that "we operated in the black for the fourth year in a row." Three districts on the zone had paid their budgets in full, and this "wonderful cooperation" meant a 21 percent jump in giving during the past year, allowing for 7.7 percent faculty and 8.3 percent staff raises. In addition they were to "do everything possible to urge our Nazarene young people to spend at least one year on the campus of NNC. PLEASE EMPHASIZE THIS." Finally the NNC envoys should tell the districts that the college would soon put in place a plan to raise a $5 million endowment for the institution, something NNC had not yet achieved.

A few weeks later the president prepared a special presentation for a lay retreat on the Colorado District. Pearsall and his successor Gordon Wetmore paid special attention to this district because Colorado, recently transferred to the NNC zone, seemed reluctant to support the college with its dollars and its students. Nazarene college graduates in the state were remembering their times at Pasadena, Bethany, or elsewhere and were neither quick nor enthusiastic about switching their loyalties to NNC. So in his talk to the Colorado Nazarenes, Pearsall practiced what he preached to others. His page and a half of notes were a litany of successes and positive descriptions. He endeavored to link these hesitant Colorado Nazarenes to a campus in faraway Idaho that many did not know. He closed his presentation with two upbeat clinchers. "Some of our finest students come to us from Colorado. Let me appoint you as unofficial recruiters for NNC," and "Last year three districts made it to 100 % [of their educational budget payment]. We are hoping that Colorado will do it this next year."

Pearsall's financial plan changed very little in the next few years. Most of all he wanted to avoid alienating persons who might cooperate financially with the college. That meant smiling one's way through some frowning times. In the midst of obvious tensions over the dorm hours issue Pearsall wrote to Riley, summarizing, briefly and explicitly, his blueprint for funding the college. The Nazarene Church needed colleges, and the schools had to have the church, he told Riley. This mutually supportive system, Pearsall was certain, embodied "a superior method [of raising funds] that is the envy of other Christian colleges and denominations. I hope that we shall never be forced to return to the summer pledging campaigns for capital improvements. While this plan served well at that time, our systematic and uniform plan is far better." Surely Pearsall failed to realize that he was writing to the prince of year-round campaigns for capital improvements who clearly thought that method of raising funds superior to other systems.

Pearsall's plans worked well until unexpected changes shook his economic edifice. Inflation rates soared following the end of the costly Vietnam War and the upsetting resignation of President Nixon in the mid-1970s. As Pearsall wrote in another letter in 1975 updating Riley, then teaching in Africa, the president and the Board of Regents hoped "to recommend a small salary increase for faculty and staff. It will perhaps have to be conditional," Pearsall cautioned, "since the economic picture is very uncertain at this time." If enrollment stayed at "a minimum" of 1,000 students and if the churches "continue[d] to cooperate" in paying their full educational budgets, "we can grant the raise." In spite of the uncertain times—"high inflation, the poor economic conditions and the unemployment"—the college was giving out to the media a picture of "optimism and excitement" because "we are very positive about the work of this school."

One of the unplanned-for challenges occurred in dealing with the athletics program of the college. The Title IX legislation that helped ignite the firestorm over dorm hours called for gender equality in sports programs. Once the implications of the new law were understood, the college moved rather quickly to begin planning for women's intercollegiate sports. A strong women's intramural program was already in place, and NNC women's teams had, informally, played competitors from other colleges. In the winter of 1973-74 Pearsall, other administrators, and the Physical Education Department worked diligently to project athletic expenses for the 1974-75 year. The slightly more than $21,000 expended for intercollegiate sports in 1973-74 (minus salaries) would be upped to roughly $25,000 for the next years, including $2,000 for all women's extramural athletics. Expenses for men's basketball (varsity and junior varsity) were bumped up $100 to $9,200. Nearly half of the budget went for travel, food, and lodging, and only $400 was set aside in 1974-75 for recruiting in all sports. New coaches and additional staff members needed to be hired and faculty teaching and coaching loads worked out to implement this expanded sports program. Fortunately for athletes and coaches, President Pearsall, a former athlete (once drafted as a professional baseball pitcher) and an avid sports fan, strongly supported these measures. If reading and academic programs were Riley's avocation and major emphases, sports and physical activity ranked high on Pearsall's interest list.

Housing for an expanding student body became an even more pressing economic issue toward the end of Pearsall's administration. In fall 1979 the college announced an all-time high enrollment of 1,332, nearly 100 students above the previous high in 1977. Two years later in 1981 registration hit an all-time high for traditional student enrollment of 1,353. Although the burgeoning enrollments brought sunshine and smiles to the business office and budget makers, they placed new dilemmas on the shoulders of campus housing officials. At first, upper-division students were allowed to live off campus in nearby apartments, an upsetting and unprotected situation that the college had usually frowned upon as very unsatisfactory. Finally, after increased, persisting needs for on-campus housing continued from the mid-1970s onward, the Olsen (1977) and Corlett (1980) apartments were erected.

In some ways the Pearsall economic plan had been so successful in the short run that it backfired in a longer view. True, churches paid their educational budgets at a higher level, and they supported the president's endowment plan. They were also sending their sons and daughters to Nampa in increasing numbers. But this plan had not made sufficient space for the successes it spawned. The expanding student body quickly outgrew available campus housing, and the administration and regents, hesitant to dream and plan ahead, were forced to borrow expensive funds rather than having set aside sufficient monies for the needed housing expansion.

In still another area Pearsall's economic outlook, and perhaps that of other administrators and the regents, did not sufficiently plan for the future. The president's modus operandi did not pay enough attention to a possible expansion of the NNC professoriate. Although the student body grew about 25 to 30 percent between 1973-74 and 1981-82, the number of faculty members did not expand accordingly. At the end of Riley's presidency, 75 faculty members were listed in the NNC catalog, but 82 at the close of Pearsall's administration, an expansion of only 8.5 percent. This modest increase in faculty numbers, in light of the strong jump in enrollments, frustrated academics, professors and scholarly students alike, yet it provided a fiscally sound 16.5 : 1 student : faculty ratio.

Pearsall had even larger problems with the academic mission of the college. If his strong, warm connections with pastors and churches out on the NNC educational zone and his diligent efforts to raise funds, increase enrollment, and balance the college's budget were his strengths as a college administrator, his role as an academic leader displayed fewer large achievements. Save for J. G. Morrison, Pearsall was the least academically trained of the NNC presidents to his time. Still, to his credit Pearsall never claimed to be an academic leader. For the most part he left academic discussions to others, relying heavily on their suggestions in making his executive decisions. Other NNC administrators, divisional or department chairs, and individual faculty members were the major sources of frequent advice. On more than a few occasions Pearsall told the NNC faculty—some thought too often—that he was not primarily an academic leader. Sometimes the faculty was clearly frustrated with what they considered Pearsall's inadequate academic leadership.

Dr. Gilbert Ford reluctantly became an NNC academic dean and served for nearly fifteen years. (Fig. 5.5)

The paucity of the president's academic comments led some to believe that he lacked a plan for NNC's academic mission. It is true that he infrequently made public statements about academic matters. In his speeches, interviews, and comments in issues of the *Messenger* he referred only glancingly to the faculty and academics. Instead, the president chose to rely heavily on Gilbert Ford for academic advice and guidance. At the outset that seemed a wise decision. Ford was already the college's chief academic officer, had been on the NNC faculty for more than twenty years when Pearsall came into office, and had the clear respect of his colleagues as a scholar and supporter of the college. Even though Ford took the position rather reluctantly when Thelma Culver retired as dean in 1970, he had worked well with Riley, and the future looked good for his continued academic leadership under Pearsall.

But Pearsall was not Riley, and that difference impacted the character of Ford's leadership. During Riley's last years he remained in the control room for operating the college's academic program; when Pearsall took over the college controls, he allowed Ford and others to manage academics. That meant Ford had to become the dreamer and planner that Riley had been. Unfortunately, that did not happen. A cautious, balanced man, Ford found it difficult if not impossible to fly into a hazy and indistinct future. As one of Ford's long-time colleagues pointed out, Ford was not so much an academic leader as a manager. Thus the academic program in Pearsall's years, though student enrollments expanded nearly 30 percent and church giving rose, remained in a somewhat steady state. Pearsall and Ford, both rather managerial in their tendencies, were reluctant to launch new or expand in-place academic programs. For example, the college's historians had difficulty talking Pearsall into hiring a political scientist, the English Department needed additional faculty, especially with completed doctorates, the innovative Non-Western studies program (widely touted in the Riley era) died without strong support, and the library holdings languished.

Ford's reluctance to move into new territory became particularly clear in his reactions to calls for extension or off-site course offerings. Several pastors, district superintendents, and even laypersons encouraged NNC to provide courses out on the zone for preachers and other interested students. Although such programs, as well as online courses, would become a central part of NNC's academic outreach in the 1990s and afterwards, Ford and President Pearsall did not favor these expansions in the 1970s.

Perhaps Ford's work with accreditation committees in the Pacific Northwest brought about his hesitancies. In a three-page, single-spaced answer to a Yakima pastor's asking for NNC courses to be offered in that city, Ford enumerated the reasons that he "personally ...[had] serious reservations about offering college credit courses at sites away from our main campus...." For one, the Northwest Association of Schools and Colleges closely watched such offerings because they often were less satisfactory than those given on campus. Such courses were expensive, Ford continued; it was difficult to arrange for strong faculty for them, and needed library support was sometimes unavailable. President Pearsall reiterated similar reservations (quoting Ford when he did so) in answering an inquiring district superintendent who wanted continuing education courses for his pastors. Although "we have had requests from several different states on our zone to offer a satellite program," Pearsall told the district leader, "we have hesitated to have any." The president urged the superintendent to send a proposal to Ford for such a program and expressed his hope the district wouldn't go to the Nazarene Bible School or seminary for professors, but he offered little or no encouragement for the extension courses in Oregon. In another overture, when two very loyal NNC laymen proposed an endowment plan to support worthy NNC professors, the president was willing to consider a proposal for such support, but he was not very encouraging of this innovative offer, and nothing came of it.

Pearsall also differed from his predecessor in his reactions to grumblers who wrote in to criticize the controversial books professors were assigning. Riley protected his faculty in these matters, often directly, sometimes bluntly. On some occasions he even wrote to critics to defend professors without bothering faculty with the petty issues. But Pearsall asked divisional or departmental chairs to respond to the letter-writers rather than to answer himself. Undoubtedly in building positive relations with Nazarenes out on the zone, and particularly with NNC alumni, this decision to have others answer complaints was a wise diplomatic decision for the president. But it probably heightened faculty discontent with Pearsall, which grew during his presidency.

Not surprisingly, discontents often attacked assigned books in literature courses. "One of the English proffesors [sic] at N. N. C.," wrote a Colorado pastor, assigned an anthology of short stories that was "trash reading...pure pornography." Upset with the reading assignment, he wrote to Marian Washburn, a thirty-year veteran in the NNC English Department and to President Pearsall about this "questionable material." The collection was so bad, the pastor was told, that the instructor had "admonished the students not to report it to their parents or pastors."

Professor Washburn answered the pastor, the president did not. After examining the controversial stories that the instructor Gaymon Bennett had assigned, Washburn agreed with Professor Bennett's decision not to use the book again. Although the class syllabus had warned students that these were the stories of "angry, frustrated, and hopeless young writers," Bennett did not think them more "offensive...than truth ever seems." Still, if students were "offended," they were requested, Bennett pointed out, to "come talk to me." Miss Washburn assured the Colorado pastor that "such material has no place at N. N. C." She and Bennett would be even more careful about future assignments.

A few weeks later an Oregon layman wrote to President Pearsall about another book, James Michener's *Sayonara*, assigned in a course of Japanese literature. "This book uses God's name in vain," "makes light of the name of Jesus," and "makes much of living in adultery." "Is there some reason for requiring this cheap reading," the layman wanted to know. "I cannot find it in my heart to support our school any longer," he warned, "if this is an example of what we are teaching." In reply President Pearsall wrote that he had handed on the letter to Marian Washburn to answer; she "is in a much better position to comment" on the questions raised. Professor Washburn explained to the gentleman that Helen Wilson, the instructor, had begun her class with an explanation of Japanese culture, including its rather "earthy" explorations of sexuality. If missionaries were to understand and communicate with Japanese people, Washburn and Wilson noted, they would need to understand Japanese sociocultural experiences and perspectives, even if these viewpoints were non-Christian. In general, Washburn concluded, NNC sometimes assigned books that were not evangelical in their orientation because Nazarene students needed to have realistic exposure to world cultures and yet "rightfully divide the word of truth."

On more than a few occasions, often controversial in content, students and faculty members commented on Pearsall as an academic leader. Some with sufficient background realized that unlike earlier presidents H. Orton Wiley, Russell V. DeLong, and John E. Riley, Pearsall was not primarily an academic. Although his speeches, sermons, and personal letters indicated a very literate man who read in varied sources, he was a derivative rather than innovative thinker. In that tendency he resembled two other NNC presidents, Lewis T. Corlett and Gordon Wetmore.

The timber of his mind probably was less important for most pastors and Nazarene laypersons, but for some faculty and academically inclined students Pearsall seemed an ineffectual scholarly leader. The president and his supporters must have winced in early 1979 when Sonja Cady, perhaps the most outspoken *Crusader* editor during his decade-long presidency, wrote a very critical editorial about Pearsall and what she considered his inadequate academic leadership.

Cady's editorial was a hard-hitting, explicit, and negative portrait of Pearsall. She compared the NNC president unfavorably with David McKenna, the president of Seattle Pacific College, who had just been on campus to deliver the Riley Intellectual Life Series lectures. Hearing McKenna speak, Cady opined, forced one to observe "the obvious lacking in our own president and other members of the NNC administration." It was "high time," she added, that Nazarene colleges, supposed institutions of "higher learning," recognized "that pastors do not necessarily make good college presidents. For too long, NNC has been without leadership in its top position strictly as a result of such an unfortunate misconception." What made it worse, Cady continued, no one on the campus was acknowledging "the inability of its president to administrate and to lead the college...for fear of losing jobs or being branded divisive or troublemaking."

In a matter of hours the student publications committee (made up of nine students, one faculty, and one administrator) met and passed a resolution to fire Cady. The resolution did not stand, but a stiff reprimand appeared in the next issue of the *Crusader,* accusing the editor of "irresponsible and ill-advised methods of journalism." Soon, the Boise *Idaho Daily Statesman* carried two articles about what it considered NNC's failure to protect freedom of speech. One of the stories, titled "Off with Sonja's Head," went even farther, pointing the finger of blame at the college administration and its false "view of dissent as an evil that must be eliminated." The *Statesman* countered that Cady's points were "well-made and well taken"; it saluted the "courage and integrity" of her actions.

Sonja Cady, editor of the campus newspaper The Crusader, *stirred up a controversy with her criticism of the NNC president. (Fig. 5.6)*

Although defending her own actions, Cady avoided further controversy until the end of the semester. In her final issue, however, she penned another editorial, which, among other things, provided backgrounds for her earlier controversial piece on President Pearsall. Cady related that just before and after Christmas break of 1979 "a number of faculty members and students expressed to me their perception of a difficulty with the lack of academic growth at NNC....At least ten members of the teaching staff confided in me their concern about the lack of leadership at the top of the system at NNC. It was a problem they felt was common to the Nazarene denomination."

How dead center were Cady's perspectives on faculty opinions about their president? Was the rumor of an impending faculty revolt during his administration nothing but hearsay or of considerable substance? The available evidence is insufficient for a definitive answer, but perhaps the comments of two long-time NNC faculty members and later administrators lift the veil, even if only slightly, on the incipient conflict. The soft-hearted Gilbert Ford, Pearsall's fellow administrator in 1979, observed nearly thirty years later that Pearsall was a diligent and commendable preacher who had difficulty understanding the faculty. Darrell Marks, who devoted nearly a half-century to NNC/NNU as professor, administrator, and volunteer, provided another illuminating perspective. In Marks's view, Pearsall and his successor Gordon Wetmore came to NNC with valuable experiences as pastors and a district superintendent, but they had not been faculty members. If the two presidents had realized that faculty wanted to be heard but not necessarily always heeded, Marks pointed out, they could have gained more loyalty and admiration from NNC professors. Unfortunately, this lack of understanding of preachers and district superintendents for college faculty was denominationally wide, not just at NNC.

Had too much been made of Pearsall's alleged shortcomings as an academic leader? Despite all the academic challenges whirling about NNC under his watch, several long-time faculty were hired who devoted twenty or more years of strong service to the college. Ralph and Lynn Neil came to the religion and English departments, he to provide balance and fairness to classroom and department, she to add clear strength to the college's writing program and to head up a time-consuming reaccreditation process. Wendell Bowes, Edwin Crawford, and Dan Berg also joined the religion department and Kevin Dennis and Daryl Wenner the English department. Janet Harman and Ernie Thompson became mainstays in education, Newell Morgan in Spanish, and Walden Hughes in music. Eventually Ralph Neil and Dan Berg would serve as divisional or college-wide deans

These were good times, too, for the scientists, mathematicians, and some areas of the social sciences. Leon Powers and William Fyffe came in biology and David Redfield in chemistry. Joining in mathematics were Gary Ganske and Kenneth Yoder. Ronald Ponsford arrived in psychology, Steve Shaw in political science, Dennis Waller in communication studies, and Jerry Hull in social work. Hull, Ponsford, and Shaw would also become administrators or divisional deans.

Kenneth Pearsall occupied the president's chair in the longest period of sustained student activism in the history of the college. On many other college campuses, student rebellion apexed and then declined before 1973. At NNC, however, student discontent reached one early high in the late 1960s and another from roughly 1973 through the decade. The voices of strident student activists were often like a Vivaldi concerto, bold and brassy. Those viewpoints and subsequent actions both enriched and frustrated—sometimes even angered—NNC administrators in the 1970s and early 1980s.

No issue exhibited student-administration tensions more clearly than controversies over the *Crusader*. At the same time, no campus source provided more information to students and furnished an outlet for their varied points of view. Part of the discord arose out of differing perspectives on the newspaper's chief purpose. Students, especially those on the *Crusader* staff, considered it a student newspaper, the voice of the student body. College administrators and faculty tried to inform laypersons critical of the periodical's content that it was not a public relations medium for NNC. Nonetheless dozens of letters each year attacked the *Crusader*. Rocky Mountain District Superintendent Ross Price told the president that the "erratic and scurrilous articles" in the *Crusader* "have hindered budget payments considerably. And if any budget is neglected it is always the Educational Budget first." Price and other critics wondered why the college administration allowed publication of a student paper that so roundly criticized NNC, particularly administrative actions.

The tone of the *Crusader* usually reflected the outlook of its annual editor. As we have seen, Sonja Cady, a talented and outspoken editor, harpooned the president in 1979. Jay Vail, named editor in 1976, lasted but a few days in the position before resigning after irreconcilable conflicts between his and administrative guidelines for the paper. Steve Arnold and Elizabeth Martin were also activist editors, with sharp views. But Del Gray and Will Merkel were more moderate in their editorship, avoiding harsh criticisms in their editorials or strident stories written by others.

Often a single topic, appearing in the first fall issues of the student newspaper, dominated its pages in that school year. In 1973 and 1974 dorm hours debates stood out in the *Crusader*. In 1979 and 1980, after a rumored sexual assault on campus, articles on rape and sexual violence were frequent. In the same years several stories in the newspaper focused on visitation rights, coed dorms, and students' sexual maturity as decisions were being made about student life in the new Olsen and Corlett apartments. Indeed, more than a few essays in the *Crusader*, often sparked by chapel presentations, dealt with sexual subjects, including two or three on the previously verboten topic of abortion.

Obviously NNC administrators and the publications board in charge of setting policy for the *Crusader* pondered often how to handle this perennially hot issue. Sometimes they asked editors to tone down their criticisms, to be less negative, and to cease printing controversial advertisements. Over time President Pearsall changed his way of handling the *Crusader*. At the outset he hoped the newspaper would speak for the students but not attack his leadership or the college's actions. When that hope was not realized, he gradually withdrew from the issue, allowing others to deal with it. When pressed in 1978 to help reform the newspaper, he upset the newspaper staff by revealing he did not read the *Crusader*. That revelation set off another round of criticism of the president. Throughout Pearsall's presidency the *Crusader* and its pointed coverage of the college and church remained a contested issue. The newspaper continued as an outspoken mouthpiece of student opinions, often alienating administrative and constituency persons. Student freedom of speech and administrative guidelines for responsible actions wobbled in the crosshairs of conflict.

Other discussions, sometimes heated and barbed, appeared in the *Crusader*. The campus was in turmoil, as was the general church, over the issues of movies and dances in the 1970s and 1980s. Attendance at movies and dances had been forbidden in the Nazarene *Manual* from 1908 onward. But in the 1960s college students and increasing numbers of laypersons were not adhering to those guidelines, sometimes trafficking in those entertainments, sometimes calling for their elision from church guidelines.

During the Riley years, Hollywood-made films were occasionally shown on campus. Usually they were previewed or acts of censorship were carried out during their showings. When Pearsall took over the presidency one district superintendent vehemently called for the end of movie showing on campus. The showings did not stop, and some pointedly referred to the "Circle Drive Theater on campus," but those screened were often censored while being shown, a measure eliciting several sharp criticisms in the *Crusader*. Such censorship, a letter-writer argued in 1974, was "an obscene insult" to movies. Some way or another NNC censors wanted to make "reality vanish." Was the administration feeling the pressure of conservative constituents and mistakenly thinking they could achieve holiness by cutting out swear words in a movie? A generation later in 1997 when the church officially dropped its stance against movie attendance, it had become a nonissue on campus. By that time for most Nazarene young people movies were not a dangerous or evil entertainment despite the church's ongoing criticism of them.

In the Pearsall period the flap over dancing persisted. The front page of the March 5, 1976, issue of the *Crusader* reported that thirty-five students were to receive a letter of "warning and reprimand" for attending a dance at the Breakers West club in Boise. It was rumored that President Pearsall favored a more stringent form of discipline for breaking the college's "no-dancing rule," but instead reprimand letters couched in "strong language" were sent to the students. Two years later newspaper editor Stephen Hauge commented negatively on the Special Rules section of the Nazarene *Manual* forbidding dancing because it, ostensibly, broke "down proper reserve between the sexes which leads to nothing less than promiscuity and fornication." That false conclusion, the editor argued, cast a "pessimistic shadow on the strength and sincerity of our fellow brothers and sisters on campus that have to be watched and regulated to ensure their continuation here at NNC." Instead, Hauge urged other students, if they felt comfortable about making their own behavioral decisions, to express themselves on the dancing issue. "Change must come from within," he concluded, "and you, the Nazarene student, have just as much right to input as your college Administration." But neither NNC nor general church leaders were ready to accept this perspective; the dancing issue would remain an ongoing campus controversy for another generation.

Other student activities raised no controversies and often replicated those of earlier NNCers, even of parents and a scattering of grandparents. Music groups and their presentations remained newsworthy on campus and out on the NNC zone. Concerts by individual performers, men and women's groups, the college music faculty, and the Crusader Choir filled many paragraphs and pages of the *Crusader* and *Messenger*. But commencing in the Riley years and continuing during the entire Pearsall period, the Northwesterners, a very select group of singers under the able and enthusiastic directorship of Dr. Double E Hill, became the premier music group of NNC. They even surpassed in notice and acceptance the summer traveling groups, which had dominated publicity efforts of the college since its inception. Gaining a first-rank reputation as performers, the Northwesterners became a USO-sponsored group, traveling to Asia, Europe, and elsewhere. A visiting Colorado layman bringing a car load of young people to NNC senior days, spoke for many when he told the president that he wished "to commend Dr. Hill for the type of good music and good fun by the Northwesterners, this is the standard I can heartily endorse." At the same time Dr. Jim Willis put together a small jazz ensemble, The Hallelujah Brass, which also entertained and drew audiences around the country and abroad.

Meanwhile, securing well-known vocalists and other musical groups willing to travel to Nampa and appealing to college-age students was not an easy assignment. Student officers tried to bring high quality and popular performers to campus, but to do so meant ladling out large amounts of student body fees, charging a high price for tickets, or both. Even then, funders were challenged because NNC was an out-of-the-way venue with higher transportation costs than for performances on the West Coast. Sometimes college students were frustrated when administrators disallowed invitations to popular but secular rock musical groups.

Intramural and intercollegiate sports programs likewise continued to capture hundreds of campus participants. A panoply of speech, dramatic, musical, and athletic activities were available to NNCers through their Athletic-Literary societies. But change loomed too. More students had their own cars and were escaping campus for social activities, and the expansion of intercollegiate sports diminished the number of participants available for intramurals. Even college departments seemed reluctant to support intramurals if those activities threatened the viability of their own programs.

Dr. Martha Hopkins and Jean Horwood directed increasingly strong women's athletic programs. (Fig. 5.7)

Intercollegiate sports programs captured the most attention. The *Messenger* and *Crusader,* chiefly, overflowed with news of NNC teams and their competitors. With the start up of women's intercollegiate sports under the inspirational coaching of Martha Hopkins and Jean Horwood, the sports pages were even more replete with news of teams. These two coaches quickly led NNC women's teams to notable status among competitors in the Pacific Northwest.

The men's basketball team continued to capture the lion's share of attention, however. When pressure from discontented alumni forced out long-time basketball coach Orin Hills, former NNC basketball player Ray Burwick came for one year before going elsewhere. His replacement was Terry Layton, a young, energetic coach and a first-rate recruiter and plumper for much bigger things for the men's round ballers. In early fall 1979, the ambitious young coach told NNC administrators that he was working hard "to make our program the best small college basketball program in the northwest." Sometimes Layton was a bit gung-ho, even for a sports fan president. When the coach pointed out the large discrepancies between NNC's financial backing for athletics and much larger funding for Boise State and other nearby teams, he lost support. Finding that he was unable to gain this added funding for his ambitious plans, Layton took another job, although on two or three later occasions he reapplied for openings at NNC.

On a handful of occasions NNC sports have featured nationally recognized athletes. In the early 1960s Gary Locke had been that for men's basketball; in the 1970s Steve Hills became another for the track team. The son of Coach Orrin Hills and

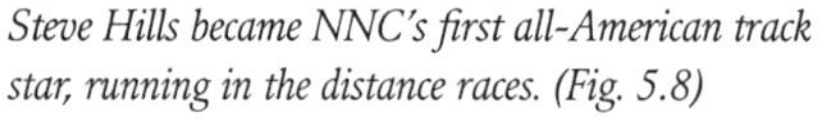

Steve Hills became NNC's first all-American track star, running in the distance races. (Fig. 5.8)

Antonette Blythe was also a superb trackster, winning a national championship in the long jump. (Fig. 5.9)

following in the steps of an older brother Lynn, Steve lowered his distance times in his years at NNC. In the spring of 1975 he became "the first full-bodied All-American...from NNC" with a 4:05:3 mile in the national NAIA meet. "It was just kind of a dream," Hills told a campus reporter after his sterling performance. Three years later in spring 1978, Hills garnered another All-American honor by winning the 1500 meters race at the national NAIA championship. In 1981 Antonnette Blythe, also a superb track star, won a national championship in the long jump, as well as performing superbly in other events.

During the 1970s, following nation-wide trends as well as those in the Church of the Nazarene, students at NNC became less and less insular in their worldviews, more inclined to see and react to national and even global events and ideas. The expanding student outlook expressed itself in several ways. Politics and political activities became more important to NNCers as local and nationally known figures came to campus, spoke, took part in campus discussions, and were interviewed. Frank Church, Idaho's senior senator, and his rival Steve Symms were among the political visitors. A periodic column "Washington Scene" and another, "Soapbox," appeared in the *Crusader*, and so did numerous other stories about national political events. Political opinions on campus seemed more balanced, too, than they had been. In a preferential straw ballot in spring 1980, about two-thirds of students indicated a preference for the Republicans, one-third for the Democrats. But the presidential race was much closer—Ronald Reagan with 49.4 percent and Jimmy Carter with 47.1 percent. This near balance between conservative and progressive voters diverged markedly from earlier student votes that often gave Republican candidates 80 to 90 percent—or more—of student support.

Student backing was especially enthusiastic and widespread for a widening of Nazarene mission programs—in the Pacific Northwest, across the country, and throughout the world. A remarkable shift that began in the late 1960s continued—and even expanded—in the 1970s. Many Nazarene young people were dissatisfied with earlier definitions of denominational missions and pushed for new kinds of domestic and foreign outreach programs. Soon after President John F. Kennedy asked American youth to think about what they could do for their country rather than for themselves, Nazarene college students were calling for programs to serve others. They promoted programs to help on mission fields, especially in Africa, Latin America, and Asia; to aid the poor and literacy-challenged peoples of the U.S. and elsewhere; and to tutor and encourage children and adolescents falling behind in their schooling. Several of these proposals became part of a very successful, denomination-wide Youth in Mission program.

Simultaneously the general church began to undertake similar efforts labeled Work and Witness, sending laypersons to help needy missions, churches, and the world's less fortunate. At least a generation before the word came into general use, college students from NNC were in the vanguard of what became known as a "missional" approach to ministry. This shift was path breaking in redefining the long-range goals of NNC. In the 1970s and early 1980s NNC students were helping to incorporate a third core value—missional outreach—into its earlier partnership of spiritual journey and academic excellence. This impulse would remain at the center of the college's identity throughout the coming decades.

When President Pearsall announced his retirement in late 1982, his supporters on campus and out on the zone—and they were clearly in the majority—spoke of him as an encouraging and good president. They saluted his positive spirit, his strong preaching, his superb work with pastors and district superintendents, and his careful financial leadership leading to balanced budgets. On the other hand, neither they nor he said much about student or faculty discontents during his administration. Nor did his backers note his seeming satisfaction with a solid, status quo administration rather than an ambitious, forward-looking one building on increasing enrollments and solid district giving. Perhaps after the strain of keeping up with the energetic and expansive Riley, the NNC constituency wanted to catch its breath and embrace a less demanding leader. More than one observer thought Pearsall connected better than Riley with Nazarenes of the NNC educational zone. In addition, the differences between Riley and Pearsall—and to some extent the next president—illustrated the cycles in NNC leadership. Periods of relaxation and even-state often followed expansive and stressful periods. After the pioneering work of Wiley and the driven leadership of DeLong, NNC seemed satisfied with the custodial, less frenetic administration of Corlett. The nearly two decades following Riley were also, largely, a respite from his strong but exacting leadership.

Even before Pearsall cleared out his office, his successor had been chosen and was waiting in the wings. In March 1983 the Board of Regents announced that A. Gordon Wetmore, the pastor of Kansas City First Church of the Nazarene would be NNC's ninth president. He would assume presidential reins the next summer and be formally inaugurated the following spring.

Wetmore both resembled and differed from Pearsall. Born in 1931 in New Brunswick, Canada, Wetmore was converted through the ministry of St. Clair Avenue Nazarene Church in Toronto, where John E. Riley was the pastor. He attended Eastern Nazarene College, graduating in 1955 with an English literature major; then followed four years at Nazarene Theological Seminary, resulting in a degree in systematic theology in 1959. Becoming an American citizen in 1960, Wetmore took a church in Wisconsin and later joined the staff at the Wollaston Church on the ENC campus and subsequently became its senior pastor. While at the Wollaston Church, he also served as dean of students and chaplain at ENC. Next were pastorates in Columbus, Ohio, and at Kansas City, Missouri, where he was when named president of NNC.

Like several of his predecessors, Wetmore spent several years as a pastor. Although he had not served as a faculty member, he was on the staff of Eastern Nazarene and had continued his education. One year after coming to Nampa, he received his Doctor of Ministry degree from Fuller Theological Seminary with a dissertation on church administration. Similar to most presidents at NNC—in fact, most chief administrators in Nazarene colleges—Wetmore came to his office from the pastorate. He was much more at home with parishioners, other pastors, and church administrators than with faculty. His contact with students was considerable but primarily as a counselor rather than as academic instructor. Again, like Pearsall, his greatest challenges at NNC would lie in the academic field; his largest achievements in good connections he forged with district superintendents and pastors out on the educational zone.

Dr. Gordon Wetmore, here with his wife Alice Jean, was a positive, encouraging leader as NNC's ninth president. (Fig. 5.10)

President Wetmore experienced a country and campus much changed from the height of student activism during the later Riley years and the Pearsall presidency. When Ronald Reagan became the U.S. president in January 1981, he promised a more patriotic and placid nation. There would be less turmoil and disruption, Reagan added, that had plagued the country since the mid-1960s. Even though many of these promises were not fulfilled, the temper of the country did shift, and with it came less frenetic times to campuses, including NNC. Tests of leadership invaded the Nampa campus, but they were not primarily of the same kind that vexed Pearsall in the previous decade. Most of Gordon Wetmore's acquaintances thought him a calm, reflective man. Years in the pastorate with a good deal of church administrative experience had taught him valuable interpersonal skills. He was a conciliator, attempting to balance the ongoing tensions between conservatives and progressives, writing letters of thanks to everyone (his files bulge with thousands of letters of appreciation), trying to encourage students and their parents in spite of rising tuition rates. Fortunately for Wetmore, he served in more temperate times, much less tempestuous than those of his two immediate predecessors.

Wetmore himself projected a temperate demeanor even before he assumed NNC's leadership. In 1968 on campus as a visiting chapel speaker, he revealed repeatedly to a *Crusader* reporter that he tried to be a middle-of-the-road Nazarene. He agreed with and supported student calls for additional activism and social responsiveness, but, as a convert to the church, he also applauded its efforts to encourage holy living and adherence to Christ's leadership. One Nampa resident and a close observer of Wetmore's presidency, persuasively summarized the new president's stance: "From his first arrival on campus Wetmore maintained a quiet self-confidence which has fostered a climate of moderation and cooperation. Faculty members have not been nervous, students have not been rowdy, and board members have not been critical, this despite the facts that enrollments have not grown and that fiscal pressure has continued."

Some successes did crown the first years of Wetmore's presidency. Through his numerous brief writings for the *Messenger* and *Crusader* he communicated well with the NNC constituency and students. The general tenor rather than the specific contents of these communiqués revealed Wetmore's desire, most of all, to manage NNC diligently and smoothly rather than to ruffle students, faculty, and trustees with outspoken, demanding leadership. He would, he told readers, do his best to bring God's blessings to the campus, watch after the budget, and ensure that NNC continued its journey as a Christian college: "A year of blessings, budget-monitoring, and being a Christian college may make this academic year one of the best we have known." Obviously a less-than-projected student enrollment prompted some of the president's caution, but as the campus community gradually learned, he was by nature a cautious leader.

Feeling the need for additional administrative training, Wetmore attended the Institute for Educational Management at Harvard in the summer of 1984. The institute offered short courses on management, educational leadership, the politics of higher education, financial planning, and several other topics. "The work at Harvard," Wetmore told a district superintendent, "was exacting but tremendously informative. I feel a little more prepared now to be a college administrator." A few months earlier he had written a congratulatory letter to the new editor of the *Crusader*, telling the talented journalist "you will bring to it [the *Crusader*] the kind of inquiry and expression that will make our student paper the positive and stimulating influence that it is intended to be on our campus." Many subsequent issues of the student newspaper carried Wetmore columns. Through this venue, and nearly all others, Wetmore established strong, noncontroversial connections.

So, clear equanimity and apparent consensus, on the surface, seemed to reign, but unexpected changes and trends also fostered disruption and sometimes upset. During Wetmore's nine-year presidency, central and support administrators played a lively game of musical chairs. Academic Vice President and Dean Gilbert Ford, frustrated in serving in a position not of his own choosing, returned to teaching after serving fifteen long years (1970-85). His replacement, another scientist, Ken Watson, began his work with much promise, but was severely injured in a near-fatal plane accident and held the position for only two years (1985-87). After two years of fill-in-time by NNC leaders, former NNC religion professor Dan Berg, with his Ph.D. from the University of Glasgow in Scotland and administrative experience at Seattle Pacific College, became academic vice president and dean from 1989 to 1992. In 1984, Hal Weber replaced Galen Olsen as business manager, and in a move of major import Richard Hagood came in 1985 to replace

Ray Lindley in a newly established position, vice-president for institutional advancement. Changes in other administrative slots also redefined leadership roles: Wanda McMichael retired in 1986 as registrar after long years of masterful service, Randall Simmons replaced Edith Lancaster as head librarian in 1987, and Ken Hills came in 1989 as dean of students and later became vice president for student development. After twelve years of yeoman service as executive director of the Alumni Association, Myron Finkbeiner transferred to another NNC position. These resignations and reassignments meant that no key administrator served during the entire Wetmore administration. Perhaps the most important addition to the administration was the placement of Hagood in institutional advancement; he came from his administrative post at Washington State University and served until being named president in 1993, following the tragic death of Leon Doane.

Dr. Ken Watson's deanship was cut short by a near-fatal plane accident. (Fig. 5.11)

This revolving door of administrative occupants chiefly impacted the academic mission of the college. No one occupied the academic vice president's office for more than three years, and there is no evidence that any of these academic leaders, in their brief stints as chief academic officers, formulated, put into practice, or led a well-organized plan of academic development. Adding to the problem, Wetmore was not a take-charge leader in the academic field. That was not his strength. What occurred was a continuation of the academic maintenance that characterized the Pearsall years. From a faculty perspective, academics lagged behind other segments of NNC during most of the 1970s and 1980s.

The first shift in academic direction occurred in 1985 when the gentle and gifted scholar Gilbert Ford resigned to return to the classroom. He did not enjoy academic administration; his first love was teaching, the classroom, and the laboratory. In all these areas he demonstrated the grace and mastery of the teaching profession. A man who favored consensus and agreement over division and any semblance of contention, Ford was too softhearted to make the demanding administrative decisions that DeLong, Culver, and Riley, for example, carried out before him.

"I did not want to be in the way," Ford told a reporter soon after his resignation. "I had always hoped to end my career teaching. Teaching is the thing I have enjoyed best in 35 years at NNC." Conversely, for Ford, the academic vice-president's job was not satisfying, a position of "day to day drudgery of little important things....I like to do intellectual things, things that are challenging." Although one could count among Ford's achievements during his fifteen years of service the establishment of a revised salary scale, a manual for faculty policy, and a bachelor of science degree, he was bothered by the recent difficult decisions he had to make. He wondered if his cutting personnel and programs, because of falling enrollments, hadn't been precipitous and whether he might have been presumptuous in those decisions. "After many months of thought," Ford had decided to resign and return to teaching, where he displayed again his premier talents as a classroom mentor. For several years afterwards he remained ambivalent about the administrative job he left and the tough decisions he had made while there.

Ford's replacement, Ken Watson, was a chemist and a graduate of NNC. After earning his doctorate in biochemistry at Oregon State and taking further work as a postdoctoral fellow, he had become a professor at the University of Montana and then accepted a very responsible administrative position at Abbott Laboratories in Chicago, where he headed up a staff of nearly forty persons in its Viral Genetics Laboratory division. The son of a Nazarene pastor he had also been active in NNC alumni relations, president of the Alumni Association, and a member of the NNC Board of Regents. Because of his numerous and long encounters with NNC and the Church of the Nazarene, his abundant strengths as a scholar, and his approachable personality, he came with the support and high hopes of administrators, faculty, and regents.

Tragically, catastrophe struck before Watson had much opportunity to lead academically. Returning from a convention in Kansas City, he was severely injured in a plane crash outside Denver on November 15, 1987. After spending more than four months in the hospital and undergoing extensive treatment in a therapy clinic, Watson returned to Nampa. But it became evident that a full return to the academic vice-presidency would be too much for him. On May 4, 1988, President Wetmore announced his decision to search for a new academic vice president. In making the announcement the president reported, "This has probably been the most difficult decision I have had to make in my five years at NNC." After a good deal of consultation with Watson's doctors, Wetmore continued, "it became evident that this decision was best for both NNC and Ken Watson." Martha Hopkins, chair of the Division of Professional Studies, was named acting academic leader. When the search in late summer 1988 for a new dean failed to turn up an acceptable candidate, Hopkins continued to serve the following year. A bit more than a year later the college announced The Watson Faculty Endowment

Project; the Watson family asked that interest from the gift (derived from the accident settlement) be used to establish an endowment for faculty research and development. At the same time when Eastern Nazarene College was looking for a new academic dean in late 1990, the search committee wrote Watson urging him to apply. "Despite the moments of excitement it [the invitation] generated for both me and my family," Watson responded, the decision had to be "negative." He had to remind himself, he told the search committee, "that [he] was not the same person [he] was." The work "would just generate too much stress," which he could not stand. Watson, meanwhile, had been named to a new position as assistant to the NNC president in December 1988, where he served ably and energetically for several years.

Late in the fall of 1988, Dr. Daniel Berg was selected as the new vice president of academic affairs. A graduate of NNC and a former professor of religion at the college, Berg had earned his doctorate in systematic theology from the University of Glasgow and had served in administration at Seattle Pacific College. "The prospects of returning to NNC and Nampa are thrilling to me and my family," Berg told a NNC reporter; "I am anxious to return to my colleagues."

With abundant energy and obvious enthusiasm, Berg arrived back on campus in mid-summer 1989. Early on he provided a realistic, provocative description of higher education as an example of "cognitive dissonance," in which "prior knowledge [was] confronted and challenged by new knowledge." Berg realized that this painful questioning of previous teachings often upset freshmen, their parents, and their churches. So, it was all the more important that professors listened carefully and extensively as young NNCers traveled these questing highways. As a Christian liberal arts college, NNC would encourage this question-asking, but the difference between this and other colleges "is the studied unwillingness of [NNC] professors to leave the student unsupported during the process." Berg's colleague Dennis Cartwright also saluted the new dean's willingness to support accreditation efforts in the teacher education field. Although Cartwright had originally "express[ed] concern regarding his [Berg's] candidacy for the position" of academic vice president, he had been "wrong." Cartwright wrote to tell President Wetmore how much he "appreciated Dan," who had "worked very hard to become aware of the issues associated with the variety of programs he supervises....I appreciate...his leadership and support."

Despite these evidences of Berg's insights, his ambition to lead, and his warm personality, he seemed unable to take charge, to provide the academic leadership NNC sorely needed during the Wetmore years. Requests for action from Berg's office went awry, and sometimes the president had to step in to make things happen. As Wetmore explained to a dissatisfied faculty member, "with the unfortunate need for changes in the office of the Academic Dean, and with some other issues about which you had no reason to hear, I have found it necessary to take some swift and summary actions." Connections with the Department of Business also presented special unsolved challenges under Berg's watch. One accounting professor quit under protest, and Berg was unable to strengthen the department, although inadequate salaries were part of the problem beyond his control. And when Berg overruled another professor's wishes on a student petition, he alienated that colleague. Still another professor felt that Berg was not an energetic administrator, sometimes working shorter days than were needed. Most of all, however, Berg, even though articulating well circumstances facing NNC's faculty and administration, could not provide specific ways to address those challenges. Too often Berg's stuttering steps led to uncertainty; he failed to gain the confidence of faculty and administration in his leadership. Behind the scenes, Wetmore encouraged Berg to step down. In fact, Wetmore hinted a bit vaguely at this move when he wrote to his successor Leon Doane, "...since it was our initiative which caused the Bergs to leave NNC...."

Berg's resignation letter in May 1992 revealed his ambivalence about his most recent role at NNC. He would leave, he wrote, "with many warm recollections of kindnesses" to him and his family, and "the sense of unbroken friendship that marks the community of God." But he also hinted that his stint in the dean's office had been "a very trying time in [his] life." In another venue, he told a reporter that in his administrative position at NNC he had "received an intense education about the nature and business of education, and that the role of dean was satisfying in some ways." Berg left Nampa to take a similar position: dean and vice president of Western Evangelical Seminary in Portland. Then, Lilburn Wesche, in charge of graduate programs at NNC, was appointed acting dean while a search for a permanent academic leader was launched.

The lack of continuity in leadership made it very difficult to sustain the college's academic programs, let alone efforts to mount new ones. Other problems conspired to make the initial Wetmore years especially difficult ones for faculty. Because of falling enrollments—tumbling from a high of 1,320 in 1979-80 to a nadir of 1,007 in 1984-1985 and continued lows for the next few years—financial shepherds at NNC were hard pressed to round up sufficient funds for salaries and other ongoing programs. Indeed, a fiscal rule of thumb obtained: a loss of twenty students equaled one faculty position, so the dip of 300 (or nearly 30 percent) student enrollment translated into the threat of losing fifteen faculty. In the fall of 1984, under the wringing pressures of these economic realities, the regents and President Wetmore made a controversial and much-debated decision to hold off on that year's three-year rolling contracts until the next spring. An even more drastic entrenchment plan, cutting budgets and laying off several faculty and staff members, waited in the wings. Instead, the three-year contracts were again frozen in the next spring's regents meetings, and three staff and faculty members were eliminated, with the larger threatened cuts withheld.

One professor, in examining these decisions, complained that "the faculty cuts and the way that they are being made are arbitrary and inequitable." In a rather familiar but realistic faculty response, the professor asserted that teaching faculty were taking the major hits, and nonteaching staff, expanded before the enrollment downturn, was not being reduced. He also noted that retiring faculty were, haphazardly, not being replaced; NNC needed to mount a careful plan to keep some departments from disproportionate losses. He might have added, but didn't, that faculty salaries had been frozen for three years. Although enrollment jumped nearly nine percent in fall 1985, the Board of Regents decided, again, "not to continue to give out new three year contracts." President Wetmore supported the regents' decision, even though he had promised three-year contracts would be back in order in spring 1985. To many faculty, the verdicts of the regents and the president's backing of these bad-news reports were alienating examples of double-speak. One disgruntled professor grumbled that putting off the three-year rolling contracts was but another evidence of "the lack of understanding and respect that Regents appear to have for the faculty of this college." During the ten years he had been at NNC, the regents had "treated the faculty in a very nonprofessional, insensitive and un-candid manner."

When enrollment began to rebound after the mid-1980s the college academic program gradually escaped from the confining crisis mode of the previous half-dozen years. That meant new faculty members could be hired, especially those replacing others who had retired or gone elsewhere. Several of the new hires stayed at NNC for well more than a decade, making memorable impressions on their students and colleagues. Brenda Miller Martin and Michael Bankston came in music and directed musical groups; Wendell Bowes, George Lyons, and C. S. Cowles in religion; Eric Forseth in physical education; Mary Curran in social work; and Elizabeth Murtland in home economics. The sciences gained in strength and number with Gilbert Ford's return to the classroom and the addition of Thomas Mangum III, and education expanded with Dennis Cartwright, Larry McMillin, and Ed Castledine.

Concurrently new graduate programs were added, with education and religion expanding in this regard. Actually NNC had been strong for many years in these fields. From the 1920s onward religion had been one of the college's notable departments; the same was true of education, especially after Thelma Culver began to teach in that department and became dean from the mid-1940s forward. One or two graduate programs were attempted in the 1940s and 1950s but were dropped after inadequate student demand.

Jerry Hull was a key and dependable figure in the advancement of a social work major and in organizing campus student activities. (Fig. 5.12)

Other departments either expanded or developed new programs. Under the dynamic leadership of Merilyn Thompson and later Dennis Waller the forensics program grew into a powerhouse program. These and other professors involved in the speech program did a superb job of notifying campus, community, and zone of the room-full of trophies and prizes NNC debaters and speakers toted home to Nampa. The social work program continued to expand during these years. Ben Sherrill, Richard Stellway, Jerry Hull, and Mary Curran built on early offerings and attracted mounting numbers of majors. More and more evangelical students at a Christian college, increasingly interested in global missions programs, found social work a natural occupational outlet for their desires to help people, much like other students joined the ranks of environmentally concerned groups. Music also continued to pull in a large number of students and majors.

One change to the NNC academic program initially stirred up considerable controversy among faculty. Since 1964 NNC had been on the three-quarter-per-year calendar, but in the fall 1990 meeting of the Board of Regents, President Wetmore presented—and the regents supported—a proposal to return to the two-semester academic year in 1993. The *Messenger*, as an arm of the college administration, did not mention that two years earlier the Academic Council of faculty had opposed the move to semesters. It merely stated that most colleges followed the semester format and that it allowed "for academic evaluation and reform." But the *Crusader* boldly reported the professorial opposition and concluded that "most faculty members...strongly oppos[ed] the change from quarters to semesters." The student newspaper also stated that in this move Wetmore was "perhaps [making] his boldest stand since assuming office...."

Faculty opposition to the semester system at the end of the previous year had been near unanimous. As one professor told the president, "Approximately twenty departments on campus came independently to the same conclusion: The semester system would hurt the quality of our academic program. Only foreign language was in favor of the change." A professor of sociology spoke to a different kind of challenge in the transition to semesters. He was concerned primarily about the "four simultaneous course preparations." When he had checked with NNC historian Dr. Bob Woodward, who had attended another Nazarene college where a four-course load was demanded, he discovered that professors at that college, under the pressure of so many preparations, often came "to class with [a] textbook and simply walk[ed] the students through the text." The sociology professor told the president, "I don't think this is what you have in mind when you talk of quality education." After the regents announced their support for the change, a special faculty meeting was convened to discuss this and other issues, including beginning moves toward university status. Following that meeting faculty opposition melted away. Had they been convinced to follow the wishes of the regents, president, and academic dean Berg? One veteran faculty member and later administrator recalled that, though the faculty, especially the scientists, favored the quarter system they chose not to continue opposing the change. The shift to semesters was delayed, however, during two subsequent presidential changes.

On another more substantive question—their salaries—faculty members had reason to be upset, but they rarely said much about this bread-and-butter issue. Yes, salaries were low; they had always been inadequate. Indeed, many who came to teach at NNC considered their work like that of a minister or missionary: they "labored for the Lord" with little remuneration. Through the years, NNC presidents and other college administrators made much of NNC's tuition and room and board charges being among the lowest—if not the lowest—in colleges like NNC in the Pacific Northwest. These low charges, they suggested, were the major reasons for poor salaries. Salaries were also clearly enrollment-driven; when numbers of students plummeted between 1980 and 1985, adequate funding was unavailable for present salaries, let alone for raises.

A report in 1983-84 revealed, comparatively, the inadequate remuneration for NNC professors. The summary of faculty salaries at fifteen "Pacific Northwest Independent Colleges" indicated that NNC faculty pay was near the bottom in all rankings: full professors in the fifteen colleges ranged from $36,145 down to $18,138, with NNC professors at $24,451; associate professors from $29,231 to $16,445, with NNC at $19, 863; assistant professors, $26,000 to $16,445, NNC at $18,434. Only one or two colleges ranked below NNC in these categories. Since NNC operated on an unranked system (no divisions into full, associate, and assistant professors), the salary breakdowns for rank had to be adjusted. Five years later, faculty remuneration ranged from the highest nine-month salaries of $32, 083 to the lowest of $18,400, with a median of $27,000. When President Wetmore came to NNC in 1983, his salary was $45,000 plus benefits; by 1987 it was $60,240, plus benefits. Wetmore's salary was also considerably lower than those of other college presidents in the Pacific Northwest.

Even though faculty said little about their inadequate compensation, they did worry about the financial pressures the low salaries imposed on their colleagues.

A chemistry professor, recalling his own monetary dilemmas on a single-salary income at NNC fifteen years earlier, feared that his department might lose another colleague to a higher-paying job. He wrote to the president and academic dean to remind them that chemistry had lost two faculty members in the past decade or so because of inadequate remuneration. Now they might lose another since he was "within about one hundred dollars per month of being able to qualify for the school hot lunch program for his children." "This is a rather sad situation," the chemist added, "for a person who has an earned doctorate in chemistry." In the same year a salary comparison with nearby public schools revealed that a professor at NNC with a master's degree and no experience would receive $14,000, approximately $1,000 less than for a beginning master's teacher in Nampa schools, and $1,200 less than for teachers in Boise. Realizing the low morale among the NNC professoriate after several years with no raises, the president and regents voted in a pay raise for faculty in fall 1986 even though that action meant accepting a budget tagged with a $250,000 shortfall. After slight increases in enrollment, added giving from the educational zone, and rising tuition charges, the college was able to increase salaries slightly toward the end of Wetmore's administration.

Despite these converging challenges to its academic program, NNC continued to receive positive affirmations from popular media and accrediting agencies. The popular and widely dispersed information about NNC's high rankings as a college in the yearly surveys in *U. S. News and World Report* and other venues (to be discussed later) were sometimes palliatives in tough times. In 1987, in another decadal evaluation from the Northwest Association of Schools and Colleges (NASC) begun in 1957, NNC gained full accreditation for ten more years. The executive director of the NASC and its Commission on Colleges congratulated NNC on its "receiving this continued recognition." He pointed out that in two years the commission would return to evaluate the college's new Master in Ministry and its Continuing Education program, but NNC's general academic program, he wanted to make clear, was receiving another important pat on the back from its regional accrediting agency. It was a much-needed salute in stretching years.

In another role, President Wetmore, as a spiritual leader on campus and throughout the educational zone, achieved more than as an academic chief. His strengths and limitations in these two areas were similar to those of his predecessor. As former pastors, Wetmore and Pearsall were experienced and successful church leaders, but academic generalship came less easy for them. Perhaps, as one observer has astutely put it, "Riley grew the faculty, but it was never so large he let it go. Pearsall and Wetmore were making a managerial change common in higher education, ceding their authority to the academic dean as the faculty grew and required more attention than these presidents could give." Interestingly, their three successors in the president's office—Doane, Hagood, Alexander, all laymen—faced opposite challenges. As laymen and business or academic persons, they had to prove to onlookers that they could be the spiritual captains expected of all NNC chief administrators.

Wetmore exhibited his religious leadership through his writings, the persons he invited to campus as chapel and religious emphasis speakers, and his reports to campus and constituency. Like a newly arrived pastor who wished to win over parishioners rumored to be inflicted with human shortcomings, Wetmore carefully worded his reports and letters to regents, faculty, and students. He accentuated NNC's strengths and achievements, downplaying or overlooking limitations. Harsh or demanding words were absent. Nor could anyone accuse the new president of gloom and doom, even when enrollments, finances, and administrative appointments went awry in his first years. Wetmore thought he could see bright lights in an unclear future—or at least he did not admit to any insurmountable ridges or darkling plains out ahead.

The president sounded positive religious notes early on to a variety of audiences. In writing to Nazarenes of the Northwest, Wetmore assured them it was "God's nature to bless," and "those who [did] His will in the implementing of the service of NNC will be blessed." To district superintendents of the NNC zone, he enthused: "the spiritual tone on campus is excellent." The president was impressed too with the upbeat mood on campus, "confirming" his "impression of NNC as a vine of God's planting." To the regents, Wetmore concluded that declining enrollment and its impacts had "not dampened the enthusiasm of the campus" but "proved to be a challenge to strengthen the commitment of us all at NNC." To students in the *Crusader*, he reported that the reason "why we mind the store here is to equip people for life....To help them grow in their faith and learn to apply it in their world."

Equipping leaders in a church or a college was a central goal in Wetmore's thinking. It was a notable emphasis in his doctoral dissertation and a topic to which he repeatedly returned. To one of the general superintendents Wetmore explained that a reoccurring concern of his was "to impress upon our Nazarene pastors and families the importance of the uniqueness of Nazarene higher education." "A Nazarene college, at its best [he added], will bring together the vital concern for Christian social holiness and the sanctified ambition for full intellectual development." An astute judge of his varied constituencies, Wetmore spoke appropriate words to all the major components of the college, hoping in that way to bring about stronger commitment to spiritual growth, additional academic development, and heightened social concern, the three core values of Nazarene higher education.

Wetmore remained remarkably sanguine about the religious atmosphere of NNC during his entire presidency. He also tried to make sure that invited speakers followed a similar positive agenda in their presentations. A generation or so earlier three or four revival or religious emphasis speakers came to campus for a series of sermons; by the 1980s fewer presenters came, not many of which were evangelists or pastors. Nor were many general or district superintendents on campus to conduct revivals.

Instead, the president and his advisors engaged speakers who reified the marriage of head and heart at the center of the NNC mission, others who encouraged students to think missionally and globally, and still others who spoke to social concerns. Timothy L. Smith, as the church's leading scholar, came again to a welcoming student body, open to and encouraged by keen preaching. Patricia Ward, ENC grad and then dean at Wheaton College, spoke about the needed balances between faith and learning; and Richard Schubert, former head of Red Cross, inspired NNC students to become world servants. These speakers, all friends of Wemore, and others reminded students and faculty of the marriage of spirit and mind in the Christian liberal arts tradition.

The increasing numbers of speakers on the NNC campus emphasizing religious global concerns reflected impulses at work in the Church of the Nazarene. When missionary Harmon Schmelzenbach mesmerized students with his dramatic storytelling sermons, he not only stood as the grandson of the Nazarene missions founder in southern Africa, he also represented the growing interest in the Nazarene church and on the NNC campus in expanding and diversifying its missions outreach. At the same time that the church was launching Work and Witness programs sending laypersons out to mission fields to erect or refurbish buildings and speak of their faith, the Nazarene Education Commission announced in 1985 that forthcoming missions of the church would include attempts to "cross frontiers" and encourage "global communion."

Numerous pages of the *Messenger* and *Crusader* carried stories about Youth in Mission, international compassionate ministries, and short-term mission work involving NNC students and faculty. One general church official, visiting the Nampa campus, found NNC students "unusually responsive" to varied mission outreach programs. After speaking in chapel, he "was swamped with requests for appointments"; his visit to speak about student involvement in missions "proved to be two of the most extraordinary days I have had on any college campus." President Wetmore, as a discerning observer of college students, and repeating one of his favorite themes, explained to the church missions official: "Those who lament a lack of commitment on the part of Nazarene students are living in a time lag. Those of us who work on Nazarene campuses are very conscious that there is a dispensational move going on in which God is actively preparing leaders for the

21st Century. The Church of the Nazarene is being shaped through the formation of these leaders."

No person in the Nazarene Church better represented its expanding social concern in the U. S. than Tom Nees, and he brought that concern to the NNC campus with large impact. Scion of Nazarene pastor and college president L. Guy Nees, NNC graduate, and former pastor of Washington, D. C. First Church, Tom Nees and his wife Pat pioneered in the nation's capital an innovative and path breaking ministry, the Community of Hope. It opened in 1976. Nees wrote that he wanted "to find a way to minister to the poor of my city." He had been particularly influenced by the life and teachings of Martin Luther King, Jr., and felt led to help bring understanding and reconciliation among urban peoples. When he returned to speak at NNC ten years later, he came with a stirring story of how housing, school, health care, and spiritual community were joined in the Community of Hope.

Nees's journey narrative warmed the hearts of Nampa audiences. He told them of a visitor to the Community of Hope who had asked, "Why feed people who are going to hell?" To answer such narrow-minded questions and to inform his own thinking, Nees undertook a concerted study of holiness movements and their social missions. His research revealed that from John Wesley onward, including holiness people like the early Nazarenes, Wesleyans had been interested in reaching out to the poor, the homeless, and those victimized by racism. Nees's findings and his experiences at the Community of Hope may have been a major influence on the "Thrust to the Cities" program that Nazarenes launched in the mid-1980s. His story also meshed neatly with trends on the Nampa campus. As one NNC professor and administrator pointed out, in the Wetmore era "more NNC students than from any of the USA-based Nazarene colleges applied and served in the summer ministry programs for the Church of the Nazarene." Another NNC professor, Irving Laird, who had been Wetmore's college roommate, was an important booster for the urban ministry programs that increased markedly in popularity on campus from the 1970s onward.

Dr. Tom Nees, NNC grad and founder of Community of Hope in Washington, D.C., warmed the hearts of and inspired missional dreams in dozens of students. (Fig. 5.13)

On one occasion Wetmore wrote that social concerns were in the DNA of holiness people. Other speakers brought to campus attempted to show that living for Christ demanded that

NNC students were increasingly motivated to reach out to the young and needy, through such programs as Operation Satisfaction. (Fig. 5.14)

they think of social needs surrounding them. Tony Campolo, a dramatic and nationally known speaker from Eastern College, threw down the gauntlet on issues of poverty and Christians' responsibility to help the needy. One student thought Campolo had laid a "guilt trip" on his audiences, but others were convinced that his presentations and writings hit dead center in their forcing listeners and readers to face the social dimensions of evangelical teachings. Mary Curran, a Point Loma graduate working with Tom Nees at the Community of Hope and who later joined the NNC's social work department, presented a "revolutionary message of Christian Holiness" in 1985. In a news story captioned "Speaker Stuns Campus," a *Crusader* writer reported that Curran had told students Nazarenes must move beyond the legalism of the special rules of the church's *Manual*—on movies, dancing, and smoking and drinking—and focus instead on the real, pressing issues of American society, such as racism. Although more outspoken than most other presenters, Curran's message was similar: the Christian gospel contained large social dimensions that Nazarenes and other evangelicals had underemphasized for too long. Another speaker, novelist Frank Peretti, drew an audience of nearly 2,000 to his talk. He took a different tack in urging his listeners to prepare for "spiritual warfare" against Satan's influences in American society. Peretti was convinced that his novels *This Present Darkness* (1988) and *Piercing The Darkness* (1989) were valuable battle manuals in combating New Age doctrines and practices.

These presenters, particularly those sounding the tocsin for more attention to the social dimensions of Wesleyanism, paralleled a gradual trend in theological teaching in the Church of the Nazarene. President Wetmore and religion professors on the NNC campus followed that trend. From their beginnings in the early twentieth century, Nazarenes taught that Christians went through two definite and separate works of grace: the first was salvation through confession, God's forgiveness of sins and the initial work of the Holy Spirit (being "saved"); then followed a "second instantaneous work of grace" (being "sanctified") through which a deeper work of the Holy Spirit eradicated an inborn sin nature and provided power for one to avoid sin. Nazarenes for at least a half century had testified to being saved and sanctified with these experiences and ideas in mind.

But challenges to the traditional Nazarene modes of theological thinking began to emerge in the post-World War II years. Most of the initial discussions about the need for clarification and perhaps redefining dealt with sanctification: how to make it clearer to laypersons, how to find some consensus among Nazarene theologians, and, gradually after the 1960s, how to define holiness in ways understandable to an expanding international church. Some discussants wanted to emphasize God's work in the holiness experience through the guidance of the Holy Spirit; others wished to stress the role of human will in sanctification; and still others desired to rediscover Wesley's teachings on a second work of grace, as seen in his glosses on the Bible.

In some ways the central tensions that arose in redefining holiness in the 1970s forward revolved around two views, one older, the other newer. The more traditional view derived from a nineteenth-century holiness leader Phoebe Palmer; from interdenominational holiness groups; and from early Nazarenes, all of whom emphasized sanctification as a second crisis spiritual experience in which an Adamic inborn sin nature was eradicated. The newer strain of thinking about sanctification came from those promoting "relational" emphases in holiness theology. Of the latter group, the writings of Mildred Bangs Wynkoop, particularly her much-discussed book *A Theology of Love* (1972), were crucial. Wynkoop, who had studied with H. Orton Wiley, served as a missionary-teacher in Japan, and later was a professor of theology at Trevecca Nazarene and at the Nazarene Theological Seminary, asserted that Wesley emphasized God's grace more than the human will. Without rejecting sanctification as a second work of grace, Wynkoop pushed the holiness discussion toward defining sanctification as a "perfect integrity," a "moral integration." It was a "'way,' a 'life.'" This new "relational" definition of sanctification, illustrated through an enlarged emphasis on the concept of love in Wynkoop and other writers, found its most popular manifestation in Reuben Welch's widely quoted book *We Really Do Need Each Other* (1981) but also later in the more scholarly, if diverse, works of H. Ray Dunning, *Grace, Faith, and Holiness: A Wesleyan Systematic Theology* (1988) and Thomas J. Oord and Michael Lodahl, *Relational Holiness: Responding to the Call of Love* (2005).

Gordon Wetmore, who stayed aloof from most theological debate during his NNC presidency, nonetheless reflected much of this new definition of holiness in his writings and presentations. In his initial issue of the *Messenger* he relayed to readers on campus and across the zone that "NNC must be a really responsible part of our community, of our state, and of our world." Individual holiness was not enough; "we are responsible for our day." The real business of NNC, he added a few years later, was "the equipping of our people." To do what? To help young people in the work of social holiness, "for the ministry in every occupation or profession." Even more explicitly, he told readers of the *Crusader* that from Wesley to Martin Luther King and throughout the history of the Church of the Nazarene, there were evidences of "Christian commitment combined with insight into social actions." Nazarenes, recovering "their vital connectedness of evangelization and social action," were once again linking "the heart on fire for God and the hand directly involved in meeting the human needs of people." It was the president's "concern that Northwest Nazarene College be at the center of this new thrust."

Even while President Wetmore tried to be upbeat in encouraging academic excellence and vital religious experience, financial pressures lurked near at hand like a group of shivaree revelers, threatening to disrupt his presidential honeymoon. Before long, however, increased giving from districts in the NNC zone, rising tuition charges, and the Competitive Edge Annual Appeal, together, helped keep the financial troublemakers at bay. A slightly expanding Nazarene population also provided a larger pool from which to draw for prospective students. By the end of the 1980s, Wetmore could tell the district assemblies of the Northwest region that financial support for the new program, *"Mission XXI,"* was increasing. The $3.5 million goal for the first phase of the program (1988-91) was in sight; $3 million had already been pledged. In addition, a Northwest Nazarene College Foundation had been organized and was at work on raising an Endowment Fund for NNC, the earnings of which would be used for student scholarships, faculty development, and other pressing needs.

Perhaps the most important new impulse to the NNC economic turnaround came with the arrival of Dr. Richard Hagood in 1985. Named to the new position of vice president for institutional advancement, Hagood brought several years of valuable experience from the University of Idaho and Washington State University to his job at NNC. He was to be responsible for several areas of college administration: alumni outreach, fund raising, marketing and communications, church connections, community and federal government links, and admissions and recruitment. All these important assignments were directly tied to the fiscal stability of the college—and to its financial future. Within weeks, Hagood had a thorough report prepared for the Board of Regents, including recommendations on budget revisions, policies on church giving, matching awards, and a development manual. Most important, Hagood recommended that the regents adopt a "three-year strategic plan as the program direction for institutional advancement through 1987-88." As a new NNC administrator Richard Hagood, like a developing point guard, was already beginning to formulate and carry out a major role in the college's game plan.

"Strategic planning"—Hagood's two favorite words, and what they implied—became crucial ingredients of NNC's upward surge in the next few years. The college had needed consistent, far-seeing planning; Richard Hagood furnished it. His superb work in strategic planning provided a new balance and foresight that the Wetmore administration had lacked.

When NNC received high rankings in national magazines, the news was spread far and wide. (Fig. 5.15)

Nothing did more to boost NNC spirits and self-confidence than its appearance among top-ranked American colleges in the October 15, 1990, issue of *U. S. News and World Report.* An October 1990 issue of the *Crusader* emblazoned on its front page a one-inch, bold headline "NNC RANKS 6TH IN THE WEST." Below the attention-grabbing headline was a photograph of President Wetmore and Vice-President Hagood in front of the Administration Building, with the caption "National recognition has NNC officials smiling." NNC was ranked sixth among "The Top Ten Regional Liberal Arts Colleges" in the West, above competitor George Fox (eighth) and below Pacific University (Oregon, second) and Evergreen State College (Washington, third). Nowhere in sight was the College of Idaho, NNC's pesky rival in everything, and no other Nazarene college made it into the rankings.

Although many colleges, their administrators, and backers pooh-poohed the subjective rankings—especially those not ranked—NNC showcased the new recognition. The college emphasized that the rankings were based, in large part, on academic reputation, strength of faculty resources, and student selectivity (the latter "measured by the school's ability to graduate the students it admits as freshman"). Nationally, NNC ranked 32nd among the 385 colleges included in the category of "small liberal arts colleges." In the coming years when the college reappeared in these surveys, NNC made news of the high rankings a cornerstone of its outreach and recruitment efforts.

From 1990 onward Wetmore and his fellow administrators were promoters, far and away, of this useful news. The November 1990 issue of the *Messenger* trumpeted on its front page the headline "NNC Receives National Recognition." The president told readers, "This recognition is most encouraging....This listing affirms NNC's superior educational process." To these enthusiastic words, Dean Dan Berg added: the headline notice confirmed NNC's strong work "faithfully done for decades" and served too as a "prod to a new vigilance over the quality of our work and a renewed commitment to our task." Vice-President Hagood called the ranking "incredibly significant"; "it means we no longer need to be quiet about the quality education we offer at NNC." Wetmore even used the news as a major point in his outreach contact letter to grocery magnate Joe Albertson, telling the Boise resident about NNC's recent rankings among "America's Best Colleges." More ambitiously, Wetmore, other NNC administrators, and Leon Doane, chair of the Board of Regents, decided to expend $11,000 for "production and mailing costs" for a "bulletin insert to all congregations of the Church of the Nazarene" in NNC's educational zone, apprising them of "NNC's national ranking... [among] America's best colleges."

The new rankings and their explosive importance to NNC's future were, in part, a product of specific programs launched earlier in the 1980s. Others, building on the influential rankings, occurred later. As falling enrollments and consequent diminishing yearly revenues became evident in Wetmore's first years, he tried several schemes to turn around the disappointing status quo. In late 1984 and early 1985 the president personally took charge of a "Quiet Campaign" to approach small groups of individuals to raise $200,000 to 500,000 "to provide financial aid both for retention and recruitment of new students." The following May he added another program, "The President's Call to Invest," to raise "scholarship and grant money" for NNC students. Later in 1985 through the counsel of Vice President Hagood, another plan, the "Competitive Edge Annual Award," was put into place to raise more funds throughout the NNC educational zone. These measures were inadequate. Something better planned and more extensive must be launched. Wetmore hoped that much-needed planning had been inaugurated by fall 1987. With the help of Hagood he put forth the planning package *"Mission XXI."* As Wetmore told the regents, he and other NNC administrators were thinking increasingly about the challenges of the next century, moving "forward with determination in planning and implementation."

Meanwhile even better aforethought was emerging from Richard Hagood's office of institutional development. Experienced and skilled in formulating and carrying out plans of action, Hagood turned on the planning switches and powered up: first in planning documents and then in specific programs to be implemented. Once the regents began to recognize the applicability and persuasiveness of these new planning blueprints and the programs they called for, they threw their strong support behind the plans. "In the past several programs to boost NNC have been marginally successful," the *Crusader* reported, but "since Dr. Hagood first began his first program for NNC, the school has grown in many ways." As proof, the reporter pointed to climbing enrollments and predicted "there should be money for more scholarships and staff salary increases."

Two years later during NNC's 75th Anniversary celebration, an improving economic picture was coming into focus. In fall 1988 enrollment had rebounded to 1,148, the highest in six years. Increasing emphases on and financial support for recruitment were paying off, and the college was doing a better job of reporting "its quality education"; the message was "being heard, and more importantly, believed," Hagood asserted. President Wetmore agreed and urged constituents to understand the tough competition NNC faced in garnering students and to provide necessary financial support for the college. In 1990 Robert Sevier, an NNC graduate and educational consultant, told NNC administrators and faculty, among other things, that they needed to spend more on student recruitment, increase their publicity on NNC's academic strengths, advertise more, and scale down the number of academic majors. Those suggestions were much discussed in the coming months—and years.

An extensive story in the Nampa *Idaho Press-Tribune* in early fall 1989 pinpointed the financial status of NNC and its future plans. Leon Doane, chair of the NNC regents, encapsulated the look ahead for the Nampa reporter. The college hoped, Doane said, to raise an endowment of $3.5 million, which would be used for "the general endowment fund, student financial aid, updating instructional equipment, improving library holdings, and establishing... [a] business chair." Doane also pointed out that the college was redoubling its student recruitment efforts with the 450 Nazarene churches on its educational districts and trying to reach out to more non-Nazarenes, especially those in the Treasure Valley of Idaho. A new NNC Foundation had been organized, and it planned, some day, to raise a $50 million endowment.

The next month another descriptor was added to the ever-expanding NNC lexicon; it would become a "destination college." Since most Nazarenes lived in the interior Pacific Northwest valley stretching southward from Bellingham, Washington, to Medford, Oregon, in towns scattered across eastern Washington, and in Colorado, Nampa, Idaho, was a distant, strange location for many of them. The image of NNC needed to be reshaped: from a backwoods, small-town Idaho to a "pleasant, attractive campus," one that would draw students "to Nampa from hundreds of miles away." The new idealistic plan called for several new buildings, an enlarged enrollment of 1,600 by the year 2000, an honors program, and other "academic 'programs of distinction.'"

One central facet of the "destination college" dream was the physical expansion of the campus, including, perhaps, the acquisition of the adjacent Kurtz Park for the college. As early as the 1950s and 1960s, plans for the widening of Holly Street through NNC had been broached. In the mid-1980s the Nampa City Council raised the possibility of expanding Holly Street to four lanes through the campus. Soon after Hagood arrived, he began approaching Nampa officials about a land swap that would give Kurtz Park to NNC in exchange for another plot of ground available for a replacement park. After careful, complicated, and long negotiations, including tracking down Kurtz family descendants on the East Coast,

NNC (especially under Hagood's leadership) succeeded in carrying out the land exchange that gave Kurtz Park to the college and a plot of land near Mercy Medical Center to the city for a planned park. The Kurtz Park addition was an extraordinary step forward in keeping NNC in Nampa (a college task force had studied the possibility of relocating to Vancouver, Washington), providing another central piece of land for development, and ending the controversy about pushing a Holly Street freeway through campus. Before long the college acquired other nearby properties and worked with the city to construct a street bypass rerouting Holly Street traffic around campus. This reroute was a significant step in NNC strategic planning and the creation of a "destination college."

As these academic and economic advancements were being worked out and captured most of the local newspaper and *Messenger* columns, the *Crusader* carried other stories depicting attitudes and activities of other kinds. Over the years the campus newspaper remained the best-published source of information about NNC students and their social life; it remained so in the Wetmore era. No subject, aside from sports news, filled more column inches in the *Crusader* during the 1980s than the Nazarene Church's lingering strictures against movies and dances. While the international church wrestled with these issues in general and district assemblies, and increased tensions on the topics surfaced among pastors, parents, and youth, most of the writers for the NNC newspaper made their convictions clear. Although the coverage of these social conflicts was neither as barbed nor demanding as campus news stories in the 1970s, campus journalists and most other students were in agreement that the Nazarene Church was out-of-date in continuing what they considered legalistic standards and, conversely, blind to other more significant issues. Early on a student complained that NNC students were being "subjected to a somewhat straight-laced sort of living," with too much negative emphasis on movies, dramatic presentations, and television. Not so wrote two students in the next issue of the newspaper. The lifestyle guidelines, one rebuttal opined, were "perfectly appropriate," representing "a middle ground between conservative and liberal elements on campus." The other critic lambasted many entertainments on the campus, such as Senior Slick, as overflowing with violence and risqué songs and language inappropriate for a Christian college.

For the most part, each year the *Crusader* issues carried several articles challenging if not strongly criticizing church and college restrictions on movies and dances. Gradually the rhetorical fallout subsided on movies as more students had access to VCR's, allowing them to see the movies they wished. On dancing, students asked why should cheerleaders, basketball half-time entertainers, and even the Northwesterners be allowed routines that included dance steps and other students not allowed to dance? Indeed, one editor argued that students raised in morally upright Nazarene homes were coming to NNC and finding "themselves suffocating under foreign behavioral expectations. The rules of the campus are much more strict and inflexible than the rules of their home," he observed. True enough, perhaps, but the rules on campus remained largely unchanged during Wetmore's presidency. Then, and later, Nazarene campuses hung on longer to earlier rules on entertainments than many Nazarene homes and home churches.

Concurrently, NNC students pointed to rampant racism in the U. S. and around the world as an issue Nazarenes were overlooking while holding fast to their outdated stances on movies and dances. Tom Nees and Mary Curran from the Community of Hope in Washington, D. C., and other campus speakers raised the consciousness of students on worldwide racism. In this vein in fall 1985 a *Crusader* essayist reminded campus readers that before they self-righteously condemned a minority white supremacy government in South Africa for upholding apartheid policies they should consider the "American Phenomenon," the negative treatment of Native Americans in the U. S. How much difference was there between reservation policies in the U. S. and segregation in South Africa?

The following January another student journalist, celebrating Martin Luther King Day, urged her fellow students to think of Dr. King as "a man with a life worthy of much honor." Six weeks later Mary Curran reminded NNC students that they and Nazarene churches must understand the special challenges facing black families and work specifically to help address these problems by recognizing both "cultural differences" between races but the similarities as well. NNC students were largely unaware of the challenges the general church faced in handling apartheid and other crucial issues in places like South Africa and Papua New Guinea. For the most part the Nazarene Church tried to avoid the road of controversy and in doing so did little to challenge segregationist or polygamist issues they should have confronted. Many NNC students in the 1980s wanted the church to face, not avoid, these challenges.

In other areas, topics of discussion by campus and visiting speakers might have surprised parents and possibly even shocked and dismayed grandparents. Again, none of these subjects appeared in the president's papers or in issues of the *Messenger* but were much reported-on in the *Crusader*. Periodic articles appeared treating controversial topics such as condoms, AIDS, and rape. There were even seminars on sexual abuse and human sexuality. But the stories creating the stormiest rebuttals were those on abortion. When editor Richard Hume, whom many considered a model of balance and re-elected him twice as the annual newspaper editor, wrote a front-page story on "Planned Parenthood Offers Service and

Opportunities," including information on birth control and unwanted pregnancies, he received a storm of responses, including one published simultaneously with Hume's piece. The editor defended his story by reminding readers—and letter writers—that the *Crusader* did "not support either pro-life or the pro-choice position as a formal editorial policy." His article "was strictly...informational, written not to persuade but to accurately describe the Planned Parenthood organization." But just publishing the article was too much for critics. A local Baptist pastor, who would later come to campus to speak against abortion, wrote to say that NNC "ought not to support an organization that winks at pre-marital sex and supports hiding the results of it behind abortion." For this dissenter, presenting information on abortion was tantamount to supporting it. The controversy over abortion continued at NNC, even as it remained a much-debated issue among Nazarenes and Americans in general during the next generation.

Although more muted and less numerous than the discussions of Nazarene standards and race issues, several articles in the *Crusader* dealt with feminism and the rights of women. In 1985 in her prize-winning essay for the Dooley creative writing contest, NNC coed Debbie Turley pointed out that from top to bottom the Church of the Nazarene was male-dominated. From the pulpit to the pew men were leading and making the major decisions in churches, and they were not accepting women as pastors. But some laywomen had reservations about feminism, such as one telling a pastor-and-wife ministerial team: "A woman's place is in the home! A man's place in the pulpit! I will not listen to that woman preach... it's unbiblical." Revealingly, Wetmore complimented Turley on the essay, telling her to "continue to deal with this [women's roles among the Nazarenes] as it is a message the church needs to continue to consider." Less than ten years later while serving as president of Nazarene Theological Seminary, Wetmore reiterated his stance on the need for Nazarenes to accept women into their pulpits. As the centennial history of the Nazarene church points out, "Wetmore was troubled that though women who attended NTS came with the clear call of God 'to be pastors, evangelists, chaplains, missionaries' and take 'other specific leadership roles' and often achieved top results in seminary classes, they were 'not placed as pastors in our local congregations.'"

If students had scrutinized the NNC and Nazarene leadership scene more carefully, they would have realized how much their college reflected its denomination in choosing men as leaders. True, Olive Winchester and Thelma Culver were selected as deans and proved to be superb academic leaders, but their selection was the exception. All other top elected NNC administrators in the 1970s and 1980s, save for JoAnn Willis as an associate dean and Martha Hopkins as acting dean for a bit more than a year, were men. Women were selected for registrar, divisional and departmental chairs, alumni director, and librarians; but as accreditation teams

Ginger Rinkenberger became the second NNC student and first Nazarene coed to win a coveted Rhodes Scholar award. (Fig. 5.16)

and other consultants noted, NNC was top-heavy with men. In this regard one NNC alumna wrote in 1989 to register her dismay about women being excluded from major NNC committees and the new foundation: "The message I clearly see is that the college does not believe women have the knowledge, expertise or critical thinking skills necessary to make a contribution to the college....What a sad message for women alumni and present women students!"

Perhaps change was in the air. Women were being moved into more leadership roles. The first woman regent, Trude Conrad, was elected in 1985, and one year later Elizabeth Mosteller Ott joined the board. Gradually others were elected alongside these two until a handful of the forty regents were women. Meanwhile, in the post-World War II years, women were also winning student body elections. In 1960, Joyce Oldenkamp was the first coed named vice president of the student body since the college's founding years, and in 1986 Dianna Fitz and in 1987 Laura Grossi became the first elected female student body presidents. Another significant breakthrough for NNC women came in 1985 when Ginger Rinkenberger was named a Rhodes Scholar. A double major in biology and psychology from Denver, Ginger was a gifted scholar and writer who, after her years in England as a Rhodes winner, became a filmmaker in New York. Alumni director Myron Finkbeiner, with his usual flair for organization, put together a Ginger Rinkenberger Day to recognize her and to bring back NNC's other Rhodes Scholar, John Luik, for a presentation. It was a grand day for Ginger and John, for NNC academics, and for the young women of NNC. By her hard-won selection Rinkenberger was among the crème de la crème of American graduates, and made NNC, at the time, the only Nazarene college with a Rhodes Scholar, let alone two.

Thankfully, in the midst of this serious push for gender equality at the college, some NNC students maintained a few chuckles. One campus male confessed to girl watching, along with many other guys. Did you notice, the writer pointed out, "that most NNC men sit facing the doorway of SAGA [dining hall]." They were "scoping-out" the new girls on campus. Why were the upperclassmen turning their attention to the freshmen girls just arriving? Maybe they had a better chance with those new coeds who did not yet recognize the shortcomings of the "scopers." Similarly, NNC students viewed the outcome of romance at work when a future NNC/NNU president and then director of the Northwesterners, David Alexander, sang a song dedicated to his wife Sandy; their matchmaking had occurred at another Nazarene college to the south. Bits of humor, boy-meets-girl stories, and long-time dating leading to engagements and marriages on the Nampa campus indicated that, in spite of demanding behavioral standards and challenging social issues, NNC was still in the matchmaking business, even though never admitting such in its guidelines or histories.

Alongside the ongoing matchmaking were competing signs of change. Interest in some aspects of the intramural program was falling. The sad end of Elmore Vail's yeoman and enthusiastic work as intramurals director; the establishment of more intercollegiate sports (especially for women); the increasing professionalization of campus music, drama, and speech programs; and the growing mobility of students, taking them more frequently off campus—all these trends undermined the strength of an intramural program that had engaged students' energies and attention for more than a half century. Interest had fallen so low that men's flag football teams had to be organized outside the Athletic-Literary societies.

Intercollegiate sports programs, at the same time, were on the rise at NNC. News of the men's and women's teams captured more pages in the *Crusader* than any other subject. Even the *Messenger* covered sports. Men's squads in basketball and baseball and women's in volleyball and basketball gained most of the attention, but other stories featured men's soccer and track and women's tennis and track teams as well. By 1992 athletic director Eric Forseth was juggling athletes, their schedules, and the cost of eight collegiate teams at NNC. A key leader in the expansion of women's athletics was Martha Hopkins, a fierce competitor herself, and a tiger in search of larger support for NNC athletic programs. Garry Matlock coached men's basketball during several impressive seasons, but problems with several of his players' actions on and off the court led to his replacement with Ed Weidenbach in late spring 1991. The next year the energetic new basketball coach, a former NNC player himself, led his team to a 26-9 record and an appearance at the national NAIA tournament, for the first time since 1956-1957.

Controversies in the sports program shadowed some of these successes. Earlier in the 1980s the women's field hockey program had been dropped even though the team had won its way into a national tournament. Tighter budgets until the mid-1980s caused other problems. But the largest brouhaha—and it may have been Wetmore's most difficult moment—came as a result of his dismissing Norman Parrish as a volunteer assistant basketball coach. A former star basketball player at NNC—and a Mormon—Parrish had accepted a verbal offer from Coach Matlock to help direct the team. President Wetmore, with reservations, supported the offer. But when an article in the Nampa *Idaho Press-Tribune* in September 1988 revealed that Parrish had taught at a Mormon seminary in Nampa, conservative Nazarenes attacked the president for hiring a "non-Christian" at odds with Nazarene teachings. Once the story of Parrish's Mormon background got out, Wetmore and NNC were hit in the next few weeks with a blizzard of negative publicity.

The stories in local newspapers ran largely to one side of the gamut—from the negative to the fiery critical. A Boise *Idaho Statesman* headline ran "Religion costs coach his job," and an opinion column read "A black eye for NNC." An editorial in the *Idaho Press-Tribune* pointed a finger with the title "Shame on NNC," and letters to the editor carried head notes "NNC president must be nutty" and "The hypocrisy of NNC." And a local educator seemed to speak for the opinions of many non-Nazarenes and non-Mormons in her story, "NNC botched Parrish affair."

Although many Nazarenes supported the president's very difficult decision, other church members were among his harshest critics. One former NNC basketball player zapped Wetmore, telling him that the writer had "no desire to witness athletic events at a higher institution of learning displaying such blatant bigotry. My excess monies will go to other causes." Wetmore thanked the man for his "sympathy in this decision-making process."

Wetmore tried to stem the tide of negative comment. He interviewed with local media to give his viewpoints and the stance of the Nazarene Church in hiring persons for the college sympathetic to the church's beliefs. Vice-President Hagood contacted local Latter-day Saint leaders, and President Wetmore sent informative and calming letters to Nazarene congregations. Most of his coreligionists seemed satisfied with the president's explanations, and local Mormon bishops responded understandingly, suggesting that, if the tables were turned, it would be difficult if not impossible to hire a Nazarene coach at BYU or Ricks College. Later in fall term 1988 the furor had died down some. Putting a positive slant on the controversy, Wetmore told an inquirer that he was convinced NNC "is coming out of this recent issue stronger than when we went in…[;] if there was any question about NNC's Christian commitment that question has been settled."

A number of other less sensational occurrences and issues challenged Wetmore. Conservatives were upset with what they considered the liberal views of NNC political science professor Steve Shaw in his newspaper columns. Wetmore defended Shaw not as a spokesman for NNC but as a Nampa resident fully free to express his own opinions in the newspaper. Creationists also charged that NNC was soft on evolution and, concomitantly, professors were not providing inerrant interpretations of the Bible in their classes, notably the Genesis account of creation. The president, urging them to examine the Nazarene church *Manual* and its statements on creation and scriptural inspiration, asserted that NNC stuck closely to those denominational guidelines. He also encouraged science scholar Gilbert Ford to prepare a statement and presentation on how an evangelical could accept theistic evolution as God's way of creation. The issue would not die, however, and resurfaced, drenched in bile, during the Hagood presidency. Although Wetmore had much less trouble with an outspoken and sometimes trouble-making *Crusader* than Pearsall, he did have to deal with the publication of an underground newspaper, the *Anti-Crusader* (1990) that stirred up some interest and minor discord.

Another controversial tete-a-tete that embroiled Wetmore came after he invited Cecil Andrus, governor of Idaho, to give the graduation address in 1990. It was Idaho's centennial year, and Wetmore wanted the governor to speak at commencement as a symbol of NNC's ties to and support for its home state. But not long before graduation time, Andrus vetoed a strong right-to-life bill that turned anti-abortion supporters livid, including many Nazarenes. More than a few of these pro-life persons wanted to know how the college president could invite a man who supported "murdering babies" to address NNC students and alumni at graduation time.

Most of the central truths of the matter got lost when emotions boiled over. Andrus explained that he vetoed the legislation because it was poorly written, probably would get challenged in court and cost Idahoans hundreds of thousands of dollars in legal fees, and would stand in the way of better right-to-life legislation. He added that he stood with most Nazarenes in their anti-abortion stance but could not endorse this bad bill. Those explanations satisfied Wetmore and some NNC faculty but were lost on critics who saw the conflict entirely as a black and white issue. Some of the harshest opponents of Andrus—and Wetmore—threatened to disrupt graduation to demonstrate their political stances. Fortunately that did not happen, but the president nonetheless suffered through several weeks of disconcerting upset leading up to graduation and even beyond the ceremony. Adding to Wetmore's burden at the time was mounting criticism of the NNC basketball coach and increased calls for his resignation. Perhaps more letters arrived in the president's box about the need to replace the coach than to cancel the governor's invitation to speak at graduation, another testimony of how important the NNC sports program had become to some die-hard alumni.

At times Wetmore appeared forced to dine on a steady diet of controversy. Thankfully that was not always the case. Supporters wrote in to encourage him during the Parrish and Andrus imbroglios and in his daily duties. His voluminous correspondence included hundreds of these missives and his letters of thanks in turn. In public, Wetmore seemed noncombative, his reactions usually calming controversy rather than adding fuel to already-burning fires.

To provide a positive turn on campus events and to encourage students and alumni to see other sides of NNC experiences, Wetmore frequently saluted the achievements of students and alumni. These communications illustrated what he thought to be the major purpose of the college: to produce a new crop of leaders to direct the Nazarene Church—and other Christian organizations—in the coming decades. Besides writing letters of congratulation such as to Ginger Rinkenberger on her Rhodes Scholar award and to students winning student body offices, the president also made sure he contacted other students and/or faculty who had achieved some kind of milestone or who were challenged with new moments of disappointment or grief. He was extraordinarily pastoral in these presidential activities.

NNC grad Rick Hieb climbed high to be the only Nazarene astronaut. (Fig. 5.17)

He also celebrated the achievements of alumni. When NNC graduate Rick Hieb was selected as an astronaut and eventually made it into space, his successes were paraded in several issues of the *Messenger*—and *Crusader*—and he was brought to Nampa to be appropriately lionized on campus and in the community. Jeff Carr, who had established an inner city work for young people in Los Angeles; Harmon Schmelzenbach, life-long missionary; Noel Riley Fitch, nationally known author; Jack Wright, lawyer and activist; Ann Kiemel Anderson, popular youth speaker—these were all Nazarene stars receiving presidential accolades and brought to campus to speak. Wetmore likewise made certain that *Messenger* readers and the campus community were aware of earlier, venerable students and graduates: they included Louise Robinson Chapman, the epitome of Nazarene missions and church executive; Jerry Johnson and George Coulter, general superintendents of the church. Sprinkled among the vignettes of well-known leaders were pen portraits of campus leaders like intramural director and coach Elmore Vail and nonpareil alumni director Myron Finkbeiner and campus servants such as Jo Kincaid, postmistress

Myron Finkbeiner redefined the Alumni Office with his nonpareil leadership as Alumni Director. (Fig. 5.18)

and Alumni House housekeeper. Had Wetmore cast his congratulatory net wider, he would have featured such life-changing teachers as retiring professors A. Elwood Sanner (religion), Double E Hill (music), Robert Woodward (history) and Helen Wilson (speech and drama). And looking back he would have emphasized the importance of his hiring Gene Schandorff as the new college chaplain. Schandorff played a key leadership role in campus religious activities for years to come.

Wetmore also appeared to enjoy and sponsor celebration. He encouraged the "big doings" that sprang up around NNC's 75th birthday in 1987-88. Under the general leadership of historian Dr. Ray Cooke and organized around the general theme of "Changing Times, Enduring Values," the 75th anniversary committee arranged a full school year of celebration. A huge Homecoming in November 1987 kicked off the months of visiting speakers, entertainments, and sports events. The next spring John E. Riley's valuable history *From Sagebush to Ivy: The Story of Northwest Nazarene College...1913-1988* appeared, providing the college with a master narrative. Later in the spring the annual NNC graduation continued the celebration. But the most dramatic event of the birthday year came after the committee secured Mel Schroeder, Nazarene-dom's master of pageant and extravaganza, as director, to put together a huge celebration entitled "There Is a Season." Linda Quanstrom wrote the script and Jerry Nelson worked with the music to fashion a sprawling festival of music, pictures, and drama, a mini-history of the college. Involving dozens of students, alumni, and faculty the four "season" presentation hinged on "Reflection, Recalling, Tribute and Building." After two presentations in Nampa the 60-person production went on the road in spring 1988 for two showings in Washington, two in Oregon, and two others in Colorado. Based on the words of Ecclesiastes 3:1—"To everything there is a season, and a time to every purpose under heaven"—the pageant did more to advertise NNC than any other presentation. During the year, alumni, the pioneers and keepers of the NNC past, were recipients of a barrage of information on the 75th year in issues of the *Messenger*. But current NNC students, for some reason, demonstrated much less interest, perhaps too busy living in the present and plotting the future than looking into the past.

The June 1992 issue of the *Messenger* announced that President Wetmore had resigned to take the presidency of Nazarene Theological Seminary. In doing so he was following in the footsteps of previous NNC president Lewis T. Corlett. (Kenneth Pearsall had also been offered but rejected the NTS presidency.) Nazarene college presidents and professors of religion and philosophy saw the NTS presidency or a professorship at the seminary as a step up in their careers; rarely had any moved in the opposite direction.

Wetmore had reason to be satisfied with his nine-year stint at the NNC helm. He had bounced back from the difficult, rudderless times of his first years in office to direct the more stable, expanding years at the close of his presidency. Stronger financing, better planning, more extensive outreach to Nampa and Idaho communities, and national rankings for the college evidenced these improvements. Weathering the Parrish and Andrus controversies, Wetmore had, with the help of Business Manager Hal Weber, Deans of Students Jerry Hull and Ken Hills, and especially institutional advancement leader Rich Hagood, provided strong foundations for what lay ahead. Some of his colleagues viewed Wetmore as a superb consensus builder, among Nazarenes and non-Nazarenes, in Nampa and out on the NNC educational zone. They also emphasized his balance of head, heart, and outreaching hand.

Revealingly, at the close of Wetmore's service in 1992, Eastern Nazarene graduates had served as NNC presidents for 52 years: DeLong (12), Riley (21), Pearsall (10), Wetmore (9). Indeed, three ENC graduates, Riley, Pearsall, and Wetmore, had led NNC for 40 consecutive years, 1952 to 1992. Had the leadership of these East Coast Nazarenes made a difference at NNC? One could point to obvious influences: all of these presidents were products of a Christian liberal arts education, majoring in either religion and philosophy or English. All had come under the sway of the Church of the Nazarene's best-known mistress of the classic liberal arts, Dean Bertha Munro. Through her tutelage and influence, as well as in the balance of mind and heart on display at the campus at Wollaston, Massachusetts, these NNC presidents-to-be had already been introduced to the major partnership to be worked out at all Nazarene campuses. Over the years, other ENC students and graduates joined them in long-term teaching assignments at NNC: among them, Marian Washburn, Donald Tillotson, Robert Woodward, Arthur Seamans, and Irving Laird. More than a few ENC persons were invited to speak at NNC: Bertha Munro, Ed Mann, Richard Schubert, and Kent Hill (the latter was an NNC grad who had become the ENC president). Most of the presidents and professors with ENC backgrounds came, as students of Nazarene culture would observe, with an evangelical outlook different from Nazarene perspectives in the Midwest,

South, and even southern California. Those direct links of socioculture influence are difficult to trace, but whatever one decides, the facts stand: in the first 79 years of its history, NNC was led for 52 years by presidents with ENC background.

Tradition and tragedy, like two unmatched horses, marched alongside one another in the year following Wetmore's resignation. In late summer 1992 tradition looked to be changing when a layman and an NNC graduate became the new president; both were tradition-breaking moves destroying older cakes of custom and establishing new ones. Then tragedy invaded the scene when the new president died in office before serving one year. With that untoward happening new traditions and tragedy seemed to be galloping in unison.

In 1992 Leon Doane became the tenth NNC president, as a result of both familiar and untypical campus customs. Like dozens of other early Nazarene families, Doane's parents brought their family to Nampa so their children could attend a Nazarene college. Doane attended NNC, as did his siblings, and he graduated in 1956 with a major in business administration. Joining West One Bank soon after graduating, he worked there for thirty-four years, serving in the bank's branches in Idaho and was vice president of the Boise Business Banking Center before he came to NNC. He had also completed training at the Pacific Coast Banking School in 1970. A member of the NNC Board of Trustees for nineteen years, he had been the board's chair for ten years. He was an active local churchman, also working for five years at the general church headquarters division of finance in Kansas City. In addition, he was elected to the General Board of the Nazarene Church. At NNC he was president of the Alumni Association for three years, named Alumnus of the Year in 1974, and awarded an honorary doctorate by his alma mater in 1980.

Doane came to the NNC presidency by an unusual route and in doing so inadvertently set precedents for the next generation of presidents. The first step in his presidential search followed familiar lines: a committee of regents, faculty, students, the alumni president, the foundation chair, and a general superintendent winnowed the applicant pool of 37 persons to 14. Next the regents stepped in to reduce the number of candidates to three. After the board interviewed those candidates, a vote followed with all three receiving the same range of votes on two different ballots: Jerry Lambert (17), Tom Nees (7), Ron Benefiel (7), and 4 blanks. After the second regent vote produced the same results, board member Jim Diehl—urging the board rescind its early actions—suggested they allow Chairman Leon Doane to become a candidate. Following Diehl's suggestion, Doane was asked to step out of the room; the regents then voted him into the presidency, with Doane receiving 27 of the 35 votes, the exact number needed for election.

Although Doane himself did not think of his election "as a change in purpose or goals, or anything," that decision illustrated a large change in the type of person selected as NNC president. Doane was the first person not a pastor or church leader, and the first businessman, to be named president. He was also the first NNC graduate to become president. He and the next two presidents were laymen, and he and Richard Hagood were NNC grads; and David Alexander, who followed Hagood in 2008, had been a professor at NNC. That meant presidential leadership at NNC had shifted to laypersons with strong ties to the NNC student body or faculty. Tragically, Doane's presidency, begun at the end of July 1992, lasted less than nine months. He was diagnosed with incurable cancer in February and remained in the hospital until his death less than two months later in April 1993. Before he had barely begun the end came.

Dr. Leon Doane, the first layman to serve, became NNC's tenth president (1992–93). His very brief administration was cut tragically short by his untimely death. (Fig. 5.19)

Even before the tide of sympathetic responses to Doane's death flooded onto and throughout the campus early in spring 1992 and made impossible an early, balanced evaluation of his leadership, students had taken to the "gentle giant" in the control room. They liked him, and he, they. Students noticed his attendance in chapel (and the absence of many faculty members), his coming to sports events, and his trying to learn and remember students' names. Student body president Rosco Williamson told the press at Doane's inauguration that in his few weeks in office the new president had revealed "his caring toward the students" and that they would "return the support."

In Doane's opening address to faculty, other administrators, and staff, he asked them to think about the hopes of Eugene Emerson and other NNC founders and whether the college was following their visions. Were they still pursuing the tenuous balance involved in a Christian liberal arts college, and were the faculty and staff yet committed to "the development of Christian character within the philosophy and framework of genuine scholarship"? After rehearsing the most recent activities and achievements of faculty and administrators, Doane laid out his first goals. He would work to "broaden the donor base and increase endowment for scholarships to departments," help raise funds for the fine arts center, begin a search for a new academic dean, address the recommendations of interim accreditation visitors, and push for more recognition of NNC as a "Destination Campus." In closing he expressed his happiness to be in the presidential harness and predicted "our greatest days are before us."

Then quickly followed hectic weeks of travel, contact with churches, districts, and pastors, and the campus activities always facing a new president. By way of his nearly twenty years on the regents, his Nampa links, and his business connections around the Pacific Northwest, Doane was well armed with experience and backgrounds in these areas. Still, no amount of experience could have prepared the new president for the usual and unexpected challenges that came his way.

All NNC presidents have received dozens—if not hundreds—of letters of complaint in their mail. Over the years the crabby and negative letters have far outnumbered those missives encouraging or supporting a chief administrator's achievements or strong leadership. Does the Church of the Nazarene give members license to "shape up" a president or to direct his attention to misdeeds or wrong attitudes the critic has perceived? Evidently so, for those dunning letters came throughout the first eighty years, and now Doane got his dose.

The first arrived from an unnamed, long-time friend. After chuckling with him about the rascally things they had done together at teenage camps and among Nampa Nazarene youth gatherings, the letter-writer paraded her discontents. First she heard professors in the religion department were not only presenting theistic evolution but also pointing to it as the theory to be heeded. Even worse they were speaking of the Biblical story of Abraham nearly sacrificing his son Isaac on an altar as "Jewish legend" and suggesting "there are no more miracles." And why should someone in a chapel presentation talk about "His/her." "Is this person trying to say that God is He or Her?" She was bothered by these and other rumors but had to admit they were "second hand knowledge....If it wasn't such a big problem [she added] I would ask [that] my tithe not to be used for paying NNC's budget. Maybe that spells how strongly I feel about the matter[s]."

Social concerns fired up three other letter-writers. Why "were there no women directly involved...in the graduation service" in the previous spring, one non-Nazarene asked? "Not to involve women in the academic leadership is an element of the twenty-first century that the school, not the theologians, needs to address." Another student wrote in about the inconsistencies in NNC standards. Students were prohibited from dancing, which was not an issue with the student; but "CONSISTENCY" was. He saw entertainers during a basketball half-time dancing "as entertainment"; and that was allowing "a double standard" that should "be resolved." Still another student was "concerned for the spiritual welfare of our school." The recent "No-so Hard Rock Café" program, with its "fake cigarette smoke, the fake drinks and the waitresses in tight skirts," was upsetting. Also, too much "perverse 'humor'" was being allowed in entertainments, especially on a campus of a "Christian" school.

In response, Doane thanked her for writing, and he promised to "pursue" these incidents and "visit with those who are responsible for these actions."

Faculty members also had queries to send and points to make. A mathematics professor asked for clarification on why Doane claimed NNC had expanded faculty in a time of flat enrollment. A faculty member in music reminded the president of the need for funded scholarships in music by re-sending a memo he had written to President Wetmore.

But the most thorough and revealing faculty letter came from a professor in religion responding to the president's request for reactions to "the initiatives for NNC for the next three years." In the extensive, well-researched letter listing annual NNC expenditures over a ten-year period (1985-94) for the president's office, academics, student development, financial affairs, and institutional advancement, he demonstrated convincingly how academics (only 26 percent expansion in ten years) and student development (2 percent expansion) had suffered in these allocations and how much institutional advancement (287 percent expansion) had received. He listed a half-dozen other needs and then leveled both guns at the library budget; it was "an absolute disaster." Proposed purchase of electronic equipment to network with Boise State University was admirable, but firstly and most importantly NNC simply needed to buy more books for its library shelves. He could "guarantee" the president that the next accreditation team would hear about the library lacks. The faculty expected "to speak very strongly on this issue." Unfortunately as this lengthy, insightful letter made its way into the president's office, he was headed to the hospital for life-threatening exploratory surgery.

Doane did not feel confident about his academic backgrounds, so he depended on Lilburn Wesche for guidance and leadership in dealing with faculty and other academic matters. Wesche, named acting dean after Dan Berg had resigned, set out to be and succeeded in being more than an interim dean. He worked closely with students, urging them to consult with him on what they wanted in the curriculum, including major changes if they wished. Wesche and Student Body President Williamson worked together well, and the *Crusader* strongly recommended that Wesche be named dean as the search for the position opened in spring 1993. When a reporter from the campus newspaper asked Wesche if he would be interested in the dean's job beyond his fill-in time, Wesche told him, "Today, yeah." His "whole preparation was for administrative assignments," Wesche added, but "one of the things about higher education is that it assigns roles to people for which they're totally unprepared." Speaking for himself, the reporter concluded that some might "see higher education as a horse-and-buggy in a jet-paced world," but he was certain that "the leadership of men like Dr. Lilburn Wesche...may bring it up to speed." Three months later another campus reporter spoke of Wesche's accomplishments as interim dean but added "despite coming from the faculty...Wesche has not been well-received by the faculty, many not agreeing with his proposed reforms....It is very likely that someone else will be selected to fill the position of academic dean permanently." The prediction proved on target. Wesche was not selected; Samuel Dunn of Seattle Pacific was chosen after Richard Hagood became the next president. Perhaps Wesche's realistic, direct, and sometimes blunt observations may have put him at odds with some of his colleagues.

Because Doane spent much of the first part of his presidency making obligatory contacts off campus and keeping up with his general church assignments before illness struck him down, others on campus filled in the gap of leadership. Wesche handled academics; Hal Weber, business details; Richard Hagood, institutional advancement; Ken Hills, student development; and Ken Watson, administrative details. Others came, like Gary Skaggs and Jerry Gunstream, to help Hagood in raising funds. Most things moved on an even keel in 1992-93: enrollment was up slightly, the budget was balanced, and planning and fund-raising moved on apace.

But a few events attracted large attention—none larger or more significant than NNC's serving as host for the national NAIA Division II men's tournament on March 11-16, 1993. The tournament brought twenty teams (and more, later) and thousands of fans to Nampa; a carnival-like atmosphere flooded over the campus. Although the previous year the NNC team had won the District 2 championship and gone to the nationals, in 1992-93 the NNC men had lost out in the first round of the playoff but gained a slot in the national tournament as the host college. Viewed as an underdog, NNC nonetheless posted three wins and made its way into the semifinals, including an unexpected win over defending champion Grace College of Indiana. But the men's dream crashed with an overtime loss to Willamette University, the eventual tourney winner. Brian Locke, the team's leading scorer, racked up a record 39 points in the game with Grace and was named to the national tournament—and several other all-tourney—teams. (His older sister Kerri had also set an all-time, one-game scoring record in 1990; they were the son and daughter of NNC's all-time leading scorer Gary Locke.) The well-attended and very successful tournament, largely under the direction of indefatigable Athletic Director Eric Forseth, put Nampa and NNC on the NAIA map. The tournament organization happily returned to the campus for several more years. The women's basketball team also finished with a flourish, winning its way into the district tournament before being ousted. Later in the spring in an otherwise lackluster baseball season, pitcher Mike Mortimer was a bright light, selected as NAIA District 2 Player of the Year as the area's leading mounds man. Obviously, sports at NNC, intercollegiate and intramural, continued to capture the attention of students and alumni alike.

Another kind of athletic—and daring—feat captured the attention of students at a May convocation. It was an extraordinary event featured in the *Crusader* but somehow overlooked in the *Messenger*. Just as a professor of English was announcing winners of the creative writing contest, three nearly naked young men dashed in front of the students gathered for convocation and out through the gym. Masked and dressed in tee shirts and sneakers, and nothing more, the streakers sprinted across the floor and out the door without being identified or apprehended. Reactions were mixed, of course. Chaplain Gene Schandorff expressed the obligatory response: "Incredibly inappropriate," but the freshman class president thought the dash "a work of art and simply beautiful." Although nothing like this had happened recently on the NNC campus, former Dean of Students Irving Laird recalled three similar events in earlier years. On one occasion, four NNC freshmen, challenged to match the streaking fad then invading Idaho college campuses, appeared in nature's wonders just outside a Meridian radio station. In reporting all these events, the *Crusader* reporter ended his story: "Streaking: today, yesterday, and forever." These varied responses, so typical of the NNC community, surfaced again in the next week's paper. In her letter to the editor one sophomore coed confessed she was "horrified" with the streakers. "This kind of behavior is not exemplary of Christian believers," she intoned, "and speaks poorly of the campus and the students of this school." Another young woman's reaction was brief and variant: "My only regret concerning the streakers" she responded, "is that they didn't trip and get raspberries."

Dr. Eric Forseth provided valuable leadership in athletics and in enrollment and marketing. (Fig. 5.20)

During the 1992-93 year members of the NNC community had experienced a full run of emotions. They had lost their president—the only NNC president to die in office—and grieved his short, unfulfilled administration. There were the uncertainties, too, of working with so many fill-in and new leaders in administrative positions. They had experienced the emotional high of hosting the dramatic, attention-catching NAIA national tournament and the totally unexpected near-success of the NNC men's and women's team. The usual gamut of classes, schedules, chapels, and student loan pressures also faced campus residents. What would the future bring to the college? Downs, ups, and uncertainties—all again jostled the campus and its constituents.

6

From College to University

THE HAGOOD YEARS: 1993-2008

They came from Oklahoma like John Steinbeck's Joads: father, mother, and six children crammed into a Ford Model T. Lining out in 1937 for the Treasure Valley that lapped over from Idaho into Oregon, the family traipsed to alien sagebrush acres, sight unseen, near Ontario, Oregon. Without capital to purchase a fully developed farm, the family lived in a tent until a rude home was erected. It was a difficult, demanding life—pushed forward by diligent and long labor. Gradually, by dint of daily drudgery, the family hacked out a living and established a home in the new, forbidding environment.

Into this home came Richard A. Hagood on Christmas day 1941. He was the seventh and last child in the family. He spent all his boyhood and adolescent years in eastern Oregon, milking cows and doing other farm chores. When Hagood was a young teenager, his father and mother left the Church of the Nazarene, and they and he became charter members of the newly launched Bible Missionary Union (Church) in the Nampa-Caldwell area. Although the strict new denomination forbade participation in interscholastic athletics, Hagood was able to play sports while in mid-school and high school, becoming an adept basketball player at Ontario High School.

Attending college appeared nearly impossible since family funding was lacking. Still, at first thinking of Eastern Oregon College or the College of Idaho, he turned to NNC when his older brother and his wife, who had attended the college, invited Hagood to live with them and go to college in Nampa. A job at Birds Eye cannery and then other campus employment allowed Hagood to move into the dorm. He also joined the basketball team. All elbows, knees, and skinny legs—his teammates called him "Goose"—Hagood played four years of varsity basketball. Playing with NNC star Gary Locke, Hagood was a scorer and playmaker too, an excellent hoopster on his own, and a baseball player. Before graduating, he married Junella Finkbeiner, from one of the best-known Nampa Nazarene families. She turned out to be a thorough, supportive partner in Hagood's demanding, upward-bound career.

Hagood became a teacher of history in the Boise area. Then after completing a master's in Interdisciplinary Studies at the University of Oregon, he enrolled in and completed a doctorate (1972) in the history and philosophy of education at the University of Illinois. Then followed two years (1972-74) on the staff at the University of Idaho in Moscow before he moved to nearby Washington State University in Pullman. In the next eleven years (1974-85) he filled several staff and administrative positions before serving as associate provost for Extended University Services (1981-85). He was much involved in the planning for and implementation of WSU branch campuses. In hindsight those were presidential apprentice years, preparing Hagood for work in the field of institutional advancement and academic planning.

Well before these positions in higher education, Hagood had experienced a dramatic life-changing moment. Even after his retirement in 2008, he remembered his "calling" of nearly forty years earlier. While on a trip to Mexico in 1969, he felt a strong tug, an urging to return to NNC. He never forgot the impact of that calling, and a decade and a half after its occurrence, when the invitation came to NNC, he accepted, feeling that he was heeding the divine urging that came to him in Mexico.

President Wetmore's invitation to come to NNC in 1985 ended Hagood's climb at Washington State and brought him to Nampa. And he hit the ground running. One of Hagood's NNC colleagues explained that everyone expected new administrators to listen a few months before speaking. Not Richard Hagood. "I joked with him that he was supposed to listen (on the [presidential] cabinet) for the first six months before he proposed anything," Jerry Hull recalled, but Hagood "chimed in at the first major meeting we had." And, as we have seen, Hagood's suggestions and his work on NNC advancement, including fund-raising and campus enhancement, were central to the "Destination Campus" concept. His energies and actions during the next eight years led some to think of him as co-president of NNC. When the presidency opened twice—at the end of the Wetmore and Doane administrations—he was touted by several as a strong presidential possibility. It almost did not happen.

Dr. Richard Hagood, here with his wife Junella, gave superb leadership as NNC/NNU's eleventh president (1993–2008). Fig. 6.1

Rumors about Hagood as a presidential candidate surfaced in spring 1992, but the stronger possibility crystallized in summer 1993 after the death of Leon Doane. Within days after President Doane's death in April 1993, the NNC regents swung into action to find a new president. The process turned out to be longer and more complex than everyone thought. Under the able, energetic leadership of Monte Chitwood, a search committee advertised the position and quickly winnowed the applicants to their two top choices, Hagood and Jim Bond, president of Point Loma Nazarene College. On August 13, after 27 long ballots were cast, a two-thirds majority finally supported Bond. The Point Loma Nazarene College president came for a campus visit but two weeks later decided not to accept the NNC presidency. As Bond told one acquaintance, "To have been elected President of NNC by the Board of Regents has been one of life's highest honors... [but] after much thought and prayer I have decided that it is God's will for me to remain at Point Loma Nazarene College." The decision was all the more difficult because Bond had pastored Nampa's College Church of the Nazarene and his wife Sally had been an NNC student. "There has been an almost irresistible attraction to accept the presidency there," he told the same acquaintance.

On September 30, the regents then moved to elect Hagood on a yes/no ballot. On the first vote he was named the new NNC president, "amidst great rejoicing!" On the next day Hagood was announced as the new NNC president, its eleventh, to the campus and community.

The complicated voting, the delays, and the initial disappointment undoubtedly led to the election's being a bittersweet moment for Hagood. Superbly trained and experienced in college administration, for more than thirty years connected in one way or another to NNC, and a man devoted to his faith and with a sense of calling, Hagood was as well prepared—on the academic and administrative side—as anyone to be NNC president. But he was nearly passed over. Finally named, Hagood's selection solidified the precedents that Doane had set: a layman and an NNC graduate assuming the presidency. To these precedents were added Hagood's doctorate in higher education and his manifold experiences as a college administrator. He would prove to be a superb NNC leader in the next fifteen years.

What kind of person was NNC's eleventh president? Most found Richard Hagood approachable and enthusiastic in his support for the college. A few others thought him retiring—even a bit shy; one long-time and close friend thought of Hagood as a "mild-mannered introvert." More like the reserved Wetmore than the other preacher presidents Riley and Pearsall, Hagood quietly and competently gained the mounting trust of regents, pastors, and students in his decade and half in the president's chair. When Hagood himself filled out a questionnaire entitled "Leadership Orientations," he ranked himself high on interpersonal skills, concern for people, toughness and aggressiveness, as a listener, a coach and developer of people, and as a "politician." Conversely, he thought of himself as less strong in analytical skills, as a visionary, as a skilled negotiator, or as a person of imagination and creativity. Junella Hagood, the president's wise and winsome helpmate, took a different tack in evaluating her husband the president. When asked about his leadership at NNC, Junella pointed to his addresses and presentations as notably important; "he led with those," she told an interviewer. "You need to pay special attention to them."

The mind and heart of Richard Hagood and his strong—even intense—attachment to NNC were readily apparent before he took hold of the presidential reins. In the eight years of his pre-presidential period, as vice president for institutional advancement from 1985 to 1993, he furnished several revealing reports and helped prepare important strategic planning documents for the campus community as well as for the board of regents. These reports foreshadowed the goals, the content, and the strategies that marked the Hagood years in the president's office.

In his first years as an NNC administrator Hagood led a revealing fast break across the NNC terrain. Arriving in July 1985 he quickly assumed leadership, as we have seen, for several important campus activities. Three months later Hagood provided a helpful report to the regents on all these segments of his new job. Even more impressive, his report included a handful of significant recommendations concerning future strategic planning, a "development manual" for the college budget matters, and matching fund guidelines. Near the close of his report he appended "several general comments about ... [his] first one hundred days" in office. He appreciated the prayer support he received in the decision-making process and indicated "that God gave us tangible indications that it is His will for us to be at NNC."

Then, at the end came the most revealing part of his significant report. "Many of the recommendations I propose for the October [1985] meeting of the Board of Trustees," he wrote, "would normally take one or two years of preparation and consideration. The Regents will decide, but I have been operating from the assumption that we do not have the time." He urged the regents to quickly gain additional financial support and aid in enlarging the college's enrollments. (NNC enrollments had dropped 100 in each of the three previous years.) It would "require extraordinary effort on the part of all of us" to do what was necessary.

The reports Hagood prepared for the college administration and the regents continued to roll out twice a year like pleasing and insightful products emerging from a smoothly running and highly efficient headquarters. Only three to four months after taking office, Richard Hagood was exhibiting the energetic, straight-ahead leadership NNC needed. The coming years, and with them his dozens of other reports, added to his quickly expanding reputation of administrative excellence.

The planning documents Hagood prepared and delivered to the NNC campus community and educational zone helped Nazarenes to think more broadly. He understood, from his previous service on the college's alumni board and its board of regents, that "NNC was not realizing its full potential, was inward looking, maintained a closed campus community, and lacked a strategic vision and plan for the future." When he came as a new administrator, he was shocked with "all of what had to be done." He "walked into" a campus where enrollments were dropping sharply, where needed funds were lacking, and no plan was in place to address these problems. Plus, previous plans of the city of Nampa to build a four-lane street through the NNC campus were still in place, had been since the early 1960s, and "nothing" could be done about that agreement seemed to be the consensus. This inward looking, unaggressive, and—in fact—defeatist attitude had to be countered. In his first months as vice-president for institutional advancement, Hagood and others formulated more forward-looking agendas to launch strategic planning. These like-minded administrators urged the regents to "authorize the initiation of an institutional planning process." After the regents accepted the proposal, a drafted *"Statement of Mission"* was prepared for the campus community in September 1986 and adopted by the regents one month later. In revised form this document became known as *"A Context for Planning"* and in several subsequent editions served as the major blueprint for strategic planning for the next decade and a half. Although the original *"Statement of Mission"* carried the name of President Wetmore, it sounds like Richard Hagood and was indeed primarily the product of his relish for strategic planning.

The organization and content of the *"Statement of Mission"* and the later *"Context for Planning"* followed a uniform format. These documents put "in context" the needs of higher education in changing times but also explicitly reiterated NNC's traditional core values. Indeed, the "central theme" of the initial planning document was "changing times—enduring values."

The key distinction in the planning documents lay in college leaders and boosters understanding shifting sociocultural and economic pressures pressing on—indeed, reshaping—higher education. Planners urged NNC's watchdogs to make sure the college maintained its holiness or Wesleyan traditions while, simultaneously, they kept the college abreast of changing times. That dual purpose was encapsulated in one sentence: "Strategic planning is characterized by its awareness of the institution's [NNC's] place in the changing environment of higher education and the development of mechanisms to adjust quickly to change while remaining true to the historical role and purpose."

In his first years as an NNC administrator, Richard Hagood engineered the agreements to secure Kurtz Park for the college and to reroute city streets around the campus. (Fig. 6.2)

Put specifically, NNC, as it planned its future, had to comprehend the shifting racial and ethnic, gender, and age-related groups wanting college educations. A liberal arts core might remain, but new professional education programs (e.g., business, nursing, and computers) had to be considered. Possible graduate programs should also be studied, especially in fields of education, business, and religion. Better community connections with Nampa and the Treasure Valley and with the greater Northwest must be forged, and more insightful understandings of competition for the same students must be comprehended. The initial planning document of 1986 closed with a probing section on how NNC must retain its mission through careful examination of its religious-academic emphases and what kind of students it was producing.

These fundamental ideas became the architectonic platform on which Richard Hagood eventually built his presidential administration. And he did not let up. Alongside the *"Context for Planning"* guides that appeared every three years in his pre-presidential period (1987, 1990, 1993) and in revised form in his presidential years, Hagood presented other more long-range plans that looked a decade or so into the future. The most significant of these far-reaching presentations early in his presidency was entitled *"At the Crossing,"* delivered to the Board of Regents in March 1995. The new president considered the imaginative address, after discussions and possible amendments, a paper that could "provide a 'planning and decision framework' for the years ahead."

Hagood borrowed the pioneer crossings of challenging rivers to reach their newer homes as an apt metaphor for evaluating, planning, and implementing the future course of NNC from 1995 to 2005. Just as the westward-moving wagon trains had to follow a "rutted route of promise," face threatening and uncertain tests, and "keep moving," so the college must courageously and energetically "guard the soul of NNC" while it kept moving into the uncertain future. As he had often done before, Hagood laid before the regents the shifting U. S. and regional contexts influencing NNC's plans for the years ahead.

Those heading up the trail had to be aware of intimidating currents and eddies, treacherous passes, and daily difficult challenges. At the same time, college planners and supporters must pay specific and close attention to the changing contexts profoundly shaping and sometimes remolding the NNC campus and community. Hagood exhorted his listeners and readers to be particularly aware of shifting demographic trends like the leveling off of Nazarene church and youth populations, the increasing spiritual openness sweeping over Nazarenes, and the emerging diversity of theological viewpoints within the church. Accompanying these changes was the willingness of many Christians to join and follow nondenominational groups like Campus Crusade for Christ, Focus on the Family, and Promise Keepers. Even more challenging were the divisions within denominations "between the liberals and the conservatives." Public policy shifts such as lessening federal aid to students and the resultant necessity of more individual borrowing, as well as a changing standard of accreditation, added other hazards confronting planners and the path-makers.

Nor must anyone overlook the transitions taking place in NNC's host community, the Treasure Valley, and on the campus itself. Idaho's population in the Boise Valley was quickly expanding: Boise had jumped from 102,249 in 1980 to 185,787 in 2000, while in the same two decades Nampa more than doubled from 25,112 to 51,867. Since NNC was the only private Christian college in western Idaho, Hagood noted, "the opportunity may exist for NNC to become the college of choice for many congregations, Nazarene or other." NNC enrollments were up a bit since the mid-1980s, and some funding was available for "new initiatives or administrative flexibility," but these dollars were small in number and increasingly difficult to gather.

With these contexts clearly in view, Hagood suggested that NNC must plan wisely and well for the next decade—into the twenty-first century. It was his view that the college must ride on—and move with rather than be swept aside—by these currents of change; NNCers must be more insightful, comprehensive, and forward-looking in their planning. Hagood made clear he was willing to show how the college and its constituency could keep atop these inundating currents instead of being buried under them. Radically optimistic and enthusiastically committed to NNC, Hagood insightfully listed the major crossings facing NNC modern pioneers. They needed to do a better job servicing their "primary constituency" (the Church of the Nazarene), expanding a constituency among non-Nazarenes, and providing graduate programs in "the helping professions" (e.g., social work and nursing). In addition, NNC wagon masters should strengthen the college's liberal arts core, expand NNC's research mission without becoming a "publish or perish" institution, and provide varied international experiences for students. At the same time they must reinforce the campus's commitment to serve and encourage a concomitant upbeat outlook that avoided cynicism, negativity, and criticism from the Nampa community.

The closing section of *"At the Crossing"* provided a step-by-step plan for implementing these goals in the near-distant future. These would include reducing the size of classes with excessively large faculty-student ratios, eliminating classes and majors with low enrollments, and proposing new graduate programs needed in the Treasure Valley and pushing forward with the "destination college" concept and its expanded master plan for the campus.

The specific content of this important presentation takes on much larger meaning when one realizes how many of those specifics became central measures of Hagood's administration. In addition, he utilized the generalizations mounted here for the three-year cycles of planning interspersed between this major address and another that came nine years later, *"Fulfilling the Promise: NNU at One Hundred"* (2004).

One can, however, make too much of Richard Hagood's power as a presenter and planner and in doing so overlook other notable facets of his personality and leadership. A closer look at other changes, connections, and controversies casts further illuminating light on the personal dimensions of Hagood's fifteen-year presidency.

In many of his presentations and his personal correspondence Hagood asserted that NNC must do better at connecting with Nampa and the larger Treasure Valley. If NNC were to expand in numbers and influence and become the comprehensive university he was envisioning , the college must link up with its immediate community even while keeping close ties with its supporting denomination, the Church of the Nazarene. These stronger and expanded connections should be personal, academic, and institutional.

Hagood led by example. Making himself available to the newspaper editors of the area, he fostered better and expanded relationships with media leaders of the Nampa and Boise areas. As Wayne Cornell, editor of the Nampa *Idaho Press-Tribune*, told Hagood, "you[r] arrival was the best thing that ever happened to the school." The president had "talked frankly about" the Nampa-NNC "relationships" with Cornell, and "out of those sessions, I believe," Hagood replied to the editor, "came the improvement." The president had made certain, too, that Cornell had received the Eugene Emerson award from the college for his service to Nampa and NNC. Hagood also made certain community administrators were thanked for their efforts in furthering NNC's expansion. He wrote to one local leader involved in the rerouting of Nampa streets around the campus and told him "you[r] willingness to listen to our needs and to take a leadership role in finding a solution remains the single most important influence in the successful resolution of the streets issue."

The president also backed Nampa facility improvements, joined several important service and community groups, and helped with other committees and boards. Hagood insisted that Nampa must have strong NNC backing for its Nampa Recreation Center. As one Nampa official told Hagood, "we want to express our gratitude for the contributions made by Northwest Nazarene in making the Recreation Center a reality." And when the center opened, Hagood issued a statement about its being "a positive force for the community" and that NNC was "a beneficiary of that [improved] quality of life." Hagood also played active roles on the Mercy Hospital board, the Boise Airport Commission, and sponsored forums that brought Treasure Valley leaders and activists to Nampa to discuss issues of concern to the valley's economy, social life, and cultural livelihood.

Hagood's personality likewise became more apparent in his dealings with campus and church communities. In his speeches, sermons, and letters the president tried to exude the calm, stable, and optimistic atmosphere that he thought best for NNC. Early on NNCers expressed their pleasure in seeing the sports-minded president at athletic events, and one student wrote on her chapel card that it's "great to have President Hagood here in chapel." The previous president "never came," she added; "we NEVER saw him [not quite true]. We as students seeing him (P. Hagood) here, makes us feel important, like we mean something to him. And in return, he means MUCH to us, because he cares."

Particular challenges faced the layman president as NNC's spiritual leader. Nazarenes, like most evangelicals, were accustomed to having pastoral and general church leaders as college administrators. Hagood had to establish and maintain the presence of a spiritual shepherd if he were to fulfill the expectations of most of his coreligionists. In a revealing self-description, Hagood told a frustrated coach disappointed about others' perceptions of his religious commitment that a person had "to establish a 'track record' of solid, authentic Christian commitment and professional achievement." The president added: "I say this from personal experience for it is the path I had to walk." Hagood added to his confidence-building image by presenting numerous campus, district assembly, and church "sermons" that stressed character building, moral values, and scriptural guidelines. One prominent parishioner at a large Nazarene Church perhaps expressed the growing confidence in Hagood's spiritual leadership by pointing out that he preached more Biblically than her own pastor. In his reading, the president stressed works on theology and religion, and during a sabbatical spent considerable devotional time discussing God's grace with Reuben Welch, a superb Nazarene speaker and former campus chaplain at Point Loma Nazarene.

Hagood adopted another strategy that removed him from several of the controversies often convulsing the campus and church during his presidency. Although he might privately respond to queries about such fiery issues as homosexuality and AIDS, nudity in art exhibits, abortion, sexuality on campus, and creationism and evolution, he carefully avoided such controversies in his public statements. None of his annual presentations on campus or to district assemblies dealt with these issues. Instead of upsetting his administration with public statements on such squabbles, he urged students, faculty, and Nazarenes in general to adopt positive attitudes about their lives and the future. As president he charged his first year of graduates (1) to learn "from the legacy of NNC's central principles"; (2) "live the legacy, in your way and in your space, but carry the legacy as your lifestyle"; and (3) "leave a legacy for the generations which will follow you." He added to this stream of optimism in telling a former NNC staff member that if she returned to the campus she would be "amazed" to "discover just how much progress we have made in the last few years. While the first few months (years) were swimming upstream, we have been able to turn the flow in a new direction. Now everyone is talking about strategic planning, the college mission and institutional advancement. Remarkable!" Shortly afterwards he reiterated the need for NNCers to "take positive stands on issues, not just negative stands."

Hagood's optimism, his strong leadership, and his apt planning were much needed at NNC. Challenges in academic and religious matters soon surfaced and called for his best efforts to deal with them.

Samuel Dunn rode to the rescue of NNC academics in 1994. Most of all he provided the needed continuity in the dean's office missing since the resignation of Gilbert Ford in 1985. Ken Watson and Dan Berg, as full-fledged deans, and Lilburn Wesche, Martha Hopkins, and Ford again, as interim deans, looked after the needs of NNC's academic mission, but none served sufficiently long to mount an enduring program that clearly strengthened academics or sent the college in new, strong directions. That continuity of energetic, insightful academic leadership occurred after Dunn arrived.

Sam Dunn, by background and experience, fit smoothly and quickly into the NNC academic scene. A Nazarene with a PhD in mathematics and later an MBA and with a passionate interest in futuristic studies, Dunn taught math and business courses at Seattle Pacific from 1968 to 1978 and then became an administrator (1978 to 1993), with appointments in the Academic Affairs office (1988 to 1993). He had written letters of contact to NNC and then became a leading candidate for the dean's slot in spring 1993 when President Doane died. The next year, in a reopened search, he was named dean and arrived on campus in summer 1994 to become the college's chief academic officer.

Dr. Sam Dunn, energetic dean and vice president, worked closely with President Hagood to plan the university's mission. (Fig. 6.3)

Dunn's vigorous, go-ahead academic leadership meshed well with President Hagood's views on NNC's college mission. In announcing Dunn's hiring, Hagood pointed out that the new dean "shares our commitment to the liberal arts, our institutional plans and strategic initiatives and our commitment to our statement of mission. I believe Dr. Dunn will contribute splendidly to NNC's aspirations for the future." All of Hagood's predictions proved true, and every one of the items he mentioned was central to his administration. In fact, Hagood and Dunn seemed entirely compatible; they "thought so much alike" that some faculty complained because "it appeared we agreed too much," Dunn later reported. The Dunn-Hagood partnership lasted from 1994 to 2002 when Mark Pitts became dean. Then Dunn returned for another year with Hagood (2007-8) when Pitts went to African Nazarene University as deputy vice-chancellor of academics. Dunn served two more years with President Alexander before retiring from the dean's office. The complementary relationship between Dunn and Hagood was particularly apparent in the restructuring of departments, the switch of the college year to semesters, the move to university status, the addition of several new graduate programs, and the launching of online degrees.

Like Hagood, Dunn moved quickly and directly. Knowing that the next accreditation visit was looming, Dunn immediately floated plans to meet accreditation needs. The library must have additional support—to expand its holdings and staff. Dunn also pointed to needed changes in curricular, faculty, operational, and learning resource structure and management.

Between late 1994 and early 1995 Dunn's ideas came into clearer focus. He began a systematic swing around the NNC curriculum, carefully scrutinizing departments and majors, looking to see if the system was operating as well as it could. He thought not. After an examination of majors, course enrollments, and graduation figures, the new dean found that there were fifty-one majors; NNC "has spread itself too thin," the dean concluded. Then looking forward, Dunn predicted: "Over the next two to five years NNC... [will] begin to focus on the institution by phasing out programs we wish to eliminate. When NNC does that we can expect to lose some students and be highly political." Again, Dunn's predictions were on target; the down-sizing, the closing of majors, and the laying off a handful of faculty members was so disruptive as to bring about mounting criticism, even the end of friendships.

The curricular revisions moved in two different directions; first, the buttressing and building up of a department that needed revitalization. In this case the Business Department. Second, some departments needed to be terminated. They were not commanding large enrollments, did not play a central role in the liberal arts, and failed to find a place in the Hagood-Dunn vision of the future. Specifically, the president and dean had in mind the Department of Home Economics, whose name had been changed to the Department of Family and Consumer Sciences. The moves to deal with the Business and Family and Consumer Sciences departments led to fiery clash and conflict.

Dunn wanted to light a fire under the Business Department. He had a strong personal interest in the field and, encouraged by the president, set out to strengthen the department. He would do so by naming a stronger departmental chair, expanding the number of faculty, and hiring as many earned doctorates as possible. It would be nothing less than the professionalization of the Business Department. Much of this occurred; the department became stronger, especially under the energetic direction of Dr. Ron Galloway. But at personal loss too. Those working in the subfield of secretarial studies without terminal degrees particularly felt marginalized in the new moves toward professionalization. Hard feelings led to harsh words, and departmental divisions turned toxic. Even as new graduate degrees, PhDs, and additional students were added to the department, it nearly self-imploded. Finally one of those most hurt by the changes was terminated. Dean Dunn was right; those changes could become dangerously "political." In the next decade, however, as new faculty came, the department of business expanded, business accreditation was achieved, and student retention increased.

Changes in the Home Economics/Family Studies program were similarly contested. While at Washington State, Hagood had been involved with the closing of Home Economics as an emphasis not central to the mission of that university; the same view informed his leadership at NNC, and Dunn agreed with him. The statistics concerning the Home Economics field were mixed. For example, between 1991 and 1994, twenty-six persons had enrolled as majors in the field, tying it for the seventh largest major at NNC. Despite those rather encouraging numbers, moves toward closing down Family Studies began—rather obliquely. Even before Dunn appeared on the scene, the president told a recent graduate of the NNC Home Economics program that he was convinced "there does need to be review of the fit this program, or certain dimensions thereof, has with the mission and future of NNC."

Then when the department was forced to change locations with the Business Department and to take lesser quarters, the die seemed cast. Evidently the two professors in the department, Liz Murtland and Kate Hohenbrink, seeing signs of diminution if not closure of their program, decided to fight back. They urged recent graduates to write letters of support to the NNC administration and asked for a name change for their program to Department of Family and Consumer Sciences. They wanted the new name because "it better defines who we are and what we do." Murtland, the departmental chair, and Hohenbrink also compiled an inch-thick "Response from the Family and Consumer Sciences Department to the Academic Dean's rationale to phase-out the Department." It was a thorough, well-organized defense for strengthening the Family and Consumer Sciences program and keeping it in existence. Although the Academic Council supported the renaming of the department, the administrative ax fell, and the program was closed.

Similar if less heated reactions surfaced when, after considerable discussions and delay, Dunn moved to drop the two-year Associate of Arts programs. The dean had suggested these two-year programs tarnished the "image" of NNC and caused problems with accreditation. Although a prominent member of the religion faculty opposed the ending of the AA programs in his department, the motion passed by a close vote. On the other hand, faculty seemed willing to accept the ending of an AA program in science and the trimming of a few other majors.

Overall, though, the administrative attempts to drop majors and departments caused bad feelings. So strong were these negative reactions that at least one family wrote the president and dean demanding repayment of their daughter's tuition when the reduced program in Home Economics at NNC was not going to be accepted at a regional state university. More personally, the Hagood and Dunn families felt uncomfortable worshipping in Nampa's College Church with former Home Economics faculty. Although apologies and forgiveness came, some residue of the closing of these departments and programs remained for several years. Were the changes worth the high costs of bad feelings and disarrayed morale? Most involved wondered.

While these administration decisions and their aftermath remained at best bittersweet, other happenings brought many smiles. For several years NNC remained highly ranked in polls of small colleges of the West. NNC leaders sometimes downplayed the rankings in *U. S. News and World Report* and the *Princeton Review*'s guide to best colleges, but more often they trumpeted this marketable news. The strong NNC rankings in *U. S. News* first appeared in the Wetmore years, although even more often during Hagood's presidency. At the end of Hagood's first year and only a few months after Dunn came onboard, NNC was rated among the top ten liberal arts colleges in the West, the third time in five years. It was "the only Idaho college and the only Nazarene college listed in the survey," according to a denominational report. These rankings derived from a survey taken among 1,400 officials in post-secondary institutions. In fall 1996, NNC won another top-ten ranking for the third consecutive year, and the fifth time in seven years. Again it was the only Idaho college so listed.

But once NNC transitioned into a university, the ranking classifications changed, placing the university in a new division, the Universities-Master's category. Now the competition was stronger, larger, and more numerous, with NNC placing in Tier 2 of western universities, or the top 50 percent, at first; and later in the first tier, or top 25 percent. President Hagood, taking a most positive view, concluded that the ranking "validates our efforts in becoming a comprehensive university that serves Idaho and the greater region as well." He added: "As a newcomer to this particular classification we're gratified that we had a strong presence this time out." But stories about NNU's rankings were less frequent when the university was no longer at the top of a new category, and sometimes those rascal rivals just up the road in Caldwell, Albertson College of Idaho, ranked above NNU. Later, when the two long-time competitors were placed in different categories, it was difficult to continue the previous comparisons. Revealingly, when NNC/NNU administrators filled out the necessary surveys for *U. S. News* to compile the rankings, they gave their own institution high marks but the College of Idaho lower rankings.

During these years NNC was transitioning to university status, to become Northwest Nazarene University. Although discussions about the move began during the Wetmore presidency, the administrative changes and the lack of continuity in the dean's office slowed the transition. Some NNC supporters wondered if the college was ready for a switch to a university, but, in fact, the Nampa college was slower in making the move than most other Nazarene schools in the U. S. Even before 1910 what later became known as Pasadena College and Point Loma University was, ambitiously though briefly named, Nazarene University. In the late 1950s the president of one Nazarene college called for serious consideration of university status but gained little denominational support for the change. Then in 1986 Bethany Nazarene College became Southern Nazarene University and Olivet Nazarene College a university. A decade later Trevecca (1995) and MidAmerica (1996) became universities. Then in 1998 Point Loma joined the Nazarene universities and NNC (1999) the following year. Mt. Vernon gained university status in 2002, leaving only Eastern Nazarene College as the non-university among the eight Nazarene liberal arts institutions.

Following the strong leadership of President Hagood and Dean Dunn, NNC became Northwest Nazarene University in 1999. (Fig. 6.4)

Several pressures were at work, some explicit and others more subtle, in the NNC transition to NNU. President Hagood pointed out that the name and status change was a normal progression of the institution—from college to university: "It's a natural evolution of an institution that's expanding its horizons and defining itself as a regional institution." In addition, as the Nazarene school expanded globally, the name shift took on more significance since many outside the U. S. considered a "college" a high school.

More subtly, the name change to Northwest Nazarene University also carried heightened prestige symbols. As NNC political scientist Steve Shaw put it bluntly, "These days in higher education, if you stand still you get run over." For Shaw, the new university status would be an action "to guarantee NNC's vitality for years to come." Many students seemed to agree. The *Crusader* reported that "the change is one that is needed because they [students] think it [the name change] will...benefit the college in the future. They feel that 'university' carries with it a more prestigious sound than 'college,' and that in many people's mind, universities are associated with having more to offer its [sic] students."

The Board of Regents unanimously adopted the change to university in its spring 1999 meeting, and when the districts of the educational zone also backed the transition, NNC officially became Northwest Nazarene University on September 1, 1999. The new university status called for a few restructurings. The academic organization of NNU would be divided into four "clusters" or schools needed for university status: (1) arts and humanities; (2) mathematics, natural sciences, and health sciences; (3) professional studies (e.g., business, philosophy and religion, education, counseling); and (4) academic support services (e.g. registrar and library). (Later, these would be expanded to six "schools," with slightly different titles and missions.) Other reorganization was put into place, and Nampa had a smoothly operating university by summer 2000.

Along with a name change the college administration wanted to shift the academic year from a quarter to a semester system. This transformation had also been in the air for several years before it finally was put into place. When the change was first broached in the late 1980s, most of the academic units at the college did not favor the shift. Ten years before the system was actually implemented it became a topic of campus discussion. The faculty opposed the change. "The semester system would hurt the quality of our academic programs," one scientist asserted. "It is my hope for NNC," he added, "that the pressure is off for changing to the semester system." But the pressure continued, with President Wetmore recommending in fall 1990 that the board of regents "authorize the President to begin the process of moving to a semester calendar by Fall 1993." A special faculty meeting convened to discuss this and other motions; the NNC professors did not support the measure. Wetmore also asked academic divisional chairs to gather information about the semester issue. Again, administrative turnover and the lack of a strong academic dean to drive the change allowed it to slip off the scene.

But soon after the administrative tag team of Hagood and Dunn linked up, they turned their joint attention to the issue. The semester controversy was back on the table. This time the administrators waited for a more auspicious time to renew the conversation, while gathering information on other programs and tracking the increasing number of U. S. colleges and universities swinging away from quarters to semesters. In a thorough, extensive memorandum the administrators listed nearly a dozen "Reasons for the Semester System," laid out a sample calendar for a two-semester year, and noted NNC's peer institutions moving toward semesters.

At the same time the president and dean prodded the campus with rumors that other Pacific Northwest schools were moving into semesters. But no groundswell for the transition surfaced on campus, so the president himself, with regent support, moved. "I have determined," he told the campus community, "that it is in the best interests of NNC, our students, and constituencies that the college move from the quarter calendar to an 'early start' semester calendar effective with the beginning of the fall term of the 2000-2001 academic years." To plan a smooth transition, the president named a "semester transition coordination team." The next year students were supplied with a *Student Handbook for Semester Conversion* to answer their questions and guide them through the touchy transformations. After some delay, effective September 1, 2000, NNC was officially on the semester system.

The decade or so stretching from the mid-1980s to the mid-1990s and beyond was a difficult time for NNC faculty. With the turnover in deans, faculty did not have a long-time, outspoken advocate for their academic interests early in these years, and then it seemed that a president had taken over whose interests were primarily in strategic planning, not on academics. When Dean Dunn arrived, it appeared that he sided more often with the president's dream for a comprehensive university than for a strong liberal arts college. Morale was not high. The feelings of dissatisfaction carried over into the twenty-first century. Indeed when the university utilized the Best Christian Workplaces survey, sponsored by the evangelical magazine *Christianity Today*, and 90 percent of faculty, staff, and administrators filled out the questionnaire on campus satisfactions, NNU ranked in the middle of the nonfinalists. That meant about half of these workers were not satisfied with NNU as a work place.

Although the specifics of that survey and others are not available, probably low salaries were a major part of the dissatisfaction. Indeed, for about half of the Hagood years faculty received no overall raises, except those within the normal step raises based on education and years of experience. For the years 1995, 1996, and 1997, records of faculty salaries are available, although NNC's unranked system (no division of faculty into professor, associate professor, assistant professor, and instructor ranks) makes exact comparisons difficult. But in 1995-96 NNC average salaries fell below those of peer institutions such as Whitworth College, Point Loma Nazarene, and George Fox College, and the top salaries provided at NNC were not as high as those at Seattle Pacific, Westmont, Azusa Pacific, and Albertson College of Idaho. Generally, however, NNC salaries were about the same

Dr. Sharon Bull, diligent and warm-hearted librarian, also served as a divisional chairperson. (Fig. 6.5)

as those at other Nazarene colleges. The next year, 1996-97, nine-month faculty salaries ranged from $27,000 to $46,000, with higher remuneration for those on eleven-month contracts. For 1997, administrative salaries also remained low in comparison to those in peer institutions: Dunn ($67,000); Hal Weber, financial affairs ($62,000); Darrell Marks, institutional advancement ($62,000); and Ken Hills, student development ($62,000). In 1996-97 when the Coalition for Christian Colleges and Universities surveyed its eighty members for faculty salaries from 1987-88 to 1996-97, NNC ranked near the bottom in most categories. The college's mean salaries were nearly flat from 1990 to 1993 and again from 1994 to 1995. Again peer institutions such as George Fox, Seattle Pacific, and Point Loma Nazarene were considerably above NNC; most other Nazarene schools were about the same; and Northwest College and Warner Pacific in the Pacific Northwest were below.

Faculty questions about low salaries were part of larger problems. Why was it, some wondered, that the president's presentations were so full and explicit on buildings to be built, new programs to be launched, and other projects to be considered, but that these presentations contained so little concrete information on faculty salaries and benefits? In budget making, they asked further, why didn't planners start with a 2 or 3 percent raise for faculty and then build a budget around that need first? If faculty were so often held up as *the* core of the NNC experience, why were their salaries so often figured at the end of the budgeting process rather than at the beginning? And if college administrators wanted to keep costs at NNC below those of most peer institutions in the Pacific Northwest, did that necessarily mean that faculty salaries had to be close to the bottom too? Of course, the complex question of faculty salaries and benefits was not a new one; NNC administrators and faculty had wrangled over these issues for most of the college's history. As one long-time faculty observed, from the 1960s onward professors seemed less willing to think of their teaching at an evangelical college as a mission and more of a job that should bring satisfactory remuneration. As NNC transitioned toward a university of increased stature, its faculty was less inclined to think of themselves as low-paid missionaries. They wanted pay scale commensurate with the stronger institution at which they were working.

Despite these questions about salary, new faculty members were coming to the campus. More than a few stayed a decade or so and made strong contributions to NNC/NNU. Among these were Glena Andrews in psychology, Karen Blacklock and Mike Poe in education, Jennifer Chase and Daniel Nogales in chemistry, Sharon Bull to the library, Diane Leclerc and Michael Lodahl in religion, and Ron Galloway and David Houghton in business. Several others joined the business department and strengthened it immensely after Galloway began to chair the department. Equally gratifying was the explosive growth in nursing, meeting the administration's market research expectations. Once the four-year program was reinstated in 1998 and several new faculty members hired, students came by the dozens. Toward the end of the first decade of the twenty-first century the nursing program enrolled more students (exceeding 200) than any other major on campus, including religion, business, education, and the other sciences, the mainstays for several decades.

As in the past, a few faculty got caught in the eye of controversy. One of these was among NNC/NNU's best and brightest, Steve Shaw. Joining the college faculty in 1980 as its pioneering political scientist, Shaw was superbly trained, a skilled teacher, and an especially energetic participant in research and writing and public presentations. He was also an outspoken advocate for ideas and causes. Before Hagood became president, Shaw launched an opinion column for local newspapers, where he clearly stood for his Democratic and progressive principles. But when he wrote columns about abortion, homosexuality, and social justice, he frequently stirred up conservatives, especially Nazarenes, in the Treasure Valley. They wrote the president. And when Shaw opined in one column that conservatives thought the country was "going to hell in a peach basket" if the U. S. didn't follow Reagan-Bush positions, a fundamentalist critic dashed off a letter to the president. Betraying his own prejudices, another critic denounced Shaw for telling the student body in a chapel devoted to the upcoming election that he would vote for Bill Clinton.

Dr. Steve Shaw, among the university's best and brightest, brought energy and enthusiasm to his courses in political science. (Fig. 6.6)

Hagood, as Wetmore had before him, spoke vigorously in support of Shaw. To one letter writer questioning Shaw's selection as a school dean in the new university setup, Hagood replied that Shaw was intensely committed "to the mission of NNC," his files contained a "strong written statement of faith," and his life evidenced his "growing, maturing as a Christian." To still two other loyal supporters of the college who queried Shaw's ideological stances, his lack of commitment to Nazarene doctrines, and (they said) his harmful classroom teaching, Hagood countered that Shaw's "statement of faith ...was exceptionally strong," he had a "strong sense of the 'social holiness' dimension of our Wesleyan roots," and that he had the endorsement of the executive board of the regents, including Nazarene pastors. Perhaps the clincher came when Hagood told one of the critics that his own daughter, who had rather conservative outlooks, had taken Shaw's classes and found him a superb teacher asking her to think about her faith and its personal and social dimensions. Quite possibly Shaw mellowed some, too: his controversial column disappeared, and fewer of his strong pronouncements appeared in print.

Similar sharp criticism came to President Hagood after Professor Glena Andrews spoke in chapel from an evangelical woman's perspective. A Boise man indicted her presentation as "intellectually disappointing, biblically offensive...looking for a fight." In all, he continued, Dr. Andrews's "arguments were very shallow and they contradict fundamental bible teaching." And, then, as was so often the case in such letters, a hint of blackmail surfaced. The critic ended his harpooning letter with a threat: "This event certainly makes me wonder if NNU is worth five times more than BSU [Boise State], especially since next year our second son will be in college." Hagood's answer was clear, direct, and supportive of Glena Andrews. He had known her since she was a little girl in Boise, he said, and "one would be mistaken to assign motives to her beyond what her clear intention was: to raise our awareness of domestic violence and that often mistaken notion that men hold a superior relationship to God than women." NNU invited such chapel presentations not to convert students to "feminism," the president added, but to release any guilt young women might feel from their mistreatment and to "help our male students view women with honor and respect." And then another Hagood clincher: after Andrews's chapel talk, a young coed came to her dorm hall assistant, telling her that she had "heard exactly what she needed to hear....She had accepted Christ as her Savior today" because the message by Dr. Andrews "was so in tune to her need." Hagood closed with: "Now that's what we're about."

Such negative letters had been a constant throughout the college's history. Richard Hagood was not immune from them. In fact, as we shall see shortly, he received even more letters—and often more critical—on issues dealing with the interpretation of Scripture and the college's teachings on creation-evolution issues.

Controversies such as these did not foreshorten developments in other academic areas. For one, graduate programs greatly expanded. As early as the beginning 1940s NNC offered a master's program in religion, but by the end of the 1950s, because of lack of interest, that program was dropped. In the 1950s and 1960s a master's degree in education was bandied about, but was held off until additional funding and faculty were available. With heightened interest in religion and education during Pearsall's presidency, graduate work was again reconsidered. By 1976-77 a master's in teaching was offered and a master's in education announced for fall 1978. A master's in ministry was added in 1987.

Hagood gave graduate work at NNC/NNU its greatest presidential impetus. As with so many plans for expansion, Dean Dunn also agreed with this move toward additional graduate programs. Finances and community relations were strengthened too with new graduate degrees. By the end of Hagood's presidency in 2008, master's programs in business, counseling, education, social work, and nursing, and religion (four different programs) were in place or in final steps of implementation. Plans for a doctorate in practical theology, with interdisciplinary work in religion, business, and education—a pet project of Dean Dunn—were also in final stages of planning. (In 2009, the board of trustees voted to begin the program, but accreditors delayed its implementation until more information was available to them.) Opinion was divided on the possible interdisciplinary doctoral program, some thinking it added luster to NNU's academic offerings, others wondering if the university had the necessary faculty, library, and other academic support for a doctorate. Other plans were underway for a doctoral program in education, which was launched in fall 2011.

Another set of academic challenges emerged later in Hagood's administration and when adopted and put into place brought probably the most marked changes to NNU's faculty organization. These shifts were the adoption of a ranking system, tenure and promotion, and the downsizing of the faculty to achieve a higher student-faculty ratio. The transformations were linked to one another since the costs saved from fewer faculty members could be redistributed to achieve a less compressed salary system following the adoption of rankings. Eventually the ranking and tenure and promotion systems gained faculty support, but downsizing the size of the faculty threatened to be much more contentious.

Dr. Mark Pitts, as dean and academic vice president, led NNU through some of its most significant academic changes. (Fig. 6.7)

This dramatic reorganization of the faculty and the concomitant push to raise the student-faculty ratio came under the generalship of a new dean. In fall 2002 Sam Dunn returned to teaching, and another educator from Seattle Pacific took his place. Mark E. Pitts, with a Nazarene background and a specialty in English education, arrived on campus in late summer 2002. During his years as dean, Pitts faced a steady cavalcade of stretching assignments. The disagreements and tensions over some of these issues were enough to break the spirit of even the most courageous educator. Pitts's first assignment was to formulate a set of institutional outcomes for the university. With the help of faculty, staff, and administrators—indeed, from all sectors of the campus—Pitts, with major aid from Eric Forseth and Jerry Hull, arrived at a group of four outcomes that adeptly summarized the mission of NNU: (1) Christ-like Character, (2) Academic Excellence, (3) Creative Engagement, (4) and Social Responsiveness. At the same time enrollment services came up with a new tag line for the university: Great minds • Great hearts • Great futures. These outcomes and tag lines were widely utilized in the early years of the twenty-first century.

The Mt. Everest challenges for Pitts were the ranking and tenure questions. Except for a ten-year period from 1937 to 1947, NNC had always followed an unranked system among its faculty. Although the unranked system was unusual, it had worked fairly well for the college. But for Hagood, as part of his professionalization push for the university, a ranking system should be put into place, since it was utilized in nearly all U. S. colleges and universities, and would allow for one method of compensating faculty on merit. The idea began to be floated before Dunn resigned, but Pitts spearheaded the drive once he arrived on campus. Intense and lengthy discussions followed, with a bare majority of the faculty favoring ranking. Pitts carried the measure, with the president's strong support, to the trustees, where it passed. The dean also labored diligently to work out the details of a new system of tenure—or a job security system—for the faculty. Legal complexities and the need for lengthy and precise language slowed that complex series of discussions and the final decision. But the trustees also backed tenure. The ranking and tenure systems were to be officially in place and implemented by 2008-9. Mark Pitts had worked overtime to engineer the passage of both of these measures.

More traumatic for everyone was the move to downsize the faculty in order to raise the student-faculty ratios and to fund the higher salary costs resulting from the new ranking system. But to achieve a student-faculty ratio in the range of 15 to 1 to 16.5 to 1 meant that 10 to 12 full-time faculty positions needed to be cut. Hearing this additional depressing news while still in the throes of wrestling with promotion and tenure issues, one faculty member told a trustee that "a tsunami has hit us [the faculty] this week." Would the dean have to hand out nearly a dozen pink slips to lay off the necessary faculty? How could one vote to terminate a colleague?

Then something remarkable occurred. Several senior faculty nearing retirement and some with thirty to forty years of service to NNU decided to take the brunt of the unusual need. Rather than see their younger colleagues terminated—following a usual university practice of "last in, first out"—these veteran professors decided to retire early. (They had been offered an early retirement option.) Most had not announced their impending retirements but would do so now to save the jobs of their younger or newer colleagues. True, the early retirement packages were tendered, but they were surprisingly modest, hardly beckoning in any way. Instead, sufficient numbers of long-time faculty retired early to meet the needed reduction of 10 to 12 in the professoriate. Theirs was another act of service for NNU.

There were other important outcomes from these changes. In the first year of the new ranking system (2008-9), some senior faculty received a $10,000 salary boost. Student-faculty ratios also went up with fewer faculty to teach classes. In these outcomes, some of Hagood's goals were clearly met.

The academic decisions were traumatic for faculty and administrators alike. Dean Mark Pitts carried an exceptionally heavy load of work—and pressure—in ramroding these large changes. Some of his colleagues thought the pressures were too great and that he resigned primarily to get out from under the load. Viewing Pitts as a warm, good man but more of a manager than a leader they wondered if the pressures had driven him out of his administrative position.

But Pitts himself told a different story. When a second invitation came in January 2007 from the Nazarene World Missions department asking Pitts and his wife Nancy to consider a three-year assignment at Africa Nazarene University (ANU) in Kenya as its chief academic officer, deputy vice chancellor academic, he at first hesitated. But after a good deal of meditation and reflection, Pitts came to agree with his wife about going to Kenya. The decision, he explained later, came after a feeling of "the fire behind me and blue skies were ahead." We "both felt a sense of God's release from the work at NNU that was motivated not by concerns of future pressure. We responded in obedience to what we believed was God's 'next chapter' for us." Although President Hagood and the chair of the NNU trustees encouraged Pitts to stay in Nampa, he felt a sense of mission accomplished at NNU and a new mission beckoning in Africa. Pitts resigned in 2007 after serving five years as dean and academic vice president. Then, after finishing their three-year stint in Kenya at ANU, Pitts and his wife returned to the U.S. and Point Loma Nazarene University, where he took a position as vice provost of academic administration.

As the new chief administrator of NNC, Richard Hagood stood before the NNC Board of Regents to give his first presidential report. He promised "to care for the soul of NNC." And he did—consistently and carefully. But quite possibly he did not know—indeed, who could know?—how much of his energy, courage, and commitment would be expended to keep his promise to tend NNC's spiritual garden. It was an enormous, emotion-gulping task, cultivating and nurturing youthful journeys, keeping faculty and staff fruitful, and judiciously culling out weedy errors.

The most vexing problems facing Hagood in NNC's religious life were also, by and large, dilemmas challenging the Church of the Nazarene. In truth, what general leaders and theologians were wrestling with became the issues that Hagood had to address from the early 1990s into the early twenty-first century. In theological terms they were primarily matters of Wesleyan holiness teaching, the nature of the inspiration of the Bible, and conflicts between Six-Day and Young Earth creationists and theistic evolutionists. Every one of these issues added dozens of speaking assignments, numerous conversations, and hundreds of personal letters to Hagood's already growing heap of duties.

From the 1960s and 1970s onward many Nazarene thinkers were cautiously moving away from the emphases in H. Orton Wiley's systematic theology to what some called neo-Wesleyan theological teaching and preaching. This new heightened interest in Wesleyanism was particularly evident among one band of Nazarenes, reflected in the preaching, teaching, and writing beginning in the 1970s of Mildred Wynkoop and later with Reuben Welch and H. Ray Dunning. These scholars and preachers emphasized an ethic of love, relational and experiential in its manifestations. Later, many of these ideas would be echoed in *Relational Holiness: Responding to the Call of Love,* coauthored by Thomas Jay Oord, an NNU professor, and Michael Lodahl, first at NNU and then at Point Loma Nazarene University.

Campus chaplain Gene Schandorff provided a steadying, positive impact on NNU spiritual life. (Fig. 6.8)

These writings and other similar presentations sparked waves of controversy among Nazarenes. The "relational" theologians, critics charged, were straying away from traditional Nazarene emphasis on sanctification as a second, definite work of grace, and they were dabbling in Neo-Orthodoxy and Postmodernism, and they were just too "liberal." Nazarene scholars like Donald Metz and Richard Taylor were among the chiefest of critics. To his credit President Hagood read widely in the theological writings, generally, of Nazarenes, holding fast to Wiley's foundational teachings but also perusing and reflecting on the alternative views of Dunning and Taylor, for example.

Early on Hagood warmly supported two efforts to bring reasoned, balanced, and stimulating Wesleyan messages and presentations to the NNC/NNU campus. Gene Schandorff, who came to NNC in 1992 as campus chaplain, did much to quiet the heated and continuing criticism of chapel presentations during the previous generation. Over the years, Hagood and much of the campus relied on Schandorff's relevant, witty, and heart-warming sermons and his columns in the *Crusader* to provide stimulating and helpful spiritual guidance. Raised in southern California and a graduate of Pasadena College, Schandorff viewed firsthand how the superlative chaplaincy of Reuben Welch could make a large difference in campus morale. Schandorff became something of a Welch clone at NNC/NNU, with students reacting to him like the sustaining and helpful pastor he was. Over the next fifteen years Schandorff did much to aid Hagood in caring for the campus soul.

Hagood also pushed hard for the establishment of a Wesley Center for Applied Theology. In these actions, the president worked in cooperation with philosophy professor Edwin Crawford. The center, like the campus chaplaincy, followed successful programs already in place among the Nazarenes. The general church had, since the 1950s, convened theological conferences bringing together church leaders, pastors, and academics to discuss theological issues among Wesleyans. In founding the NNC Wesley Center in June 1994 (the same year Point Loma opened its Wesley Center), the president had done so, he told a church leader, "out of concern for preserving and enhancing the Wesleyan Holiness tradition and message." The center was designed, Hagood added, "to give a positive expression to our distinctive as a denomination and college. I am finding a keen interest among our constituency to reassert our call to holy living." Throughout the next dozen years the center, by way of its conferences and other programs, achieved much of what Hagood hoped. Well-known evangelical and fundamentalist speakers came to campus, conference papers were collected in books, major Wesleyan holiness volumes were placed online, and a Compassionate Care program reached out to help community organizations and churches with their social missions. Overall the center provided a measure of stability and tradition on a campus whose religious life seemed always in high gear, often ahead of off-campus laypersons. In addition, a decade into the twenty-first century the Wesley On-Line arm of the center had become the world's largest online resource for Wesley data.

In some years Wesley Center programs addressed contemporary religious disputes, but more often these upsets involved faculty and administrators in private conversations and correspondence rather than in public conferences. In fact, an informal conversation between President Hagood and a member of the Board of Trustees helps to set this scene. The trustee asked the president what were the most controversial departments on campus. The conversation, creatively recalled, went thus: President: "Would you believe the religion department is the most controversial." And the second most? President: "Oh, probably biology and the struggle over creation and evolution." A third? "Perhaps behaviorist psychology." And what about historians? "Nope, you guys are not controversial at all." President Hagood's bulging correspondence files attest to these and other debates that embroiled perplexed administrators, faculty, and laypersons in matters pertaining to religion and theology and the creation-evolution debate. Sometimes the tempests were magnified, with the two controversies conjoined.

Few major ideological-theological storms sallied forth from the NNC religion department before the 1970s. In the 1940s John Riley and in the 1950s through the 1980s A. Elwood Sanner trolled without muddying theological waters. D. Shelby Corlett consistently followed Nazarene doctrine in the 1950s, although Carl Hanson ran into some problems in the same decade with his introduction of critical-analytical methods into introductory Bible courses. But from the 1970s and 1980s onward, when NNC theologians were more highly trained and more willing to bring modern Biblical scholarship into their classes, disputes arose that sometimes eroded good feelings among religion faculty, district superintendents, pastors, and laypersons.

Indeed, a two-part scenario seemed at work. As the neo-Wesleyan approach allowed for varied perspectives and became more widespread among Nazarenes, there was a concomitant upsurge of conservative reaction. Was a cause-and-effect dualism at work: did a rising "liberalism" among Nazarene academic theologians—in its seminary and liberal arts colleges—spawn a negative anti-liberal, or conservative, response? Were the reactionary elements all the more outspoken because they feared that Biblical modernists or liberals, having taken control of Nazarene colleges, would determine the future? Or was the controversy primarily a conflict between the previously mentioned Wesleyan and American holiness advocates? Whatever the causes of the debates, many conservatives felt they must fight back or lose their beloved denomination.

Dr. Michael Lodahl, provocative theologian, stimulated students and colleagues but upset some Wesleyan conservatives. (Fig. 6.9)

Two incidents illustrate the sometimes fractious relationships between NNC theologians and conservative constituents. The first involved the young professor Michael Lodahl. An NNC grad, Lodahl returned to teach at NNC in 1988 and published his first book in 1992: *Shekhinah/Spirit: Divine Presence in Jewish and Christian Tradition.* Some laymen did not like the scholarly book (it was Lodahl's revised dissertation) and accused him of straying too far from acceptable American holiness and popular theology. President Hagood, new in his presidency and perhaps a bit uncertain how to handle such blitzing controversies, carefully put together a review/conversation for May 1994. Unfortunately, it was something of a repeat performance. Two years earlier an outspoken NNC graduate had attacked Lodahl's writing and teaching. A hearing conducted on these charges had cleared Lodahl. Now Oregon laymen and pastors were coming after the young professor again. Hagood told the Board of Regents he wanted "to resolve the issues surrounding the writings" of Dr. Lodahl. Warning that "this is an incredibly serious and delicate situation," the president invited Dr. William Greathouse, general superintendent emeritus and a keen student of Wesleyan theology, to lead the discussion. General Superintendent James Diehl would be in attendance; so would Dr. Ralph Neil, chair of the NNU religion department, and other theologians and colleagues.

More than fifteen years later Professor Lodahl remembered much about the gathering. It seemed to him less than a heresy trial, more than a pat on the back, something akin to a hearing. Lodahl was given a series of questions beforehand to which he replied, and then at the meeting Greathouse followed up on those comments and raised other questions. Lodahl had decided ahead of time he would not come off as a smart-alecky upstart—because that path could lead to loss of his job, and perhaps the revoking of his church credentials. Neither would he simply apologize and give way on everything. He would follow a middle-of-the-road path, attempting to show in his written and oral comments that he was a loyal Wesleyan and Nazarene.

After the hearing, President Hagood wrote an extended letter explaining the group's findings. He reported that Dr. Lodhal had "answered each question posed in written and oral form to the total and complete satisfaction of the inquiry committee." The Board of Regents, after reading the committee's report, "endorsed the findings." "Now this matter is closed," the president concluded. The meeting cleared the air and, in essence, rebutted the criticisms arriving in Hagood's office from crabby critics. Lodahl had been vindicated and gained the strong support of Dr. Greathouse, other Nazarene theologians, the regents—and the president.

Two years later the second incident embroiled a more seasoned faculty member, C. S. Cowles, who had been Lodahl's undergraduate mentor. The son of missionaries from another denomination, Cowles became a Nazarene, gained a doctorate, pastored for more than fifteen years, and then in 1977 came to NNC to teach. He taught in the religion department until 1984, resigned to pastor a church in Spokane, and then returned to NNC, where he remained until his retirement

Dr. C.S. Cowles, able teacher and preacher, sometimes stirred up dissent on the NNU educational zone. (Fig. 6.10)

in 2001. C. S. Cowles was a widely acknowledged preacher, a skillful teacher, and a writer for several Nazarene publications. He also liked to stimulate his listeners and readers with provocative assertions and conclusions. For example, his preaching on forgiveness, genocide in the Old Testament, the differences between the two Testaments, and his questioning of Abraham's sacrificing Isaac upset traditionalists, who argued that this preaching undermined the faith of students. Cowles loved to play "devil's advocate," but sometimes he alienated students and laypersons with this approach. When pressed about Cowles and these issues, the chair of the NNC Religion Department Ralph Neil, himself a model of balance, replied: "Well, that Cowles can be a rascal sometimes."

The criticisms of Cowles, storming out of the Soldotna, Alaska, Church of the Nazarene, were strong and persisting. The church's pastor, a former student of Cowles, along with a key layman in that church, filled Hagood's mailbox with strong indictments of Cowles's preaching and teaching. As a result of these criticisms, and others as well, Hagood promised the Board of Regents to "assess the nature of these issues, and conduct an inquiry—either internal or external—with interim reports" to the regents. At the same time, Hagood had to remind the outspoken critics that the president did not answer to them but to the regents; Hagood would not be forced "into a time line of ... [their] making."

After the spring 1996 meeting of the regents and before its fall convening, Hagood undertook an "administrative inquiry" into the Cowles situation. In this inquiry, the president informed several interested parties (mostly critics of Cowles), that "several specific and direct questions regarding his [Cowles's] understanding and commitment to the doctrines and teachings of the Church of the Nazarene" were put to the professor; his responses were also requested. The president and Dean Dunn also examined Cowles's lecture notes, student evaluations, and consulted with his colleagues. "It was an intense and thorough review," Hagood reported. A preliminary report was filed with the Board of Directors, the executive committee of the regents, asking their reactions; then a final full report was sent to the full Board of Regents. Their unanimous decision found Cowles "within the bounds of his employment contract with NNC and within the bounds of the theology and doctrines of the Church of the Nazarene."

The Cowles inquiry findings did not satisfy critics. One long-time Nazarene family, after reading the report, expressed "a great deal of sadness." They would "no longer be able to support NNC." Theologian Richard Taylor, professor emeritus of Nazarene Theological Seminary, was also unhappy about the outcome of the inquiry and so informed the president. How could the board imply "full endorsement of Dr. Cowle's [sic] beliefs and teachings"? Hagood clarified the conclusion of the inquiry by telling Taylor that it did "not endorse nor deny endorsement." Plus, the president added, without much clarification, Cowles "has proactively participated in agreements of which you have no knowledge."

Even more intense were the attacks on NNC/NNU professors accused of misreading the Genesis story and of teaching anything but a literal, Six-Day or Young Earth interpretation of creation. A few such criticisms surfaced in the evolution battles of the 1920s and continued to come to NNC presidents through the next half-century. But beginning in the 1980s the civil war over creation-evolution reached a fiery intensity. For a small but very vocal group of conservative laypersons and pastors the creation-evolution warfare was centrally important; it became a nonnegotiable of their faith. For these persons, readings of the Bible must be literal and founded on the belief of the inerrancy of the Scriptures. No one should think of the Garden of Eden, Abraham and Isaac, the parting of the Red Sea, Jonah, or any stories of Jesus as anything but actual, in-history events. In addition, when the Bible spoke of the six days of creation it was referring to six, twenty-four hour days. Nor should anyone think that human errors had made their way, like noxious weeds, into the Bible. God had dictated the Scriptures; they were His words and ideas and thus without error, inerrant.

When NNC's president reminded the critics that these conclusions were not Wesleyan or Nazarene, he seemed to make little headway with absolute inerrantists or creationists. Even more surprising, many of the objectors were of Nazarene background, some life-long Nazarenes or graduates of the denomination's colleges. But they did not know their Nazarene *Manual*, they had been won over to other traditions, and now they were tossing the sharpest of critical darts at NNC/NNU.

Certainly what happened at NNC/NNU was part of a larger Nazarene story. Creation-evolution incidents and debates popped up on other Nazarene campuses as well. At NNC/NNU the creation-evolution imbroglio was not tied to a specific person or a controversial publication, but followed the general pattern emerging elsewhere among the Nazarenes. The college's scientists all believed in God as creator, accepting the opening words of Genesis 1:1: "In the beginning God created...." Yet several of these scholars were theistic evolutionists, concluding that God's method of creation, if one followed both the Bible and the best findings of the biological sciences, was a gradual one—hence "theistic evolution," God's evolutionary way of creating the world and humans. This point of view accepted neither the Six-day nor Young Earth (the earth was at most 5-10,000 years old) interpretations.

Not all creationists writing to NNC/NNU leaders were of the same stripe. Some vigorously accepted the Six-Day or Young Earth views; others, adopting a later set of ideas and positions known as Intelligent Design, were less critical of theistic evolution. But nearly all creationists had trouble with the evolutionary ingredients of theistic evolution. They thought of evolution-believing scientists as atheists or at best materialists in their emphases. One exuberant creationist and Nazarene pastor from California referred to evolution as "anti-biblical, relativistic, humanistic, anti-traditional liberal subjectivism." Like-minded critics of evolution among the Nazarenes organized a group known as Nazarenes in Creation and sponsored publication of a magazine of the same name. In the Pacific Northwest, Pastor Dennis Swift of the Beaverton, Oregon, Church of the Nazarene and later pastor of his own independent group, harshly criticized scientists at NNC who taught theistic evolution. Swift and his disciples flooded the NNC president's office with letters calling for changes in the science curriculum and urging the invitation of creationist speakers to campus.

NNC had invited to campus Ken Ham, a leading spokesman for the creation movement and president of the organization Answers in Genesis, USA. The visit did not turn out well. Besides concluding that NNC was not entirely friendly to him, Ham thought the college scientists were wrongly traveling the evolution road. When asked at a Christian School gathering on the West Coast of nearly 3,000 persons where parents ought to send their young people to a college or a university, he replied, "I know where I wouldn't send them—to that Nazarene college over by Boise. They are theistic evolutionists in that science department." As Hagood wrote to one advocate of creationism, after Ham's "visit to our campus, in what I regard as an act of disrespect for the position we take as an institution of the Church of the Nazarene, he put us on a 'black list' of places where parents should not send their students. That is unacceptable to me." The president also pointed out that there were creationists on the NNU faculty, among them a recently hired scientist who was a traveling speaker for creationist viewpoints. NNU had also invited to campus Philip Johnson, a major spokesman for the Intelligent Design approach to creation.

The wrangles over creation-evolution climbed to a more intense level of conflict when they were yoked to differences of opinion on scriptural inspiration.

Biblical literalists asserted that if theologians and other scholars did not accept their Six-Day and Young Earth interpretations of Genesis, chapters one to eleven, these academics were reading the Bible incorrectly, failing to see it as the inerrant (without error) word of God. Creationism linked to inerrancy had invaded the Wetmore administration by the late 1980s, but escalated to a new high plateau of contention during Hagood's watch.

Nearly always Hagood tried to explain to creationists and inerrantists that the historical position of Wesleyans and Nazarenes, which NNC/NNU followed, differed from their stances. He quoted from the Nazarene *Manual* to one layman what he wrote to nearly all questioners about NNC/NNU and creation: "The Church of the Nazarene believes in the biblical account of creation...Genesis 1:1. We oppose a godless interpretation of the evolutionary hypothesis. However, the church accepts as valid all scientifically verifiable discoveries in geology and other natural phenomena, for we firmly believe that God is creator." And when letter writers spoke of the necessity of adopting an inerrancy position, Hagood quoted another section from the *Manual*: "We believe in the plenary inspiration of the Holy Scriptures, by which we understand the sixty-six books of the Old and New Testaments, given by divine inspiration, inerrantly revealing the will of God concerning us in all things necessary to our salvation, so that whatever is not contained therein is not to be enjoined as an article of faith."

On most other occasions the president added information from H. Orton Wiley's *Christian Theology* (1940), the church's accepted theological exposition. He used Wiley's comments to explain Nazarenes' avoidance of Six-Day or Young Earth interpretations of creation. These references from Wiley illuminated the church's middle of the road position on scriptural interpretation: avoidance of liberal higher criticism on the left and a fundamentalist, literalist, inerrant interpretation on the right. Nazarenes believed the Bible inerrant in "all things necessary to our salvation" but not inerrant in all matters of science and history, for example.

On a few occasions the president was pleased to hear from laypersons supporting what he had done with the creation controversy. Such a person was Dr. John Sutherland, son of the long-time NNC professor Francis Sutherland. Dr. Sutherland wrote to thank the president but also to tell him about the overreactions of Nazarene laymen to ENC Professor Karl Giberson's book *Worlds Apart*. At an Arizona district assembly in Phoenix, two men, showing their distaste for Giberson's ideas and their disagreements with general church leaders who supported those conclusions, "constructed 6 life-size, cardboard gorillas, each with a face of one of the general superintendents. They displayed them on a sidewalk across the street." Hagood replied to thank Dr. Sutherland for the update and added that "the continuing (forever) discussion on creation and evolution...has, of course, been a part of my presidential life from day one."

Revival, Time Out, and private prayer times stimulated spiritual stirrings on campus and in the Nampa area, blessing NNU leaders, students, and laypersons alike. (Fig. 6.11)

Happily, Hagood could also report on other more upbeat religious experiences at NNC/NNU. He often praised Chaplain Schandorff's diligent and supportive work in chapel services and out across campus. In addition, he told a leading Nazarene educator in 1998 that the student-led "Time Out" gatherings on Wednesday evenings were drawing 500 to 600 students. Watching these enthusiastic gatherings and students' religious journeys, the president was beginning to realize that "the 'new wine' of this generation will be placed in the 'new wineskins' of their own forms and methods." These heart-warming and expanding moments on campus also convinced Hagood that "these are truly days when students are seeking an authentic relationship with Jesus Christ."

Even more exhilarating to President Hagood was the spiritual awakening that, like an electric shock, pulsated quickly across campus in late spring 1997. A mini-revival in the Chapman Hall men's dorm sprang, the president was convinced, from a year-long student involvement in Bible study, prayer and fasting, special times in the new prayer chapel, and "a concerted effort on the part of students to be genuinely authentic in and on their own lives." An unusual evening prayer service stretched out to three hours and then spilled over into Chapman Hall and on to the other dorms. Many students experienced spiritual victory, including new conversions and recommitments by dozens of students. As Hagood told a general superintendent, the "renewal movement" brought "excitement...to our community knowing that God continues to move in mighty ways on the campus of Northwest Nazarene College." In the midst of the spiritual upsurge Hagood also wrote to another Nazarene president: "We are experiencing a genuine revival on our campus and enjoying the presence of the Holy Spirit in chapels, regular and impromptu student prayer and praise meetings, and numerous dorm gatherings....Praise the Lord!"

Hagood attempted to remain in center-of-the-road positions theologically, the place where most Nazarenes had stood during the past century. One of the ironies of NNC/NNU's expansion during the Hagood years, an enlargement that the president encouraged and often engineered, was the theological challenges that students of Reformed or Calvinist persuasions brought to a Wesleyan campus. As Hagood told one long-time college supporter, "Our denomination is experiencing a growing pressure to graft more and more Reformed [or Calvinist] positions onto our Wesleyan-holiness 'branches' of tradition and doctrine. The archivist for our church calls what we are experiencing the 'baptistification' of our fellowship, i.e. the trend in our church to be influenced by the doctrines and teachings of varied Baptist groups."

When evangelistic Nazarenes and non-Nazarenes alike tried to sow Reformist seeds of creationism and inerrancy among NNC/NNU students, Hagood called for a meeting of pastors from large Nazarene churches in the Treasure Valley. The president asked Edwin Crawford, director of the Wesley Center and professor of philosophy, to prepare a brief comparison of Reformed and Wesleyan traditions to show differences between the two groups (it was a masterful abbreviated overview), and then he himself spoke extemporaneously on the university's attempt to hew a middle path between liberals and fundamentalists, asserting that NNU stood more closely to conservatives than to liberals.

Another example of Hagood's mediating stances came in his contacts with the Nampa Christian schools. Nampa Christian High (as College High) had been a part of NNC until the late 1950s when it became a separate school—and flourished. It also came under the increasing influences of Reformist faculty and parents. Several teachers at the school, holding to inerrancy views, criticized NNC for teaching "an alternative creation theory." Hearing of these negative comments and rumors that some Nampa Christian teachers "were advising students not to consider NNC as their college of choice," Hagood met with one Nampa Christian principal and others to explain Wesleyan and NNC beliefs about Scriptural inspiration. He hoped that the meetings and his comments would help "all of us in the Christian community [to] focus on those elements which unite us rather than those which can divide."

Richard Hagood became a strong spiritual leader at NNC/NNU. Not a few district superintendents and pastors worried at the outset of his presidency if he, a layman, could be the shepherd the college needed. No one expressed these doubts after Hagood had been in office a few years. Critics might zap faculty for teaching theistic evolution, failing to hold to strict inerrancy, and being too liberal in their politics; but they did not mount any objections to Hagood's spiritual directions. He led well in troubled and changing times theologically within the Nazarene church and during a tempestuous time when American society and culture was sometimes nearly rent with escalating culture wars. General Superintendent Jerald Johnson put his stamp of approval on Hagood's leadership early in his presidency as he tried to sort out the increasing upset over creationist and inerrancy controversies. What Johnson said about Hagood toward the end of his third year in the presidency rang true for the remainder of his presidency. "This has been a difficult time for him," Johnson wrote to one of the NNC questioners, but "he has been thorough and fair. We all may be very grateful for the kind of leadership Dr. Hagood is giving NNC. I personally feel very comfortable with his direct and decisive manner in dealing with issues, which are as important to him as they are to all of us. He has my full support...."

It was October 1993 and Richard Hagood's first formal address as president of NNC. Early on in his speech he borrowed Abraham Lincoln's Gettysburg Address for his own purposes. "My fervent hope is that alumni and friends of NNC will little note, nor long remember what I say here tonight, but will never forget...years hence...what we will have done here at NNC...together...within the Providence of God." Looking to the future he asked his listeners to join him in agreeing to "a reinforcement of moral imperative," going "back to the roots of our tradition and Wesleyan heritage," pushing for the "academic enhancement" of the college, and in working to "preserve, protect, and promote the mission and well-being of this college."

But this initial presentation also called attention to several significant economic factors. The NNC community needed to improve the appearance of the campus and update its residential facilities, raise funds for a fine arts center in Kurtz Park, and expand the college's support base in the Treasure Valley and greater Northwest. These and other economic goals such as expanding student enrollments, raising faculty salaries, and constructing other new buildings were at the center of Hagood's current thinking and future planning in early fall 1993. If as a successful president he was to be an academic enabler and a spiritual leader, he must also keep the NNC financial ship afloat and headed in the right direction.

Hagood's strong oversight of NNC's economic vessel may have been his outstanding contribution as a college administrator. He could captain academics and foster a warm spiritual climate, but keen financial leadership and apt forecasting were his forte. Those clear achievements are not surprising, for Hagood had been thinking about such matters for nearly a generation. He had been eyebrow deep in economic matters for more than a decade at Washington State University and since 1985 at NNC. So it was natural and expected that he could bring his experiences to bear in raising more funds to help enlarge enrollments, add to the college's financial support, and erect new buildings—and to achieve this before crisis times hit the campus.

Hagood disclosed his thinking about some of these economic changes soon after his arrival in 1985. He was struck, he told an interviewer much later, how much needed to be done—and quickly. As President Wetmore's most influential and active cabinet member he worked with several of these issues in the late 1980s and into the next decade. They came to him in a series of questions: How could enrollments be boosted to the planned-for 1,500 undergraduates? Was it possible to find other sources of funding to finance the construction of needed buildings and the remodeling and updating of others? Would there be sufficient financial flexibility to pay for an expanded sports program and technological installations and improvements? How could tuition and board costs be kept sufficiently low that Nazarenes could afford to send their young people to NNC and yet bring in enough income to pay decent salaries to faculty and staff? In what specific ways could NNC reach out to the Treasure Valley and demonstrate both its importance as a Christian liberal arts college and also as an economic contributor to the Treasure Valley? These were major economic issues facing the new president; several of them became central to his administration in the next fifteen years.

When Hagood took the president's chair in 1993, the NNC undergraduate enrollment stood at 1,288. Five years later that enrollment had dipped slightly to 1,243. In another five years, in 2003, enrollment had jumped to 1,572, including 1,163 undergraduates and 409 graduate students. What happened to enrollments in those first five years, and then in the second five years, illustrates a pressing challenge the college faced and what the school and president did in addressing the challenge. Undergraduate enrollments remained flat during Hagood's presidency. Indeed, there were more undergraduates at Nampa in the 1993 and 1994 school years than in the next dozen years of his administration. The forward-looking president could see the writing on the enrollment sheets; he saw a dangerous trend and didn't like it. So, he suggested a change and led the college in a new direction.

Other notable trends helped lead to the fresh course of action. Nazarene church populations in the NNC educational zone—in fact in most of the U. S.—had plateaued. Key parts of the NNC educational district, chiefly Oregon and Washington, were also some of the least church-affiliated areas of the entire country. And in NNC's own Idaho backyard, Latter-day Saint (Mormon) numbers bulked larger than evangelical populations. The pressures of these unpromising contexts added to the impetus for new policies.

Evidences of change gradually began to appear on the NNC campus. First, Hagood was convinced that NNC could do better in recruiting and pleasing incoming students. Understanding the increasing competition to secure and keep enrollees, he moved to hire more professionally trained persons for the recruitment and counseling arms of the college. The new recruiters were urged to make additional and more persistent contacts with prospective students, to involve faculty in speaking with possible recruits, and to pay more caring attention to student needs and desires once they arrived on campus. The president wanted to raise student satisfaction so that they, in turn, would become personal "recruiters" for the college. Overall, this was an attempt to professionalize the student recruitment and management processes of the college.

Another two-pronged plan was mounted to address enrollment challenges. If competition for undergraduates was becoming so fierce, perhaps new graduate programs would not only add needed numbers but also expand new connections with NNC's host, the Treasure Valley. At the inception of Hagood's presidency, "academic enhancement" plans included "development of selected activities and offerings which strengthen the entire educational program and draw attention to the quality of the entirety of the College's academic program (perhaps to include an honors program, programs of distinction, pre-college experiences for college-bound high school students, etc.)"

Signs of Hagood's new plans soon multiplied. In the next edition of the *Context for Planning*, which the president prepared in three-year cycles, he called for an "aggressive reallocation" of more than "$600,000 in salary savings" by reducing "previously planned remuneration levels through position reductions and a moderation of salary increases for all category [sic] of employees...and revenue enhancement through continuing education programs." At the same time he recommended closing the Speech-Language Pathology and Audiology program and the Department of Family and Consumer Sciences but the launching of a new graduate degree, a Master of Business Administration. The president was not blind to all the reactions of those whose oxen were to be gored in these controversial changes. He knew salary raises might be put off or canceled, and two programs would be closed, with faculty losing their jobs. These changes were not likely to please faculty and staff. Hinting at these possible negative reactions but nonetheless trying to put a positive face on his recommendations, Hagood told the regents in spring 1996: "I am unspeakably grateful for the willingness of our campus community to tackle the challenge of institutional change, to work with colleagues and administration to determine the best course of action among less than ideal choices, and to keep focus on institutional mission. Understandably, these are the times that strain relationships and challenge our concepts of role and responsibilities." The president chose to place an upbeat reading on these traumatic transitions; more than a few faculty and staff, especially those losing their jobs or having to change positions, had more difficulty accepting the changes. Some were upset, too, when professional recruiters were hired and the very popular Bruce Webb, the writer of thousands of hand-written letters to prospective and returning students, was let go. Had the personal touch of a committed senior staff member been sacrificed in the name of professionalization?

Symbols of change were increasingly coming into focus. Strengthening and expanding student enrollment management, cutting undergraduate programs and majors not at the center of the college's mission, and growing graduate and continuing education programs—here were explicit changes in the works. Most of the graduate programs thus far had been in two very strong fields at NNC: religion and education. New graduate degree programs were added in these fields, and then new master's offerings in business, social work, counseling, and nursing. There was even talk of a doctoral program in practical theology toward the end of Hagood's presidency. These graduate programs brought in much-needed revenue, added to the academic prestige of the university, and forged multiple links with the Treasure Valley, particularly in the fields of education, business, and nursing. Once online programs were begun, academic connections with new cohorts of graduate students were added, throughout NNC's zone and virtually around the globe. Enrollment outcomes displayed the successes and less than successes in Hagood's institutional changes. Graduate enrollments steadily bounded upwards: 83 in 1996, 202 in 1999, 403 in 2003, and 622 in 2009. Continuing education headcounts zipped up from 298 in 1995 to 543 in 1999, and to an amazing 8,000 in 2010. Pastoral training and concurrent enrollments for strong high school students (2,300 high school students by 2010) also added to enrollment totals. These were the successes—rapidly growing graduate and continuing education enrollments and substantial rising revenues from them. But despite all the energetic and professionalization put to work on undergraduate enrollments, they remained flat: 1,118 in 1996, 1,104 in 1999; 1,163 in 2003, and 1,156 in 2009. This was a disappointing outcome—in planning and in financial return.

Hagood also pushed for different methods of fund raising to help pay for the expansion of the NNC/NNU campus. His record of accomplishment in this area, supported by the complementary work of unusually talented and energetic colleagues, was remarkable. Notably important buildings were erected and other campus improvements put in place, clear results of these new fund-raising efforts. Hagood reached out to specific individuals and families, even explicitly courted them, to provide lead gifts to kick-start the funding for needed buildings. For example he wrote to a contemporary who had done well in the media field, asking him to consider "making a leadership gift at the $1 million dollar level toward" a "technology learning center." A year later he was back at the prospective donor requesting he think about "participating...as a major donor," particularly in the "athletic facilities and...the business building." And to another very successful investor in the Boise valley he wrote asking that he and his wife consider becoming heavily involved in funding the "facility need we have in our School of Health and Science." Some worried, however, that the direct, personal calls for these additional funds for buildings, renovations, and sports programs would undermine other fund-raising efforts. With limited money in the funding buckets, if much of it was poured out for special building projects would anything be left to finance academic and other staff programs and positions?

The completed Brandt Center (1997) signaled a new, important expansion of the NNC campus. (Fig. 6.12)

Early on as an administrative newcomer at Nampa, Hagood became enamored with the idea of NNC as a "destination college" and began to push the concept while still vice-president for institutional advancement. Linked to that bent was his conviction that a foundation organization ought to be established primarily for raising funds for the college. By fall of 1987, just two years after he arrived, Hagood was recommending to the Board of Regents that a "Development Foundation" be established, that a campus master plan be put in place, that a list of "capital development projects" be proposed, that a capital funds list be prioritized, and that the regents work with the city to close public streets crossing the campus. With Hagood's foot on the accelerator every one of these recommendations was put into effect in the next few years.

Hagood rode with that agenda of recommendations and possible implementations into the president's office on October 1, 1993. His first presidential report to the regents five weeks later included plans for establishing a Wesleyan Center of Applied Theology, a concerted move toward erecting a fine arts center, the completion of a new baseball field (later named after long-time and much-admired coach Elmore Vail), and what became eventually known as the Byron Lee Athletic Complex. If raising enrollments and locating additional sources of funding were at the front of the new president's strategic financial goals, so was the construction of new buildings. He euphorically requested of the board less than a year later that they "receive the largest donation in the history of NNC." John H. Brandt, local realtor and strong churchman, was offering NNC "a lead trust funded by income producing agricultural property in the amount of $2,000,000 for the Fine Arts and Convocation center project." Hagood was also asking the board to name the building the Brandt Center, the first time NNC would be naming a building "for someone who is not directly linked to the college faculty or staff or to the Church of the Nazarene." A fund-raising campaign was mounted to gather another $3.5 million, and groundbreaking took place in 1996. It was the first academic building on the campus in twenty-three years. The Hagood building bonanza was roaring into action.

The first building completed of several was the Kirkeide Apartments. Ken and Dolly Kirkeide, dedicated Nazarenes from western Washington, funded the construction of a married student housing complex of twenty units, which were dedicated in 1995. At the same time work began on a small prayer chapel (the Little Prayer Chapel) and a four-story freshman dormitory (Ford Hall). They were completed in 1997 and 1998, respectively. Meanwhile, the most significant of the buildings, the Brandt Center in Kurtz Park, was completed and dedicated in 1997. In a four-year period two major buildings went up, a prayer chapel and married student apartments completed, and major city streets through campus rerouted.

Other new projects began three years later. Businessman/educator Bob Helstrom and his wife Yvonne provided the lead gift for the Helstrom Business center, which opened in 2002. Others, including the Harter, Ellis, and Walden families, were major contributors to erection of the center. That new building not only helped the expansion of NNU's Business Department and its multiplying programs; it also housed the degree completion programs in continuing education and Student Educational Employment Program (STEP). Together they fit nicely into Hagood's plans to extend NNU's influences beyond the boundaries of Nampa. As the energetic chair of the Business Department Ronald Galloway put it, the new Helstrom Building allowed "NNU to carry on its mission of service" to students, the campus, and the surrounding community. At the same time Loren and Roz Rader worked out a trust to eventually deed their 20-unit Holly Apartments to the college. These apartments were located on the edge of the campus. In

The dedication of the Johnson Sports Center (2004) symbolized NNU's advancement in its sports program. (Fig. 6.13)

the same year, 2002, NNU opened its Admissions Welcome Center in the former headquarters of the Nazarene Financial Credit Union, also adjacent to NNU. A second stage of Hagood's expansion program had been completed.

A third and final stage was even more impressive. The sports-minded president wanted to enlarge the university's athletic facilities, particularly after it became an official member of the NCAA Division II in 2002 and needed to compete with second-tier universities (the two Alaska state universities, Western and Central Washington, and Seattle Pacific, among others) throughout the PNW. Again a lead gift, from Harmon and Liz Johnson, made possible the expansion of the Montgomery Gym into the Johnson Sports Center (2004), including a new field house, fitness center, and other sports facilities.

Then in quick fashion other major gifts allowed for the planning of two additional expensive buildings. One family provided the lead funding for what became a new science center, The Thomas Family Health and Science Center, dedicated in 2009. For the first time in NNU's history, the science departments and the enlarging nursing program would have spacious and up-to-date facilities for their strong and expanding programs. Finally, in an intriguing story of memory, contact, and encouragement, NNU announced that Leah Peterson, an Alaskan teacher who had attended NNC for one year in the 1920s, was contributing between $6.5 and 7.5 million for the construction of a new building or the expansion of the existing Riley Library into a huge "learning commons." The resulting edifice would be a greatly enlarged center for books and state-of-the-art technology needed for a small but comprehensive university.

Dr. Joel Pearsall served ably as NNU's vice president for financial affairs, vice president of university advancement, and general counsel. (Fig. 6.14)

Hagood pioneered these programs and helped to plan the construction of these buildings. Then as president, he enlisted a cadre of able lieutenants to help him. Hal Weber and Joel Pearsall kept budgets balanced, freeing the president from worrying about the college/university sliding into the red. Early on Jerry Gunstream, as director of major gifts, made vital contacts with donors. Ernie McNaught, B. Edgar Johnson, Barry Swanson, and Michael Pitts kept connections with pastors and churches warm and open to adding to their support for NNC/NNU. In fact for several years during the Hagood administration the per capita giving on the college/university's educational zone was the highest in the entire Church of the Nazarene. Darrell Marks also served well as vice president for institutional advancement and then generously as a volunteer in that office after retiring.

But perhaps the kingpin of fundraisers was Gary Skaggs. He first worked as director of planned giving before becoming Marks's replacement in 1998. Until his untimely death in 2008, Skaggs linked up with key families. His close contact with Leah Peterson, in which he became essentially her personal pastor and financial advisor, led to her contributing approximately $7 million to the university. Overall, Hagood and his colleagues did remarkably well in raising large lead gifts and other needed monies for several construction projects. Concurrently, endowment growth zoomed up from almost nothing to $22 million at the end of 2007, with another nearly $20 million in deferred gifts.

Across the front page of the *Crusader* in bold and black-and-white large print read the word **CENSORED**. No one would know from the NNC/NNU presidential correspondence, regents' minutes, or stories in the *Messenger* that there were topics discussed only in the student newspaper or in the student development files and not elsewhere. Had these and other such controversies been "censored" or elided from descriptions of the college? Or, more precisely, if the *Crusader* reflected the topics students were frequently debating on campus, was there much more to the college's socio-cultural life than met the eye in official campus sources? Whatever the best answer, NNC/NNU students talked about and participated in events and actions missing from most information sent out from the college.

Take sex, for example. NNC/NNU students wanted to talk about that complicated subject. Rarely a year went by in the 1990s and early 2000s without several articles appearing in the *Crusader* on varied facets of that controversial topic. Obviously raging hormones on campus were packed down, full, and often running over—frequently to the consternation of student development leaders and administrators, but evidently to the joy of many young men and their coed companions. Sex in all its manifold mysteries and manifestations spilled out on campus in dozens of essays in the *Crusader*, chapel presentations, and campus workshops. No topic seemed more "censored" in official NNC/NNU media and yet more alive in campus conversations.

Some of those stories and conversations were open, explicit, and revealing. A cover story "S-E-X at N-N-C?" in the February 11, 1997, issue of the *Crusader* carried the results of an informal survey among 230 students about sexuality on campus. When asked about premarital sex, 84 percent of the respondents thought it unacceptable, 4 percent "sometimes acceptable," and 4 percent "acceptable." Nearly 90 percent taking the survey had not participated in premarital sex, with about 10 percent claiming they had. The outspoken newspaper editor doubted these findings: he thought "far fewer than 89 percent of students have been abstinent during their NNC years." The same issue carried the sad story of an NNC student who had been sexually active in a premarital experience that turned out badly. Even more revealing was an interview in 2003 that the newspaper editor recorded with about ten students in the dining hall. She asked them about their first sexual knowledge, "making-out," girls and their dress, limits on dating activity, what their honeymoons might be like, and sexuality in marriage. Evidently an "uncensored version [of the story] was even more elaborate." The editor correctly concluded that the conversation proved that Christian college students "can openly and maturely discuss something often considered taboo."

The limited number of extant records of student life and development indicate other vexing challenges in dealing with campus sexuality. In trying to become more proactive, student development leaders, hoping to head off major dilemmas, sponsored date rape prevention and sexual choices seminars. They also offered counseling on marriage and marriage enrichment conversations for interested students. Sometimes, weekly reports from the student development offices included sex-related incidents. For instance, two girls, wanting to avoid conflict in their dormitory, "chose to solve it by going to a motel over the weekend. This was no problem to us except they took two boys with them," one student counselor reported. Some constituents worried, too, about the new freshman dorm, with its connected men's and women's wings; hadn't it compromised NNC's "standards to attract the secular crowd with its secular offering of a co-ed dorm"? "Whose idea was it to make opportunity for the flesh here?" the questioner continued. The president answered that the residence was not the threat the writer saw it to be; "we have not had a single infraction of the house rules....We do not describe our residence halls as 'co-ed.'"

A surprising number of essays also appeared in the *Crusader* dealing with condoms, homosexuality, AIDS, and pornography. Those treating homosexuality were the most numerous. A majority of these stories called for more understanding, hoping that Nazarenes and Christians in general might accept homosexuals among them without necessarily accepting homosexual acts. An anonymous "John Doe" wrote a story for the *Crusader* asking that anti-homosexual statements on his dormitory board be stopped. The next issue of the newspaper carried two responses, both calling for Christian attitudes of love and understanding, not harassment, toward homosexuals. Still two other comments came in the following issue, one requesting Christians to be less judgmental and more informed about homosexuality and the other entitled "Homosexuals will not go to heaven."

On another occasion it was difficult for all involved—administration, faculty, students, and regents—when Soul Force, a national organization for gay and lesbians asked to visit campus. After a good deal of campus thinking and planning, the group was allowed to come. For the most part, the visit went off without any major problems. In allowing the visit, NNU followed the path most evangelical colleges and universities took in regard to Soul Force, but a few more conservative schools chose not to have the controversial group on their campuses. Obviously the NNU campus was divided on these much-debated issues, but most of those who spoke out on the controversies wanted Christians to be open to homosexuals.

These sexual topics, when they involved faculty and staff, were not easy for administrators to manage. When one professor became too flirtatious with his female assistant, he was reprimanded and then eventually left the faculty. Another faculty member, accused of infidelity by his wife, took a leave of absence and then resigned. Still another prominent staff member, who disclosed his homosexual identity, left NNC. Full information on his disclosure and his leaving and specifics on the other two incidents are missing from their personnel files.

Happily, other relationships between the sexes often led to smiling results on campus. Dating was a continuing, favorite activity on campus, and students wanted to talk about it. The tenor of a majority of the comments in the *Crusader*—perhaps because most editors during the Hagood years were young women—urged NNC/NNU men to look up, to realize and value the attractions and achievements of coeds. Presumably the increasing ratio of young women over young men—a national trend, and about 60 to 40 percent ratio at NNC—encouraged these editorial thumbs-in-the-backs directed at young men. For instance, two freshman girls contributed a provocative piece to the newspaper, "Why boys are stupid: Two single girls speak out." They put it directly: "One can't help but wonder what the boys at NNC are doing." Why not a few dates—not expensive, big events or meals, leading to "life-time commitment," but those just for fun. They wanted others to know their definition of a real Man: "A male creature with the guts to ask a girl on a friendly, nonthreatening, pleasant, chivalric, generous, fun outing (a.k.a. a date)."

No response came to that jab in masculine ribs, but other comments on the dating game spilled out in the *Crusader*, especially in the annual Valentine's Day issues. TWIRP week also got yearly coverage. On these TWIRP dates—when The Woman Is Required to Pay—couples went off to Nampa or Boise hangouts for an evening of fun. As one young woman opined, TWIRP time was "the best weekend of the entire school year." A later two-part question/answer interview summarized what young men looked for in coeds and what they, in turn, looked for in guys.

Another journalist took a varying, revealing slant. A married woman in her fifties living off campus, she encouraged students to look around to see how many of the NNC administrators, faculty, and staff members had found their mates on their campus. Although "a degree without a mate is not a lethal combination," she concluded, looking for a lifetime partner at the college was "an idea well worth pursuing." A Hagood story added substance to her contention about NNC matching. Recalling his own college years, the president told an interviewer that the first time he saw Junella Finkbeiner, he declared: "I'll marry her some day." And he did.

With all that was happening, NNC/NNU was remarkably free from major disciplinary hiccups, with but a few upsets of unsatisfactory behavior. Part of the disciplinary disconnect resulted from changing standards and enforcement of them. As NNC/NNU increasingly expanded its course offerings into the Boise Valley to attract students, particularly adult graduate students, the school was less inclined to dictate the lifestyles of these off-campus students. Noting this lack of enforcement, young men living on campus began calling for more freedom of actions when off campus. When they were called before the student life leaders, those being disciplined pointed to what they considered a double set of standards for dormitory and off-campus students. The complaints did not work; on-campus students drinking off campus were warned, and then if guilty of repeated rule breaking were dismissed. But not many were sent home.

Another dislocation came on the dancing issue. That conflict took on new urgency when the Church of the Nazarene changed its stance on dancing in the 1990s. Previous to 1993, the church forbade all forms of dancing, even in school physical education classes. Now the church would stand only against those types of dancing "that detract from spiritual growth and break down proper moral inhibitions and reserve." That inexact statement opened the door for a good deal of high school dancing, meaning that many Nazarene young people came to campus having participated in dances. But they were not allowed to dance or sponsor dances at NNC/NNU. Issue after issue of the *Crusader* carried stories on this unresolved issue. Early on, one student journalist called for a clarification on dancing. As he put it, "For those of you who have wondered on occasion why NNC holds the stand it has against dancing, or for that matter, what exactly that stand is, you're not alone. I'm not sure the college itself is sure." The student handbook, he pointed out, called for no dancing on or off campus or campus-sponsored dances, following general Nazarene guidelines. But the handbook also stated that those attending a church that sponsored dances or students invited to a church dance would not be disciplined. Waffling like this, the writer continued, would not help the issue; clear, straightforward guidelines were needed. The journalist failed to see the box in which NNC/NNU was caught: as long as the general Church of the Nazarene was inconsistent on matters of dancing, so too the college.

The dilemmas surrounding dancing continued throughout the Hagood presidency, conundrums that all Nazarene college educators faced. When a student asked the president in 2001 for permission to establish a "swing dance team,"

Hagood pointed to a Board of Regents policy not to sponsor entertainments "including all forms of dancing that detract from spiritual growth and break down proper moral inhibitions and reserve." The wife of a retired Nazarene pastor also wrote the president, worried about dancing on campus. Hagood clarified that NNU followed Nazarene Church guidelines, and that it allowed only "choreography that is part of musical and dramatic productions, if done with proper standards of modesty and without sexual suggestion." Generally speaking, the Church of the Nazarene had punted on the issue, neither disallowing nor totally allowing it. Nazarene colleges would likely remain in this quagmire of indecision until generations of anti-dancing Nazarenes passed from the scene.

Another area of entertainment and physical activity—the sports program—greatly expanded and blossomed during the Hagood presidency. As a former NNC athlete, Hagood retained a strong interest in sports. Illustrating that long-held attraction, he told a former teammate: "As you might expect, I maintain a keen interest

NAIA national tournaments held on the NNC campus drew large, enthusiastic crowds and many teams to the college and Nampa. (Fig. 6.15)

in basketball here at NNC." That continuing attention, coupled with the president's desire to expand the mission and reach of NNC/NNU, led to strong administrative support for the college's athletic programs. The college and then university reached the apex of its athletic prowess and notoriety during the Hagood years.

In the 1990s NNC rose to prominence in its NAIA region and also gained stature nationally. The men's basketball team, the mainstay for many years of NNC's sports program, experienced a huge, immediate upturn when Ed Weidenbach, a former NNC basketball player, returned to coach at his alma mater. In his first year as NNC's coach, following a very disappointing season under the previous coach, Widenbach took his team to the NAIA Division II nationals. An even greater leap upward occurred the next year when NNC was selected to host the NAIA Division II national tournament. For seven years, from 1993 through 1999, hundreds of players and thousands of fans invaded Nampa for this sports spectacle. Tourney participants and their supporters filled motel rooms and restaurants, spent much-appreciated dollars in the Nampa-Boise areas, and generally expanded NNC's reputation as an institution on the move. In all these years, as the victor in its NAIA district or as host of the national finals, NNC played in the tournament. And they did very well, advancing into the final eight or even final four for several years. Under the talented, tireless efforts of Eric Forseth, the tournament worked smoothly and added luster to NNC's expanding reputation. Nary a discouraging word was heard on the Nampa and Northwest ranges about NNC's central role in the NAIA extravaganza.

But an ambitious president wanted to move NNC to university status, and along with that transition, change to a higher level for the sports program. Hagood

NNC's women's basketball team won the national NAIA Division 2 championship in 1997. (Fig. 6.16)

believed, as he told the campus community in March 1999, "the time seems right for us to turn our attention to the task of broadening and strengthening our intercollegiate athletic program. We believe that our undergraduate enrollment can be enhanced with the introduction of several sports approved by the Board of Regents...." Realizing the differences of opinions that might explode out of these changes, he asked that "our community rally around these new initiatives with the same spirit and support displayed with the NAIA championships." Part of that transition, it turned out, was a switch to NCAA Division II status. After five years of probationary status, NNU became a full-fledged member of the Great Northwest Athletic Conference (GNAC) in 2002.

Ironically, even though most of the publicity focused on the men's basketball team, the women's teams were beginning to enjoy more successes than the men. In fact, the women's basketball program, under Coach Roger Schmidt, was the only NNC/NNU team to win a national NAIA Division II championship, in 1997, except for the women's field hockey team in 1980. After NNU joined the GNAC the women's volleyball and basketball teams fared better than the men's basketball and baseball squads. (The men's cross-country team had won the GNAC championship, however, in 2001.) Perhaps because NNU enrolled more women than men, perhaps because the women's teams won more often—and played more exciting games, some fans thought—attendance at the women's games moved beyond that at men's contests.

The new construction and expansion of playing fields and buildings illustrated how much NNU had enlarged its sports program. The Byron Lee Athletic complex reached out to embrace the Vail Baseball Field (1994), the track and field complex (2000), the Halle Softball Field (2003), and other soccer fields. The jewel of the complex was the much-expanded Johnson Sports Center, dedicated in 2004. By the end of Hagood's presidency NNU had a fully laid out athletic complex, more than standard for the major and minor women's and men's sports teams the university sponsored.

But some alumni and faculty fretted about the costs of athletics at the university. Those misgivings surfaced in a number of probing questions: Why had NNC left the NAIA division, which allowed them to play long-time rivals such as Albertson College of Idaho, Eastern Oregon, and Whitman, and compete with other evangelical schools, George Fox, Warner Pacific, Western Baptist, and Whitworth? What about the expensive trips to play Alaska teams, and why so few conference games in the Nazarene population centers of Portland, Spokane, Walla Walla, Denver, and Colorado Springs? Were the costly sports programs, with several coaches and many exorbitant trips, necessary for a Christian liberal arts college or university? Hadn't the institution taken on too much in trying to compete above its head in cost and competition?

Hagood had good answers for several of these queries. The move to NCAA II status came, largely, because the NAIA was losing strength in the Pacific Northwest. Schools such as Seattle Pacific, Central Washington, and Western Washington had moved to the NCAA. Also, Hagood rhetorically asked an interviewer, "What institutions do you want to be identified with academically?" He had hoped, too, that even more private funding would come from alumni, especially those involved in the Crusader Athletic Association. The group had done well, but, the president thought, had not reached its full potential in financially supporting NNU sports. He was also convinced that an athletic program was a central part of educating "the whole person," a long-time objective of NNC/NNU. Yes, athletics were expensive, but they also helped undergraduate enrollments by bringing new students to campus. As he pointed out, in 1998, 98 students were involved in intercollegiate sports at NNC; two years later 250 were participating, with perhaps as many as 95 not enrolled if the college lacked a competitive sports program. Hagood was also quick to note that each year more than $900,000 came from external sources to support the NNC/NNU sports program.

One of the fiercest tempests in the post-2000 period was the upset that erupted over a possible change of the NNU mascot, the Crusader. Earlier in 2001, President Hagood had formed an ad-hoc committee to discuss the idea of such a switch but decided the issue was too divisive among NNU alumni. NNU students had also proposed dropping "Crusader" as the name for the student newspaper, but the president had vetoed that idea. In 2005 the chair of the board of trustees initiated a discussion to reconsider dropping the name Crusader and finding a less controversial mascot. The trustees agreed to take up the issue, and the president wrote to thousands of NNU alumni for their reactions to a possible change. The feedback was surprising—and emotional. A clear majority of the alumni opposed the change, accusing the trustees and administration of kowtowing to "political correctness," a term unfortunately appearing in the president's letter to alumni. Tradition, evangelical "crusading," and athletic recognition were among the reasons trotted out to oppose the name change. One bristling letter writer, an alumnus and minister, told the president, if the Crusader name is changed, "I will choose to not be associated with Northwest Nazarene University—or whatever you may change its' [sic] name to." Another alumnus in Wyoming warned the president, "Should there be a name change, just take me off your calling list and mailing list for any of your drives." And, he added, "another NNU graduate that lives in Wyoming...said that if they change the name NNU will never receive a donation from their household. That is noteworthy for I have been told their net worth is between [$]8-10,000,000." Equally forceful was a letter from a group supporting and funding NNU athletics that warned their support would end or greatly diminish if the Crusader name were dropped.

Letters supporting the elimination of the Crusader insignia were less numerous and, for the most part, less contentious. Missionaries who had served in non-Christian areas, many Nazarene travelers, and several faculty members agreed that a change in mascot name would remove a controversial calling card of the university. They pointed to times when "Crusader" had not been used in the past in foreign areas because the name was freighted with too much controversial baggage. As one supporter of the change put it, with NNU accepting its "challenge to become more engaged around the world, there will be even more opportunities for the adverse name to raise bad feelings. We must not let that name get in the way of our ability to teach around the world." In support of a name change, the Church of the Nazarene archivist made an interesting historical point: when Nazarenes dropped the controversial word "Pentecostal" from their name in 1919, they did so because "Time had caught up with them, and the popular use of the word no longer reflected the image they wished to project." Was the same true of the Crusader?

NNU alumni, students, faculty, and administrators were clearly divided on the polarized issue. A task force that the administration named, composed of missionaries, alumni, faculty, and students, voted overwhelmingly to support a mascot name change. The trustees seemed split down the middle, but those writing to the president ran about 60 to 40 against the change. Hagood, pondering whether the change would be too controversial among NNU supporters, decided on a compromise. He brought to the executive committee of the trustees a suggestion to keep the Crusader name but to change the graphics to try to make depictions of the Crusader emblem less offensive. The executive committee, equally divided on the issue, eagerly accepted the president's suggestion, and so did the full board of trustees. Just before he made his suggestion of compromise, Hagood told one trustee he had been reading Doris Kearns Goodwin's magnificent study of Abraham Lincoln, *A Team of Rivals* (2005) and other writings by and about Lincoln, and realized how he might, Lincoln-like, find a middle-of-the-road position between the two extremes of opinion. That compromise measure and its implementation remains a sterling example of Hagood's wise leadership.

While students were wrestling with controversies over sexual identity, dating, sports, and the Crusader issue, they were also dealing with religious issues. In the long run this may have been their most significant issue, but attempting to understand the nuances of the struggle is like trying to catch sand in a sieve: much more skips through than is caught and identified.

Not much hard data is available on persisting or changing religious views of NNC/NNU students from the 1980s forward. But in information gathered from freshman and seniors in 1997 and from statistics compiled at two other Nazarene colleges (Point Loma and MidAmerica), a few intriguing glimpses of student attitudes and lifestyles and changes over time come into better focus. And when considering this information, we should keep in mind the apt observation of two of the pollsters: "As to change over time, there is little that concerns us Nazarenes more than the possibility that slowly but surely we are somehow losing our calling, our identity and ultimately our reason for being."

Similarities and differences appear in the surveys of NNC freshman and seniors in 1997. Students in both classes were nearly all Caucasian (more than 90 percent); most saw themselves as conservative or middle of the road in politics (freshman, 75 percent; seniors, 92 percent); nearly all identified themselves as born-again Christians (freshman, 93 percent; not asked of seniors); and almost all attended weekly religious services (freshman, 100 percent; seniors, 95 percent).

There was some evidence of shifting points of view on a few controversial issues, as one would expect after three years of study at a Christian liberal arts college. Although 67 percent of the freshmen thought homosexual relations should be prohibited, 37 percent of the seniors so thought. Where 6 percent of freshmen agreed that abortions should be legal, 13 percent of the seniors did. In 1997, most freshmen came with little experience with alcohol, but beer drinking (12 percent) and wine or other liquor (17 percent) increased during the year.

NNC/NNU students during the Hagood years mirrored new religious trends and ideas common throughout the Church of the Nazarene and American culture in general. Some of the campus religious currents were running in the same channels as those emanating out of the Nazarene headquarters in Kansas City. For example, NNC/NNUers maintained the strong missional interests that emerged in the 1960s and continued for the next two generations. Summer and short-term mission trips still caught the eyes and warmed the hearts of NNC/NNU students; they raised the necessary funds to go on these trips and reported back on their meaningfulness. Others found their mission calls close at hand, working with the elderly, the needy, and children—in the Nampa-Boise area and in their home churches.

On occasion student reactions to religious issues could be edgy. When a popular student and talented singer from the NNC of the 1950s returned for her class's 40th reunion she was horrified with "a terrible slanderous and offensive article" titled, "Stupid Christian Tricks" in the *Crusader*. As a strong admirer of television evangelist Pat Robertson she was particularly upset to hear that she and others were "hopelessly devoted self-conscious whackos" for following Robertson. She wrote to President Hagood, telling him that the article's author would have "to answer to God on the Day of Judgment" for his slandering of Robertson, whom she considered "God's favorite person in all the world." The president reminded her that the *Crusader* most often reflected student opinion alone and that the story she objected so vociferously to represented the views of one notoriously outspoken student. When the woman's letter to Hagood was reprinted in the student newspaper, it elicited several responses, mostly negative. She sent another letter to the *Crusader* explaining her especially warm regard for Pat Robertson. Overall, the original pointed essay, the woman's responses, and the letters to the editor reacting to her opinions illustrated how much NNC/NNU, as well as the Church of the Nazarene, had changed in forty years and the difficulty of speaking and understanding across the chasm of two generations.

As usual, the individualistic and independent-minded editors of the *Crusader* prided themselves in exercising their freedom to print a variety of controversial stories. In doing so they presented a spectrum of writings from right to left, probably reflecting fairly well the gamut of religious, political, and sociocultural opinions among students. Most essays on religion veered toward the conservative side. Conversely, each year some students felt free to write stories or letters to the editor challenging Nazarene standards and beliefs. Others called for the liberalizing of codes of conduct, dropping required chapels, and ending the denominational domination at the college. The latter opinions, often labeled "liberal," were particularly upsetting to alumni fearful that their alma mater was falling into the hands of secularists.

Two of NNU's spokesmen provide helpful descriptions of what students were attempting to achieve religiously while at the university. When an NNC graduate of the 1940s wrote of his earlier alienation from and his more recent re-attraction to his alma mater, President Hagood answered the grad with a superb, succinct definition of NNU student goals in their religious lives. "I am persuaded," he wrote discerningly, "that young people of today are as idealistic, as desirous of a relationship with Christ, as earnest in seeking for meaning with eternal significance as any time in our history. While they are less interested in forms and systems, they are most interested in authentic worship and lifestyle."

Perhaps NNU theologian Thomas J. Oord also had it right a bit later. He was convinced that Nazarenes were living out a neo-Wesleyan theology of love. Students at NNU, as well as Nazarenes out on the educational zone, were displaying lives in relationship—with God and other humans. If that definition seemed a bit vague and illusive to some hard-core traditionalists, NNU students were certainly displaying a relational holiness or Wesleyanism in their missional desires. They wanted to embrace the world's problems and needs, to attempt to become answerers and problem-solvers. And in their idealism and commitment were they any more or less evangelical than the "holiness folk" of early NNC or advocates of Arminian-Wesleyan ideas of mid-twentieth century NNC who were convinced that missionaries and pastors somehow were more spirit-driven than laypersons? The two generations of Nazarene students following the 1960s were bent on becoming new kinds of missionaries and ministers. They desired to "break out of the bubble" that threatened to confine and encapsulate them in faraway Nampa. They wanted to get off campus, go into the educational zone, and travel out into the world. There, to borrow words of Lincoln's second inaugural, they would "bind up the [world's] wounds," "care for [those] who shall have borne the battle," and for their widows and orphans. And they would hope to do all this without malice and with charity for all, as God gave them insights. A new generation of students had come to Nampa, less tied to saved, sanctified, and satisfied and more driven by conversion, Christ-likeness, and missional commitment.

Even before Richard Hagood retired in summer 2008, pundits were beginning to assess his legacy. What kind of leader had he been, how did his presidency compare with those of his predecessors, and what lasting marks had he made on NNC/NNU? As he closed his office door in retirement, observers were already making their opinions known.

Nearly everyone was impressed with Hagood's bent toward planning. Whether in his doctoral work, in his experience at Washington State University, or through an inborn desire to keep things organized—no one seemed to know whence came his ties to strategic planning. He arrived at NNC with that bias in 1985, immediately put it to good work, and continued his ten-year and three-year planning cycles thereafter. He seemed to know from the beginning the administrative mountains he wished to climb and how to lay out the routes to those peaks.

Out from that planning center naturally flowed apt leadership in matters of the spirit and bricks and mortar. Hagood did "care for the soul" of NNC/NNU, as he had promised. Facing and fronting false worries, he proved a layman could be the spiritual shepherd the university needed. He also expanded the campus, protected it from intruding, widening streets, and planted several new and imposing buildings. He also made large strides in balancing the college's finances, expanding its endowments, and raising enrollments in most student sectors.

It was in the areas of academics and athletics that most questions about Hagood's leadership arose. Not all faculty agreed with large changes the president and his deans Dunn and Pitts instituted. (What strong president has ever gained unanimity from his faculty on *any* issue?) They wondered if in closing some programs and in adding others he hadn't undercut the liberal arts core of the college. Were these leaders putting so much emphasis on business, nursing, education, and technology that professorial positions in economics, literature, languages, and sociology, for example, were not being filled? Others were certain that all the money used in expanding athletic programs when NNC moved from the NAIA to the NCAA was weakening academic programs. One discontented alumna was convinced the president was "nothing but a jock." And others thought Hagood failed to establish the warm, supportive relationships that some of his predecessors had sustained between the president and the faculty.

Did these questions, in the aggregate, go too far? Yes, additional funding was needed to expand the professional programs in business and nursing, for example; but bold, clear numbers proved these departments and the graduate programs generated new dollars and were funding key liberal arts positions. Hagood had not so much shifted away from liberal arts as built on those trends already in existence when he came.

Richard Hagood was anything but a caretaker leader. Unlike his two immediate predecessors (leaving out the too-short Doane presidency), Hagood looked far ahead and planned diligently for the paths from here to there. To employ clichés for larger meaning, he was not a reactive but a proactive leader. Hagood's mindset differed dramatically from the caretaker approach. In the face of shrinking enrollments and tighter funding, he wanted to "make it happen," find ways to turn around these negative trends as soon as possible. Leading by example, he examined the contextual circumstances, peered into the future, and set on paper an agenda of active, energetic plans. Seen in the larger spectrum of long-time NNC presidents, Hagood most resembled Russell V. DeLong and John E. Riley in his strong leadership. Hagood often quoted the words of the first principal of what became NNC: that some day there would be "a great school here in Nampa." He also encapsulated his own look forward in one memorable sentence: "The promise of greatness lies before us as an ever-escalating challenge, never static; at once fulfilled and always yet to be fulfilled." Richard Hagood took Northwest Nazarene University far into that promised land during his fifteen years at the helm.

Epilogue

AT THE CENTENNIAL

David Alexander of Southern Nazarene University was elected NNU's twelfth president in spring 2008. Although he became the new chief administrator at the university, he was not new to kingdom work, to NNU, or to such challenges. As the first months of his administration sped by, many came to believe he was the ideal successor to Richard Hagood as NNU president.

Alexander had strong Nazarene roots and close links to NNU. The son of a long-time Nazarene pastor and his wife—both NNU alumni—Alexander had attended Point Loma Nazarene College after growing up in interior California towns. He graduated as a music major in 1977. After completing a master's in choral conducting at California State University, Fullerton, Alexander earned a doctorate in music education at the University of Illinois. In 1986 he came to NNC as a professor of music, directed the Northwesterners singing group, and stayed until 1991. Then he transferred to Southern Nazarene University where he remained seventeen years, first chairing the Music Department and then serving as vice president for institutional advancement. He returned to Nampa well acquainted with NNU and well trained as a university administrator.

Alexander's new administration opened on a positive, upbeat note in 2008. Fall enrollments hit an all-time new high of 1,944, with 1,329 undergraduates and 615 graduate students. Those impressive numbers represented a 6 percent increase from the previous year. Contributors had given large amounts of new scholarship money, allowing the university to fund many more new scholarships and to expand the university's capital funds reserve to nearly $13 million. During the year, the transition from Richard Hagood's active fifteen-year administration to Alexander's presidency also went smoothly. From his

Dr. David Alexander, here with his wife Sandy, early on revealed his spiritual and warm-hearted leadership as NNU's twelfth president (2008–). Fig. 7.1

The completion of the Thomas Family Health and Science Center (2009) symbolized NNU's continuing institutional advancement. (Fig. 7.2)

opening presentation through his inauguration in spring 2009, Alexander clarified his goal of unifying warm hearts and expanding minds, the central partnership of NNU's history.

Good financial news also emanated out from the Nampa campus at the beginning of Alexander's second year. The budgets were balanced, scholarship funding remained high, and enrollments kept steady. Five years earlier NNU enrolled 416 graduate students, but in 2009 that number had climbed to 622. With NNU supporters furnishing the necessary funds, the university was also able to provide even more scholarships for needy students. Even though the U. S. economy was in bad shape, NNU was doing well.

More than any other event, the completion of the impressive new Thomas Family Health and Science Center in 2009 provided a forward-looking, positive symbol for the NNU campus and community. The $10 million, 50,000-square-foot structure was the largest building in the history of the university. It would provide the much-needed space for science classes and laboratories and especially for the nursing program, which was now the largest department on campus, enrolling more than 200 majors. Nursing students would have five times the amount of space for their studies as they previously had on the cramped top floor of the ancient administration building. The new Thomas Center would also free up the old Science Building, which, after refurbishing, would become the new home of the education, counseling, and social work departments.

The erection of the Thomas Center and other expansions on campus illustrated the university's increasingly successful attempts to reach out to friends and alumni of the institution. Under the skillful and energetic guidance of Gary Skaggs and then Joel Pearsall, the university gained the necessary financial support to plan and construct new buildings as well as to renovate older ones and update other necessary campus facilities. The Alumni Office was also helping NNU expand. Building on the pioneering first-rate leadership of Myron Finkbeiner, Darl Bruner and April McNeiece, through their energetic work as directors, were linking up with thousands of former students who wished to nourish their NNC/NNU roots and to support the university. Homecoming celebrations each November, annual Golden Grad roundups at spring graduation, and gatherings across the NNU zone were particularly popular with alumni.

The faculty and administration were united in maintaining NNU's long-held mission. They wanted to keep the traditional balances between heart and head that had characterized the institution's earlier years. As the new president reminded his listeners in fall 2010, NNU's mission remained the "transformation of the whole person," with emphasis on Christlikeness and on becoming "God's creative and redemptive agent in the world." NNU had become and would remain a "Christian university of the liberal arts, professional and graduate studies." This multifaceted mission would both build on as well as further NNU's core values.

Keeping the university's mission and core values in mind, the new administration laid out in the fall of 2010 a vision for the next fifteen years. It would include an expansion of the Wesley Center to deliver programs across campus, to the NNU region, and even to global sites. Through its emphases on nurturing disciples, serving the church, and fostering the expansion of learning experiences, NNU would support the development of a Residential Village living arrangement, which would allow students to live in apartment-like complexes. The college would also work toward establishing a semester abroad site.

At the center of the forward-looking plan were several academic ingredients. In summer 2010 the arrival of a new academic dean, Dr. Burton Webb, with a strong background in the sciences and helpful administrative experience, gave promise of renewed academic direction in the coming years. Another key segment was the planned erection of a large new "Learning Commons" at the north entrance of campus. It would be a learning center, true enough, but also a "living room" for the university. It would be the new front door to campus. Centennial plans called for raising $10 million to construct this cornerstone building. At the same time the university would attempt to recruit faculty of more diverse backgrounds. Several other features of the plan would address student scholarship. NNU would establish an honors program, offer more interdisciplinary and cross-cultural courses, and attempt to attract students of color and need.

Similar upbeat signs emerged from student campus life. Scholarships were available, new courses and programs came on line, and a fresh crop of faculty members were in their places. A few gripes surfaced about the food, a steady discontent for decades, but the new friendships in the dorms and on campus seemed to outweigh negative feelings. Indeed, student life was remarkably quiescent during President Alexander's first years in office.

That did not mean students were without strong opinions, however. The *Crusader* continued to be a mouthpiece for undergraduates. And the subjects the newspaper dealt with were often different from those of administrators, faculty, and alumni, frequently discomfiting these groups but also providing glimpses into student thoughts

Distance runner Ashley Puga was the first NNU student to win a NCAA Division 2 national track championship. (Fig. 7.3)

and actions. These subjects were not so much new topics as reiterations of ones under campus discussion for more than a decade: more acceptance of and love for persons of homosexual orientation; more interest in "missional" work; additional volunteerism to help with national and global problems; and allowance for more campus input for student living arrangements, especially for upper-division students.

The student newspaper also provided stories focused on academic and recreational experiences. In the 1990s the *Crusader* began to carry movie reviews, especially after the Church of the Nazarene changed its stand on movie attendance, but the periodical did not publish notices of dance clubs in the Hagood or Alexander years, even though the Nazarene guidelines had changed too on that entertainment. In fact, on one occasion when the newspaper devoted a full page ad for a Boise dance club, the editor received a strong letter of criticism from the faculty advisor.

Sports activities continued to garner as many column inches as any NNU activity. The women's volleyball team competed well, and the women's basketball teams made it into the district NCAA II playoffs. Men's basketball players won preseason games but had difficulty in their GNAC conference. The baseball team, facing even more challenges previously, made a giant comeback in spring 2010 and gained national rankings the next spring with its front-rank efforts.

But the story of stories in NNU athletics was that of Ashley Puga, who became the university's all-time outstanding athlete by the end of her senior year in spring 2009. A graduate of Nampa Christian High, Puga began to surge to the top of regional indoor and outdoor track meets early in her career at NNU. When she closed out her collegiate running by winning the national NCAA II indoor and outdoor 800-meter races in 2009, she had become an NCAA II All-American several times. In addition she had been honored twice as regional Women's Athlete of the Year and was a finalist for the U. S. women's athlete of the year award. Only Steve Hills (1978) and Antonette Blythe (1981) had won national competitions when the college competed in the NAIA bracket.

In addressing the campus community in early 2010, President Alexander called the audience's attention to Charles Wesley's words on the chapel wall:

"Unite the pair so long disjoined, / Knowledge and vital piety." New buildings and programs might be erected and launched, and everyone should be thankful for those achievements. Even more important and significant, however, was the ongoing union of heart and head that had characterized the university through its nearly century of existence. Alexander asked "what do the words on the wall mean to this place, our faculty and our students," and then answered his own question. "For us, these words imply a call to be like Christ," the president began, and added "to live lives of faith, to utilize our capacity to reason and explore so that we might know Him more fully and serve Him more ably." It was a presidential statement uniting NNU's past and present and pointing his listeners and NNU toward goals they should pursue.

In the academic year of 2010-11, on the eve of its centennial, NNU remained in remarkably good shape. Despite the overshadowing economic downturn vexing the U. S. and much of the world, the Nampa college was on solid financial ground. Sufficient money was available for salaries, scholarships, and other fiscal needs on the expanding campus. Part of the optimism at NNU derived from the continuously increasing enrollments. In fall 2010, the combined undergraduate and graduate enrollment hit a new, all-time high of 2020 students. In the following spring semester, enrollments persisted at a lofty level.

Academic programs were also growing. Students could choose from more than 60 areas of study. New programs in electrical and mechanical engineering were in place, and 18 master's programs in 7 areas were available. And then in late spring 2011, NNU announced the launching of a new doctoral program in education. The EdD program would be the university's first doctoral offering, providing further evidence of its advancement as a university. Another doctoral program in religion was also in an advanced planning stage.

Outreach efforts were widening out from Nampa to the Boise Valley, the Northwest Educational Zone, and on to even larger areas. Online programs were now available in several world areas, with 8,000 enrolled in continuing education

NNU enrollment exceeds 2,000

▼ **EDUCATION:** Fall figures show number of students tops milestone for first time

Idaho Press-Tribune staff
newsroom@idahopress.com

NAMPA — Northwest Nazarene University has enrolled more than 2,000 students for the fall semester, the first time in the university's history its enrollment has passed that mark, officials said Wednesday.

Overall, 2010 numbers indicate a substantial 12 percent growth in graduate students and a small increase in undergraduate students from 2009 fall enrollment. The registrar reported 1,322 undergraduate and 698 graduate students registered for a total enrollment of 2,020 compared with 1,934 students for fall 2009.

"The campus welcomed 144 new undergraduate transfer and adult students," said Stacey Berggren, vice president for enrollment and marketing. "The youngest among us is 17, the oldest is 76. Increased diversity among the degree programs available to adult professionals is also telling of our commitment to provide a quality educational opportunity to students of all ages."

NNU President David Alexander said exceeding the 2,000-student threshold marks a great day for NNU.

"The investment by NNU faculty in each student's life, both graduate and undergraduate, put feet to our commitment to instill habits of heart, soul, mind and strength in each student to become redemptive agents in the world," he said. "This transformative learning community ignites intellectual discovery in her students."

In fall 2010, NNU's enrollment passed the 2,000 mark for the first time. (Fig. 7.4)

NNU announces first doctorate program

Idaho Press-Tribune staff
newsroom@idahopress.com

NAMPA — Northwest Nazarene University officials have announced the launch of a doctor of education program, the local institution's first doctoral degree.

The program, approved by the Northwest Commission on Colleges and Universities, will begin in September.

Officials said the program will provide advanced study and research for educators interested in educational leadership in school administration, and provide opportunities for in-depth exploration, study, research and analysis regarding administrative practices in the school and school district setting.

"We are delighted that NNU is poised to launch its first doctoral degree; it is truly an historic day," NNU President David Alexander said in a press release. "As a regional university of significance and graduate study substance, we will now be able to build upon NNU's century-long tradition of educating some of the most highly sought-after elementary and secondary teachers and school administrators in the Northwest. The doctorate in education will become the capstone of educational offerings in the NNU Department of Education."

The program consists of a minimum of 60 semester credits and will take approximately four years to complete.

The announcement of NNU's first doctoral program in 2011, in education, signaled the university's academic advancement. (Fig. 7.5)

programs and 2,300 high school students studying in concurrent credit courses. And in February 2011, more than 500 church officials, pastors and laypersons, and students attended a conference on Biblical inspiration sponsored by the university's Wesley Center. The Nampa cocoon seemed to have burst; NNU had become a global institution.

Step back and ponder the meanings of this century-long series of events. Picture an aged but still ageless observer who can see and understand the 100-year history of Northwest Nazarene College/University. If our insightful onlooker is attuned to changes and continuities on the Nampa campus as well as in the Church of the Nazarene and in wider worlds, what shifts and persisting trends will he or she pinpoint in attempting to portray the college's history?

Our imagined spectator would undoubtedly mention several notable changes both shaping and emerging from the Nampa campus. Chief among these is the transformation from a school of a dozen beginning students housed in a rented church to a university of 2,000 undergraduates and graduates hosted on an 85-acre, sprawling campus of numerous buildings. Immense new and imposing structures such as the Brandt Center, the Johnson Sports Center, and the Thomas Family Health and Science Center dwarf the oldest and refurbished buildings, the Emerson Administration building and Elmore Hall. With fully accredited graduate and undergraduate programs in 60 areas of study and national accreditation in such programs as teacher education, social work, music, counseling, and nursing, NNU is receiving national rankings in journals such as *U. S. News & World Report* that pre-World War II NNCers could not have thought possible. NNU is "on the map," more and more an around-the-world university.

Change marked NNC/NNU in other ways. Presidential leaders until the

1990s were pastors, former pastors, district superintendents, or teachers of theology. But the three most recent presidents—in office since 1992—have all been laymen with strong links to NNU as former students or faculty. The influential presence of the university is increasingly felt, too, in the Treasure Valley and even out on the educational zone of the Pacific Northwest and the Intermountain West. As recently as the 1970s, students expressed a desire to get out of the "NNC bubble in Nampa." They and the college have done that since the 1980s, including bringing many more non-Nazarene students to campus.

A series of tipping point events would catch our observer's attention. Among these are President DeLong's dramatic Out-of-Debt Campaign (1927-28) and his full-throttle drive to full four-year accreditation (1937). The shaping influences of the Great Depression and World War II also changed the character of NNC. Even more transformative was the powerful leadership of President Riley and his *"Campus Plateau 1970"* program launched in 1964, during which several major buildings were erected and student enrollments doubled. No less significant was the move from the college of NNC to the university of NNU in 1999 and the professionalization of the campus and its manifold planning and academic programs under the strong direction of President Hagood.

But our all-knowing spectator would avoid overemphasizing change; he or she would also point to the notable continuities in the history of NNU. The motto of the school—"Seek Ye First the Kingdom of God"—remains in place and is frequently invoked. The goal of a balanced head and heart that pioneering President Wiley appealed to in the college's opening years and that Riley, Hagood, and others continued remains at the center of NNU's mission. The university still enjoys the strong financial support of its educational zone, so strong that accrediting agencies often consider it as an important addition to the university's otherwise very modest endowment. But some long-lasting challenges persist. It is still not easy to entice undergraduates, especially first-year students, from Colorado and the western regions of Oregon and Washington to distant Idaho for their college work.

Perhaps the most important of the clear continuities that stabilizes NNU is its continuing strong leadership. None of the presidents was a failure or even below average. Leaving out the administrations of J. G. Morrison and Leon Doane, which lasted less than a year, one can confidently state that all the NNC/NNU presidents have been strong or superior. True, President Gilmore was wrongly encouraged to leave after three years, but in the long run his administration proves to have addressed, successfully, pressing problems of a terrible depression. In Presidents Wiley, DeLong, Riley, and Hagood the university enjoyed superlative leadership at the presidential helm. In addition, Presidents Corlett, Pearsall, and Wetmore kept the college in the black, added new faculty, and looked after other needs. And in the redoubtable founder Eugene Emerson, in deans Olive Winchester, Thelma Culver, and Sam Dunn, and in alumni director Myron Finkbeiner NNU has enjoyed other first-rate leaders. And, of course, in dozens of legendary faculty members who served at the academic and spiritual centers of the college through the decades.

Our all-seeing onlooker would also point to the notable graduates of the college as further evidence of its continuing strength. Besides the hundreds of missionaries, pastors, and church workers, numerous talented scholars, athletes, writers, and public servants have marched through NNU's classrooms, laboratories, and sports facilities. Think, for example, of Rhodes Scholars John Luik and Ginger Rinkenberger and the numerous PhD's, MD's, and research scholars emerging from NNU. Consider athletes like Morris Chalfant, Gary Locke, Steve Hills, and Ashley Puga. Recall, too, Kent Hill and Richard Hagood, later Nazarene college presidents; writers Noel Riley Fitch, Donna Fletcher Crow, and Jill Williamson; historians Gary Topping and Ron Butchart; Rick Hieb, astronaut; Jeff Carr, Los Angeles counselor for innercity work; and Tom Nees, key figure in Nazarene missional outreach and Compassionate Ministries. All these and hundreds of others stand out as testimonies to the persisting excellence of NNU, its academic programs, and its superb graduates.

In the end, our astute onlooker would find an oxymoronic truth in NNU's history: in the midst of change, continuities persist. Think pictorially. Stand in the middle of Holly Street (now South University Boulevard), facing the Emerson Administration Building, with the Brandt Center at back. Look around the circle from Williams Hall, Elmore Hall, and the Student Center on the left, and the Riley Library, the Thomas Science Center, and the Wiley Learning Center to the right. And beyond, the Johnson Sports Center and the athletic fields. Turn about to take in the Fine Arts building, Helstrom Business Center, and dorms to the left, and other dorms and the prayer chapel to the right.

Then ask: what has kept these places together—in spite of the pull of the library and science on one side and religion and philosophy on the other. The tug of Fine Arts, physical education, and education in still other directions. What web of values, what equilibriums, have kept these places and the disciplines they represent unified and in community rather than falling into conflict and disuniting?

Three core values—two from the beginning, a third more recent—have provided cohering community. In the opening years of Northwest Nazarene College, from the union of Jerusalem (heart, religion) and Athens (head, learning) came its offspring: a Christian liberal arts college. Vital piety and knowledge were the two core values in the hearts and minds of Eugene Emerson, H. Orton Wiley, and other founders. The attempts to marry heart and mind in the next half century were often stuttering steps toward synthesis. Perhaps President Riley did most to combine these two strands, which he labeled conscience and competency.

Another core value—known variously as evangelism, outreach, and more recently as "missional"—was among the major goals of Nazarene founder Phineas F. Bresee. But this mission of social outreach seemed to get lost at NNC and in the Church of the Nazarene from the 1920s through the 1950s, save in the outpouring of thousands of missionaries and pastors. A remarkable shift occurred in the late 1960s and 1970s. Many Nazarene young people became dissatisfied with earlier denominational definitions of missions and pushed for new kinds of domestic and global outreach programs. Gradually, another core value was grafted onto the earlier heart-and-head duo; a helping or outreached hand was added. Perhaps the NNU community already understood the contention of sociologist James Davison Hunter in his provocative book, *To Change a Culture* (2010): evangelicals should practice a "faithful presence" in the arenas of need rather than championing a more militant and eventually unsuccessful and alienating "change the culture" agenda. Whatever the impulse, NNU students and graduates were increasingly motivated—even driven—to communicate a worldview that united warm hearts, trained minds, and outstretching hands.

Think ahead. As Northwest Nazarene University pushes farther into the twenty-first century and into its second 100 years, it will face the ongoing challenges of communicating spiritual journey, academic excellence, and mission outreach. Together, these impulses continue to be the summum bonum of everything NNU does. Our observant onlooker—and other witnesses as well—will realize that these three values, combined, are at the university's core, as if in its DNA. So they have become, so they can continue to be.

By its centennial year (2012-13), NNU had expanded well beyond the original footprint of the campus, demonstrating its continued growth and development through the years. (Fig. 7.6)

Afterword

PRESIDENT DAVID ALEXANDER

The mission of Northwest Nazarene University is the transformation of the whole person. Centered in Jesus Christ the NNU education instills habits of heart, soul, mind and strength to enable each student to become God's creative and redemptive agent in the world.

~NNU Mission

Centennial observances provide a vista—a vantage point from which to look across a one hundred year span. Centennial history books become a record of the people and events in that span, a chronicle of possibility and progress, hardship and sacrifice, faithfulness and achievement. *Seeking First the Kingdom: Northwest Nazarene University, A Centennial History* is indeed such a ledger.

Certainly, the NNU history may be read in a merely factual manner, a list of characters and programs, an array of statistics. Yet this work is more than a record; it captures a story—a story worth telling and re-telling. A story of an idea that became a calling, the people who answered that call and their legacy, the founding and flourishing of Northwest Nazarene University.

This is a story of a people in pursuit of a divine imperative—a command. This is a story written in response to seven words. Seven powerful words.

Seek ye first the Kingdom of God.

~Matthew 6:33

For over one hundred years the people of NNU have pursued the essence and spirit of Christ's command. These seven words became their motto, guiding and compelling men and women of successive generations to answer the call to serve the cause of Christ in Christian higher education. Their acts of service and self have resulted in the institutional legacy recorded within this work of history.

For the caring reader, the individual vested in the NNU story, it is fitting and proper, upon completion of this good work to pause and celebrate and give thanks. I invite those captured by the spirit of the place called Northwest Nazarene University to raise their hearts, minds and voices in praise and gratitude.

Join me in giving thanks for the author of the NNU centennial history, Dr. Richard Etulain, a man who answered the call to tell the story. He accepted the challenge to live within the tension of being both seasoned historian, writing with a sense of scholarly rigor, and a favorite son, a university alumnus writing as one shaped by his subject matter. We give thanks to Dr. Etulain for his two and a half year labor of love.

Let us raise our voices in praise of leaders. Men and women of faith and vision—Emerson, Wiley and Winchester—whose founding courage and sacrifice made something out of nothing. And for those leaders who followed them—DeLong and Riley, Culver and Ford—truly scores of individuals took ideas and birthed programs, secured resources in times of want and occasionally in times of abundance. Each leader guided by a kingdom calling.

Join me in giving thanks for the church. Since the university's founding, the church has always been a constant—governing, guiding, and sustaining the institution. Even in the infancy of the Church of the Nazarene her people dreamt of a place at which their children could be fitted for life and service. Northwest Nazarene University has always been and will always be that place—an instrument and an arm of the church.

Let us give praise to the people of NNU. Though written records are naturally organized around eras of leadership, the heart of history is written by the lives of the people. The chapters of the NNU story are forged by hundreds of laborers in the cause of Christ—teachers possessing a passion for their discipline and their Lord—each of them exercising the sacred privilege of shaping lives through learning. Joining them are rank upon rank of secretaries, craftsmen, technicians and representatives—each a servant ambassador of their university.

And if there are hundreds of laborers, there are thousands of NNU students. Let us honor and celebrate those young women and men and their faithful families, who because of their faith, sacrifice and hard work chose to enter the transformational world of Northwest Nazarene University. As they studied and learned, words became flesh, ideas were incarnated; and then, with lessons learned, they left NNU poised to be God's creative and redemptive agents in the world.

We also do well to remember and enjoy the place to which we have been called—the land of the northwest. Let us be grateful for the providence of place. Northwest Nazarene University is fortunate to be planted in the northwest, a land of beauty and breadth, of sea and mountains, prairie and plains. We are privileged to live in this fertile land populated by a people of independence and creativity, passion and generosity. We are blessed to be citizens of this town, this state and this region. We have been shaped by it and we have been called to write our story upon it.

To read and reflect upon the story captured in *Seeking First the Kingdom: Northwest Nazarene University, A Centennial History* is to inevitably turn one's heart and mind to

God. It is God who our forefathers sought. It is God who called and provided. It is the seeking and pursuing of God that drew generation after generation of students to NNU. It is God to whom we offer thanksgiving. It is the providence and blessing of God that we trace in the telling of this century-long story. Ultimately it is God and God alone who is worthy of our praise.

Centennial observances tempt us to celebrate arrival. Indeed, we have marked the milestones in a one hundred year journey; we have highlighted heroes and remembered the faithful, yet we have not arrived. We have looked back and remembered, we looked around and surveyed, but now, most importantly, we must look ahead and recommit to answer the call of the divine imperative—to seek first the Kingdom of God.

Though the centennial history book is concluded, the story continues. It is now our turn. Our chapter. We have the privilege and responsibility of continuing to seek to be a university that proclaims the triumph of good over evil, the difference between right and wrong, to explore the wonder of God's creative activity and to bring about redemption and restoration in ways large and small. We are bearers of the good news, a community of scholars and disciples committed to living in relationship with God and one another, actively engaged in this world, yet not of it—citizens of the Kingdom of God.

Guided by a vision of the Kingdom of God
Northwest Nazarene University seeks a more excellent way,
to be a transformative learning community by
forming scholars, nurturing disciples, serving the church,
shaping the culture, redeeming the world.
~NNU Vision

Sources and Acknowledgments

This centennial history of Northwest Nazarene University is based, in large part, on primary manuscript and published sources on file in the NNU Archives in the John E. Riley Library. Most of all, I have utilized the presidential papers of all twelve presidents, the minutes of the NNC Board of Regents/Trustees, and the various files of university deans and other administrators. I have also used the personnel files of dozens of faculty, staff members, and other persons associated with the university. In these collections I may have perused between 75,000 and 100,000 documents.

The files of the *(Nazarene) Messenger,* running back to the presidency of H. Orton Wiley, are also important for campus news and the administrative viewpoints through the years. The *Crusader*, the student newspaper in existence for roughly sixty years, is the most revealing source for student viewpoints, particularly since the 1960s. In addition, the interviews of NNU professor and former archivist Robert C. Woodward with administrators, faculty, and staff persons furnished valuable personal perspectives on the university's history.

Three book-length sources—two published, one in manuscript—contributed invaluable information. More than any other sources these extensive accounts furnish reliable narratives for specific periods of the college's history. The Silver Anniversary publication, *Northwest Nazarene College: Twenty-five Years of Progress* (Np:np, [1938?], covers the story from 1913 to 1938 and evidently was coauthored by President Russell V. DeLong and Dean Albert Harper, and with, perhaps, additions from Bertha Dooley and Emma French (Smith). "The History of Northwest Nazarene College," intended as a Golden Anniversary publication, was authored by Francis C. Sutherland but never published. It covers NNC's history into the Riley period of the 1960s but is, unfortunately, incomplete and avoids most controversies. The fullest and best of the NNC stories is John E. Riley, *From Sagebrush to Ivy: The Story of Northwest Nazarene College 1913-1988* (Nampa: Northwest Nazarene College, 1988). This seventy-fifth anniversary volume makes especially thorough use of the *Messenger* and *Crusader* files and clearly benefits from Riley's long and close contact with NNC administrators, faculty, alumni, and students.

The history of NNU's sponsoring institution, the Church of the Nazarene, is treated in several volumes. The best of these is Timothy L. Smith, *Called Unto Holiness:The Story of the Nazarenes: The Formative Years* (Kansas City, MO: Nazarene Publishing House, 1962). This model volume, which covers Nazarene holiness origins and the church from its founding in 1908 into the early 1930s, is exhaustively researched and appealingly written. Less strong but still satisfactory is W. T. Purkiser, *Called Unto Holiness, Volume 2: The Second Twenty-five Years, 1933-58* (Kansas

City, MO: Nazarene Publishing House, 1983). The most comprehensive and recent story of the Nazarenes is its 100-year history, Floyd Cunningham, et al., *Our Watchword and Song: The Centennial History of the Church of the Nazarene* (Kansas City, MO: Beacon Hill Press, 2009). This mammoth 733-page overview is a global history with helpful coverage of the church's full story. A readable, interesting collection of biographical vignettes of notable Nazarenes and their precursors by the church's archivist appears in Stan Ingersol, *Nazarene Roots: Pastors, Prophets, Revivalists and Reformers* (Kansas City, MO: Beacon Hill Press, 2009). The coverage in this volume of women reformers, leaders, and evangelists and pastors is particularly impressive.

Also helpful is a handful or so of general studies of recent American evangelicals and evangelicalism. See, for example, George Marsden, *Fundamentalism and American Culture: The Shaping of Twentieth-Century Evangelicalism, 1870-1925* (New York: Oxford University Press, 1980), and Marsden, *Understanding Fundamentalism and Evangelicalism* (Grand Rapids, MI: William B. Eerdmans, 1991); Joel A. Carpenter, *Revive Us Again: The Reawakening of American Fundamentalism* (New York: Oxford University Press, 1997); and Ferenc Morton Szasz, *Religion in the Modern American West* (Tucson: University of Arizona Press, 2000).

Several other books have been useful in preparing this volume. For an excellent history of NNU's sister institution (from which I have learned a great deal), consult Ronald Kirkemo, *For Zion's Sake: A History of Pasadena/Point Loma College* (San Diego: Point Loma Press, 1992, 2008). Another extensive history of a Nazarene college is the thoroughly researched two-volume history by James C. Cameron: *Eastern Nazarene College: The First Fifty Years 1900-1950* (Kansas City, MO: Nazarene Publishing House, 1968); and Cameron, *The Spirit Makes a Difference: The History of Eastern Nazarene College, Part II, 1950-2000* (Quincy, MA: ENC Press, 2000). The best study of the leading Nazarene founder is Carl Bangs, *Phineas F. Bresee: His Life...* (Kansas City, MO: Beacon Hill Press, 1995). We lack a much-needed intellectual biography of H. Orton Wiley, chief theologian and NNC's founding president; until that volume is available, see John J. Griffin, "Yours in His Service: H. Orton Wiley as Evangelical Theologian and Educator" (PhD dissertation, University of New Mexico, 1997). Two volumes helpful for understanding long-time and recent influences on NNC/NNU are Michael Lodahl, *"All Things Necessary to Our Salvation":... The Article on the Holy Scripture* in the *Manual of the Church of the Nazarene* (San Diego: Point Loma Press, 2004) and Thomas J. Oord and Michael Lodahl, *Relational Holiness: Responding to the Call of Love* (Kansas City, MO: Beacon Hill Press, 2005).

For general historical backgrounds on the Pacific Northwest and American West, I have relied on Carlos Schwantes, *The Pacific Northwest: An Interpretive History* (Seattle: University of Washington Press, 1989), and Richard W. Etulain, *Beyond the Missouri: The Story of the American West* (Albuquerque: University of New Mexico Press, 2006).

I am indebted to several people in the preparation of this volume. President Richard Hagood persisted in thinking that I ought to write this history. Others thought so too. During an unforgettable year spent in Nampa—from September 2008 to September 2009—I lived in the NNU Archives in Riley Library and benefitted from the invaluable library staff. Sharon Bull, the library director, and her staff members Deanna Wilde and Lance McGrath were very helpful. So were Lois Roberts, Coral Mattei, and LaRita Schandorff.

During my research at the general Church of the Nazarene archives in Kansas City/Lenexa, Kansas, Nazarene archivist Stan Ingersol and his assistant Meri Janssen were very supportive. So was Linda Hasper while I was working at the library archives at Point Loma Nazarene University in San Diego.

Later, President David Alexander and his able executive assistant Cindy Rodes helped me with several details during my stays in Nampa. Joel Pearsall also aided in the effort.

Along the way, Bob Woodward, Ray Cooke, Myron Finkbeiner, Larry Bunts, Harrold Curl, and Loring Beals were Wednesday morning sources of memory and information in treating the NNC/NNU's past. I've been warmed, too, by the delightful memories of Jo Kincaid and the stimulating chats with Chaplain Gene Schandorff and professors Jerry Hull, George Lyons, and Darrell Marks. Several persons also read and commented on the manuscript. They include Bob Woodward, Ray Cooke, Ralph Neil, Lynn Riley Neil, Jerry Hull, Sharon Bull, Jackie Etulain Partch, Fred Fullerton, David Ralph, John Berggren, Richard Hagood, and David Alexander. I'm especially indebted to my much-esteemed mentor, Bob Woodward, for his generous help with and insightful comments about this project.

I also want to thank Sharon Bull, Deanna Wilde, and Brad Elsberg for their help in the time-consuming endeavor to select and prepare photos for this project, and Paul Kinsman for designing the cover and laying out the pages of this book. Thanks too to Double E Hill and Mel Schroeder for their photos.

I am also much indebted to my wife Joyce Oldenkamp Etulain for putting up with my year and more of absences, for accepting the overload of NNC/NNU information I shoveled in her direction, and for reading and commenting on this manuscript.

More recently Carol Wight's editing of the manuscript improved its readability, and her careful eye caught and corrected dozens of errors.

Altogether, this historical journey has been one of self-discovery and expanded meaning. I am grateful for the voyage.

Index

Boldface numbers indicate an extended treatment of the subject.

About the Author

Richard W. Etulain is a lifetime Nazarene. He grew up attending small Nazarene churches in eastern Washington and graduated with high honors from NNC with a BA in English and a BA in history in 1960. He earned a master's degree (1962) in American literature and a PhD (1966) in American history and literature at the University of Oregon. He taught at NNC (1966-1968), Idaho State University (1970-79), and the University of New Mexico (1979-2001).

He has authored or edited 50 books and pamphlets. The best-known of these volumes are *Conversations with Wallace Stegner on Western History and Literature* (1983, 1996); *The American West: A Twentieth-Century History* (with Michael P. Malone, 1989, 2007); *Re-imagining the Modern American West: A Century of Fiction, History, and Art* (1996); and *Beyond the Missouri: The Story of the American West* (2006). His most recent work is *Lincoln Looks West: From the Mississippi to the Pacific* (2010).

He is also coeditor, with Noel Riley Fitch, of *Faith and Imagination: Essays on Evangelicals and Literature Honoring Marian B. Washburn* (1985), and, with Raymond M. Cooke, *Religion and Culture: Historical Essays in Honor of Robert C. Woodward* (1991).

His writings have won several awards, and he was honored as president of both the Western Literature and Western History associations. He was chosen as the NNC Alumnus of the Year in 1975. In 2000, NNU awarded him a Doctorate of Humane Letters, and he served on its Board of Trustees, 2003-6.